THREE-HUNDRED-MILE TIGER

Also by the First Zen Institute:

*Original Nature: Zen Comments
on the Sixth Patriarch's Platform Sutra*

Holding the Lotus to the Rock

The Zen Eye

Zen Pivots

Cat's Yawn

THREE-HUNDRED-MILE TIGER

THE RECORD OF LIN-CHI

Translation and Commentary by
Sokei-an Sasaki

Edited by
Mary Farkas, Robert Lopez, Peter Haskel

iUniverse LLC
Bloomington

THREE-HUNDRED-MILE TIGER
THE RECORD OF LIN-CHI Translation and Commentary by Sokei-an

iUniverse books may be ordered through booksellers or by contacting:

iUniverse LLC
1663 Liberty Drive
Bloomington, IN 47403
www.iuniverse.com
1-800-Authors (1-800-288-4677)

ISBN: 978-1-4917-0645-9 (sc)
ISBN: 978-1-4917-0646-6 (e)

Library of Congress Control Number: 2013916535

Printed in the United States of America

iUniverse rev. date: 11/09/2013

Table of Contents

For the Note-Takers, Audrey and Edna,
And For Mary

Kuei-shan and Yang-shan were disciples of Huai-hai, whose teacher was Ma-tsu, another famous master. Kuei-shan was asking who Lin-chi's real teacher was. However, Huang-po (Lin-chi's teacher) and Ta-yu were not two men. From this angle, Ta-yu was the head of the tiger and Huang-po its tail. What a huge tiger! Three hundred miles long!

Sokei-an

Preface

Shigetsu Sasaki (1882-1945), known as Sokei-an, was the first Zen master to settle permanently in America. Sokei-an studied sculpture and graduated from the Imperial Academy of Art in Tokyo. During this time, he undertook Zen study with the Rinzai Zen master Sokatsu Shaku (1859-1954). Sokatsu, a Dharma heir of the noted Zen master Soyen Shaku (1859-1919), continued Soyen's interest in attracting educated lay people to Zen. In 1905, Sokei-an accompanied Sokatsu to California with the mission of building America's first Zen center. After this mission failed, Sokei-an wandered the American West in a restless search for the American character and the meaning of Zen. He was the original Dharma bum. Settling into Washington Square in 1915, Sokei-an began writing stories about his experiences for Japanese magazines and published four books of humorous essays about America. During the 1920's Sokei-an also supported himself repairing antiques, and returned to Japan several times to complete his formal Zen training. Sokei-an received Dharma transmission from Sokatsu, founding the First Zen Institute of America in New York in 1930. During the next decade Sokei-an offered a mixture of koan study and lectures on Buddhist and Zen texts based on his own translations to a group of dedicated students. The details of Sokei-an's life in his own words can be found in, *Holding the Lotus to the Rock* (2002).

Sokei-an translated the *Record of Lin-chi* (*Lin-chi lu*) from 1931 to 1933, in his first series of lectures. He felt that Americans needed original Chinese Zen source materials, translated and commented upon by a Zen master, and there were no such materials in those early days. Sokei-an was the first Zen master to translate the *Record of Lin-chi* and to give a commentary in English to Western students. The real historic value of Sokei-an's *Lin-chi* is in his commentary with its manifestation of Lin-chi's Zen.

Sokei-an's handwritten translation sits in a weathered box in the FZI publications office. We have reproduced sample pages to illustrate how Sokei-an worked on the text using Chinese, Japanese, and English. Sokei-an's father, a Shinto priest and scholar of medieval Japanese, had taught Sokei-an Chinese from early childhood. Moreover, besides his works in Japanese, Sokei-an wrote short stories and poems in English. Although he spoke with a strong accent, Sokei-an prided himself on finding the right English equivalents as he translated Buddhist terms. Sokei-an had studied the *Lin-chi* with his Zen master, Sokatsu, and had finished the Zen koans that relate to passages of the text. These experiences had prepared him as each week he sat at his desk with his unabridged Webster's dictionary, his large map of Chinese Zen sites, and his Chinese- and Japanese-language Tripitaka texts, translating and preparing his commentary. Chaka, Sokei-an's cat sat contentedly on his lap assisting. This is Chaka on the cover of Three-Hundred-Mile Tiger.

What makes Sokei-an's commentary so enjoyable is his ironic wit and his dramatic recounting of his vivid experiences in Japan and America as a young Zen student. Manifesting Lin-chi's Zen before the eyes of those lucky enough to come to his little temple on West 70th Street in 1930's New York, Sokei-an apparently also liked to act out the dramatic parts of the text's encounters.

In November 1941, disatisfied with his original, Sokei-an began a second series of translations and commentaries on the *Lin-chi*. Shortly before Japan attacked Pearl Harbor in 1941, the institute moved into the home of Ruth Fuller, a Chicago heiress and longtime Zen practitioner, who had joined the group in 1938. Following the outbreak of the Pacific War, Sokei-an was interned at Ellis Island as an enemy alien and was later sent to a camp in Fort Meade, Maryland. Sokei-an had completed only twenty-seven of the new commentaries, assisted by Ruth. He was released in 1943, subsequently married Ruth Fuller, and resumed teaching and giving *sanzen* (private zen interveiws) until his death in 1945.

Ruth Sasaki, then vice president of the First Zen Institute of America, had intended to publish Sokei-an's *Lin-chi* after his death. The 1932-33 commentary and the original translation however, existed only in the notes of Sokei-an's original students. After starting the First Zen Institute of America in Japan, and conferring with Japanese and American experts in Zen and early Chinese texts, Ruth decided to launch upon a more accurate translation for use by Western students using Sokei-an's second translation as a first draft. The excellent version edited by Ruth Sasaki is now available with the notes and a fine introduction in the edition edited by Thomas Kirchner (Kyoto: 2009). Only a Zen master, however, may comment on the Zen meaning of this material. As Sokei-an stated: "When other teachers of Zen come after me to this country, they should note what I have just said about transmitting Zen to American people. They should not transmit that particular poetic feeling that comes from Chinese sentences. I am trying to transmit Zen itself to American people, not Chinese literature."

Back in New York, Sokei-an's commentary, which had been given orally, was gradually rescued from the notebooks of his students by Mary Farkas, who had also joined the institute in 1938 and served as secretary of the First Zen Institute until her death in 1993. Sokei-an's lectures and translations from 1932-33 were painstakingly collated and edited by her over the 1960's and 70's. This is the version presented here. Mary was then editor of the Institute's periodical, *Zen Notes*, and it was there that she first published the *Lin-chi* in installments. Mary laughed to herself as she put together each new installment of Sokei-an's *Lin-chi*, and we would receive animated demonstrations and exclamations from her about the stories in the text. She was loathe to explain Lin-chi's actions, but wanted us to grab hold of the mighty principle. When Mary was asked why we needed this awakening of mind, she simply answered, "Well, that's what a human being is."

"Sokei-an emphasized that he wasn't teaching anything," Mary wrote. "To learn spoken ways to do things is not, in my mind, Zen. Zen in the art of daily life with Sokei-an was his real transmission to me. I tell stories about Sokei-an many times, but students do not understand them. I would tell them again and explain the point, which of course destroys the possibility of its getting across. Zen is like lightning. It illuminates when least expected, but it can be appreciated only if your mind is awake and absolutely clear."

As Sokei-an stated in his own brief introduction to the *Record of Lin-chi*, he changed the traditional order of the text and begins with Discourses X(b)—XXII. Sokei-an was concerned that the opening Zen encounters depicted in the "Pilgramages" and in the early "Discources" were too difficult an introduction for Western students as yet unacquainted with Zen. So *Three-Hundred-Mile Tiger* concludes with these encounters like the flicking of the tiger's tail. The 1941-42 translation and commentary follow the traditional order, and the commentary clearly speaks to a more sophisticated audience of Sokei-an's *sanzen* students. Sokei-an states, "Lin-chi used a short dagger and pointed it directly into the heart, and it was very sharp." Sokei-an also comments on the difficulty of reading the Lin-chi because of the "colloquial expressions throughout".

Buddhist terms are explained in the glossary. Lotus icons (borrowed from Sokei-an's personal copy of the Taisho Tripitaka) separate the lectures. Sokei-an used "Lin-chi" and the Japanese reading of Lin-chi's name, "Rinzai," interchangeably with no particular logic. In the book, "Lin-chi" has been used for clarity, and all the record's names are given in Chinese for consistency, employing the Wade-Giles system of transliteration but dropping the diacritical marks.

Sokei-an spoke about the importance of the *Record of Lin-chi* as a foundation for this pivotal moment in the transmission of Zen to America. "No translation of Lin-chi's sayings has been made from the Chinese until now," he observed. "This is the first time it has been recorded in English. In Lin-chi's time, Buddhism in China had reached the highest point of its metaphysical phase. The Chinese had accepted Buddhism from India with their brains. Now they realized it was a 'brainy' Buddhism. It is the same in America. It will probably take five hundred years for Buddhism to reach America's heart. An impasse had been reached from which it was impossible to take another step. Lin-chi broke out a new channel through which the slow flow poured into a quick stream."

For eighty years three generations of Zen students at The First Zen Institute of America have enjoyed the resonance of Sokei-an's commentary on the Lin-chi in their own notebooks, zendo readings, and in *Zen Notes*. We bring it forth here before your eyes, as Sokei-an intended. I think he would have liked its title. Most importantly, we also transmit Sokei-an's insistence that, like Lin-chi, American Zen students do something original to demonstrate awakened mind.

Michael Hotz, President,
First Zen Institute of America
New York City, Spring 2013

Introduction by Sokei-an

In China, where the Zen sect originated, five major houses or schools of Zen developed. Lin-chi I-hsuan [*d.* 866], a Chinese master of the ninth century, was the founder of one of them. All Buddhism is from the Buddha's teaching, came from his golden lips. This teaching came from those giant disciples and patriarchs from generation to generation. All these will be included in these lectures.

No translation of Lin-chi's sayings has been made from the Chinese until now. This is the first time it has been translated into English or any language other than the Chinese. So this is the first spoken in English.

It was during the Tang dynasty [618-907] that the Zen school of Buddhism swept throughout China. This golden age in Chinese history was distinguished by a struggle against fierce invaders, the blue-eyed and purple-bearded Tartars and Turks from the West. The succeeding Sung Dynasty (960-1127) was brilliant, but decadent compared with the Tang. The spirit of China was strong and warlike, so Zen was influenced by the blunt and forceful atmosphere of the time, not so fine-grained as it is today. Buddhism once more took on its original form, its original face, as if the Buddha spoke it directly from his own heart. The Zen masters of China at this time were not reading from moth-eaten sutras, but spoke Buddhism as it was written in their own hearts, spoke from the innermost man. Lin-chi died in 866. It is over a thousand years since his death.

It is through the study of *The Record of Lin-chi,* noted by one of his disciples, San-sheng Hui-jan [*n.d.*], that you will understand Zen as expressed in the China of that time. The dialogues of this record are good examples of how those early Zen students dealt with one another and exchanged views. Lin-chi's catechism, which precedes the part with which

I am beginning, is difficult to explain to those not familiar with the Zen school, so I will begin with his teachings, proceed to his enlightenment, and end with the dialogues.

Discourses
X(b)

The Master said: "Today, whoever wishes to learn Buddha's Dharma must find true understanding. Attaining true understanding, he need not conform to life and death. He is at liberty to go or to stay. He does not seek the extraordinary, but gains it naturally.

"Brothers! The ancients had ways of making men. What I want to point out for you is that you should not be confused by others. If you wish to use [true understanding], use it! Do not hesitate!"

SOKEI-AN SAYS:

Lin-chi's says "today" for a reason. Buddhism in China at that time had reached its highest metaphysical development. The Chinese had accepted the Buddha's Dharma, the teaching from India, with their brains. Now they realized it was a "brainy" Buddhism. An impasse had been reached from which it was impossible to take another step. Lin-chi broke that impasse and created a new channel from which the slow flow of the time poured into a quick stream. It is the same here in America now. It will probably take another five hundred years for Buddhism to reach its heart.

Lin-chi says, *"Whoever wishes to learn Buddha's Dharma must find true understanding."* True understanding is the Buddha's true teaching— the Dharma. And it is not to be attained through brainpower; nor is it to be attained through the emotions. Buddhism tells us how to come to it in the Eightfold Path. The Eightfold Path, the fourth of the Four Noble Truths (suffering, the origin of suffering, the cessation of suffering, and the path towards the cessation of suffering), is the path that brings us

1

to what Lin-chi calls "true understanding." True understanding is not knowledge gained from the outside but is inherent wisdom, the faculty of gathering experience and creating ideas. This faculty manifests in us through meditation. The gathering is the sharpening of the sword of wisdom. To understand its sharp point one must meditate and realize it— that is, attain it.

"Attaining true understanding, he need not conform to life and death." In other words, he is not subject to *samsara*, the course of nature that is life and death.

In the autumn when a red maple leaf falls into a pool of water we see the water as red, but scooping up a handful we see that the water is not stained but pure. As the lotus is not stained when it grows from the mud, the soul is not touched by life and death as it struggles through— according to Buddhism—the realms of the three worlds, the *tridhatu*: the three stages of our observation of the universe.

The first world or stage is *kamadhatu*, the world of desire. In this stage our observation is through the five senses where all is agony. And in our agony, we observe the world in five ways: as hell-dweller, hungry spirit, angry spirit, beast, and human being.

The second world or stage is *rupadhatu*, the world of form. In this stage our observation is without desire but through the senses. Here we observe the world in the sixth way as a god or angel, what Buddhists would call a *deva*.

In the third world, that of *arupadhatu*, our observation is without the senses but with the mind. It is the formless stage.

These stages or worlds have been described in Buddhism as a staircase of meditation for our ascent to the state of complete annihilation and the cessation of suffering, the third of the Four Noble Truths. When one has attained the knowledge of the fourfold, not dualistic view, one knows that life and death taken together are one. This life is not to be changed—*this* is life in heaven. So it is from the pure consciousness of the *arupadhatu* stage that realization is, as Zen says, instantaneous. It is not necessary to deny or to affirm anything—one *is* reality. Speak reality with great SILENCE! In Sanskrit this "unspeakable" reality is called *avyakrita*, for it is unrecordable. When you reach here, you understand that all phenomena *are* reality.

"He is at liberty to go or to stay." That is, he can live in any of the three stages of understanding at will. The three stages have many divisions,

comprising all the abodes of sentient beings constantly transmigrating through them. These stages form the backbone of Buddhism. All ascending and descending experiences are to be found here, and he who understands may go or stay as he wills. The mass of mankind, however, knows only the first two stages, the world of desire and the world of form. Even the stage of formlessness, the third world, is still in the realm of conception. It is, however, the highest point for man.

"*He does not seek the extraordinary, but gains it naturally.*" He has attained the stage of Buddha's true understanding and has proved his buddhahood. Yet, at the same time, he is able to enter into the life of any sentient being with sympathy.

"*Brothers! The ancients had ways of making men.*" Previous Zen masters knew how to make good disciples with their sticks. Under their blows one proved one's cognition of nonexistence, bearing any shame or torture as so many feathers. It is under the shout of a Zen master that one suddenly opens one's eye to reality—that existence is nonexistence.

"*What I want to point out for you is that you should not be confused by others. If you wish to use [true understanding], use it! Do not hesitate!*" Once the Buddha told his disciples to do so-and-so and another time he said to do something else. What do you do then? Lin-chi is telling you not to be confused by others but to believe in your own judgment. Use it and do not hesitate. But are you able to use it in everyday life? And what is this "it"? [Here, Sokei-an held up his *nyo-i*, a small scepter symbolizing his rank as Zen master.] Do you understand? "It" is the power that you attain through true understanding.

Lin-chi is speaking to those, of course, who are of a capacity for enlightenment equal to his own.

"*Why, students of today, are you unable to attain true understanding? What infirmity renders you unable to attain it? It is because you lack self-confidence. Unless you have self-confidence, you will lose the very thing that is essential to you. At a loss, you will be involved in circumstances and inverted by innumerable phenomena. When your mind ceases to bustle about, you will in no way differ from Buddha. Do you wish to*

*know Buddha? He is none other than the one behind your face,
listening to my sermon.*

*"It is difficult for students to have faith in this, so they busy
themselves with external matters. They may gain something, but
it will only be words. In the end, they will fail to grasp the vital
point of the patriarchs' teachings."*

SOKEI-AN SAYS:

Lin-chi is asking you what sickness prevents you from having
confidence in your own ability to attain buddhahood? Truth is not to be
sought outside yourself; though, of course, if you deny the outside, you
have to deny the inside as well, for it is relative to the outside. Truth is
neither the one nor the other. So where is it at this instant? As Lin-chi has
repeatedly said, "There is no time for hesitation."

Faith is important in any religion. The Buddha said that faith is the
mother who brings you to earth, the existence of reality. If you wish to
reach the highest point of Buddhism, your task is like that of an alpine
climber struggling from the foot of the mountain to its peak. If you
decide to attain the truth of the world, or beyond the world, see reality
in both phenomena and noumena. In other words: you must seek IT in
yourself until IT manifests its power in the mirror of your shrine. If you
do not have confidence in the power you have intrinsically, you will have
no ground to stand upon, you will be at a loss, and you will not know
what to do.

A Zen teacher does not teach Zen. If you plant a seed and it sprouts,
all of nature has answered you. When you dig into the ground of your
soul, all phenomena answers you as well and tells you that the thing that
you manifest in your mind is true, and the eighty-four thousand buddhas
and bodhisattvas will acknowledge your attainment. But the man whose
observation of the world is inverted, who sees mutable things as eternal
and feels agony as joy, is just like the crow that looks to constantly
changing clouds to guide him to the tree where he has stored his food. It
is the same with human beings and their mutable pleasures. Attachment
to the mutable is like slipping into quicksand. But if you discontinue the
bustle of your mind, running around and pursuing mind-stuff, you will
immediately prove that you are a buddha. And he who realizes Buddha
in himself, "the one behind your face, listening to my sermon," lives in
self-confidence. When you have heard the sound of the single hand, you

have proved the microcosm in yourself and there is nothing more to talk about.

But, as Lin-chi points out, it is hard for the student to have faith in this, for it means you must *prove* the Buddha in yourself. Everyone listening to his lecture is the Buddha, but not all of them believe it. They are seeking the truth externally, in books, in others' teachings, in superstitions. They are nothing but words, ideas, and notions. When the words change, their conceptions change with them. This is not true understanding, and it is not the vital point of Buddhism. The vital point of the Buddha's teaching is the Middle Way.

Once a Brahmin asked the Buddha, "Without speaking, without remaining silent, please express your attainment." This question is something like a twofold door, isn't it? The Buddha answered by keeping himself in SILENCE. That was all, but it was as if he broke open those twofold doors with his feet—Bang!—crushing the twofold doors and throwing them away.

This moment of SILENCE has great significance. The Buddha did not fall into ordinary silence, nor did he fall into "speaking," neither into the negative nor the positive. As the first Zen patriarch Bodhidharma said, "Without using words, I point out man's soul directly. It is not necessary to talk about it." Later, when the second patriarch Hui-k'o came as a student to see Bodhidharma, Hui-k'o said, "My soul is not yet relaxed. Please make my soul relax." Bodhidharma replied, "Where is your soul? Show it to me!"

"Noble Zen students, do not be deceived! Unless you meet [the Buddha] in this life, you will transmigrate through the three worlds for kalpas of time and innumerable lives. Carried along by the circumstances to which you cling, you will be born in the bosom of an ass or a cow."

SOKEI-AN SAYS:

The three worlds are the worlds of desire, (*kamadhatu*), form (*rupadhatu*), and formlessness (*arupadhatu*). The human being transmigrates through, as I've said many times, the six labyrinthine ways in the worlds of desire and form. We go along according to the circumstances with which we are stitched together, for if we are not free from the outside, not emancipated from attachment, we get carried away with our circumstances, just as a small boat is carried along with the waves and is broken on the rocks. Of course, the bosom of a cow or an ass mentioned by Lin-chi is not an actual place but the mind of man.

I am always repeating that the outside does not really exist, that our desire comes from ignorance, that is, our attachment to circumstances. Ordinarily we are just carried along, but if we know *all of this* is only phenomena, if we have proved the state of non-existence, we can be free from these surroundings. When what ropes us to phenomena is cut, we are freed from bondage. Whatever we wish to "take" is our own choice. To attach or not to attach is our own choice as well. In this way, we are not carried along by karma. We are the masters of karma, not its slaves. This is the emancipation spoken of by the Buddha.

However, carried along by the karma you made in the past, you make karma in your own mind, not outside. With it you travel through the three worlds. But if you attain the highest understanding, if you destroy the stage of *arupadhatu*, the world of formlessness, and attain the stage above this notion of nothingness, you can come into any state as you wish. In *arupadhatu*, however, you think that you are in a formless world, but that is really just "big ego," and you will still receive karma. So the stage of *arupadhatu* is not really the highest stage.

There is a koan: The tea-dipper goes into burning water and into icy water but feels no pain because it has no soul, no ego. In this koan you have to prove why the dipper has no soul (the dipper is yourself). The tea-dipper does not go through these stages and is never born in the bosom of anything.

In Lin-chi's time there was once an artist who painted horses so marvelously that a Zen master of the time said to him, "You must stop making such paintings or you will be born in the bosom of a horse. Your face already resembles one and your manner also." The painter changed his subject to Avalokiteshvara, the bodhisattva of compassion.

Then there was the poet who made wonderful poems, sort of erotic love songs. The poems were so bewitching they influenced people to take up the romantic life. The master said to him, "You must stop making such enchanting love songs." The poet laughed and said, "So you think I will also be born in the bosom of a horse?" The master said, "No, you will be born in the mind of a flea."

The belief in transmigration was in existence before the time of the Buddha. He took this hypothesis into Buddhism and used it as a tool to help one wake up from illusion and come to true understanding. Knowing the real point of Buddhism, I don't think the Buddha really believed the hypothesis of transmigration. But if you do not grasp the Buddha's point, you are transmigrating every moment—you will never find yourself, never come back to yourself.

In Buddhism, you do not try to be wise. Buddhism is not a theory to make you wise. It is a religion that makes you very plain and simple. A Zen master once said that to become wise is easy, but to become an idiot is hard. Of course, a common, garden-variety idiot is nothing. The soul of a great idiot must look something like a huge stone top. A top made of wood is not a great enough symbol for the heart of an idiot.

So Lin-chi says you must meet the Buddha in this lifetime. Meet what? Meet the vital point, the Buddha in yourself.

A Zen master called to himself every morning, "Master!" and answered himself, "Yes?" One of his disciples had been with him for ten years. When the master called "Master!" one morning, the disciple answered "Yes?" The master said, "But you are my disciple," and hit him with his stick. The disciple grasped the stick and pushed the master over in his chair. It looks wild, but the truth of the universe must be handled vividly.

"Brothers, as I understand it, you differ in no way from Shakya. Is there anything you lack to perform your manifold functions today? The light of your six divine senses has never ceased to shine. Once you understand this, you need not seek any further.

"Good brothers, the three worlds are like a house afire. They are not places in which to dwell for long! The demon death, the hand of mutability, does not for one moment discriminate between rich and poor, old and young. So if you do not want to

differ from the Buddha, do not search for Buddha in the outer world."

SOKEI-AN SAYS:

In this passage, Lin-chi is emphasizing the Buddha in oneself, the "personal" Buddha. When you realize buddha-nature in yourself, you are Buddha. Therefore, it is not necessary to seek Buddha outside.

Today there are students of Buddhism who are attempting to recreate the Buddha's own original Buddhism, the teaching that came from the Buddha's own golden lips. These modern students imagine that the Buddha's own original Buddhism might be found somewhere in the so-called *tripitaka*, the three baskets of Buddhist teachings, which are the *sutras*, the *abhidharma*, and the *vinaya*. Of course, the Buddha's words can be comparatively studied in the records of various languages. But in Zen there is a shortcut to what the Buddha really taught: instead of looking through the *sutras* for it, you can look for it in your own soul. After all, the Buddha found his religion in his own soul, and we are the same human beings. So if we dig deeply into our own hearts, we will find that same religion. There is no difference. That is the reason Lin-chi does not refer to the Buddha as Lokanatha ("Lord of the World") or Tathagata ("Thus come"), but as "Shakya," a man of the same rank as himself. So when you meditate upon your own soul and open your own eye to reality, your vital point will be no different from the Buddha's, and it will not be necessary to call it Buddhism.

Is there anything you lack to perform your manifold functions today! The light of your six divine senses has never ceased to shine." According to the Buddha's teaching, all the infinite functions of the human body are important, so Lin-chi is referring to the five senses and the mind. They are the elemental powers of the universe, the six divine senses. It is with our senses that we observe various universes. We sense color and form with the eyes, sound with the ears, odor with the nose, taste with the tongue, touch with the skin, and with the mind, Dharma.

Can you imagine anything that is not observable with one of these senses? If we had different eyes, perhaps we would see something that is not color or form, but it is impossible for us to imagine it. The root of these senses is *this* consciousness. To *this* consciousness the whole universe is one—Dharma. The philosophers call it noumenon—reality. Of course, this is a metaphytsical conception. This [holding up a box] is phenomenon, but if we hide it away and say "box," this is no phenomenon but a conception. The five senses create the physical base but do not function as perception; it is another function. So altogether there are six. These days scientists are trying to find more, but so far they have not been successful.

"*Once you undertand this, you need not seek any further.* A table has legs; a snake has none. If a snake had legs, the legs would be a nuisance to him. We have everything we need to perform our daily functions. More would be a nuisance.

"*Good brothers, the three worlds are like a house afire. They are not places in which to dwell for long.*" Well, where shall I go?

In the world of desire, we are pursuing something from morning to evening. Our viewpoint is not right. We have to separate our view from our desire and look at everything with a cool mind, as an artist looks at a field and observes the green grass and the blue sky, not like a farmer who looks at the same field with desire. In the world of form, we discriminate between the beautiful and the ugly. We see by understanding. In the world of formlessness, all is pure existence, there is no purity or impurity. All is real manifestation; nothing is good or bad.

To really live in this life, you must know the existence of formlessness. Here, one observation is the truth. It is necessary at least once in your life to separate from the phenomenal and come upon noumenal understanding. The world of form must be practiced as well. However, if in your meditation you attach to form or formlessness, you are still in the world of desire. Do not be deceived by theory.

The Buddha said that there are four inverted views or wrong observations of the universe: thinking it is eternal; thinking life is a joy; believing in ego; thinking this existence of desire is pure. That is why the Buddha pointed out that all our conceptions about the world are inverted. To cure these inversions, we practice meditation. These stages of meditation are written within you, ascending to the opening of the universal eye.

Buddha also taught us about the three diseases or poisons: ignorance, passion, and anger. To cure these sicknesses, we need not seek remedies outside ourselves. For ignorance the remedy is to educate ourselves, to open our inner eye with which to see the reality of the universe. At seventeen or eighteen we can only open a doubtful eye. Why do we live? Where do we come from? Where do we go? What is our relation to our father and mother? Were we here before? After death is there only nothing? So we peer into books or go to teachers. We become like animals searching for water. For everyone it is the same problem. If you have never sought to understand these great questions, I would say you are sleeping. They come to everyone, even before we open our eye to sex. Sex, like a flower, will come a little later; but first, a leaf appears, the questioning of everything. This is wisdom curing ignorance. As for passion, we have the power to control it. It is not necessary to take a vow: all commandments are written within us. And we have tranquillity with which to cure anger.

"*The demon death, the hand of mutability, does not for one moment discriminate between rich and poor, old and young.*" In "one moment" there are nine *ksanas*, the smallest unit of time, and in one *ksana* sentient beings reincarnate nine hundred times. We think we are living now, and we think we are not dead, but in one *ksana* we repeat life and death nine hundred times, and that *ksana* is not different from our fifty years, and nine hundred lives are not different from one *ksana*.

"*So if you do not want to differ from the Buddha, do not search for Buddha in the outer world.*" The Buddha said we must give up all theories and conceptions and observe the universe from our own hearts. It is not necessary to search outside of ourselves; all is within. This is emancipation from all names and all conceptions. In the *sanzen* room, if you understand the real existence of the universe, you can take the Himalayan Mountains out of an incense box, pass through a keyhole, and so forth.

"*The pure light that resides in a single pulse of your soul is the Dharmakaya Buddha within your shrine. The light that discerns nothing in a single pulse of your soul is the Sambhogakaya Buddha within your shrine. The light that does not discriminate in a single pulse of soul is the Nirmanakaya Buddha within your shrine. This triune body is none other than the one in your presence who is listening to my sermon. Thus will it be revealed when you cease to search in the outer world.*

"According to the authoritative masters of the sutras and shastras the triune body is the fundamental principle, but according to my view this is not the case. The triune body is merely a name, and the three bodies denoted by this name are conceptual. The ancients said, 'These bodies exist theoretically. Their fields exist as a natural consequence of the bodies themselves.' The essential body and the essential field of Buddha are now evident. They are the light and shadow of one's own mind. Good brothers, you must recognize the one who operates them! He is the very source of all the buddhas. The very place you are now is the home to which you long to return."

SOKEI-AN SAYS:

This is a very important passage. Lin-chi is talking about the triune body of Buddha, the Buddhist theory of the *trikaya: Dharmakaya, sambhogakaya,* and *nirmanakaya*. Zen Master Lin-chi, however, is criticizing this theory. He is telling us that the three bodies are not existing in the sky or somewhere far away. The triune body of Buddha is our own body. Everyone is a Buddha, everyone has buddha-nature, whether we know it or not.

"The pure light that resides in a single pulse of your soul is the Dharmakaya Buddha within your shrine." The pure light of which Lin-chi speaks has two meanings: the light of nirvana and the light of pure wisdom. Pure wisdom is complete annihilation. To come to this nirvanic wisdom—if I may coin this phrase—you must annihilate all notions, all mind-stuff. To attain pure wisdom one must attain pure nirvana first.

Dharmakaya Buddha is not manifesting its own existence, but exists as essence. Its light does not perceive anything. Your tongue tastes and your eyes see, but they do not say, "I wish to taste, and I wish to see." This Buddha is the intrinsic world of *arupadhatu*, the non-seeming or formless world of *Dharmakaya*; it is the Knower of the universe.

"The light that discerns nothing in a single pulse of your soul is the Sambhogakaya Buddha within your shrine." Sambhogakaya Buddha is the "responding" or "enjoyment" Buddha and has two functions: perceiving the inside and perceiving the outside. So it is the body of actual consciousness. This Buddha is of the world of *rupadhatu* and perceives without attachment. This light or consciousness knows its own nature without phenomenal existence. Perceiving phenomena, it proves

that it sees. The first state is unmanifested consciousness. It perceives its own being without having contact with phenomenal existence; it knows its own vibration and realizes it is living. The second state is manifested: making contact with its own vibration, it realizes the whole universe.

"The light that does not discriminate in a single pulse of soul is the Nirmanakaya Buddha within your shrine." The light of the Nirmanakaya Buddha, the Buddha of "transformation," is the world of desire. It is through various transformations that it achieves its aim. This Buddha is pure. Though this Buddha uses the words "like" and "dislike," it is different from attachment or human discrimination. It chooses cotton in summer and wool in winter.

Please understand the three Buddhas or bodies are all *Dharmakaya*. *Dharmakaya* includes *sambhogakaya* and *nirmanakaya*. In *sanzen*, to show your understanding in *Dharmakaya*, you must prove the two other stages are included. So *Dharmakaya* is the body of *sambhogakaya* and *nirmanakaya*. In the *sanzen* room, *sambhogakaya* is observed in its function as wisdom, the body of response. When someone slaps your face, you feel pain. *Nirmanakaya* is your life from morning to evening. These bodies together are the *tathagata*, and they do not exist anywhere else but in your body. Your body is the body of *tathagata*, three bodies in one. There is no mystery to this; it can be clearly proved.

When you have passed the first koan, you prove *Dharmakaya*, *sambhogakaya*, as well as *nirmanakaya* within it.

The Sixth Patriarch, Hui-neng, proved *sambhogakaya* in the koan, "The flag is not moving; wind is not moving; the soul is moving."

Consciousness does not belong to the outside or the inside. Its wisdom shines through *Dharmakaya* and the whole phenomenal world. If you do not attach to any particular point in the outer world, you will prove nirvana in your physical body, in this flesh, and enter any part of outer or inner existence. That is transformation—*nirmanakaya*.

"This triune body is none other than the one in your presence who is listening to my sermon. Thus will it be revealed when you cease to search in the outer world." You can attain nirvana and reveal this mysterious body in this existence on earth. This is your merit. When you prove the reality of the universe you accumulate merit in your daily life because you are not searching in the outer world. You are proving the merit in yourself. This merit also includes "function" and "revelation."

"According to the authoritative masters of the sutras and shastras the triune body is the fundamental principle. But according to my view this is not the case." The authoritative masters Lin-chi is referring to are the *sutra* and commentary masters of his time. They said the triune body was the fundamental principle, but Lin-chi disagreed. He said the triune body was merely a name and conceptual. We cannot prove existence with words, whether they be *Dharmakaya, sambhogakaya, nirmanakaya,* or Father, Son, and Holy Ghost. For Lin-chi, a name or word is like the cane of an old man. Without it the old man cannot stand. He is trying to tell us that truth originally has no name, that we put one on it, like a robe, worn, and not very clear. Then we try another and another, and soon we have three sets of robes completing our conception. So names are convenient but also troublesome.

"The ancients said, 'These bodies exist theoretically. Their fields exist as a natural consequence of the bodies themselves.' The essential body and the essential field of Buddha are now evident. They are the light and shadow of one's own mind." So the essential bodies and the essential fields are Buddha-itself—universal nature; and they are created by the light of your own mind. It is like a moving picture on a screen where the brain is the machine operating the film. The triune body appears on the screen of your mind and you think that it is the Father, Son, and Holy Ghost, and then you pray to it. No wonder there is no answer.

"Good brothers, you must recognize the one who operates them! He is the very source of all the buddhas." He who operates these bodies and fields is the master, not your body, not your mind-stuff, but your own light. Mind is body and mind-stuff is the field of this light. You see light and cast it into bronze or write it in a character and pray to it. This is all nonsense. The master is *here.* The physical body is *nirmanakaya,* the soul is *sambhogakaya,* and the source of it all is *Dharmakaya.*

"The very place you are now is the home to which you long to return." That place is your own mind, Buddha. Man searches for truth in outward form. God is everywhere. But someday you will come to your own shrine that is supported by your own two feet, and you will find Buddha in the very place where you stand.

"My sermon to which you are listening cannot be comprehended by the four great elements of which your body is composed, and it cannot be comprehended by your stomach, liver, and heart. My sermon to which you are listening cannot be comprehended by the empty sky. Who, then, is the one who can comprehend my sermon to which you are listening? He who has no visible figure but illumines brightly in your presence comprehends the sermon to which you are listening. If you realize who 'he' is, your understanding of the true view does not differ from that of Buddha. He exists unceasingly throughout space and throughout time. Everything that meets your eyes is his manifestation.

"But when you entertain any notion, true wisdom is shattered, and when you harbor any doubt, the original body is misconceived. Consequently, you will transmigrate throughout the three worlds and will suffer from various afflictions. According to my view, there is [no moment of life] that does not touch the bottom of wisdom or reach [the height of] emancipation."

SOKEI-AN SAYS:

The four great elements that Lin-chi-chi is talking about are earth, water, fire and air. In Buddhist theory sometimes a fifth and sixth elements are added: *akasha* and consciousness. *Akasha* is Lin-chi's "empty sky"; it is the material that fills the void. Consciousness is awareness, whether manifested or unmanifested. In an intricate body, consciousness is manifested; in a simple body like air, it is unmanifested. Lin-chi is telling us his sermon cannot be comprehended by any of these elements.

"Who, then, is the one who can comprehend my sermon to which you are listening? He who has no visible figure but illumines brightly in your presence comprehends the sermon to which you are listening. If you realize who 'he' is, your understanding of the true view does not differ from that of Buddha." In other words, "he" has no name but is in everyone.

If I could say "impersonal person," it would be that. He is not living in worldly existence but in purified existence. He is the "one" of the triune body. But Lin-chi is fooling us. He thinks we are children, so he tells us a fairy story. If he had said "he" had a figure, you would attach to that figure.

"He exists unceasingly throughout space and throughout time." Everything that meets your eyes is his manifestation." Wonderful conception! Mountains! Rivers! Stars! Sun! Flowers! Birds and insects! All live everlastingly! That is the true ground of religion and Buddhism.

"But when you entertain any notion, true wisdom is shattered, and when you harbor any doubt, the original body is misconceived." The true ground or true existence is undemonstrable by words; it is not a notion. Notions are the material of logic, and logic can only bring us to the gate of religion. So you must not seek true understanding in notions, the material that comes from outer existence. The material, the stuff that we have in our minds, is the shadow of our sense-impressions. True understanding is different from sense-impressions. The true ground of religion is as pure as *akasha,* but a flake of delusion, like a small cloud in the clear sky, comes into your mind and creates mind-stuff. Then you do not see true existence anymore. You never see the fact of existence. You think this mind-stuff is mind, but mind-stuff and mind are different; one is the outer existence of mind and the other is neutral mind. When you perceive without delusion, it is altered. If you perceive with the five senses and cling to that, you think it is true existence. As they say in China, "When your form has been changed, you are carried away from the true body, the essential body—reality."

"Consequently, you will transmigrate throughout the three worlds and will suffer from various afflictions." That is, as a man, an ox, a dog or cat. You will experience torture and joy.

"According to my view, there is [no moment of life] that does not touch the bottom of wisdom or reach [the height of] emancipation." That is, true universal wisdom.

"Brothers, the soul is without form, yet penetrates in all directions. In the eyes, it is seeing; in the ears, hearing; in the nose, smelling; in the mouth, speaking; in the hands, holding; in the feet, carrying. Originally, it is one essential light divided into the six harmonious senses. If you do not cling to the thoughts in your mind, wherever you stand you are emancipated.

"Brothers, why do I say this? Only because you cannot keep your minds from wandering, and you are trapped in the useless devices of the ancients."

SOKEI-AN SAYS:

Last time, Zen Master Lin-chi was talking about the true soul, the original soul in ourselves. He said that everyone thinks the soul has various features, so everyone conceives delusion. This delusion shatters the true faith of the soul.

"Brothers, the soul is without form, yet penetrates in all directions. In the eyes, it is seeing; in the ears, hearing; in the nose, smelling; in the mouth, speaking; in the hands, holding; in the feet, carrying. Originally, it is one essential light divided into the six harmonious senses." It is very difficult to see the shape of a naked soul. We clothe it as we would a body in many garments—superstition, education, various acquirements and attainments. Our minds have many sets of garments. We can see the shape of other forms even with our clothes on, but no one sees the shape of another's naked soul so easily. You notice the ugly proportions of a naked body, but most of the time you never see the unbalanced proportions of a soul. Sometimes we see a naked soul in the form of a *preta*, a hungry ghost, but we cannot see the soul that has the beautiful form of the Buddha in perfect balance with our conceptions.

Reality is not anything when it gives you more garments to put on your soul. True reality suggests that you take off your shabby clothes. It makes you see the original body of the soul that you got from your spiritual mother in the Tushita Heaven, the creatress; not the creator of *maya*, delusion, but the creator of true existence.

When the old garments are discarded, you will choose your own clothes. In summer, you will don gossamer and in winter velvet. If you realize you wear a seamless fur coat like Noodle, my cat, you will need no other garments. If you realize where you are, on what spot of the universe you are standing and in what shape your soul is, you will know what to do, and you will be emancipated at that moment. However, in summertime you may have forgotten how you put on your heavy winter clothes, so you are unable to disrobe and emancipate yourself.

As I've said before, it was during the Tang dynasty that Buddhism once again took on its original form in China, its original face, like the Buddha speaking directly from his own heart. The Zen masters at that time were not reading from moth-eaten old *sutras* but spoke Buddhism as it was written in their own hearts. They were speaking from the innermost part of themselves. At that time, Buddhism became very clear, but it can be criticized, for these great masters forgot the atmosphere of Buddhism. They grasped the vital point and were satisfied, like the scientist of today who goes to a drug store instead of a restaurant and says, "Give me Vitamin D!" and eats it instead of a meal. If you go to the Ta-yu restaurant in the neighborhood, you will probably have a cocktail, some soup, the main dish and dessert, then, perhaps a cigarette and some coffee. Real Buddhism must be a full course meal, too. Lin-chi gives us a vitamin and we swallow it—"The Essence of Buddhism!" The vitamin is only good in theory, but when you eat food that comes from the garden, you also see the farm, the chickens, and the dogs. You must see it all. I wish to show you all of Buddhism, not just Vitamin D.

So Lin-chi says the soul is without form yet penetrates in all directions like electricity or water. We look at the sun, moon, and so forth with objectivity, with our senses, but if we become the sun and moon, we see subjectively. Then all becomes one great fire, for the soul cannot visualize itself from its subjective viewpoint. So one essential light is subdivided into different universal manifestations.

"If you do not cling to the thoughts in your mind, wherever you stand you are emancipated." It is easy to talk about annihilating the human mind, but it is not easy to do so. This human mind is made by the karma of nature, the human mind that we have made through the actions of karma. If you realize buddha-nature, you are emancipated, but you cannot see it with your two eyes. Your logical understanding will only lead you to the gate of real existence, it does not have the ability to bring you to the center of real existence; no word will take you there. You have to take off the drapery of words and enter. That is emancipation. If you really enter, this very body is the body of Buddha. That is why your teacher will say you must enter by yourself. He cannot take you in.

If you do not know how to attain this, you may think you must suppress this or that. But that way is too slow! To have the fruits of buddha-nature, it is not necessary to cut off the root and trunk. When the time comes, your mind will open the petals of the true flower and you will see the white lotus of original nature. Do not destroy its pond! However, you must separate from the three worlds of desire, form and formlessness. And it is not necessary to go into a deep sleep, separate from your body, and so on; you cannot separate from the universal body.

Why is this such a deep mystery? It cannot be understood with the understanding that you received from your mother's teaching. It is by your own effort that you will understand the phenomenal world. In this realm both realities are the same. This is the mystery.

"Brothers, why do I say this? Only because you cannot keep your minds from wandering, and you are trapped in the useless devices of the ancients." The ancient Buddhists used wonderful methods or devices—meditation and such—to carry you into the real understanding of Buddhism. When I give you *koans* like, "Sitting in your chair stand upon the Himalayas," "Pass through the keyhole," "Hide yourself in the wall," and "Walk on the surface of the water," you cannot answer because you are trapped in the meaning of words.

A koan is a device to free you from all devices, to train you to see through words and get to the meaning behind them so you are not trapped by words. I do not think my meaning is different from that of Christians who really penetrate their words and find the real meaning of phrases such as "Pass over the surface of the water." These koans point to real existence, the reality of the universe beyond phenomena. But when I say "beyond," you probably think "sky," and so forth. What can I say? Do not be bothered by the shades of meaning in words. As Lin-chi said, do not be trapped in the useless devices of the ancients.

The Buddha, however, taught us how to meditate. In meditation, you separate yourself from the circumference of your environment and realize the Buddha is yourself. The master is here. You have to knock at the door and ask to meet the master! The answer comes from the inside, not the outside. But to call, you must make an effort, must knock at the door of your heart. When you meet him, give up the knocking. At midnight, if you try to get into a monastery, banging on the door with your fist, there will be no answer. Then with a stone, Bang! Bang! Bang! "Yes?" Then you throw away the stone. Meditation and concentration are stones to find the master; there comes a time when you do not need them anymore. The door of the temple is not the master, Do not mistake it. Many people think that meditation and concentration are Buddhism, but they are not.

I need not say anything more because if I say something more you will cling to it, will forget the Buddha in yourself, and search outside from the lips of a teacher, from an image carved in wood. You will study a word from the outside, or a word made of mind-stuff. You will forget how to search for the searcher who is Buddha. The object with which you search is not Buddha. You must find Buddha in the searcher. You need no devices. Give up all devices, all methods, and when you come to yourself—"Hmmm! I understand."

In such a way you must find the Buddha.

"Brothers, if you accord with my view you will cut off the heads of the Sambogakaya and Nirmanakaya Buddhas. A bodhisattva who is content with the tenth stage of enlightenment is merely a hanger-on in an alien land. A bodhisattva whose attainment is equal to that of the Buddha is a criminal in stocks. An arhat and a pratyekabuddha are the filth in drains. Bodhi and nirvana are hitching posts for mules and asses. Why? It is because, brothers, you have failed to attain the full annihilation of countless kalpas that you have barriers."

SOKEI-AN SAYS:

To "cut off the heads" is an expression that is very difficult to translate. What it means is that you must "sit" on the head of the Buddha, sit upon the seat of meditation, sit upon the universe to realize the Buddha in oneself. You are Buddha. There is none other in the universe.

"A bodhisattva who is content with the tenth stage of enlightenment is merely a hanger-on in an alien land." The bodhisattva has exterminated his ego and embodied himself in the universal body. The human being has a separated soul and lives in blind desire. But when he opens his Eye, he realizes there is no separated soul: there is only one soul, a tree of soul, and you are one branch of that tree. You perform your own functions, but you are not separate. When you realize that soul is universal, your body is also universal, and you are a bodhisattva.

The bodhisattva that is "content with the tenth stage of enlightenment" is only observing phenomena and noumena as conceptions. This is not like the arhat who keeps himself in a corner of annihilation, separated from the rest. The highest bodhisattva knows reality in both phenomena and noumena. The arhat thinks the phenomenal is not existing, so he hides in annihilation, or nothingness. This is not true annihilation. It is only the annihilation of conception.

Nevertheless, according to Lin-chi, if anyone conceives that these stages are really existing (such stages exist hypothetically as a mode of thinking to bring one to enlightenment), he has not attained to reality but is still in a hypothetical cloud.

"A bodhisattva whose attainment is equal to that of the Buddha is a criminal in stocks." If he thinks he is a bodhisattva or a Buddha, or a plain man, he is not living in his own light. In such a case, he is merely a "hanger-on," and he is not standing on his own two feet.

There are two kinds of bodhisattvas: the one whose understanding is co-equal with the Buddha's but not the Buddha's, and the one whose understanding is the Buddha's. The first type of bodhisattva has enlightened himself and attained the understanding that is co-equal with that of the Buddha. He has gone against the stream and come to buddha-nature. He has ceased to desire and made many efforts to come to it. The second type of bodhisattva from that point turns himself into everyone's heart. Having attained buddhahood, he comes back to promulgate his own understanding. Then he will go away and return no more. According to Lin-chi, neither of these bodhisattvas are truly emancipated. The truly enlightened one is himself—neither Buddha nor the same as Buddha.

Lin-chi uses a poisonous tongue in criticizing those who are satisfied with hypothetical Buddhism.

"An arhat and a pratyekabuddha are the filth in drains. Bodhi and nirvana are hitching posts for mules and asses." The arhat has attained the annihilation of agony and the cause of agony. He has annihilated desire, but not superstition; therefore, his attainment is not complete annihilation. The pratyekabuddha has enlightened himself, but he is like the dry leaves of autumn. He has passed the twelve stages of cause and result, has attained the truth of the universe, lives alone and understands, but he cannot teach.

To Lin-chi, bodhi, knowledge, the goal of nirvana, reached with the great knowledge and theory of Buddhism, the system built by the Buddha, are all like hitching posts for mules and asses. You cannot move as long as you are hitched to any hypothetical sort of Buddhism.

"Why? It is because, brothers, you have failed to attain the full annihilation of countless kalpas that you have barriers." Kalpa means endless time. In Lin-chi's view, if you attain full annihilation, one moment equals a million years. You must realize this or the definition of the system and theory of Buddhism stays in your brain and you are never free. You have to attain throughout all *kalpas*. Even "oneness" is not existing in this entire annihilation.

These are barriers because you have not attained full annihilation. However, if you annihilate your mind immediately, you will emancipate yourself. Cutting one handful of weeds you cut all weeds. If you cut off your human mind, that is the end of all connection with this delusion. You have emancipated yourself from all agony and darkness and have attained the Ocean of Nirvana. If you cut one, you can cut all with the sword of Manjushri, the *bodhisattva* of original wisdom. Cut off human karma—I hate, I feel nice, and so forth. As for *samskara*, the subconscious, you can cut it off with the sword of Manjushri that you originally have.

"If you are a real Buddhist, you are not like them. You expiate past karma by your daily deeds. You wear whatever you please. You go or sit at will. You seek none of the attainments of Buddha, even for a moment. Why? The ancients said, 'If you attempt to see Buddha by having recourse to any device, Buddha becomes the cause of birth and death.'

"Good brothers, you must value every moment of life. Yet you run about studying Zen, memorizing terms and phrases, looking for a teacher, and restlessly searching house to house for Buddha and the patriarchs."

SOKEI-AN SAYS:

Last time Lin-chi said that you do not have freedom of mind because you have not annihilated your mind. A Chinese master after this criticism of Lin-chi said you cannot grow mushrooms upon bamboo leaves; they need soil. A mushroom that grows upon bamboo leaves dries up in one hot day. Growing upon the earth, it will survive a long time. If one's mind does not grow from the real ground of life, it disappears very soon. For once in your life you must clear away the piling leaves, that thicket of bamboo in your mind, and see the real ground of mind. If you can answer the crystal bell koan and "Where is Mahakashyapa now?" you will really see the ground of soul. If you attain real annihilation, you will know. Otherwise, you are like a mushroom upon a dry leaf.

If you do not reach the real ground of mind, you cannot see the law of the universe written in your mind. Lin-chi tells us that we must turn our blind instinct into enlightenment. When the turn takes place at the bottom of the true ground of mind, we realize that our blind instinct is wisdom calling us.

"If you are a real Buddhist, you are not like them." There was a Buddhist congregation on the Pacific Coast—not the San Francisco one— where the youngsters talked things over and made the decision that the way to deeply enter into Buddhism was to read all the books of foreign scholars in English. They were of the Pure Land sect. The founder of the Pure Land sect said that to become a true Buddhist it is not necessary to do anything but call the Buddha's name from your heart; that makes you a true Buddhist. This is a popularized form of Buddhism. It can penetrate into everyone's mind. Every moment of the day, whatever you do or think, you call the name of Amida Buddha. But the Pure Land teacher on the Pacific Coast did not teach this, Instead he said, "Read books." Lin-chi would not agree!

"You expiate past karma by your daily deeds. You wear whatever you please. You go or sit at will. You seek none of the attainments of Buddha, even for a moment." Take a drink, fan yourself, and at noon, lunch; in the evening, supper. Expiating past karma? Yes. Not hiding the past or making new karma. You must turn the karma, the judgment in you, which is the result of your past life, into true wisdom.

"Why? The ancients said, 'If you attempt to see Buddha by having recourse to any device, Buddha becomes the cause of birth and death.'" The fox never sleeps in his hole, always outside. If the wind blows from the north, he will sleep on the north side; if from the south, he will sleep on that side. So if someone approaches the hole, the fox gets the scent and enters the hole. He never sleeps there, for a fire could be set, burning the grass in the hole. No one told the fox about it. He has this knowledge naturally. However, the poor fox does not know the artificial mind, so it can be caught by a hunter who knows its instinctive ways.

We human beings are almost entirely living in our instinctual mind. Whatever we do we are expiating past karma—passion, anger, and ignorance. With true, intrinsic wisdom we turn these into virtues. Willfulness turns into willpower; anger turns into meditation; ignorance turns into wisdom. After gathering all information and knowledge, you must come back to the real ground of mind. What was once called ignorance is now intrinsic wisdom. Total ignorance is nirvana!

According to Buddhist theory, our eight consciousnesses turn into four great wisdoms. The *alayavijnana*, the eighth or root consciousness, turns into "mirror-like wisdom." The seventh consciousness, *manovijnana*, becomes "discerning wisdom." The sixth consciousness, this present consciousness, becomes "observing wisdom." The fifth consciousness, including the five senses, becomes "performing wisdom."

The mirror-like consciousness reflects; nothing but the mirror is there. There is no reflection on it, but it exists—a black ox sleeping in pitch dark. If you hear the caw of the crow that is not cawing, you can see your father before your birth, the father you cannot meet. The mirror is here, but it reflects nothing. It is *akasha*, the mirror made of sky, unmanifested consciousness.

Undiscerning wisdom is "equalizing wisdom," or "coinciding wisdom"—two clear mirrors that reflect each other with nothing between—your mirror and my mirror reflect each other as sky and ocean reflect each other. An Indian sage who visited a Buddhist master dropped a needle into a silver bowl filled with water. The master understood and admitted him to his presence.

Observing wisdom, the wisdom of insight, sees everything inside and outside. With it you perceive all color and sound with present consciousness, with Buddha's wisdom. We all have this innate wisdom with which to decide, with which to create our daily life. With it, we know time and position. So we must use it.

We all have these four fundamental wisdoms, but we use them blindly, instinctively; therefore, we make many mistakes—that is our life. We must make our wisdom sure and shining. We can be an expert in any line we wish, use it in any direction. We are rewarded and punished by its use. So by knowing it and using it, our *alaya*-consciousness can be turned from mere blind instinct into mirror-like wisdom.

The first of the four wisdoms is immobile, like the earth, and the other three depend upon it; it perceives all as Oneness. When you attain this, your consciousness becomes wisdom. We are then free in daily life and wear whatever we wish, put on whatever thoughts we wish. We can be "Zennists" or Christians, for if we have taken off everything, we can put on any garb that pleases us, go or stay at will. Mirror-like wisdom is not blind instinct but enlightened intuition. If we understand this, there is no more Buddhism. The two hundred and fifty commandments of the Buddhist monk become daily life. We need no books, no meditation.

"*Good brothers, you must value every moment of life. Yet you run about studying Zen, memorizing terms and phrases, looking for a teacher, and restlessly searching house to house for Buddha and the patriarchs.*" Buddhism came to its height of metaphysical understanding in the Tang dynasty. At that time it had reached an impasse and become stagnant. Bodhidharma came in the fifth century, and three hundred years later his disciples started destroying that metaphysical theory by actually trying to realize Buddhism in themselves. That school is called Zen. It is this Buddhism that I am trying to carry into America. You, as modern mankind, must not be blind to superstition. You must open your Eye to see the real source of Buddhism, which has real flesh, a beautiful form, and a shining body.

Today in China, Buddhism is a form without soul. The other extreme, of which Lin-chi spoke, has soul but no body. Pointing to the soul, they have forgotten the beauty of the body. Lin-chi used a short dagger and pointed it directly into the heart, and it was very sharp.

"*Do not be deceived, brothers! Have you not a father and a mother? Why should you seek to acquire something more? Turn your gaze deep into your own consciousness. The ancients said, 'Yajnadatta mislaid his head and could not find it. When he abandoned his desire to seek, he found there was nothing further for him to do.*"

"*Good brothers, be yourselves! Do not be pretentious!*"

SOKEI-AN SAYS:

Last time Lin-chi told his disciples how to be a true Buddhist. He said a real Buddhist seeks Buddhism in himself, not in the sky, under the earth, or in books. It is nowhere but in yourself. But how do you enter?

Shariputra, a disciple of the Buddha, told his disciples that we have six gates, the six senses, through which we enter Buddhism. The five senses go out from the one sense that is the root. With the senses we see color and form, and we hear sound. That is how we know the outside. But if we had no eyes, we could not be sure whether sound is inside or outside. The same with smell, taste, and touch. Of course, it is all in the sense organ, not outside. We cut our finger and say the knife is painful, but the pain is not in the knife. We say this color is red, but color is in the eye, and so on with all the senses. The five senses create phenomena in you, not outside. The creator, the Goddess Maya, is in you. The five senses perceive phenomena and the sixth, the root, perceives reality.

Then what is really existing outside? If we had no senses, what would exist in the universe? There is essential existence that is not color, form, and so forth. We must see this with the one sense. Essential existence is called by many names: reality, noumena, eternal atom, and so on. This part of Buddhism is the same as Western philosophy; it is the real ground upon which to build religion. If you do not understand reality, you cannot understand religion. So the entrance of Buddhism is this consciousness within you. Of course, this consciousness is not your self. You must realize that this consciousness and that reality are not two, but one elemental existence. You must drop the conception of ego existence. Buddhism is in that which has no name. We cannot say it is inside, for that is merely relative to the outside. Yet, Buddhism is visible and tangible within you. Do not see it in anything outside.

Lin-chi is certainly talking about non-ego. He dislikes the Buddhists of his time who kept themselves above human beings and took a pretentious attitude. So he pulled them down to earth.

"Do not be deceived, brothers! Have you not a father and a mother? Why should you seek to acquire something more?" Lin-chi is saying, Haven't you a mother and father from whom you have inherited the source of wisdom and love?

According to Buddhism, the father within you is *avidya*, ignorance; and *trishna*, craving, is your mother. *Avidya*, the father, is the darkness of ignorance when you were in your mother's bosom—we do not know time or space and have no consciousness of self. After birth, you open your eye and use your ear, but you are still sleeping. You see the blue sky with wide-open eyes, yet you are snoring. That is your life. So you must open your inner eye. *Trishna,* desire—smiling, crying, anger—is pursuing you from morning to evening; it is by them that you are destroying yourself.

But in this case, in its primitive sense, Lin-chi is not talking about this kind of *avidya*. He is talking about *avidya* as intrinsic wisdom, as the sky-mirror. *Akasha* is the mirror that has consciousness when something is reflected; thus *avidya* becomes nirvana to the enlightened mind. *Trishna* becomes love. The enlightened one creates happiness on earth, the universal love of Maitreya, the bodhisattva that will appear in the future. You have this intrinsic wisdom and universal love in yourself.

"Turn your gaze deep into your own consciousness. The ancients said, 'Yajnadatta mislaid his head and could not find it." Yajnadatta was a man who once lived in Shravasti, India. Each morning as he looked into his mirror, he saw a beautiful man and was enchanted with his own reflection. But one morning he couldn't find his image, nothing was reflected in his mirror. He was so distressed, he ran out crying, "I lost my head! I lost my head! Please help me find it!" Of course, he did not know he was looking at the back of the mirror. This is an allegory for consciousness seeking consciousness, something like looking in the encyclopedia for yourself, or searching the sky for nirvana. Truth-itself is undemonstrable, cannot be proved by something else. The logical function of the brain can identify truth, but truth is undemonstrable. So if you try to find your own consciousness by using the mind, you are like the one in the story. You need not laugh, for some do this today. When the Second Patriarch met Bodhidharma, Bodhidharma asked him what he was seeking. The Second Patriarch said, "My soul is not emancipated." "Oh," said Bodhidharma. "Where is your soul? Let me see it!" In that moment the Second Patriarch was emancipated.

"When he abandoned his desire to seek, he found there was nothing further for him to do." That is, you come back home and meet your own father and mother.

"Good brothers, be yourselves! Do not be pretentious!" This is very good; ordinary everyday life is more valuable than anything else. If one asks a Buddhist, "Do you understand?" and he dramatizes himself, we would say, "Do not be pretentious."

"Certain baldheaded monks who are unable to tell good from evil; admit the existence of spirits and demons; point to the East and point to the West; fancy a clear day, a rainy day. All such monks must someday pay their debts before old Yama by gulping down red-hot iron balls.

"Honest men and women of good families, possessed by the spirits of wild foxes, you are bewitched. Blind idiots! Someday you will be required to pay for your portion of rice!"

SOKEI-AN SAYS:

In the last lecture, Lin-chi called attention to the blind religious teachers who are always talking and making sounds but whose words have no substance. They are like birds that imitate human words without knowing what they say. If you ask such a teacher a question, he just starts talking without even knowing what the question is. Lin-chi despised such teachers. A real teacher knows how to guide a disciple into the channel of real religion. If a student does not get into the true channel, he may spend many years studying philosophy or elaborate metaphysics without its meaning anything real to him. Lin-chi is independent, however. Observing the decline of the old type of Buddhism, the metaphysical type, he tried to open a new channel. That is why he abuses all the teachers of his time with such a fiery and venomous tongue.

There are monks—here called "baldheads"—who have nothing in their heads, no enlightenment or third eye opened to reality. There are many such. They wear the robes of monks, but they do not have the eye to see beyond phenomena. Beyond phenomena to them is a mystery with no reality to it. They do not know how to discriminate, or, as Lin-chi says, "tell good from evil," for they have no criterion, no standard of judgement.

In the East, as you know, many people worship local gods or spirits, so one of these gods may be selected by a friend as a guardian for a newborn baby. Superstitious precautions are carefully taken. For instance, there was a novelist who always stepped on his left foot upon leaving his house. If he forgot which foot he had used, he would have to go back and step out on the left foot to make sure. Another man was supposed to visit his uncle in the hospital but it was on a day the diviner warned him not to go north, so he remained home—"War is declared on a dragon day."

One day the Buddha made a pot of soup that had a hundred flavors. He asked a disciple to sip it and asked him, "Did you taste the hundred flavors?"

The disciple said, "Yes."

"Do you think there is an ego in this soup?"

"No," said the disciple.

The Buddha agreed. "It is exactly as you said."

There is no particular ego in anything in the universe. When you understand this, you give up all clinging, desire, and selfishness. What we feel to be a separate ego is a combination; when combination disappears, nothing is left.

Today, biology has demonstrated that consciousness arises "between" cells. One cell alone has no consciousness; it is contact that creates consciousness. A million things making contact within us create our consciousness. According to Buddhism, our body is a composite of the four elements and our mind is composed of the five *skandhas*, or shadows. When these dissolve, they return to the eternal atom, *akasha*, as water goes back to the ocean. *Akasha* and consciousness always go together. So we know we have no ego. If you have realized non-ego, your true nature permeates all nature.

The Buddha told his disciples that flavor comes from the combination of elements. If one element is too strong, the taste is not good. Harmony is natural to the universe. When the elements contact each other, first there is love, then balance and symmetry, straightness. The whole Eightfold Path, the body of commandment, is innately in us. Without it, we cannot live. But there is no teacher for this, no disciple. It is the nature of the universe; harmony, balance, right consideration. It is all in us. If a monk enters a temple, sees that a piece of paper on a table is crooked and passes on, the teacher will call him back. The natural commandment is in everyone. Music is an excellent example of commandment, as are all the arts. If you realize that this body of commandment is in you, it is not necessary to study the commandments. But we have been blind so long that we do not see our own nature.

When the light of Dharma begins to shine in us, when we realize the dignity of the soul, then our Eye will see the law of the universe, and we will know what to do and feel what we must not do. Agony directs us to make everything straight. When somebody feels pain, nature is fighting for him; he can recover. This is the criterion written within us.

XI

The Master said to his followers: "Brothers, you must endeavor to attain true understanding so your path upon the earth will be free from the delusion of bewitching spirits. Attaining the stage where there is nothing further for you to do, you will be worthy of true reverence. You must not be artificial. Be your ordinary self. Seeking in the external world, however, you run to your neighbors searching for your hands and feet. You are committing an error!"

SOKEI-AN SAYS:

One of the eight principles of the Eightfold Path is particularly important to us as students of Buddhism: to make right effort to attain true understanding, or right view. The system of Buddhism is a device to trap students into philosophical entanglements, to take them into true understanding gradually. We in the Zen School do not need this device. It is in meditation that we realize we have everything within us. Passing through three stages of meditation we come to reality.

In the first stage, we free ourselves from desire. This is a necessary device. If we wish to reach the other shore, we use a boat; cessation of desire is such a contrivance. By this boat we can reach the other shore. When you attain this stage, you know what desire really is, and then desire exists no more. You have an eye that can see through the whole universe, and you are no longer trapped by the torture of color and form as are those who desire to grasp everything. When you have exterminated this desire for a while, you will pass that stage, (perhaps in thirty years, and will see everything without the desire to grab it. I am a man, so when I go to a department store I can look at ladies' garments without desiring to buy them even though I see their beauty. A lady, on the other hand, can look at the best baseball suit without desire. Once, when I was a woodcarving student, I was looking at my teacher. Seeing me look at him, he said, "You are trained to see everything as insentient. Be careful! I am not wood." It was true. I saw everything as wood and stone.

Next we free ourselves from form, so we enter the stage to which we can give no name. In the West, this is temporarily called noumena. However, this is just one aspect of essential existence. To enter into Buddhism, you must enter the stage in which there is nothing but consciousness.

In the third stage, we free ourselves from formlessness where consciousness perceiving time and space sees that there is nothing in it; two mirrors are reflecting each other. Consciousness has no object to perceive, so it cannot be proved. There is no ego, no self. All is one and that one is the whole universe, a universe small as a pinpoint; but that pinpoint is as large as the universe, and one moment is as a million years. If you reach there, you realize the body that has all the commandments written in it.

One such commandment is not to kill. To deny the existence of the universe—that is killing. To deny God is also killing. In this stage we can perceive consciousness, but we cannot prove it. It is emptiness, *shunyata*. However, since from this emptiness the whole universe will be recreated (after the future *kalpa* fire destroys all and reduces it to the eternal atom), this is not nothingness. But as it is impossible to conceive, we call it nothingness. If we could conceive it, it would not be real nothingness. If you think all of this is existence—I exist, you exist—then you are stealing. In the third stage, nothing actually belongs to you, nothing belongs to me. The universe is one body. In this *shunyata*, emptiness, you cannot keep anything in your hand, cannot attach. Nor can you give anything away. Such indulgence is committing adultery. This emptiness is not a void. It is really the conservation of energy; everything is in it. If you try to call it by the name of Buddha or God, you are lying.

Another commandment forbids indulgence in intoxicants. Ignorance is intoxicating. If you believe that there is something called ego that is really opposing the true nature of the universe, you are in darkness, *avidya*. In this intoxication you do not know where you are, and you do not know light, dark, east or west, This is the first darkness from which we all came, the bosom of our mothers.

All these commandments are really written in your essential body. When you enter the desireless, nameless stage, you will find the essence of all commandments written in yourself. Do you want to go East? You can. If you wish to enter into any entanglement, you can do so without danger. Those who wish to distract you are teachers who teach untruths, who do not know the real body of commandment, do not realize the real body of the universe. Their eyes are not enlightened. They have learned from a book, not from their own experience, so they do not know what they are talking about.

If you attain the stage of reality you will come back once more to form, color, and so forth. Then you will step out further. Before, it was desire; now it is great universal love that takes you out. You give and take without desire because the ego is exterminated. The realization of the universal spirit can manifest in your everyday deed because the spirit on earth comes from heaven. The power to digest food is not my own. Nor is the power to see and to hear mine. Nothing is done with selfish desire. At this stage there is nothing further to study, nothing further to prove. The million laws of the universe are written in your self. You will be worthy of respect and a true aristocrat. You will not need a castle. If we enter into nirvana, *we* are really the precious one. It is not necessary to do anything, to use any device to make yourself appear great. You realize that this body is the eternal atom that has existed from the beginning and that your consciousness is the eternal consciousness of the universe. Then why be artificial? Be natural, and everything will manifest naturally.

Book? Teacher? Church? You will find nothing there but fragments of knowledge. Truth is not a mosaic but a spring. It springs out from your own heart. That is where to seek it.

> "If you only seek Buddha, 'Buddha' turns out to be a mere name. Rather know the one who seeks! All the Buddhas of the past, present and future and the ten directions appear only to seek the Dharma.
>
> "Students of today in pursuit of knowledge have only to seek that same Dharma. When you attain it, your pursuit comes to an end. But if you have not attained it, you will continue to transmigrate in the five realms."

SOKEI-AN SAYS:

Previously, Lin-chi has been speaking of those who try to gather fragments of knowledge from others. No matter how much information such a one gathers, he will never understand true Buddhism, for true Buddhism is to be found only in oneself. All is written in yourself, not outside. You cannot come to true understanding by devouring books.

When Lin-chi speaks of seeking Buddha, it is not the Buddha who incarnated as Prince Siddhartha in India. This Buddha is the knower. All the elements in the universe have the power of reacting to that something we call "another." The function of "knowing" is in IT, itself, the whole universe. That is Buddha. It is in no form or human figure, but is the power of knowing in every atom; IT is omnipresent. That is Buddha.

You, however, devour books and try to conceive it. What you conceive is a name, not Buddha-itself. It is not necessary to pay attention to what is thought. Pay attention to the one who does the seeking: that one is the knower. But you are like a grandmother who asks her grandchild to find her spectacles—"Oh, I've got them on!" Though you search outside for a thousand years, you will never meet the Buddha that is in you.

Do you know the one who is seeking? This mysterious Buddha enters many different states and knows the feeling and taste of everything in all of them. We speak of many states of consciousness, but really there is just one soul who enters those states as an actor puts on different garments. One Buddha in you enters all the different states. You scratch your skin, and Buddha enters your skin, feeling that sensation. Good, evil—there is not a different type of animal in your body for each sensation, only one Buddha.

But Lin-chi-chi says, "*Students of today in pursuit of knowledge have only to seek that same Dharma. When you attain it, your pursuit comes to an end. But if you have not attained it, you will continue to transmigrate in the five realms.*" The five paths of deluded beings are the six realms in the stage of desire—hell, hungry ghost, animal, man, and angel.

"*What is Dharma? Dharma is the law of your mind. The law of your mind has no external form, yet extends in manifold directions, manifesting its power before your eyes. He who has no faith in this chases after words and names, conjecturing about*

the Buddha's Dharma. He and the Dharma are as far apart as
heaven and earth.
　　"Brothers, what is the law that I am talking about? I am
talking about the law that is the ground of your mind by which
the mind enters the secular and the sacred, the pure and the
profane, the real and the temporal."

SOKEI-AN SAYS:

Little of Shakyamuni Buddha's Dharma or teaching was actually recorded at the time, for in his day what he said was recited by his disciples to others from memory, passed from lips to ears only. Two hundred years later, Maharaja Ashoka ordered the monks to engrave some of the important doctrines of the Buddha on stone and copper. We can still see these engravings in India. However, it was hundreds of years before the Buddha's teachings were written down in Pali, so they did not come directly from the Buddha's golden lips. The teachings we have come from the *sutras* told by disciples of the Buddha or by disciples of his disciples.

Now Lin-chi asks: *"What is Dharma?"* And then answers: *"Dharma is the law of your mind."* The Sanskrit word Dharma is difficult to translate into English. European scholars have often translated it as "law," but Dharma is not always used with that sense. Sometimes it means reality, the nature of man, conscience, compunction, commandment, scientific law, sometimes noumenal existence as distinguished from phenomenal existence. Here, in this passage, Lin-chi is saying Dharma is the law of your mind, or soul. Soul is not a good word, but I am using it here in the sense of consciousness, mind, and heart, as these words are commonly used for that something within us that masters daily life. Perhaps it could be called cosmic consciousness or cosmic law. And it was for this Dharma that the Buddha threw away his kingdom as he would a pair of sandals. For six years he suppressed all desire, lived on one bowl of rice a day, and meditated in the woods. Of course, he was not always in meditation. He asked the sages questions. But it was at the end of six years of meditation under the Bodhi Tree that he enlightened himself.

In Sanskrit there are three terms you can use for soul: *amala, hridaya, citta.* The first, *amala,* means the soul in elemental existence—fire, water, sea, moon, stars, the pure soul of the universe. The second, *hridaya,* is the soul of sentient beings—trees, weeds, insects, man. The third, *citta,* means the intellect. The first includes all beings, sentient and insentient; the second includes only sentient beings. This can be expressed in English as heart, but not brain, which is *citta*. A tree has no brain, but it has a "heart" that breathes, exposing itself to the sunlight, purifying the water from the root and bringing it out into the branches and leaves. When we sleep and are not conscious of ourselves, we are on the same level as the tree. The third is the faculty of mind, or intellect. When Lin-chi speaks of the law of mind, he means all three meanings. This law is unwritten. It has no particular form. But if you pour water on fire, you can read it; and if you touch your face, the skin feels it.

"*The law of your mind has no external form, yet extends in manifold directions, manifesting its power before your eyes.*" The "manifold directions" means all directions, all the senses of the body, not just the five we usually refer to. The Buddha said that the body has eight million senses. Each spot has a different feeling. The whole universe is one body and one soul. It manifests "its power before your eyes" in crying, anger, gladness, or regret. From morning to evening, what you feel is the law. Perhaps it is not operating as the true law. Superstition or misconception may be misguiding you, but the true function of the law is always in you. Finally, you will feel the real law written in your inmost heart. Agony is your unconscious effort to operate that true law.

"*He who has no faith in this chases after words and names, conjecturing about the Buddha's Dharma. He and the Dharma are as far apart as heaven and earth.*" Such a splendid law you carry, yet you have no faith in it. You run to words and try to grasp their meaning. What is reality? What is nirvana? That is Buddhism and Christianity, too. You think they are talking about different laws, but the one true law cannot be located in such a way.

"*Brothers, what is the law that I am talking about?*" Here, I, Sokei-an, have been speaking about Buddhism for a few years. One of you asks a question, and I feel that my three years of effort is reduced to nothing. We have to know what we are thinking—talking about—that is the most important thing. Why study religion, for what reason? To invent something useful in daily life you must study something other than Buddhism.

"*I am talking about the law that is the ground of your mind by which the mind enters the secular and the sacred, the pure and the profane, the real and the temporal.*" From the ground, trees sprout and flowers bloom. The Buddha was teaching for forty-nine years and five thousand forty-eight volumes of the texts of Buddhism sprang from this ground of soul. Where is it? In the stomach? In the brain? Where is this soul?

The Second Patriarch came to Bodhidharma and said, "I feel that my soul is not emancipated." Bodhidharma said, "Oh, you are asking me to deliver your soul? Where is your soul, show me." That is the Zen School, no philosophical explanations. If you speak of soul, show me! If you speak of reality, show me! But you cannot show reality. It is inconceivable. With what do you conceive phenomena? With the five senses? Well, are the five senses phenomenal or noumenal? The five senses are the connecting point between phenomena and noumena. Oh, so the connecting point is the five senses. Show me that connecting point. How do you explain this? If the conscious point is not in your eyes, where is it? If there is nothing outside, where is it? And if there is nothing outside, how can you prove consciousness at all? Well, without consciousness you cannot prove it.

When you are asked where your consciousness is, outside or inside, you can get lost in a maze of philosophy. Talking makes it more complicated. Without talking, we can know the truth, the ground of soul. The ground of soul is not created by anyone; it exists, has existed, and will exist forever. If I ask you, "Before father and mother, what were you?" how would you answer?

Through the conflagration at the end of the *kalpa* destroys all phenomena, the ground of soul will exist forever—not mine, not yours, but the soul of the universe. You cannot keep it privately. If you say, "It is mine," you are violating the commandment that you will not steal.

The ground of soul exists forever; its manifestation is as changeable as a cloud in the sky. When you understand that one thousand years equals one minute, it will decompose and disappear as you watch. You do not adhere to anything. If you do, you will always be struggling. Why attach a name to it? Why call it God, Buddha, Allah? If you do not know the ground of soul, you cannot understand the true meaning of commandment.

"You, however, are neither real nor temporal, secular nor sacred, even though you attach these names to the real and the

temporal, the secular and the sacred. Nevertheless, the real and
the temporal, the secular and the sacred cannot attach a name to
you. Brothers, use it, but do not name it. This is the fundamental
principle."

SOKEI-AN SAYS:

Lin-chi is again speaking about the law of the ground of soul. From the soul everything is produced, as all plants sprout from the ground. The soul is a law in itself, as the earth is its own law. In winter it holds the seeds; in spring it gives life to the seeds; in summer it gives strength to trees; in autumn it receives the fruit of the trees and again holds their seeds. Anyone who cultivates a garden knows the earth's law. In the same way, anyone who wishes to do something in this life must know the law of this ground.

Lin-chi said the law of this ground is unwritten, but that it manifests itself in you. You feel sad, angry; by this feeling you know what you are going to do. Your reaction is your guide. When you are insulted, you feel angry; when you are smiled at you become quiet. That is the law operating in you. But you must understand this law, not abuse it. If you follow the law that is written in your heart, it is not much trouble to go through life. But even though all law is written in your own heart, you do not realize it until the day Tathagata Buddha comes to you and proves it. The teaching is like the coming of spring; it shakes you into the realization of what is in you, as seeds in the ground sprout when spring comes. You may say, "My conscience is the guide that tells me to do this or not." But how obedient are you to that whisper of conscience? Do you follow it faithfully? If you do, you are not different from Buddha.

When a ship swings to the left, its compass points to the right, and vice versa. A weight in your mind tells you exactly how to take a balance. If you are deceived by preconceived ideas and do not hear the true voice, you do not get the message. So man's real work is to destroy preconceived ideas and old habits and to listen at every moment to the directions of the law that is written within. This human life can then be a new adventure at every moment. If you cultivate your awareness of the law, it will tell you the exact truth, like the hand of a boxer that moves for defense or offense. If you do not cultivate this, it grows faint and loses the power of commanding. The true man does not need to listen for this voice; it is always guiding him. Of course, one must understand all three laws—the individual law, the group law, and the universal law.

"Brothers, use it, but do not name it. This is the fundamental principle." Lin-chi tells us to grasp and use it, but to put no name to it; it is fundamental.

Soul embodies everything, as electric current enters every lamp of the city, as water enters utensils. Soul enters man, woman, black and white, good and bad. The Buddha's teaching of just one soul is peculiar to Buddhism—no cat no dog soul, frog or snake soul, man or woman soul, dragon or tiger soul, but just one soul in everything. It may seem that each one has a different soul. Buddha tells us that variety is made by the conditions of time and place. Soul itself has no differentiation, receives no karma. Karma itself makes karma. One who has a logical mind knows that the essential power of the universe must be one power, yet diversified, like a tree and its branches, flowers, and fruit, which is the result of the power that is in the tree.

"My discourse on the Buddha's Dharma differs from that of everyone else under the sun. Even if Manjushri or Samantabhadra were to appear before me, manifesting themselves in my presence to ask me about the Dharma, the moment they open their mouths I would understand [the falseness of their attainment]."

SOKEI-AN SAYS:
The Buddhism of Lin-chi is different from that of other Buddhists of his time. As a Zen master he did not speak much philosophy. Other Buddhist of the time differentiated the subjective from the objective, outer phenomena from inner phenomena—that is, phenomena from noumena. In this way, they classified all existence until finally coming to a conclusion, giving it such names as "God," "Buddha," "universal consciousness," and so forth. Lin-chi did not care to name anything, however:

"What is this?" "This is that."

"What is the universe?" "Where are you?"

"What is consciousness?" "Can't you prove your own?"

Very simple. If you ask a Zen master, What is silence? he gives no answer; he *is* the answer. The others will say that silence has profound meanings, that if you penetrate Buddhism you will enter nirvana. The Zen method puts you into IT directly—take it and use it; do not put a name to it! *This* is fundamental. The Buddha's Buddhism was the same sort of religion. When some Brahman asked him the question, Are you eternal or mutable? the Buddha's answer was silence. But this silence is speaking louder than thunder, so loud the human being cannot hear it.

In Zen all words are symbols. They have nothing to do with reality. Calling this glass of water "phenomena" or "noumena" has nothing to do with it. All concepts are relative; if it is absolute you cannot speak of it. Oneness exists relative to many, monism to pluralism, and so on. Logically, the theory of monism is wrong because they insist on oneness that is proved only by the many. When a monist has to affirm the many, it is no longer monism. Nothing can stand absolutely alone. All is relative. If you deny pluralism, you must deny monism and dualism; if you affirm one, you must affirm the other. So none of these views are logical. In philosophy, consciousness cannot prove anything, nor can it prove the absolute. This is the point of our school. In this school there is no word for anything. It says just take it and use it. However, you cannot bend the elbow in all directions, going against nature. This "take it and use it" must be understood or it can be dangerous. If you understand, you are emancipated from a useless puzzle. The law of the temporal is in words, but the law of the sacred has no words; it is written in our hearts. And, though it is not written in any terms, we know it.

"*Even if Manjushri or Samantabhadra were to appear before me, manifesting themselves in my presence to ask me about the Dharma . . .*" Samantabhadra and Manjushri are bodhisattvas. They are in Buddhism the personified doctrines of fundamental wisdom. All sentient beings have fundamental wisdom, not knowledge or intellect or information, but the wisdom that everything has innately. It is wisdom in the absolute, not relative, stage. So when the *kalpa* fire reduces all to nothingness, this is not pure nothingness; it is energy itself, not manifested but waiting for manifestation. In Buddhism that stage is not pure materialism like the atom. In Buddhism, every atom has consciousness, BEING. Even dust has consciousness. Look at the dust in a sun ray dancing; it is a gliding, microcosm of the great universe moving in perfect harmony.

Manjushri is absolute consciousness. Samantabhadra is the consciousness in each existence, the same consciousness. Lin-chi uses Manjushri and Samantabhadra to symbolize the student. Any wise monk who understands would be called a Manjushri or a Samantabhadra.

"... *The moment they opened their mouths, I would understand [the falseness of their attainment]*." So how do you manifest your consciousness without uttering a word? Such a person understands that state of Samantabhadra, which is *sambhogakaya*. If you say no word, you cannot demonstrate that simultaneous consciousness, for you are in the absolute. If you do say a word, you are in the stage of variegated consciousness. So how do you manifest?

Such states of realization cannot be expressed in words, and if you try to demonstrate them you will fail. Lin-chi is saying even if Manjushri and Samantabhadra never said a word, is there any question to ask? "Ha!" Lin-chi understands the falseness of their attainment.

If a student went to Lin-chi declaring he understood absolute consciousness, Lin-chi would just shout, "HAAAA!" It was as if a small tower made by an ant is suddenly crushed by a thunderbolt. Religion endeavors to attain something fundamental. You cannot invent anything. We cannot use this for personal ends, but we can safely sit upon it. There is nothing utilitarian in Oriental religion, but it brings us the real ground of our life. Without it we cannot live.

"When I am quietly seated and someone comes to see me, I instantly pierce his soul. How am I able to do this? My understanding of Dharma differs from others. I do not affirm the sacred or the secular in the objective world, nor do I remain in the essential ground [of wisdom] in the subjective world. Penetrating both, I have no doubts of any kind."

SOKEI-AN SAYS:

When Lin-chi seats himself he is different from other people. He has nothing in his mind, no mind-stuff. His sitting comprises the three stages of enlightenment—*tathagata*, man, and *deva*. It should be the same with everyone. Really there are more stages but from our standpoint the manifested body is the body of *tathagata*; the body of the invisible Buddha manifesting in his "usable" body as *nirmanakaya*. Perhaps you could say the body of God, the universal Buddha, is manifested in his body. The *nirmanakaya* of *tathagata* is a man's *Dharmakaya*.

The *nirmanakaya* of the fundamental stage is the *Dharmakaya* of the middle stage, and the *nirmanakaya* of the middle stage is the *Dharmakaya* of a higher stage. So enlightenment becomes ever brighter. Lin-chi called this the three mystic fundamentals and the three principles. Three principles in three mystic fundamentals equal the nine points. Of course there must be more stages, but the being existing in this universe now can attain these nine stages.

So the Buddha's enlightenment is different from that of the consciousness of a human being. The consciousness of the universe is unmanifested consciousness. The consciousness in our hearts is one of the consciousnesses of *tathagata*, but the unmanifested consciousness has no knowledge in it, no wisdom in it; it is the creator. The consciousness in man's heart is the consciousness of plants, that is, of great existence.

As Lin-chi sits in quiet, he has all these stages in him. If you go to Japan, you will see pagodas that signify the enlightenment stages of *tathagata*, manu, and *deva*. All knowledge is a stage in which man uses *deva* as foundation and creates another essential body on top of it. Everyone can see the man's body, but not the mental body.

"*When I am quietly seated and someone comes to see me, I instantly pierce his soul.*" The disciple wishes to see the master's *deva*-body, but Lin-chi sees through the three stages of enlightenment: enlightened body, soul and substance. Nature is the substantial body. Lin-chi penetrates all three stages without saying a word.

"*How am I able to do this? My understanding of Dharma differs from others.*" Others do not try to see through the mind. The Zen master sees through the mind-stuff that the disciple creates. Is the student in *kamadhatu*, the desire stage? Is he in *rupadhatu*, the form stage? Is he in *arupadhatu*, the formless stage? He sees through the soul, sees through its enlightenment, it's faculties, and so forth.

"*I do not affirm the sacred or the secular in the objective world, nor do I remain in the essential ground [of wisdom] in the subjective world.*" He does not differentiate between the spiritual and the material, the sacred or profane—all that belongs to the outside. Anyone who has knowledge such as Manjushri and Samantabhadra, he calls sacred; his disciples, he calls secular. Nature gives all nine points to each of us, though we may not be aware of this.

The prime or essential ground of wisdom is *Dharmakaya*, the three *Dharmakaya*s: the *Dharmakaya* of *tathagata*, of *manu*, and of *deva*. Lin-chi does not stay in any of these, the root, trunk, or branches. He penetrates all.

"*Penetrating both, I have no doubts of any kind.*" In meditating, he creates his wisdom from the lower stage of consciousness, which is in plants and animals. Plants create animals; the animal is the *nirmanakaya* of plants. Animal creates man, and man creates something else.

These days, man does not control his thoughts; thoughts control him. But man's real ground is thought—our life is therefore different from that of animals. If our mind is not enlightened, however, we are just the same as animals. Our material in the human struggle is thoughts; this is the *Dharmakaya* of a new being. Wisdom in the body of thoughts creates a higher understanding. There is one thing that you must have at the highest point of the struggle for knowing. Lin-chi did not express this in words, but he carried it into one sharp point—"Ha!" This means nothing if you think it is just a shout. It was his expression of the highest point that man can reach.

XII

The Master said to his followers: "Brothers, Buddha's Dharma requires no effort. There is nothing further for you to do but be yourself, as you are. Stand or sit. Dress yourself, eat, defecate and urinate. Sleep when fatigued. The ignoramus derides me, but the wise man understands. The ancients said, 'Those who devise ways and means to deal with the external world are stubborn idiots.'"

SOKEI-AN SAYS:

When Master Lin-chi tells his disciples that Buddha's Dharma requires no effort, he is talking about a principle called in Chinese *wu-wei*, or purposelessness. In other words, you cannot use Buddhism for any purpose. Of course this is said by those of the stature of Lin-chi, whose understanding is like that of the Buddha. But for those of us whose attainment has not reached such a high level, Buddhism is a wonderful device with which to govern our everyday lives. Lin-chi is speaking from his own understanding and his own view of Buddhism.

From the viewpoint of Shintoism, you are not living, you are not doing anything. If you think you are, you are doing something, and you are profaning the power of God, because the entire substance of the universe is the body of God. In Shintoism there are eight million gods and goddesses because all the elements of the universe are gods and goddesses, and it is the body of the human being that is the shrine of those deities. We cannot see them, but they see us.

A Shinto priest once told this story: "One day a very old pine tree in a garden was drying up and beginning to die. The gardener seeing this happen, dug around the old tree and put fertilizer near its roots. Later, he overheard the tree talking to another old tree, "Well, somehow I feel a little pepped up today. Looks like I'll live for a while longer." The other tree said, "My, isn't it wonderful we still have some strength left in us after so many years!"

The tree did not know, of course, of the gardener, as we do not know of the invisible [force] guarding us from outside our bodies and giving us thoughts of encouragement. We think such thoughts are coming from inside, but it is not so.

You could say the faith of Buddhism is in this one word purposelessness or effortlessness. We think we are making ourselves strong, pursuing desire, or handling one particular thing tenaciously, but this too is purposelessness, if we understand the law of the universe, that all one does is not one's own work. Some great power pushes. If an individual understands this, he does not struggle, but those who do not understand must be saved by devices, or as the Buddhists say, *upaya*, skillful means. The bodhisattva, to save someone lying on the ground, lies beside him. If someone is drowning, the bodhisattva enters the water. Buddha's Dharma, however, is motionless, not going, not saving. The Buddha said that it is not necessary to proclaim nirvana. There is no nirvana, no sentient being to be saved. This is said from the Buddha's understanding. So from that standpoint, Lin-chi says:

"There is nothing further for you to do but be yourself, as you are." That is Buddha's Dharma! You must not misunderstand this. There is nothing further for a bird to *do*, nothing further for a cat to *do*. A bird flies in the sky. That is its natural condition. If fastened in a cage, it is not the perfect condition for a bird. When a cat dances, that is not its perfect condition. If any notion bewitches you to keep yourself apart in a mountain, it is not perfect Buddhism. Be as you are, nothing more. This is Lin-chi's standpoint.

"Stand or sit. Dress yourself. Eat. Defecate and urinate. Sleep when fatigued." Daily life. My teacher, lecturing on this subject once said that many people believe morality is religion, but that is not so. Religion is the foundation of morality.

Lin-chi is content with the necessities of life, but one has to struggle to reach that stage, using many methods, *sanzen*, and so on.

"The ignoramus derides me, but the wise man understands." Time will do it, I need not push. If you push, you will be pushed back; you will not be connected with nature. You have to know the time, the place, and the conditions. To bring Buddhism to America we must await the time, the place, and the conditions.

"The ancients said, 'Those who devise ways and means to deal with the external world are stubborn idiots.'" Lin-chi is saying that we are trying to find a universal law *outside* of ourselves; we are not looking *in* ourselves. The three bodies are one body, but the human being who has this body searches for the truth outside somewhere. He is an idiot. Lin-chi says to search inside.

"If you are master of every circumstance, wherever you stand is the true ground and circumstances cannot divert you. Even if you are perfumed by the evil of your past karma, or possessed of the five nefarious crimes, they themselves are the ocean of deliverance."

SOKEI-AN SAYS:

Perhaps we can agree that consciousness is the best term to express the one in which we have faith. God is the name the West gives to the highest being. Consciousness is in everything: in the microcosm and macrocosm, in water and in fire, in a dog or a cat, a lion or a man, in all existence, sentient and insentient. The consciousness of the insentient, we call latent. It will be manifested when the time comes, but until then it is concealed. It is not necessary to prove that we are conscious by reason; we know we are—consciousness is manifested in all stages of development. In each state it is given a name, such as vegetable, animal, human being, even "group soul," but all are just one consciousness.

Lin-chi has been calling this consciousness "Master." In Zen, we worship this master in ourselves and behind ourselves. We cannot express it using terms such as depth or height; it is not ours. From the human standpoint, how can we express it in some way not related to the five senses? The master's master, the master that operates the power in the master, though it is not he? For there is no He, you, or I as separate individuals. We are inter-individual; we relate as you-and-I. We do not call this God, and we do not worship this as God. We worship the power that manifests in us from morning to evening in every word that we speak, in every deed we perform. So our religious life goes on twenty-four hours a day. There is no particular time for worshipping.

The five nefarious crimes Lin-chi is talking about are to profane or kill a mother or fully ordained nun, to kill an *arhat*, parricide, to shed the blood of a Buddha, and to destroy the harmony of the *sangha*, the Buddhist community. He is saying that even though you bear the karma of past evildoing, even the karma of the five worst crimes is itself the ocean of deliverance. In a word you are not overcome by the environment, by the circumstances of your life. If you master your body, you can wear silk hose in winter without feeling the chill. When you have mastered all words, they will have but one meaning. But unfortunately the human being is not using words but is rather used by them.

The true standpoint is one consciousness and form, color and sound are operated by it and take the form of men, women, and children. But that "one soul" is different from the human soul that has been altered from its original nature. The one soul or one body is omnipresent, omnipotent consciousness. We are that if we master ourselves. When we are not being deluded by form and color, we are that only one in the universe. It is so clear. There is nothing to talk about any more, but sentient beings are deluded and are transmigrating in six ways. When you understand what consciousness is, the torture of the past ceases. For this consciousness is not yours, but is inter-individual. There is just one being in the universe.

"Today, students do not know the Dharma. They are like goats that instantly take whatever their noses touch into their mouths. They do not distinguish between master and slave, host and guest. Because their motives for entering the Way are wrong, they enter clamorous places. We cannot call them world-renouncers. No! They are the worldly ones."

SOKEI-AN SAYS:

Once the Dragon King came from the bottom of the sea to offer the Buddha a huge blue stone gong for the Buddha's Jetavana Garden. The Buddha built a bell tower for it. Its size can be imagined from the fact that five hundred monks could sit under it at one time to recite *sutras*. The bell's vibrations were so marvelous that when *sutras* were recited beneath it, it resounded to the chanting and recited *sutras* right along with the monks. The gong, of course, is a symbol of our consciousness, our body; so each temple has a large gong as well as smaller ones.

In its natural condition, a gong vibrates clearly; under unnatural conditions, the vibration is impeded. [Sokei-an covered the gong on his table with his hand, then struck it.] If our consciousness is held back by something—false reasoning, superstition, or circumstances—it is the same as when a gong's vibration is stopped.

Buddhism is very simple. In meditation our practice is nothing but how to place ourselves on the natural ground of mind as a gong sits on its cushion. We observe how mind naturally functions in us. To understand this we have to hold this mind temporarily still to find out how it functions. The first practice in meditation is not to think anything, not to give your mind any force with which to move. Then you will see how your subconscious functions. By holding your mind still for a little while, you allow the subconscious to come up into consciousness. You cannot hold all the small movements of mind still for they belong to nature, not to you, so you can observe the way mind moves. Next, take your attention off holding your mind still and give reinforcement to the movement of your mind. You will realize that there is no ego, no man's mind. All is nature's movement. Carry this into your daily life, observing how you feel, how you react. This is the way to study Buddhism. There is nothing else we can do. It is no use to meditate when we do not know what we are doing. In meditation we learn how our body operates and how our mind operates. We do not think of meanings; meanings are in words rather than in us. Whatever meaning a word carries into your mind is not yourself. All words have one meaning only. One word can transmit all meanings. What is this one word? It is the present situation of our mind, so we concentrate to this present attitude of our mind and welcome the words carrying many meanings. Then all words and meanings are just like the sound of the gong. Let it resound, let your brain think many words. The brain is not a word, not a meaning, as the bell is not a sound. But if the mind is not clear, it does not carry the one meaning.

If you want to know the marvelous work of the mind, you must understand that your present attitude of mind conceives a million meanings at once. When you see another's present attitude of mind, you can read his mind, but only when the attitude of mind is clear as a bell on the cushion. You must keep mind in a healthy condition as you do your body; refrain from all attachment that brings sickness into it. For a little while each day, put yourself into this perfect attitude. Do not beat your mind around from morning to evening. If someone asks you what is Buddhism, what is the practice of Buddhism, there is just one answer— sound a clear bell. The koan is a device to take all attachments from your mind—all superstition and illogical reasoning. Dig to the bottom of the mind, make it bottomless. Climb to the highest reasoning and make it topless. You will then know what true Dharma is.

When you know what true Dharma is, you will know how to discriminate between the true and the false. All true religion gives you some sort of idea of purity: "Be pure as the snow," "Be pure as crystal." Some think that all desire is profane, that to smoke, drink and indulge in sex is impure, so abstaining, to become celibate, will make you pure. But purity is in your mind. You must know all the stages of purity. As a sentient being you are pure. Do not fall into any superstition. Every student must go through these stages of practice. If you study Japanese swordsmanship, you begin with straw dolls, not a real opponent. So the Buddhist student practices how to carry out the teacher's commandments with a pure mind. Devices themselves are not Buddhism but only to carry you into true understanding through the many stages.

In Japan some Buddhist abbots put on golden robes and sit upon vermilion chairs, eat no meat, speak no human word, think no human desire, just like living buddhas, but this is not true *Dharma*. His mind may be just like a layman's if his eye is not open to reality. Wrapped in the five senses, he never sees the substance of this existence. There are some who cannot even write a letter. Really, they should go back to grammar school, but there they sit! We do not call them masters; they are slaves of ignorance, undertakers just performing funeral services—yet, they call themselves Buddhists. Do you think because a man is a patriarch of a great temple he must be a great monk? Not so! There are not many real teachers today, teachers who have the eye to see the Dharma of Shakyamuni Buddha. It is not easy to meet a real teacher.

"*Today, students do not know the Dharma. They are like goats that instantly take whatever their noses touch into their mouths. They do not distinguish between master and slave, host and guest.*" According to Lin-chi's theory, there are four positions, of subject and object, or, as here, master and dependent: the master is in the master's place; the dependent is in the dependent's position; the dependent is in the master's place, and so on. A master in a master's position is like a wise king on the throne, or in the Chinese idiom, "a dragon in the sun."

But nature hides everything precious; to find a diamond is not so easy. Nature does not produce many precious things—there are not many sages in the world. How many do we know? The Buddha? Christ? Sometimes it takes hundreds of years to convince people of the true position of a great teacher. Even in the Buddha's time, two thirds of the citizens of Shravasti did not even hear his voice proclaiming his Dharma. In that great city of India, only a few listened, and how many really heard? Today, nearly all mankind knows the name of Buddha.

"*Because their motives for entering the Way are wrong, they enter clamorous places.*" One may live on a mountaintop and be calm there, but if when he enters the city and meets an insult, in an instant he has lost his quietude. How can he save others? Such people do not enter Buddhism through love of mankind, but are actuated by inferior motives. They hate the world. Because everything is against their desires, they feel that everything is impure, when nothing is impure but their own minds. All is made of pure earth, fire, and so forth. Such a person puts himself into a temple and cuts off relations with other human beings. He calls himself sacred, but his mind is not sacred as long as he hates the world. He may hide in a grotto, temple, or mountain, but he cannot hide from his own impure mind. The Buddha entered the Way through love of those in darkness. To enlighten and teach them, free them, he let them know how his mind purely resounded.

"We cannot call them world-renouncers. No! They are the worldly ones." Lin-chi thought that one is not a real recluse when he has renounced just the physical world—as if someone today were to renounce the subway and radio and all restaurants—but has not renounced the world from his mind. To the real recluse, the mountaintop and the bottom of the sea are just one thing; the whole universe is made of one substance. If one is really settled in that substantial understanding, then everything is reduced to one. But he who runs from the sounds of the city is afraid of desire. By suppressing it, he puts himself on the level of desire. If his desire is pure, then in whatever place he stays, he is pure and sacred. Though the nature of his mind may change from morning to evening, he himself does not change. He understands the changes in his body and his vibrations in accordance with others. Whatever he may see with the eye, his eye is unstained; and this is so with his consciousness.

"He who claims to have renounced the world must exert himself to acquire the knowledge of true Dharma, distinguishing between Buddha and mara, true and false, sacred and secular. When he can do this, he deserves to be called a world-renouncer. But if he is unable to discriminate between Buddha and Mara, he is one who has merely renounced one worldly home for another. Call him a karma-maker, not a world-renouncer."

SOKEI-AN SAYS:

As Buddhists we must know about what is called "The Buddha's great cause." That Shakyamuni Buddha renounced home life and became a recluse is not the important point for us. For the Buddhist, renouncing the world means to know our original nature. This is the foundation of our lives.

When you take *sanzen*, your Zen master will give you the question: "Before father and mother, what were you?" If you think and philosophize to answer this question, your answer is a concept you have manifested to identify reality and your original nature, but your answer is not original nature. Therefore, to find your original nature you must use a method entirely different from philosophizing. Original nature is not a concept. It is, to use another word, buddha-nature.

This question was the great cause for which the Buddha renounced the world. Were you there or not? If not, you could not be here. If you are here, you must have been there. If you think you were there, what were you? In Buddhism our study from the beginning to the end, from the time of entering the temple as a novice to the time of coming out as a teacher—whatever we study—is reduced to this one point: to know our buddha-nature.

A monk in China asked Chao-chou Ts'ung-shen [778-896], a famous Zen master: "Does a dog possess buddha-nature?" Chao-chou said: "MU!"—NO!

If you try to understand this by reasoning, you will never understand. It is just one word, but it includes a million meanings all reduced to this one word, "NO!"

In a legend, Brahma created the first *bija* sound, the diamond sound of AH. In Sanskrit, "AH" means "none," "negative," "no." The priests of the mantra sect say that AH is in every word, that it was there when God was there, and that it will always be there. A Zen master may ask you, "What was before AH?" All these questions point to original nature. Buddhism is not hard to study. It is as simple as your hand, clear as the sound of a silver bell.

In Buddha's time one of the great questions was the cause of the universe. Today, we know that the earth is round and how the solar system was created. But in the Buddha's time, it was thought the earth was flat, that the stars were the spirits of dead men having some connection with the souls living on earth, that the sun was no larger than the earth, and that the moon was not a dead planet. They thought that water supported the earth and that the water was supported by a whirling wind. Mount Sumeru was in the water with sun and moon circling it, and the water was dammed up by an iron mountain. This was the concept of the world at the time of the Buddha. But the Buddha thought our world was only one of a million worlds.

Today, when we observe anything, we analyze it into atoms and electrons and prove the original substance materially. We know that all the varied forms of the sentient and the insentient worlds reduce to one essential substance. We have no doubt of this. Even primary school children know it. If we compare this with the belief of the Buddhists, we can find no difference between them.

In the future a religion based purely on scientific thinking will be created. Even now, if the scientists would grasp original nature as a living substance rather than dead, they would be in agreement with us. But I fear that when the future faith comes to the human being, he will have forgotten to love and to worship. Perhaps that will be the sign for the Buddha of the future to appear—Maitreya, the Buddha of love.

Lin-chi is saying that if a Buddhist has no understanding of original nature, he is a mere toiler, a man of the world, not a real recluse. But the one who understands, though in the world, is a true recluse, a true renouncer of the world. So it is our task to find the first great cause of the universe and of man. How to live, how to teach and cure are just branches of the creative law, or Dharma. When one understands buddha-nature, he renounces two secular "homes." Our one body is living in two homes. One is that relating to our relatives—father, mother, wife, and so forth; and the other is our mind-stuff. Mind and mind-stuff must be discriminated from each other. Mind is fire and mind-stuff is a lump of coal. Of course, if there is no coal there is no fire, so without mind-stuff we cannot prove the mind. If you discriminate mind from mind-stuff, you will know buddha-nature. It is very simple to know. Mind-stuff is home, and mind is master, so mind without mind-stuff is Buddha. There is no fire if there is no wood, but wood and fire are not the same thing. When wood is reduced to ashes, the fire expires; when mind-stuff is annihilated, you return to nirvana, to total annihilation. Then you will understand buddha-nature—"Ah! I see." You need not take a long time. Understanding can come in a moment, but you must do it yourself. It is not necessary to sit in long meditation. Just pay attention, and at any moment—"Ah!" Like the monk who swept a pebble against a bamboo trunk and in the sound of its striking—"Ah! Yes, I understand!" Real substance, that is it. So if you exterminate mind-stuff, the first mind returns to you. You have renounced the physical home and the mental home; they are two dead houses.

The Buddha said these two homes are a corpse with no living soul, no understanding of buddha-nature. Such are the living dead of which Christ spoke: "Let the dead bury the dead." If you renounce these two homes, it doesn't matter whether you wear robes or ordinary clothes, whether you recite the sutras or read a newspaper. If you find original nature, you are a real recluse. The Buddha taught that this was preferable to withdrawal into the mountains. But one who leaves the physical home to enter a temple but does not leave his mental home is a recluse of the body but not of the soul. He may shave his head and wear robes but keep his wife and children in the temple and keep his mind-stuff. Such a one will never know buddha-nature. He is just an undertaker, that is all. There will be an army of donkeys in his temple!

If you understand buddha-nature, you will discriminate easily between Buddha and *mara*. We all come from the root of *maya*; we are all children of *Maya* the "creatress." As her children, we did not pass through man and woman whose nature is animal. This is the meaning of the "virgin birth."

"Now, if there were a Buddha-Mara inseparably embodied in one flesh—like the mixture of water and milk of which the Goose King Hamsaraja drank only the milk—he who has the clear Dharma eye can distinguish Buddha from Mara within that one flesh. But if you favor the sacred and abominate the secular, you sink or swim in the sea of life and death."

SOKEI-AN SAYS:

If you examine Lin-chi's words carefully, you will see that he was trying to simplify the Buddhism of his time, which had become very complicated. He was really trying to popularize Buddhism so everyone in China might understand its true principle. But today, when we read this record, we feel as though we are climbing a mountain instead of coming down from its top to the town below. We realize that our time is an intellectual one compared with the Tang dynasty when such a simple Buddhism was being proclaimed. Such simplicity is difficult for our minds to understand. When I read this record, I always feel that if someone were to call "Ah!" and another were to answer "Ah!" that would be the whole story of Lin-chi's Buddhism. Perhaps we might find someone with such a simple mind in the American Far West. In the deep woods where no ax has touched a tree, if we were to call to him, "Hey!" he would just answer "Hey!" He would not be afraid to look at anything, he would not hesitate to answer; he would be very simple. In the city, however, if you call "Hey!" they'll think you're a pickpocket!

When I was out West I thought America was the natural ground for Zen Buddhism. Comparing American students with ours, ours are putting on rouge and white paint and hanging trinkets on themselves. The Easterner has lived so long in his complicated thoughts that his mind is enwrapped with artificial affectations, while the American is very simple. Of course, in the cities there are many complicated people, but I cannot believe that any artificial, sophisticated, metaphysical type of religion will fit the American heart.

In striving to understand many things in my own past—and I haven't had much time to come to a conclusion—I feel now that I would rather make a solid foundation on the same ground than spread new branches from the trunk of this tree. My nature demands that I converge my effort to the center, to the root, to simplify life. Perhaps I have become lazy—lazier than in my youth, though I was lazy then also—but I like to see everything going on as it is without analysis by philosophy or logic.

I hold my glass in my hand and know that its colors—white, yellow, blue and red—come from various sources that I can observe logically, but this observation has nothing to do with the fact that *this* is *that*. Even when we know this simple reality, however, our life never stands upon it, but upon the results of our artificial brain activity. Perhaps we should not blame ourselves for the fact that while animals live in nature, man must live in his brain. We enjoy a landscape, but we value a landscape that is painted more. We see the beauty of the human body on canvas, in marble, or ivory, better than the living body of a human being because the beauty of the form is abstracted from natural conditions. It seems to me that a human being that lives abstracted from nature is like someone who intoxicates himself with alcohol, which is abstracted from a natural source. There is a real drama on every street corner, but we do not use it as drama; we can appreciate it only on the stage where it is simplified. My friend asked me to go to the country. But I prefer to observe human life rather than nature. It is nature abstracted from the wild state that I love represented. I draw a line distinctly between a being that lives in nature and one who lives in his brain. Standing upon that viewpoint, I see what is called evil or virtue, but to me there is no mixture. It is a shortcoming of the human being that he always mixes up nature and art. The human being took the food from nature, ate it, and created art. Then he abominated returning to his natural home. When we think of nature, we think of art, but do not mistake nature for art. Art is abstracted nature.

"*Now, if there were a Buddha-Mara inseparably embodied in one flesh . . .*" If Buddha is wisdom, what is Buddha-Mara? Mara is evil, darkness, *avidya*. A word like Buddha-Mara gives us a portrait of Lin-chi. Of course he is confessing what he is, someone who has creative and destructive power at the same time, who understands nirvana and evil. He is in darkness, *avidya*, and understands entire annihilation—in other words, Buddha. The evil of which Lin-chi speaks is complete darkness.

In Mahayana theory, the *alaya*-consciousness comes from the hidden consciousness, like heat that has not permeated the air or light, that has not come into the circle where light may be seen. The Buddha called this nirvana, and also *avidya*. Before we understand it, it is darkness, and when we understand it, it is nirvana.

Someone said, "What is it that makes the difference? If you know, then you are emancipated." Someone else said, "Though you do not know where you came from, you will be emancipated anyway." In *sanzen*, when I realized entire annihilation, I felt as though I had broken through the bottom of a bucket, and I understood the poetry of the ancient Buddhists describing the bottomless pail holding the full moon. I appreciate it; I have broken through the bottomless pail of my mind.

"*. . . Like the mixture of water and milk of which the Goose King Hamsaraja drank only the milk . . .*" Lin-chi borrowed the story of the Goose King from an old *sutra*. Water is enlightenment and milk is ignorance. We come from original darkness, *avidya*, and therefore do not know the real in us; we use it unconsciously, not knowing how we do it. Using this instinct from the darkness of *avidya*, we make many mistakes without realizing it, for we are a mixture of both. Hamsaraja, the Goose King, sucks the milk of original darkness and leaves the clear water of buddha-nature. The Buddha teaches the same. By destroying the darkness in the mind, one leaves the buddha-nature, the real enlightened nature. Since it is in everything, when the cloud of illusion is blown off the mind, the sun shines naturally. So Buddha is the Goose King drinking the milk of ignorance and leaving the clear water of enlightenment.

"... He who has the clear Dharma eye can distinguish Buddha from Mara within that one flesh." In what stage was your consciousness in the past? In what stage will it be in the future? Now? Is your mind emancipated? Where is the trouble in your mind? Is it in darkness or not? If Lin-chi has experienced all the different stages of his own consciousness, he knows the consciousness of others.

"But if you favor the sacred and abominate the secular, you sink or swim in the sea of life and death." From Lin-chi's standpoint, you must not love the condition called sacred nor abominate the condition called secular. Why sacred? Why secular? No reason, for these exist in the human mind but not in the true mind. If you attach to such ideas, you sink or swim in the sea of life-and-death where you cannot attain absolute understanding. You always live in the relative, you have to live in your mind and cannot reach a stage higher than that. But when you have experienced all the stages, you will find that you are nothing but consciousness—the tip of your finger, the toe, the nose and tongue—you realize all is consciousness.

XIII

Someone asked the Master, "What is Buddha and what is Mara?"

The Master said: "If you harbor a moment of doubt in your mind, that is mara. If you realize that nothing in the cosmos has been created, that your mind is like a phantom, and that nothing exists, not even an atom of dust or a fragment of thought, there is no place that is not pure. That is Buddha. Buddha and Mara are different circumstances. One is pure, and the other is profane.

"According to my understanding, there is no Buddha, no sentient being, no past, no present. Anyone capable of apprehending this may do so without wasting time. It does not require discipline or realization, attainment or abandonment.

Throughout eternity, no other Dharma exists. Even though there may appear to be some truth better than this, I say it is like a dream or a phantom. Everything I preach comes to this."

SOKEI-AN SAYS:

Many Japanese think that Zen is a grotesque religion, that the Zen teachers of China are grotesque. I do not feel this way. To me, Zen is very plain and the Chinese Zen teachers were plain, honest men. Why do Japanese students feel that the Chinese teachers were like demons or savages living in the mountains? Perhaps to the Japanese, Chinese sentences have some grotesque nature, some sharp strong force that is lacking in Japanese sentences, even thought they are composed of Chinese characters. When I translate the Chinese into English and then read the English version, my feeling about what is said is entirely different from my feeling when I read the Chinese characters. A Zen teacher must understand this when he is transmitting such a special school of Buddhism to Westerners. He must transmit Zen itself. As religion, Zen is pure with no mystic or grotesque element in it.

When other teachers of Zen come after me to this country, they should note what I have just said about transmitting Zen to American people. They should not transmit that particular poetic feeling that comes from Chinese sentences. I am trying to transmit Zen itself, not Chinese literature, to American people.

Someone asked the Master, "What is Buddha and what is Mara?" The Master said: "If you harbor a moment of doubt in your mind, that is Mara. If you realize that nothing in the cosmos has been created, that your mind is like a phantom, and that nothing exists, not even an atom of dust or a fragment of thought, there is no place that is not pure. That is Buddha. Buddha and Mara are different circumstances. One is pure, and the other is profane. The important point here is that you must have true understanding as the foundation of your life. Doubt brings fear. If you are not sure of your ground, you cannot succeed; you live in a blind struggle in the darkness from which we all come. From morning to evening you act at the instigation of instinct, not in accordance with your true understanding. It is through the eight stages of *rupadhatu* and *arupadhatu* that the bodhisattva comes to the realization that nothing has been created. From the standpoint of reality, he discovers all phenomena are included in it. It is not necessary to destroy phenomena,; phenomena *are* reality; and reality *is* phenomena, which is a vision, a phantom created by our sense organs.

Everything has its own inherent law. The branches of a tree always grow symmetrically. We have our law, too. We call it Dharma. But it is not good to be too exact. Confucius said if you try to follow the rule exactly, you will be under a strain and it will take all your attention. There is a rule to follow, but if you try to follow it too closely, you will bother yourself and others. In other words, act spontaneously. The Buddha made all the laws of the *sangha*, but he did not enforce them indiscriminately. This is the law that is not created.

"According to my understanding . . ." Lin-chi's understanding is very important. He means the understanding he attained under the rod of his teacher Huang-po [*d.ca.* 850]. When Lin-chi returned to Huang-po after visiting Ta-yu at his direction, Huang-po asked him about their meeting. When Lin-chi told him what had happened, Huang-po said: "Hmmm, he's a character isn't he? If he comes here, I'll give him a slap." "Why wait?" said Lin-chi, "I'll let you have it now." And Lin-chi slapped Huang-po. Lin-chi's understanding was that there were not three persons, only one, that it wasn't necessary to wait for Ta-yu or Lin-chi.

Slapping, of course, has no meaning. The Zen masters were deaf-mutes who did not explain reality in philosophical terms but only manifested the original substance. In the Zen school we use the real thing. Today, however, our Zen is polished and developed, not crude as it was then.

At the time Lin-chi was young, just out of the shell, strong, shining, and crude, like a thunderbolt, standing on the viewpoint that he had realized after he came back from Ta-yu's. He saw that there was just one person in the universe, neither Buddha nor man, neither beast nor vegetable; just one thing in the universe. Of course, when there is just one thing, it is not necessary to call it "one."

Once a Zen master was sitting with three of his disciples under a full moon in autumn. This group had come together for a tea ceremony, but the master didn't make any tea. He just sat watching the moon. All three disciples as well were watching the moon rising through the pine trees. After a while he asked one of the disciples: "What are you thinking at this moment?" The disciple answered, "A nice moment to realize the whole teaching." The moon is the symbol of *tathata*, original consciousness of the universe., and the whole universe manifests the symbols of its own nature.

Then the master asked a second disciple the same question. He answered: "This is a wonderful moment to practice."

When the master asked the third, the disciple stood up, swept his sleeves back and disappeared—no answer. Nothing was left, not even a shadow.

The master said to the first disciple, "You understand Buddhism." To the second he said, "You understand Zen." To the third, he said: "You are the only one who understands nothing." And this one became his torch-holder.

"There is no Buddha, no sentient being, no past, no present. How do you understand this? Would you call it Dharmakaya? If so, you do not understand Buddhism. This is the stage of Manjushri, the god of latent wisdom, concealed, incomprehensible wisdom. Samantabhadra is the god of manifested wisdom. Philosophy can explain the stage of Manjushri as original wisdom that lies dormant, but as an experience in meditation, how do you explain it?

As for the disciple that disappeared leaving not even a shadow, it took five hundred arhats five hundred years to explain it in the Mahaprajnaparamita Sutra. When you hear that, you have some idea of the greatness of the Zen student who can realize it and express it in one moment. You cannot speak a word to express "nothing."

"Anyone capable of apprehending this may do so without wasting time." You do not need fifteen years. If you do not understand at this moment, you will not understand though you transmigrate for three kalpas. "It does not require discipline or realization, attainment or abandonment." Lin-chi destroyed all Buddhism, all religion, all realization, all meditation, all trying to attain, all practicing commandments—nothing left!

He means you must not dream. You must abandon wisdom, all that is accumulated in your mind, and come to the bare ground. What does this mean? Compare this with all the sayings, the sutras, the systems and the teachings of Zen—all these he pulled down. He smashed everything, leaving no Buddhism, no Zen, no teaching, just leaving the one who is here—eating, sleeping waking. That is all.

"Throughout eternity, no other Dharma exists." Just this. We did not look at this. We were looking for something else. But this was existing and has existed and will exist. This is the only one and there is no Dharma but *this*! We forgot for a long time, but now we realize it. *This* is all we have and it is real. Whatever a teaching may say, *this* cannot be destroyed.

"*Even though there may appear to be some truth better than this, I say it is like a dream or a phantom.*" The *Avatamsaka Sutra* is wonderful. It contains many viewpoints of religion, all the viewpoints in the world. But Lin-chi said all this is but a dream and a phantom!

"*Everything I preach comes to this.*" Lin-chi preached in many different ways, used many different terms, but all comes to this: there is neither Buddha nor man, neither past nor present.

When you see this clear as crystal, do not touch it, for you will spoil it. When you realize pure Dharma, even a word will spoil it. Take care.

"*Brothers, he who at this moment shines brightly and is listening to my sermon is the one who abides nowhere, who penetrates in manifold directions and is at liberty in the three worlds. Though he enters into diverse circumstances, he is not diverted. In a moment he penetrates the cosmos. When he meets a buddha, he wins over the buddha. When he meets a Patriarch, he wins over the Patriarch. When he meets an arhat, he wins over the arhat. When he meets a preta, he wins over the preta. No matter what lands he traverses enlightening all beings, he never abandons a moment of mind. Wherever he is, is pure. His light radiates in every direction, and everything is one with him.*"

SOKEI-AN SAYS:

When Lin-chi says "at this moment," "this moment" covers the past, present and future, that is, before the creation and annihilation of the universe. If you understand this, you will know the one who abides nowhere, who penetrates in manifold directions and is at liberty in the three worlds. This One, of course, is *this* consciousness, *this* present consciousness. This consciousness, however, though it shines so brightly, is not God. It is said in an early *sutra*, Mahabrahma appeared to the Buddha during his deep meditation, saying: "I am the father of all fathers, the king of all kings, the spirit of all spirits." The Buddha told him: "You, mortal Mahabrahma, are not the father of all fathers, king of all kings, spirit of all spirits." "Then," asked Mahabrahma, "who is the father of all fathers?" "There is none," said the Buddha, "HE is the father of all fathers."

This is our understanding exactly. For the Buddhist, God is non-existence. Anything existing as consciousness (Mahabrahma represents the highest consciousness) is not the father. Mahabrahma is the king of light. He speaks the one heavenly word of light that contains all the meanings of all words spoken by human beings. When this light is once embodied in human beings, however, it can never return to its heavenly origin.

There is no word we can use to indicate non-existence, that is, latent consciousness. Here, even Lin-chi must keep his mouth shut. This is *dharmakaya*. In Buddhism, this mortal consciousness is always the secondary part of consciousness. We understand *dharmakaya* through *sambhogakaya*. It is through *sambhogakaya* consciousness that we reach the father of consciousness. We can call this consciousness by name but we cannot prove it with our consciousness, we cannot identify the stage of that latent consciousness. Anyone who says Buddhism is a religion of non-ego must point to that particular latent consciousness.

This consciousness is here, which is to say nowhere. Throughout the stages of the three worlds, he who is non-existent penetrates but never leaves a trace, as the moon shrines upon the water but leaves no mark. There is a very important point here. Mortal consciousness also penetrates everywhere, in all directions, but is always constrained by the circumference, the objective sensation of the body. When the body returns to its original substance, *akasha*, consciousness has no abode, no place to stay.

In China, Buddhists always return to their temples for the three months of the rainy season. One time, Lin-chi did not return until late, disobeying the rules of the monastery. Days before the end of the three months, he came to the quarters of Huang-po, who was reading a *sutra*.

Lin-chi said, "I have come to pay my respects to you, I am now leaving."

Huang-po said, "You have broken the order of the monks of this temple, coming late and now you are breaking it to leave early."

Lin-chi said, pointing to Huang-po's *sutra*, "I tell you that you are a mere pigeon picking up the black beans (characters) of charity from the *sutra* and eating them."

Huang-po seized Lin-chi and slapped him. Lin-chi was puzzled. How should he respond to Huang-po's slap? (This incident took place just before Lin-chi was ordained Huang-po's successor. Lin-chi spent two or three weeks in doubt after this encounter.)

Lin-chi said, "Huang-po's consciousness and my consciousness are the same consciousness. Why do we have an order of monks, wear robes, and remain in the temple? This is nonsense!"

When he told this to Huang-po, Huang-po slapped him again, and again Lin-chi did not know what to answer. Lin-chi must have been thinking it was strange—there must be something beyond my understanding!

Lin-chi stayed at his teacher's temple for the rest of the summer. When the summer was over, the monks went on pilgrimages. Lin-chi went to Huang-po's quarters again. "Teacher, I am leaving now."

"Where are you going?" asked Huang-po.

"I am going across the river to the north or to the south. It's all the same. At the mercy of the wind."

Huang-po grabbed him and struck him again. Lin-chi returned Huang-po's blow. Then more blows were exchanged as if they were two men in an argument.

Lin-chi did not stay in the small circle of his consciousness. He did not stay in any conception of consciousness, not as the master of the universe, nor in any particular place; he freely permeated all the dimensions of the three worlds. This is a difficult point to grasp. A Zen student may take fifteen years to grasp the real point of non-ego. When Huang-po clutched and slapped Lin-chi, Lin-chi clutched and slapped him back. Is this a sign of non-ego? Certainly not in the Western view!

"Though he enters into diverse circumstances, he is not diverted." Because he is not in any particular place, not in ego and not in non-ego. He knows he is not mortal consciousness. His consciousness is not square, triangular, nor round; he can stay in all the stars of heaven, yet not remain in one.

"In a moment he penetrates the cosmos." This is the cosmos of *dharmadhatu*, the phenomenal-noumenal existence—just one *dharmadhatu*.

"When he meets a buddha, he wins over the buddha." How do you "win over" a Buddha? Lin-chi is a little obscure here, but what he is saying is that you become Buddha.

"*When he meets a Patriarch, he wins over the Patriarch.*" When Bodhidharma met the Emperor Wu, the Emperor asked him, "Sage, what is your doctrine?" Bodhidharma answered, "There is no sage." "Who then are you?" Bodhidharma said, "I do not know."

He is not consciousness. If he is not consciousness, he does not know. How could he know? Bodhidharma gave the right answer. I agree with him. When we meet Bodhidharma, how do we preach to him? Do you know?

"*When he meets an arhat, he wins over the arhat. When he meets a preta, he wins over the preta.*" A *preta* is a hungry-spirit. An *arhat* is one who attains the highest enlightenment, gives up his self. The whole cosmos offers him his life. An *arhat* is the conclusion reached immediately through our own mind.

This religion, therefore, has an entrance immediately here. The shrine is right here. Temporarily, I call it Buddha. Not the Buddha who was born in India, but that Buddha who exists everywhere. I can call him "THIS Buddha." Yes, the answer is *here*, immediately.

Shakyamuni Buddha decided this was his religion. To us, the discovery of this religion by him has great significance. We say that a human being has reached true religion, and that the avenue through which he reached it is straight and without hindrance. Buddhism can be explained very easily and plainly, and you can have faith in it immediately without doubt. Others, however, try to reach something higher than themselves. They are always looking upward, joining their hands in prayer to someone in the sky. From our standpoint this is wrong, and it is not very convenient. Why must we search for it in the sky? Why try to get something we hope for by asking someone else for it? Prayer is the expression of man's immediate desire, and he offers a gift to ensure an answer. To us, prayer is our hope, our immediate desire, but we work to get an answer; work, therefore, is our gift. Without the offering of gifts, prayer is not answered. If our desire is natural, it will be answered naturally; if it is unnatural, it will not be answered.

We do not need any image to worship. Our self is Buddha, and our Mind is the entrance to the shrine of Buddha. The Buddha's birth brought this religion into the world and we follow it.

"*No matter what lands he traverses enlightening all beings,* The "lands" referred to are not actual places, of course. Lin-chi speaks of a subjective place. Everyone's mind is a land according to certain Buddhist *sutras*.

The meaning of the statement that Buddha travels through myriad lands in the cosmos is that the Buddha's splendor simmers through everyone's mind, like magnetic waves. In the *sutras*, although these lands are always described objectively, you must understand that a subjective meaning is intended.

So "enlightening all beings" means that God enshrines in the human heart. Each one he meets becomes one with him and is enlightened by him. Lin-chi would say when I meet water I drink (thus enlightening it). This is all we can do from morning to evening; this is the manifestation of *nirmanakaya*, the transforming body. Meet a noodle, eat it, enlighten it; meet a fish eat him, enlighten him; there is no him, no you. Wherever you go, you are one with that. This is enlightenment. No particular place. No place that you cannot go, penetrate at liberty though the three worlds. This is true consciousness. He travels through all places, pure and impure and enlightens everyone there. Certainly, this is not a usual sermon; it is not usual to give this wisdom to those of lesser understanding.

"He never abandons a moment of mind." Ksana is a Sanskrit term meaning a minimum of time, a moment. Mind, particularly subconscious mind, floats in our consciousness so swiftly it is almost incomprehensible. Sometimes the word *ksana* is used to express it. What is this *ksana*-mind?

Whenever the Buddha said "now" or "at this moment," it was very important. "Today" from the lips of the Buddha means not only this moment but also the past, present and future. *Ksana* means the cosmos that has no time or space. So when the Buddha seated himself and held SILENCE before his disciples, that was the *ksana* moment, the deepest and highest manifestation of Buddhism.

The Second Patriarch of China met Bodhidharma and said, "My mind is not liberated." Bodhidharma told him: "Where is your mind? Show it to me!" You will observe this koan in *sanzen*; then you will realize and understand the *ksana*-moment.

Wherever he is, is pure. His light radiates in every direction, and everything is one with him." "He" is without form or body but penetrates in multifold directions. This is the Master who transforms himself into numerous bodies and preaches his *Dharma* to whomever he meets. This *Dharma* of Lin-chi is not the preaching that goes on in churches or temples but is our actual life from morning to evening.

Lin-chi, of course, is poking fun at those who seek truth in externals, forgetting their own consciousness that is the *sambhogakaya* of the invisible *dharmakaya*. This is the fundamental principle among all the doctrines of Buddhism.

The radiant splendor of the Buddha became one with the light and the myriadfold existence became one with him. This is the important *ksana*-moment; all is reduced to one.

In the Gospel of St. Luke, it is said, "That they all may be as one in Thee." One in us is the same. Lin-chi, in the ninth century, had the same conception of the truth. All sages speak the same truth, the same word, not two different ones.

> "Brothers, today those who are mighty know there is nothing further to do. However, as you have no faith in yourself, you continually run about. Having thrown away your head, you go about trying to find it, unable to stop yourself. You are like the bodhisattva whose enlightenment is instantaneous and perfect. By his awakened power he manifests himself in the world of phenomena and enters into the cosmos of pureness. However, he favors the sacred and shows repugnance for the secular. Such a bodhisattva is unable to abandon his predisposition that conceives notions such as pure and impure. But the view of the Zen sect differs. Enlightenment is instantaneous; there is no time to await anything. No matter what I say, it all comes to this. Remedies are prescribed according to the degree of illness. There is no fixed rule. If you understand, you are a true renouncer of the world and may spend ten thousand coins a day."

SOKEI-AN SAYS:

In this passage, Lin-chi is talking about the worship of the bodhisattva, a universal enlightened being that has an inter-individual nature and no ego. The bodhisattva's power is not his own but the power of the universe. One who understands this is called a bodhisattva. At the Buddha's time, this was the title of all lay followers, of kings and wealthy followers of the Buddha. The monks were called *arhats*. Later on, the title bodhisattva was appended to the names of the major deities of Buddhism. These bodhisattvas would indicate highly spiritualized human beings whose understanding was very close to that of the Buddha himself. In Mahayana Buddhism he is a highly enlightened one. Today, however, you will find Kuan-yin Bodhisattva, the goddess of mercy, in the art shops as an incense burner. I think Kuan-yin, the bodhisattva who hears the cries of the world, never expected to be burning incense in her hand!

"*Brothers, today those who are mighty know there is nothing further to do.*" In other words, if we know about the truth, through the Father in us, then this is the end of all doubt and we are emancipated from seeking. Daily life is the splendor of the universal consciousness. The law is written in it. If we know that we are emancipated, we can observe everything *exactly as it is*—that is the ultimate form of enlightenment.

"*However, as you have no faith in yourself, you continually run about. Having thrown away your head, you go about trying to find it, unable to stop yourself.*" This consciousness, though mutable and not eternal, is the Son of the Father; it came directly from him and embodied in the Mother (flesh, earth) and manifests all the capacities of his nature, in this life, from morning to evening. But we do not have faith in this so we search outside. To return to ourselves, to find God in ourselves, is easy, but to search outside, philosophizing, is very hard. You will find the same teaching from St. Paul. The way of all true religion is the same. If you seek for your own head, there is no end to the search.

Lin-chi has humor and a sharp tongue.

"*You are like the bodhisattva whose enlightenment is instantaneous and perfect.*" This bodhisattva has no need to meditate for years. This bodhisattva's meditation is "instantaneous and perfect." At any time, perhaps while peeling potatoes, the time comes and he opens his Eye to the reality of the cosmos. We cannot speak a word, but he understands everything at once.

"*By his awakened power he manifests himself in the world of phenomena and enters into the cosmos of pureness.*" His enlightenment is in the first stage; he is born into the pure cosmos. This is the stage of existence not related to the five senses. In philosophical terms of the West, it is the noumenal stage; the five senses cannot conceive it, but our wisdom can identify it as the cosmos of the Pure Land, the entrance to all enlightenment. The *bodhisattva's* consciousness has expanded into the infinite cosmos. All those of a religious nature, philosophers, and scientists understand this first stage of awakening.

From this first stage of awakening, he no longer manifests himself by his own consciousness but naturally manifests once more into the phenomenal world, for example, as a flower or a man. This is the second stage of enlightenment, bringing heaven to earth. The *bodhisattva* comes from the Pure Land to this phenomenal stage. There he finds the blind and the sleeping, and he shakes them into awakening from their dark viewpoint and shoves them into the Pure Land. Lin-chi is saying that the function of the *bodhisattva* is to bring all sleeping souls into this "cosmos of pureness," the noumenal stage, that they may see the real awakening stage of life.

Lin-chi is talking about his own understanding as a Zen master.

"However, he"—the *bodhisattva*—*"favors the sacred and shows repugnance for the secular."* Why favor one and abominate the other? That is not real enlightenment. When a heavenly king manifests on earth, then earth is heaven. Everything exists in your understanding, not outside. Once you enter pure noumenal enlightenment, all is noumena, even though you are manifesting yourself in phenomena. However, as phenomena are the essence of noumena, all is reality, the same substance in phenomena and noumena.

"Such a bodhisattva is unable to abandon his predisposition that conceives notions such as pure and impure." Everyone has this predisposition, the tendency toward favoring the sacred over the secular. But Lin-chi takes the standpoint that such a notion is not true. This notion gives religious teachers a hard job to open up that understanding and give pure light. If one has a relative notion of pure and impure, one's life cannot be happy because the mind is not entirely free from attachment to the notions of human beings. This is Lin-chi's understanding.

"But the view of the Zen sect differs, enlightenment is instantaneous; there is no time to await anything. No matter what I say, it all comes to this." Our sect is called Zen today; in Chinese, it is called *ch'an*, which originally came from the Sanskrit word *dhyana*. *Dhyana* means to practice meditation, quietude, and total annihilation. It also means to become one with others. If a husband thinks of his wife who is in a faraway land and concentrates, he forgets himself. His soul and his wife becomes one. Then all that his wife thinks at that moment, he feels, he knows. This is real meditation. When we train ourselves in meditation

for five, ten years, we will have that power. But a letter is quicker. Why meditate ten years?

When I observe water at the beach, I plunge in not with my body but with my soul and mind. I drop out of my own being, move with the rhythm of the waves. That is meditating—you are one with the whole universe. Forget the boundary of the body. Become boundless. Realize that the soul of the universe and your soul are one. That is meditation.

Lin-chi, comparing Buddhist schools, tells us that Zen enlightenment is instantaneous—it happens in no time at all. The ascent is not by gradual steps, nor any devices used. When the time comes, the student opens his eye wide and sees reality and buddha-nature in that reality and the law written in that buddha-nature, and he understands the life of the human being. No matter what Lin-chi says, it all comes to the same point of instantaneous enlightenment as the ultimate of Zen study.

Zen is a school of meditation, not philosophy. Zen was really the brand of Buddhism started by the Buddha that was non-specialized. It was called the Eye of Buddhism. It does not depend upon *sutras* but upon our own experience. In this brand of Buddhism, we can plunge into anything and at that moment understand the whole universe from the inside—playing tennis, baseball, boxing. When we do, we burst into noumenal existence, realize that Being is not one's own but belongs to the universe. Through our training we can meditate anyplace, any time. This means enlightenment. There is no Pure Land to enter into or to come out from. Everything belongs to the nature of the human being if you prove the absolute. It is not necessary to wait. Realize yourself at this moment!

"Remedies are prescribed according to the degree of illness. There is no fixed rule." Even though he speaks in many ways according to the stages of men's minds, as a doctor writes prescriptions for each patient according to the stage of his illness. And *koans* are like prescriptions. One who has been deluded for a long, long time needs a stiff dose to clear the mind of all delusions, so the Zen master gives a koan that destroys everything and brings him into nothingness. It destroys the outside and the inside, and lets him see the absolute state of the universe. Then, according to the state of his mind, the master will give him another type of koan. When the student passes that one, he will find something that is like consciousness in that monotonous nothingness. He will find a new ego that is entirely different from the one before. Then, by another type of koan, that ego is destroyed, and through that next ego he will reach

buddha-nature. Until finally another koan, like poison, will kill that buddha-nature. Then he will find his own human nature and become a natural, everyday human being. He returns once more to the human stage—"Ahhh! Here I am."

In such a way, one may pass through many kinds of sickness, progressing step by step, until one comes to the true realization. This is like preparing a remedy for each stage of a malady. There is no set rule. If there is no sickness, the doctor will not prescribe, for the medicine relates to the sickness. Whatever religion you believe, that religion is your remedy. When cured, you do not need religion. There is no absolute medium, no fixed idea, no settled conviction, no particular faith in religion. If there is anything that you could call "set," it is an obstacle against the truth of buddha-nature.

Buddha-nature is like a gong, like an echo. When someone says "AH!" the answer is "AH!" If you strike it strongly; its response is strong. If a telephone girl has something on her mind, she cannot answer you correctly. The law of nature or the universe is reaction. Your mind center does not create thoughts; all thoughts are echoes of your reaction and experience from that reaction. If you study physics or law in the lower animals, you will find that all movement is reaction. The animal reacts unconsciously; there is no particular creation in that reaction. Of course, in a lower stage, the animal reacts so precisely that we can make a clear record. In the higher, human stage, this reaction has developed into a complicated system so that it takes on the appearance that the human being is thinking something to deal with the circumstances. But if you think about this carefully, you will see that it is nothing but a complicated reaction. If you free your mind, you will react according to its own law. However, every mind is deflected from its true way of reaction by past karma, so it cannot react exactly according to the law of reaction but to its past karma, having developed certain tendencies.

So in Zen studies, we must meditate unceasingly, observing the normal function of reaction of the mind force. Let your mind be free, as free as the strings of a harp. Let it vibrate clearly. Stop straining. Let your mind move freely. Then you will see the fine skeins of mind spreading their magical spell through the sky. The whisper we think is nature does not always tell us the truth because of the tendencies the mind has developed. If there are no such tendencies, the true whisper of nature will flow from our mind. When you come to this stage, you attain a mystic power to see through and think through all visible phenomena.

The true man of no ego has the power of wood to echo—even the tiniest flake of mind is a record of reaction. These take many different forms, as though we are inventing a new law, or doing something beyond experience, but that is just our imagination. We are just receiving something that has already been thought by the power of nature. Before man thinks, some other power has already settled the question. No man can manage the universal center; the whole buddha-nature is one and is that clear system of reaction, as the pineal gland is the center of reaction our biological functions. Therefore there is no absolute fixed idea. No such thing exists.

If you understand this (the law of the universe) you are a sage. When you are reacting, not from your own ego, body and mind, you are free; like a compass needle, your buddha-nature is always pointing to the North Pole. It never misses pointing truly; there is no particular point at which it settles. The center of mind of the sage never conceives any particular idea. It is empty, ready to react to whatever comes along. The mind is always taking a balance, signaling how to move. This balance is the symbol of non-ego, of clear reaction.

"If you understand, you are a true renouncer of the world and may spend ten thousand coins a day." You may lay out a million a day! If you really enlighten yourself to act freely, you can do something for others. Nature invests the sage with authority to give charity. But you cannot do this for your own purposes. If I cannot find the state of mind that will make me content, there is no use in my giving my knowledge to others. When I am struggling for food, shelter, clothing, I am far away from the ideal law of Buddhism. This applies to knowledge also. When you find the real center of reaction, your mind center will reach the center of the universe and the law written in *you* will become clear. When you reach such a point, of course you will teach it to others.

"Brothers, just because you have been stamped with the seal of approval of some old master or other, do not go around saying, 'I understand Zen! I understand the Way!' Even though

*your eloquence flows like a river from heaven, It is nothing but
hell-making karma. If you are a real Dharma student, you will
not look to the world for [the right] and wrong of anything; you
will urgently require true understanding, an understanding that
is clear and perfect. Thus you will really finish [your study of the
Dharma] once and for all."*

SOKEI-AN SAYS:

When a Zen master acknowledges your understanding, we call
it "the seal of sanction." With this "sealing" you may say, "I understand
Zen and Dharma." But Lin-chi gives warning that you should not blindly
call yourself an enlightened one simply because some Zen master has
stamped you with his seal of approval. I think that in Lin-chi's time some
Zen masters were not good enough to be the masters of students. There
were also other Buddhists of different schools giving lectures with whom
Lin-chi did not agree. Not only were there false Zen masters in the golden
age of Tang, but here and there in Japan there are false masters today also,
though not so many because the country is civilized and false teachers
(foxes and badgers) can be pulled from the temples. In Lin-chi's time,
however, many were giving false teachings.

To pass a koan given by a teacher is not so difficult, but to pass a koan
given by actual life, that is wonderful! Studying Zen in the sanctuary of a
Zen master is like learning to swim in a pool. But to swim in the ocean of
life is the koan given by *Tathagata*—that is the koan we have to pass.

Lin-chi did not like too much talking. Some teachers give beautiful
lectures, like vaudeville artists, but it is nothing but hell-making karma.
The information they give is only for the brain, causing more brain-stuff
and more torment. The real Zen student does not look to others for the
right-and-wrong of things. Until you understand for yourself, you cannot
call yourself enlightened, nor do you really know what to do, nor can
you love or help others. One who cannot swim is not equipped to be a
lifesaver. Without understanding, you cannot know what is right, what is
wrong. Confucius said, "Anyone who comes to me to speak of right or
wrong is a man of right and wrong; the wise man never talks about it."
From the standpoint of the Dharma, you see through everything.

When you attain true understanding, everything will become
perfectly clear. This is how you will really finish your study of the
Dharma once and for all.

You may think you finished Zen long ago. I thought so when I completed all my teacher's koans, but I know now that I did not finish Zen at that time.

The real understanding that you conceal in your mind must be clear and perfect. You must not show it like a bouquet; it is dangerous to show it to everybody. If you come to real understanding—"Ah, this is it once and for all!" That is the end.

Love is the first thing in daily life. You cannot promulgate the law without love. Without love a bodhisattva can do nothing.

XIV

Someone asked, "What is true understanding?"

The Master said: "Entering into all circumstances—into the secular, into the sacred, into the impure, into the pure, into all buddha states, into the Tower of Maitreya and the Field of Vairocana you manifest all the worlds of birth, growth, decay, and annihilation.

"Buddha came to this world and turned the Great Wheel of Dharma and entered into nirvana, yet there is no trace of him coming or going. To seek the evidence of his birth and death is impossible. Thus you enter into the Birthless Dharma World traveling about in various states, and as you enter the Lotus Treasury, you prove that all existence is nothing but emptiness, that there is no actual existence. There is only the one who is not dependent upon anything and listens to my sermon. That one is the mother of all Buddhas. Therefore, a buddha is born not dependent upon anything. Awaken to not being dependent upon anything . . .

"If your understanding is like this, it is true understanding."

SOKEI-AN SAYS:

In this passage, Lin-chi is observing buddha-nature from the point of view of dharmakaya—essential existence, an important term in Buddhism. According to this view, dharmakaya entered the world incarnated in the body of Shakyamuni Buddha and then entered nirvana. But there was no trace by which to grasp that evidence, just as there is no evidence of the shadow of the bamboo in the moonlight sweeping the dust from a veranda. Even though this world is born, grows, decays, and is eventually annihilated, nothing has ever happened. This dharmakaya point of view is most important. However, even some Buddhists complain there is too much attachment to this view, that there is not enough attention to the actual existence of the body. Even though *dharmakaya* is usually explained as the essential "body" (*kaya*), to grasp its real nature you must take *sanzen*. In the study of koans, you will find the real basis upon which to depend.

Someone asked, "What is true understanding?" This is Lin-chi's favorite topic. In the Zen school we ask this question, while other religions ask, "What is God?" One question is observed from the outside, the other from the inside. The Buddhist sometimes must understand first and then gain faith. The Christian creates faith first and then tries to understand God.

The Master said: "Entering into all circumstances into the secular, into the sacred, into the impure, into the pure, into all buddha states, into the Tower of Maitreya and the Field of Vairocana you manifest all the worlds of birth, growth, decay, and annihilation." This "you," of course, is not the one who has a selfish and egoistic attitude. This "you" is one with the universe; it enters into all circumstances. A Christian might say God emanating throughout multifold directions enters all circumstances; but the Zen student says "I" enter into all circumstances. Lin-chi has his own particular observations to make about entering into everything. Others think that the power of God would never extend into the secular or profane, only into pureness.

The tower of Maitreya is the heart of egolessness, tranquillity, and love—no differentiation. And the field of Vairocana, the sun, is the manifested state of oneness of the unmanifested God. The field is his body, existing in substance but not as color and form. The whole universe is manifested through your mind as the light of Vairocana. It emanates through your mind and you see the whole world. The reality you are now feeling is not color, not form: the mountain is transparent, the water in the river is transparent; the wind, rain, and fire are all transparent. You see color and form in this transparency: noumenon is the body, and the variety is noumena—we cannot grasp it as phenomena. But pure wisdom will grasp it (see it) and will know that there is just one noumenon. Our eyes see color in it, but it is not there, it is in the eyes. It is the same in all the senses—through you this world manifests. If your mind is like a devil, then all the world is evil. You will see each one's devilish nature. If you are a gambler, you will see all as gambling. You see everything from your own standpoint. But if you are a Buddhist, everything is seen as emanating from dharmakaya.

All these symbols and elements, of course, are in ourselves, and we enter into all these states. If you understand this, you will not be afraid of entering. Someone will say, "Oh, I must not think anything like that!" But he, of course, has been thinking it a long time. And anyone who practices without knowing the principle behind his practice is like a monkey in human garments playing on the stage. Good and bad conduct is important to human life, but to know the principle is more important. To know the principle and not use it is like having a million dollars and not using it. So when you can enter into all these states, that is true understanding. This is not only the highest and purest state but also all evil and profane states. To save the one who is in a ditch, one must know his condition.

"Buddha came to this world and turned the Great Wheel of Dharma and entered into nirvana, yet there is no trace of him coming or going. To seek the evidence of his birth and death is impossible." In the transparent sky, there was a transparent bird—can you trace the flight of this bird? Nothing has happened! This is the *dharmakaya* observation.

To have tranquillity in your life, you must understand this view, and though you are living in this manifested world—attached, suffering, screaming—you must know that really there is nothing! There is nothing to attach to. But do not hesitate, go ahead, attach. Do not take a false attitude. Attach knowing there is nothing. If you once experience it, you will truly understand *dharmakaya*. You will be delivered from your old egoistic self. You will have a new birth, a new body and mind. The Christian is baptized with water, but the Buddhist is baptized with this nothingness!

"Thus you enter into the Birthless Dharma World traveling about in various states . . ." States of every kind, from immaterial (insentient) to the mental (sentient). But He is in the world of essence, which is non-existent; He is at home yet travels. He travels yet stays at home.

Very queer! He is sitting upon a chair yet running around the world—impossible one!

". . . And as you enter the Lotus Treasury, you prove that all existence is nothing but emptiness, that there is no actual existence." All is reduced to One, so nothing really exists. Every fish tastes the salt in the ocean but does not notice it.

The "Lotus Treasury" is the world womb. It is the receptacle or storehouse of everything. "All existence" is the essential body of God (Vairocana) who divided his body into numberless lotus flowers. Vairocana or God manifests his own form upon each individual lotus flower, and every god who stands upon each flower is exactly the same as the God of the Universal Vairocana in his form, nature, and virtue. The Lotus Treasury includes all these millions of lotus flowers with each minor god upon it. This is the world or womb of the holy lotus. It is the symbol of the One Consciousness, sambhogakaya—one god divided into millions of individual gods. In Christianity, God is spirit and each soul is emanated from the soul of God. In Buddhism, all is emanated spirit, all is exactly the same nature—individual but one. Actually, all these individual gods are manifested states of one consciousness; and as they respond to those states, they transform their bodies—sometimes to a smiling god, or sometimes to an angry god, or a sympathetic god. There are many different figures representing this transformation, but the greatest one is Avalokiteshvara. Avalokiteshvara transforms into millions of different bodies, but all are one consciousness. It is from this standpoint that we observe all individual existence. This is the main column of Buddhist morality.

"There is only the one who is not dependent upon anything and listens to my sermon." He is spontaneously born, like God himself—does not depend upon anything.

Man always relies upon something, but not God, he creates the law directly from his own mind, spontaneously. But man must be like God in some way, for Consciousness is originally the same, like Vairocana, omnipresent Buddha. If you understand this, you will grasp the ultimatum of Buddhism.

Who is listening to the sermon? A Zen master often asks this question of his disciples. When Yang-shan went to Tan-yuan and asked him how to save oneself from the bottomless well, Tan-yuan said: "Fool! Idiot! *Who* is in the well?" "Ah . . ." said Yang-shan, but he did not grasp it exactly, so he went to Kuei-shan with the same question. Kuei-shan said, "Ah!" "Yes?" "Did you come out?" Who answered, "Yes?" From whence came the answer?

So *that one* listening to the sermon, who is that? Do you know his name?

"*That one . . .*" says Lin-chi, "*. . . is the mother of all Buddhas.*" Transcendent wisdom? Sasaki? Yes? *That one* is the Mother.

A Zen master asked, "What's the sound outside the gate?' The monk said, "Rain." The master said: "The Buddha taught us that all are inverted, deluded by the outside. What is the rain? Who listens?"

This is an interesting koan. It is hard to grasp it in the Zen room. One must open the Eye of *prajna*, the Eye of Wisdom, the Mother of all Buddhas.

"*Therefore, a buddha is born not dependent upon anything. Awaken to not being dependent upon anything . . .*" It is spontaneous but not blind.

"*If your understanding is like this, it is true understanding.*" So how do you manage yourself in daily life? You dig deeply into your nature and scrape out your mind and kill every worm in it. No one can help you with this. You must do it yourself. Dig a little deeper every day until you hear the real voice of *tathagata*!

It is said when you are near to the mountain, you will hear the sound of the wind. When you are near to the sea, you will hear the sound of the waves. When you are near to tathagata, you will hear the sound of one hand. The sound cannot be proved, cannot depend upon anything, but you will understand.

"*Students, however, do not understand this. Cleaving to the meaning of words, their view is restricted and confined to such terms as 'sacred' and 'secular.' This is the reason their view of the Dharma can never be clear. Such teachings as the twelve divisions of the teachings are merely a display of ideas. Unable to comprehend this, students invent imagined meanings for the written words. This means, of course, they are dependent [upon something that is not real]. Falling into the pit of cause and*

effect, they will never be delivered from birth and death in the
three worlds.

SOKEI-AN SAYS:

Lin-chi is repeating the same subject again, the principle of true understanding, the principle of all sentient beings, the one point that is most important for us. This true understanding is very difficult to comprehend; so when I speak of it directly, you do not appreciate it. For example, when you hear the word "sacred," I am sure you approve of it; and when if you hear the word "profane," I am also sure you disapprove of it; but you do not really know why one is better than the other. In Buddhist understanding, "sacred" and "secular" really only have skin-deep meanings. You could say the ones who are sacred are those who do not care for the life of the world and live on mountaintops and eat tree bark, weeds, and mushrooms. They do not use fire to cook their meals or put any special flavor into it. They are usually referred to as sages. Some of these hermits never take a bath for three or four years; yet, they are clean and pure. But the one who eats three times a day and does actual work from morning to evening, such a one is profane. So when a student does not know the real meaning and just surmises something from words, he cannot conceive of a deeper understanding. In this way it is impossible to grasp the law of the universe. It is like a man of law who is restricted and is never clear.

This is the reason Lin-chi says the "twelve divisions of the teachings," the Dharma of the Buddha which contains the whole teaching of Buddhism, is nothing but a display of words that restrict and narrow the real meaning of true understanding. If you surmise anything from it, it is not the true understanding. You are only making karma for yourself that will bind you in the invisible laws of cause and effect. If that is true, what shall you do? What's the use? And what is salvation? If you understand the Buddha's teaching, it is not new; it is the old, old thing; it is in our blood vessels and we carry it in our hearts. If you do not know it, you do not know Buddhism. So you must understand this before you decide to become a Buddhist.

The key to this understanding in Buddhism is in our term dharmakaya. It is a term that contains the real view of this actual, existing universe. And that view has three points: The first is everyday desire. I wish to learn this more than that, to make myself or another happier. In other words, I try to fulfill my desire or that of another. The world is a place of struggle and each being exists as an egotistic individual, but one also needs to give, to love, and to sympathize. However, sympathy towards others sometimes is like giving candy to a crying child. In this viewpoint, this ego idea, there is no rest or salvation, no peace and no emancipation.

The second point is that although my consciousness takes on all manner of different existences, it is one because it comes from one consciousness and returns to one consciousness; therefore, we must not have this kind of ego idea, as well. A commandment says that you shall not talk of another's faults and be pleased that you are better; you are part of the universe. But this idea will not save you from agony and disturbance either. You cannot save yourself.

The third point is the highest, the knowledge of non-existence. This view says this world has no value to cling to, this desire has no end to pursue; this is just a dream. The dream you experience at night comes from your subconscious, but *this* dream comes from our *alaya*-consciousness, the deepest part of our minds, the link between nature and man—all this existence is the production of our senses. This is the Buddhist idea of emptiness, of reality: I am hungry; I will eat. That is all. This is pain. That is all. You live in two worlds, the visible and invisible. That is true observation. And if you understand this, you will find that you are different from others, and you will see it. The others are running about seeking this and that, for beauty in art, and so on, but you can see emptiness and can transcend this world. I am beaten, why should I be sorry? I am dying, why grieve? If you carefully observe this viewpoint, you will see that all great men stand upon it. The one who sacrifices, always has this viewpoint. Sometimes a poet will write something sweet, yet have something dark in it, some kind of unworldly enchantment that draws all hearts into the belief that the poet has understanding. A monk will never be able to cast away his daily desire until he takes the viewpoint that all is a dream.

The emptiness of true existence is the theory of the Buddha. The beauty and the depth and the charm of Buddhism arise from it. If we understand, we do not need words. There is not much value in just talking about true understanding and true Buddhism. If we observe the great religious giants, we will see that their indifference toward their own life and death, their wonderful power and their great beauty, all come from this point of view—in Buddhist terms, dharmakaya. For them, this emptiness is not empty in the relative sense. This phenomenal existence, this desire, is just a temporal mutable existence, and they do take it seriously. But they give it no value and make no attachment; they enjoy its beauty, but this enjoyment of beauty is not eternal existence. They stand upon emptiness and realize true existence. This is true salvation.

"If you wish to be at liberty, to live or to die, to go or to stay, to put on or to take off, you must at this moment comprehend the one listening to my sermon. He is without form or appearance, root or ground, or any abode, but he is full of vitality. Performing manifold functions, he responds to all circumstances and leaves no trace. Therefore, if you seek him, he recedes; if you pursue him, he turns away. Thus, this is called the "Mystery."

Of course, in this passage Lin-chi is speaking of the Master, this universal man we might call consciousness. He has no root because he is beginningless; no ground because the original form, original existence, is pure space and time—there is nothing in which to root this originality. (I think you will understand this when you pass the koan "Before father and mother.") He has no abode because he penetrates the whole universe but does not stay anyplace—there is no place to stay.

You must understand that your consciousness is performing manifold functions from morning to evening. It is tangible; you can feel it. You may sing and dance in your dreams, but when you awake, you find no trace of these performances. If you try to catch the dance of this Consciousness, you cannot! In the koan, "The wooden man dances and the stone woman sings," it is impossible to find a trace of this song and dance. One answer was, "The dragon peacock circles in the scarlet sky." This was an answer given by a disciple to his master when their candle flame was blown out, leaving them in darkness. Who can trace the dragon peacock circling the sky? Although we can see everything in this stage, if we shift into the dharmakaya stage, then we cannot trace anything anymore.

Of course, Lin-chi is speaking from his own standpoint. He is standing upon the transcendental existence of dharmakaya. One who has an egotistic viewpoint cannot understand his words. But one who transcends this physical and individual world and lives entirely from the universal standpoint, such a one will understand. Such faith is very difficult to explain from the Zen standpoint. Christianity explains it simply by saying that we have nothing to do with staying or going, living or dying. All is in the power of the Almighty, a part of his omnipotence. Man must give up his desires, his clinging to life. He should be modest and humble, and welcome the will of God. To grasp the real understanding of that almighty power and to live in it, one cannot have any pride and Selfishness. This is the Christian view.

It is a shortcoming, however, of some Zen students to put too much importance on themselves. These kinds of Zen students think they can act in any way they want, to stay or to go as they wish, but they do not really understand that stage. They must give up something, make their slate clean, must be annihilated once and so gain that great relaxation of true understanding. When Lin-chi speaks of being at liberty, this liberty is not a selfish one; it is the liberty of the universal one, the one with the universal mind. Such a one can attain this liberty, can stay in this stage or go, put on any state of mind and take it off, not acting or dramatizing. Nature performs this wonderful function for him. To live, to die, you do not know how to do it. But if that one with the universal power of nature carries you away and brings you back, it is just the same as though you did it yourself!

Sometimes a man will attain this liberty at the moment of death, because his hardship will annihilate his egoistic mind and he will know Nature's arrangement to be much better than his own egoistic desire. We already have this faith in our nature anytime that we meet with difficulty and we can say, "I am ready; I have some understanding." In the last moment, you have infinite tranquility. A soldier in the last battle will say, "I was afraid, but now I am ready, settled in my mind. At this moment death may come. I have no regrets." There is this dream, and there is the eternal world.

"*Therefore,*" Lin-chi says, "*if you seek him, he recedes; if you pursue him, he turns away. Thus, this is called the "Mystery."* If you say no, it turns to yes. You say yes, it turns to no. Nothing exists in the universe; all is existing; even nothing is one existence.

In Zen if a koan is presented from the dharmakaya view, you must answer from nirmanakaya and vice versa. That is a trick to pass through a koan. A teacher always tries to present it from an entirely different angle. When the Zen master is indicating something very small, he will speak of something very large because in the dharmakaya state both are the same—the poppy seed contains the universe and a hair swallows the ocean. If you try to "take four-thousand volumes of sutras out of a violin case," this koan is impossible to handle from the phenomenal viewpoint because this is not the real ground from which to settle the question. You must go back to the cause of creation of this phenomenal existence. If you enter into this, then you will see from that standpoint. You will see that all is mutable, like the waves on the ocean, always moving. To grasp real understanding, you must see from all standpoints, from knowledge, emotion, and desire. You must reach it from all angles. In koan study, you will realize it when the teacher says, "Your word is alright, but not yet!" There is something more to understand.

There was once a disciple of Nan-ch'uan [748-835], who went far from his temple and then returned after about ten years. He walked into the temple and met the Abbot. "But where is Nan-ch'uan?" The Abbot said, "Oh, your teacher Nan-ch'uan is dead." He laughed at the news. The Abbot looked at him and said, "You must not laugh!" He then cried bitterly. We see, from his understanding, his action was spontaneous, not dramatic. The attitude of the Buddhist is sometimes very different from others.

"Brothers, do not cling to your attendant the body. It is a phantom and a dream. Sooner or later it will fall into insubstantiality. Why are you searching in this world for emancipation? Instead of searching for a mouthful of food and wasting time repairing your garments, find a teacher! Do not day after day pursue your ease. Be provident of every moment; every moment of life is full of uncertainty. The coarser part of your body is being controlled by the four great elements of earth, water, fire, and air; the finer part of your body is being controlled by the phases of birth, growth, decay, and annihilation. Brothers! Today you must understand these four states of formlessness. Stop being dragged about by circumstances!"

SOKEI-AN SAYS:

Zen Master Lin-chi is calling this body the "attendant" because wherever the soul goes the body follows, just like a shadow in the moonlight. He says the body is a phantom, a dream created by the senses. In other words, all phenomena are the perception of our five senses; yet, something exists. But how do you prove it? And as reality, how does it exist?

Lin-chi is telling us that all will return to the void where you cannot see, feel, smell, or hear. That is our home. We came from that void as a seed grows and consciousness develops. At birth, you do not know your mother, day or night, time or space. Then your eyes see colors but not distance, just flat space without perspective. Day by day you make contact with the outside, and gradually you create your own universe according to circumstances.

The whole universe, you know, has been really created by your own experience and is seen from that one angle, one-dimensionally. If one is a being in hell, then the whole world is a hell. And if one is a *deva* then everything is seen from that stage. So the world is created by consciousness, by soul, and the body is its attendant. However, one who sees original substance and views the world from that standpoint does not make the distinction between life and death; to him they are the same. One who recognizes just one soul in the universe is never trapped in transmigration. There is no life or death or reincarnation. He transcends the egoistic viewpoint and lives from the standpoint of eternal life. We detach from the physical and individual viewpoint, yet observe mutability. So how can you call anything that you find in this world emancipation? God is just a name. In Japan you can go to a shrine and get the name of God written on a huge beautiful piece of paper. This is then pasted on a wall and worshipped. You can't call this salvation!

"Do not day after day pursue your ease. Be provident of every moment; every moment of life is full of uncertainty." A monk was once asked what he thought the most important line in a certain *sutra* was. He answered the one about spontaneity. An old woman, overhearing the conversation, decided to follow his example to do nothing artificially but to act spontaneously. So she started to recite the line again and again. Well, the real observation of that line is not on this earth and cannot come from a wandering mind. But if you truly understand spontaneity, you need no observation.

"Why are you searching in this world for emancipation? Instead of searching for a mouthful of food and wasting time repairing your garments, find a teacher!" There are sometimes two tendencies or two extremes in Buddhism. The first extreme or tendency is to live like a string—slender and long. This Buddhist eats very little and does not use his body for

perception but stays in solitude and lives as a hermit—sometimes for two hundred years! But what use is that?

The second tendency is to see life as *just* a phantom or a dream: you can do anything you want; there is no difference between good and bad. Some wonderful men have thought like this. They shine like lightning and die like air bubbles. Why should I care? I'm one with the universe. I am everybody, and I am myself. Punishment or reward? I don't care! (A bad bodhisattva may take this view that there is nothing wrong, but I am sure he is uncomfortable.)

These two tendencies are called "the thick and short way."

So there must be some harmony and beauty while living in this phenomenal world. You can live like music or like thunder—live as you want—but there is one thing that you must know: This life *is* a dream and a phantom, and if you are wandering, you will find no emancipation, even though you keep the laws and commandments. You have to get real understanding—you must transcend phenomenal existence. Life and death in a moment of your mind is really this essential mutability. Even consciousness cannot conceive of such changeableness of mind.

Really, Lin-chi looks at all students as fluffy chicks. His type lives only to seek enlightenment, and do not understand why people live only to make money, or eat a nice beefsteak, or become famous. The one who seeks truth wants nothing, neither wealth nor fame. All he wants is to be true to himself—and he needs a teacher!

"*The coarser part of your body is being controlled by the four great elements of earth, water, fire, and air; the finer part of your body is being controlled by the phases of birth, growth, decay, and annihilation.*" When we see this existence with the physical eye, it is in seven colors, and it has three dimensions—depth, width and length. But if we use the ear, it is nothing but sound. To the tongue, it is nothing but taste, and so forth. All these difference universes are the result of the different sense organs, or the result of many grades of consciousness. When we see this existence with the mental eye, it is nothing but light, without space or time—or, pure space and time.

From our standpoint in Buddhism, there are three aspects to this substantial existence: dharmakaya, sambhogakaya and nirmanakaya. But in the Zen understanding, reality and consciousness are just one. Sometimes we express it with the eyes or the voice, but all comes from oneness, which is expressed by the different functions in answer to different points of view. We do not usually separate body and soul, or matter and spirit, but sometimes we make a temporary separation between the coarse and the finer parts of this body—the physical and mental. So when Lin-chi is talking about the coarser and finer parts, he is talking according to the ancient, natural science. Today we use different terms like oxygen, nitrogen, hydrogen, and so forth. Today you are enjoying, fighting, sympathizing, agonizing; tomorrow you are up in smoke, cremated in Long Island! Just a streak—nothing left. If there is no body, there is no soul. Just as there is no hotel without a guest.

"Brothers! Today you must understand these four states of formlessness." In these four states there are no-characteristics, having no signs or marks.

"Stop being dragged about by circumstances!" We do not use, but are used by circumstances. We have to change that inverted view. That is Buddhism. *You* are the Master, not your circumstances!

There was a great bandit in Japan. He pitied the poor and stole from the rich to give to the poor. One day he revisited those whom he had made rich, but they were still poor! And the rich were still rich! He realized that riches are in the *nature* of man and not in his property.

XV

Someone asked, "What are the four states of formlessness?"

The Master said: "A moment of doubt in your mind you are obstructed by earth. A moment of attachment in your mind and you are drowned by water. A moment of wrath in your mind and you are burned by fire. A moment of joy in your mind and you are stirred by air. If you understand this, you will not be dragged about by circumstances, but will master circumstances everywhere. You will appear in the East and disappear in the West; appear in the South and disappear in the North; appear at the center and disappear at the periphery; appear at the periphery and disappear at the center. You will step across the surface of water as you step across the surface of earth. You will step across the surface of the earth as you step across the surface of water.

"Why is this so? Because you will have realized that the four elements are but phantoms and dreams. Brothers, at this moment the one who is listening to my sermon is not the body of the four great elements but he who uses the four great elements. If you understand this, you may go or stay at will."

SOKEI-AN SAYS:

In this passage, Lin-chi is illustrating the vital function of the one who can appear and disappear at will in various supernatural transformations. This vital function is present in everyone.

Most people believe that our physical bodies are not who we really are, that they are just the houses in which we dwell. Our mental condition, our emotions, our notions are also not who we really are. They are just the garments that we put on and take off. You know quite well that when the spring wind blows your sleeve, it is the wind and not yourself that is moving the sleeve—so your own joy flutters your mind. You cannot objectify it, but joy is part of your vesture. This is the difference that Lin-chi is trying to make between circumstances and the self. But practice and theory are very different. Drinking a glass of soy sauce instead of water to be calm during an earthquake is a good example of this difference.

"What are the four states of formlessness?" Lin-chi is talking about the four great elements—earth, water, fire and air—and the four mental states—birth, growth, decay, and annihilation. The one enters into these elements and mental states, yet always remains pure, like a lotus flower growing from muddy water—always safe and not mutable.

The Master said: "A moment of doubt in your mind you are obstructed by earth." You feel something like a lump of clay in your breast and you cannot eat or digest. I had this sickness of doubt in my youth. I could not read, study or eat. I was shivering and pale. I was called "Grasshopper-legs" and "Blue-spike." Somehow I had to settle the question.

I was a spoiled child, who thought no one was like myself. I was that type of young man. It was not till after thirty-seven that I came into a world of some sunshine, where I could enjoy the outside and associate with friends. Before that, I was ill natured and quick tempered. I really felt that the earth filled up the mind, and it was the end of joy. If I could not pass my koan within a month, I was sick and could enjoy nothing. Sometimes I wondered how anyone could live, and what would happen after death. Reincarnation was just talk. Transmigration was just talk. Karma was just talk. I have five senses, but how were they connected after death? What senses would stay, and what would go? So many questions. What is love? What is morality?

Then I settled from corner to corner. It was like peeling the skin of an orange. I did very careful work, very tedious work; otherwise I thought there is no use living. I am doing something very important, but will I starve to death? Even so, I had to get everything settled and come to terms with myself. Otherwise, I could not go on. It was like settling one's accounts at the end of the month. If you can't find the error, you can't sleep. The question of everyday life is the same. You must think deeply into it, for no one else's sake but for your own. Otherwise, your life is just nonsense. If I don't know what will happen after death, how can I lie down comfortably to die?

Heaven and hell—just talk. Angels and gods—just talk. Can I go to death believing such things? Life is a little more serious than that! If I am not clear as to the conclusion of life, I cannot continue!

"A moment of attachment in your mind and you are drowned by water." When I was young, I went down to a foreign bookshop in Tokyo and saw a volume of poetry by Poe. I had heard of his fame and I wanted to buy it, but I had no money. That night I could not sleep, so I got up at six o'clock and ran to the shop and stood at the entrance for fear someone would get the book before me. I read it, cleaving to it, drowning myself in its poetry. Most love is cleaving, and it is like water. You do not mind if the water takes your body away if you can swim back to shore. But sometimes the water takes you away from the shore, and if you go too far you cannot come back.

"A moment of wrath in your mind and you are burned by fire." Shakyamuni Buddha said: "Wrath is the fire in the mind which burns the forest of consciousness." He thought that anger was more dangerous than sensuous passion; passion can be controlled more easily than anger. One must not be angry for one's own sake—but the father can be angry for the child's sake. The angry god does not agree with the Western idea of love. In the East, the mother gives to the child, but the father takes everything away. To our idea the Western father is just like a sweet uncle.

"*A moment of joy in your mind and you are stirred by air.*" In the happy nature, there is too much air in the mind; in the melancholy one, too much water; but the four elemental states are circumstances, not yourself, they are just your vesture.

"*If you understand this, you will not be dragged about by circumstances, but will master circumstances everywhere.*" In the East, a gentleman will not show his feelings; he will not express anger, sadness, or joy. When a Russian admiral met General Maresuke Nogi, who had lost two sons—young officers—on the battlefield in one night—he told him that he was very sorry. Nogi just grunted. To him there was nothing to say. There is fear of being controlled by emotion, but then it is very hard to be one's self.

The Zen Buddhist always grunts because he is taught to put has strength in the abdomen, but it is not good to do, this is artificially. You must learn how to find your own center of balance.

"*You will appear in the East and disappear in the West; appear in the South and disappear in the North; appear at the center and disappear at the periphery; appear at the periphery and disappear at the center.*" This is exactly what I do—appear in the West, appear in the South, appear in the North and East, center and periphery. Every standpoint is the true standpoint. For example, I am reading a newspaper in Japan while this body is seated upon this chair—this is not strange, but true. If you stand upon your own particular base it is no good; but if you stand upon the One as base, you do all. After all, religion is to see through all this personal existence, to observe the whole universe as one person. This is *dharmakaya*. It has emotion in it like a human being. But if a scientist looks at it, he will not find any emotion in it. He cannot kneel down before this great universe; he cannot weep.

A religion such as Zen is almost not a religion. The Zen monk just sits in quiet and meditates. He has no tears. But every standpoint is a true standpoint. It is not necessary to attach to just one standpoint. Most religious people confine their lives within a narrow scale, for they do not observe from the many different angles, and that is no good.

To "appear at the center" is the same as non-existence. As an example, I ask you: "Before father and mother" (standing in the center), "what is your original countenance?"

As for the periphery: "There is a stone at a fathomless depth. How do you bring it up without wetting your sleeve?" When you can bring this stone up from the depth of the ocean, that is your appearance at the periphery.

"*You will step across the surface of water as you step across the surface of earth. You will step across the surface of the earth as you step across the surface of water.*" When Christ walked upon the waters, his disciples suddenly discerned his real body. But the blind do not understand. To take this liberty of transportation, one must transcend the four great elements of the physical, mental and emotional body—growing, subsisting, decaying and annihilating.

"*Why is this the truth? Because you will have realized that the four elements are but phantoms and dreams.*" The real base upon which we stand has no name. All that we can perceive by the five senses—on the ground of that sense—does not cover the whole reality that has no color or form. We cannot conceive this reality. No one can conceive wholeness from his own standpoint. He sees only a part. The great "one-horned ox" is impossible to demonstrate. In koan study, we have to prove this impossible one. It is difficult. We can realize it, but how to prove it? The Buddha said to Subhuti, "If you try to see the *tathagata* or to hear him, you are using the wrong method." This point is always emphasized in Buddhism.

"*Brothers, at this moment the one who is listening to my sermon is not the body of the four great elements but he who uses the four great elements. If you understand this, you may go or stay at will.*" Who is this "one"? Mahakashyapa called, "Ananda!" and Ananda answered, "Yes?" But Ananda did not understand who had answered—not Ananda but some one in Ananda answered the call.

A Chinese Zen student was once asked (from the *dharmakaya* standpoint): "The universe is long and broad. Why do you put on a robe and go to the temple when the gong sounds?" Terrible question! The answer comes to purposelessness, to egolessness.

You may think, If the universe has no particular purpose, what can I do? You feel helpless. All your plans, all your ideas are no good. Your life has no meaning. But the Buddha told us that ego has no purpose and Dharma has no purpose. I hesitated to enter Buddhism when I heard this!

Can you learn to trust this life? You must think deep, really attain faith in this universe without purpose, the faith to sit, to sit to attain enlightenment.

"In my view, there is nothing to be abhorred. If you cherish the sacred, the sacred is nothing but a word. But there are some students who seek Manjushri on Mount Wu-t'ai-shan. Wrong! There is no Manjushri on Mount Wu-t'ai-shan. Would you like to know Manjushri? Your present function of mind, constant at all times and without hesitation, wherever you are, is the living Manjushri. The undiscriminated light of a moment of mind is the true Samantabhadra. The moment of mind that of itself delivers you from bondage wherever you are is the samadhi of Avalokiteshvara. These three alternate with each other as master and attendants. When they appear, they appear together—one is three and three are one. If you understand this, you can follow the teachings."

SOKEI-AN SAYS:

Lin-chi has been saying that the reality of the universe, if it can be expressed in words, is oneness. Men observe this from many different standpoints and conceive its particular phases according to their point of view. The scientist observing from his standpoint detests the view of the religious man, and vice versa, but neither one understands reality itself. All of this is brain function. Reality has nothing to do with the logical observations of the human being. Reality transcends all such observations. Some Buddhists say all life comes from one source, is subdivided and then returns to this oneness after death. This, too, is just a logical idea, having nothing to do with the wholeness of reality. It is from this standpoint that Lin-chi says:

"In my view, there is nothing to be abhorred. If you cherish the sacred, the sacred is nothing but a word." Lin-chi is suggesting a reality not related to our five senses—pureness.

"But there are some students who seek Manjushri on Mount Wu-t'ai-shan. Wrong! There is no Manjushri on Mount Wu-t'ai-shan! Would you like to know Manjushri? Your present function of mind, constant at all times and without hesitation, wherever you are, is the living Manjushri." Wu-t'ai-shan is the sacred temple and mountain of Manjushri in China. Manjushri is the *bodhisattva* of wisdom, the personified doctrine of original wisdom, the law that is written in man. It is intrinsic; no one created this man. From Manjushri's standpoint, man is not man. God enshrines in the heart of man. But "enshrines" is a queer word.

And hatred and love have nothing to do with this mind. They arise from phenomenal existence. You must meditate in the pure, white fire of this mind. Never mind all the mind-stuff. It is your own decision whether you use it or not. That is the living Manjushri—your self!

"The undiscriminated light of a moment of mind is the true Samantabhadra" The undiscriminated (indivisible) mysterious, incomprehensible faculty—the light of a moment of your mind, anywhere—is the true Samantabhadra. When you see pictures of Samantabhadra, he is mounted upon a white elephant with six tusks. He holds a lotus in his hand and sometimes a sword. He is the symbol of non-discrimination, indivisibility; you cannot part this oneness and make it two. This undiscriminating light is in you, in him, in us; it is the same light. It differentiates, yes, but it has the same nature, the same elements coming from the same wholeness. Mind is the same, but it takes different shapes—it differentiates. Mind-stuff is the debris in your mind.

Some say that this conception of oneness in Buddhism is different from the Christian idea of soul. I am not so sure. In Buddhism, soul is like the waves related to the ocean, subdivided from oneness. But whether the soul has a monistic existence or a pluralistic existence (just the same from its own viewpoint) has nothing to do with reality. As Manjushri, we see the whole. As Samantabhadra, we see the part.

"The moment of mind that of itself delivers you from bondage wherever you are is the samadhi of Avalokiteshvara." Our mind is always in the jail of mind-stuff. We cannot see reality; we just repeat the name. A parrot can repeat words without knowing the meaning, and there are many like that. How can they be delivered from agony? But if you grasp the real flame of wisdom—the real mind—at any moment you can be emancipated. This is the force of Avalokiteshvara. In the female form, she is the Goddess of Mercy. Lotus flower in hand, this goddess transforms into different bodies, representing the different natures she wishes to save. So we see all types of Avalokiteshvaras, that is, seen according to the condition of the one who sees her. This is the way we view the world—as our own creation. How do you find the perfect standpoint from which to view the world? You must destroy everything that binds you in ignorance.

I realize this is not easy, to find the true compass pointing to the true way. But everything is written intrinsically in your heart, your soul, your mind. You have but to clear out all previous conceptions and become like a sheet of white paper, and you will find the real law written in your own heart. It is worth a whole lifetime of struggle to come to this!

"These three alternate with each other as master and attendants." Look at the whole world from the standpoint of wholeness. Then look at the different colors, tastes—the waves standing up as attendants—see the harmony! Observe the consonance and dissonance played by this ocean of waves and learn how to apply this law, how to apply truth to your daily life. For every moment there is a written code of moral life, but it takes thought and time to learn how to apply it. This is actual living. You cannot apply a moral or religious code. You must change your standpoint and look at the ocean and the waves, the part and the whole.

When you observe Buddhism, you must observe its wholeness, the whole body of the universe. You call it by many names: ocean of wisdom, universal love, boundless light—all are just names. But you must actually realize it, as it is. If you see the wholeness, you will see the parts, the phases of the wholeness. If you see the ocean, you will see the waves. If you see no waves, you will see no ocean. And you must taste the ocean. There are many different tastes and colors—the Yellow Sea, the Black Tide, and so forth. You must see the ocean as wholeness and the waves as parts, and you must observe their functions.

"When they appear, they appear together—one is three and three are one. If you understand this, you can follow the teachings." Lin-chi speaks from his experience of deep meditation, and from that, coming out into the realization of the whole universe. If you realize these three standpoints in your self at the same time—no self, no cosmos—you are Buddha.

However, to observe this "present function of mind," your mind must be separated from mind-stuff, the impressions from outside, which are not mind. Of course, without mind-stuff, you cannot recognize your mind movement. This is like a white fire flaming within you. You must live in this white flame—this flaming mind. Do not attach to this from the outside.

So Lin-chi is speaking of Mind-Itself. If you swim in clear water, you will see all the debris—wood, dead fish, shoes—all sorts of stuff as in your mind. You can use all these as instruments, but sometimes you are *used* by the debris and become inverted, and then it is not life at all.

Lin-chi speaks of the mind that is constant at all times, never hesitates, always flowing like the ocean tides. Wherever you are, you are Manjushri. No one can create this intrinsic wisdom, not even God, for it exists with him. God is not created. He Is. That is, the Universe. Every element that we see displayed here was there before creation, all differentiated through the five senses. Manjushri is the symbol of wholeness. Everything is in it—wisdom, love, sympathy, and so forth., and that is the function of the universe.

XVI

The Master said to the multitude: "Students of today must have faith in themselves. Do not seek it on the outside. Influenced by useless circumstances, you will be unable to discriminate right from wrong. The evidence for the existence of buddhas and patriarchs is nothing but the external traces of Buddhism. If, for instance, someone selects a phrase from a sutra, or appears from the hidden or from the manifested, you are bewildered, calling upon heaven and earth. Not knowing what to do, you ask your neighbor about it. A man must not spend his days in useless discourse and discussion about masters and rebels, right and wrong, lust and wealth."

SOKEI-AN SAYS:

The whole law is written in yourself—even the first law is written in your heart. This mysterious power is also written in consciousness. We never get it from the outside, all springs from within. But we try to find protection in outside power. The Zen student is, however, different; he finds it inside.

The Master said to the multitude: "Students of today must have faith in themselves. Do not seek it on the outside." So what is this faith? We have it innately, as the universe has it. This innate power is symbolized by the sun—not the visible sun but the spiritual sun of the universe, the buddha-nature of the universe. This buddha-nature is self-created exists in the past, present and future, so every manifestation has this buddha-nature. Knowing it or not, every action of daily life comes from this nature, that which the Christians call God.

"*Influenced by useless circumstances, you will be unable to discriminate right from wrong.*" By "circumstances" Lin-chi means the written records of Buddhism, the laws, commandments, and so forth. You will be influenced by that record and believe that such laws really exist, and having faith in the written law, you will be commanded from the outside and forget your self. So you will not live your own life, but will live through someone else. So how do we apply the law of nature to daily life? You can ask no one. You must think everything out very carefully for yourself. That's why you have a brain. You have judgment. Why not use it?

"*The evidence for the existence of buddhas and patriarchs is nothing but the external traces of Buddhism.*" Just like the traces of animals, or of men. Looking at them, you know that something or someone has passed—a snake here, a rabbit there; but you will not see the one who has passed. Why don't you catch the real man instead of running after his traces? That is what Lin-chi is saying.

If, for instance, someone selects a phrase from a *sutra*, or appears from the hidden or from the manifested, you are bewildered, calling upon heaven and earth. Not knowing what to do, you ask your neighbor about it. Zen is not manifested in the written law; it is transmitted from heart to heart.

"*A man must not spend his days in useless discourse and discussion about masters and rebels, right and wrong, lust and wealth.*" Meditation is the best way. I meditated for six years to attain the six mysterious powers, not as a fairy story but in an entirely different way. You can do this too.

"*In this place, I do not discriminate between layman and monk. If you appear here, you will be discerned through and through. From whatever position you appear, it is nothing but a name. All is a dream. But if you are one who avails himself of all circumstances, you are observing the fundamental law of all buddhas. Buddhahood, however, does not profess to be buddhahood, saying, "I am Buddha!" It is he who does not depend upon anything who avails himself of all circumstances.*"

If you come into my presence seeking Buddha, I will appear in accordance with the state of pureness. If you come into my presence asking about bodhisattvas, I will appear in accordance with the state of compassion. If you come into my presence asking about bodhi, I will appear in accordance with the state of mystery. If you come into my presence asking about nirvana, I will appear in accordance with the state of serenity. Although there are manifold circumstances, there is only this one and no other. Therefore, this one manifests in accordance with circumstances like the moon in water."

SOKEI-AN SAYS:

If you really understand Lin-chi's attainment, you will grasp the very point of Buddhism through this lecture.

"In this place, I do not discriminate between layman and monk. If you appear here, you will be discerned through and through." Just as you appear in the sanctuary of a Zen master during *sanzen.* Lin-chi will see you from head to foot, from outer skin to inner heart whether you are a layman or a monk. He will observe your spirit, your emotions, your every gesture and word to find out what your understanding is. Perhaps you will say, "Well, I'm glad." But your attitude is different if your face is sad. So the master compares both your attitudes and knows whether you have understanding or not. Your answers are judged by his knowledge authorized from generation to generation, from Bodhidharma to our teachers of today. The student's answer is judged by this authorized knowledge. We have faith in this.

"From whatever position you appear, it is nothing but a name. All is a dream." Whether from *dharmakaya, sambhogakaya,* or *nirmanakaya; kamadhatu, rupadhatu,* or *arupadhatu;* from whatever position you appear, it is nothing but a name. All is a dream. If you come to real understanding in the Zen room, you will understand the iron rule—the koan must be answered from all angles, but all the answers must touch reality.

"But if you are one who avails himself of all circumstances, you are observing the fundamental law of all buddhas." It is like the training of a horse. In the beginning the man is managed by the horse—you could say, there is nothing but the horse, and no man on his back. In the next stage, there is nothing but the man and no horse; the man's will controls the

horse. In the third stage, there is no man and no horse. If he is a pianist, there is no piano and no player.

The "one who avails himself of all circumstances" must be a master, utilizing mind-stuff, wisdom, emotion and power. Mind-itself is Master, and the body of mind is its motion. Mind-stuff and all that is external is just the material expression of this Mind.

"*Buddhahood, however, does not profess to be buddhahood, saying, 'I am Buddha!'*" When one attains nirvana, one has a body before entering into entire annihilation. But the mind is already in nirvana. This is buddhahood: to be one with the universe. But in this state, one does not call oneself a buddha. Someone must master this state that is the Buddha.

"*It is he who does not depend upon anything who avails himself of all circumstances.*" He does not depend upon any notion or any name. He does not depend upon anything. He avails himself of all circumstances; that is, he depends upon no circumstance, no conception, no idea. Such a one utilizes all circumstances.

"*If you come into my presence seeking Buddha. I will appear in accordance with the state of pureness.*" Lin-chi does not want to use a term like *dharmakaya* or *tathagata*, so he just says pureness. Buddhists are always talking about pureness, but it is not snobbishness. It is but one aspect of Buddhism, but there are others.

The universe was not created by anyone. It is, was, and will be existing without beginning and without end. From this standpoint, the Buddhist does not understand creation by will power; there is no scheme, no plan; there is just existence. There is no man in the world, but just one power. Man is empty and the law of the universe has no self-existence. There is no God thinking," I have to do this or that, punish or reward." There is no such God. If you know that you are just an element, that all is just one element, one stretch of ocean with a million waves, then what can be thinking? At the end of the universe when the *kalpa* fire annihilates everything, what will be existing, and what is evolution? This is one aspect, but there is another.

We cannot attain by the five senses nor conceive by knowledge; it is undemonstrable. "Pureness" is not a good translation to express this. There is no word to express it. Lin-chi knows it, grasps it. To speak of it in words means nothing.

Once a Zen master and his disciple were taking a walk. They passed over a stone bridge with many arches. The master asked his disciple which stone was actually laid first. The disciple thought it over and said, "Which element was created first?" but he could not answer. The teacher said, "All I asked about was a mere stone bridge, and you do not understand."

The teacher had transformed himself from the pure state into a man's state. The human standpoint is not wrong, of course, but there is the other viewpoint. From the human standpoint, as man has will power the whole universe must have will power. But we say that no one creates and there is no annihilation.

So what is Buddha? Wonderful question!

"If you come into my presence asking about bodhisattvas, I will appear in accordance with the state of compassion." Bodhisattva has many meanings, but here it means the incarnated power of purity. The bodhisattva is one who is ever-embodied, compared to one who is disembodied. Perhaps, in the Christian sense, it is the ever-embodied Christ, the one who is pure, possessing the whole nature of the Father, of God.

The *bodhisattva* is pure being appearing in separate bodies, but its Selfhood is one, like the light of millions electric bulbs that are lit from one current. The human being, however, is not like the bodhisattva; he has ego, ideas and desires. So the soul is divided as in this body. For the bodhisattva, the soul is all alike in whatever body, so whatever task each performs, he unites with the other and helps the other. This is the ideal personality of the Buddhist, and we all try to attain it. The element of this personality is love and compassion. It is a false human attitude to have an idea, a scheme, or a plan about the universe. From our standpoint as Buddhists, we observe the universe as love and compassion.

This "I," of course, that Lin-chi is talking about means the One who enshrines in the innermost self, the sacred self. It is a microcosm, the consciousness of the universe. If you think Lin-chi is talking about himself, then you do not understand his heart. This "I" is not ego, the separated self. It is really the one who does not depend upon anything, the One in your presence who does not depend upon anything, buddha-nature-itself, transcendental Selfhood.

Lin-chi always speaks this way. You must grasp this "I" of which he is speaking. But it is not so easy.

"If you come into my presence asking about bodhi, I will appear in accordance with the state of mystery." Bodhi is wisdom—knowing, performing knowledge; knowing the Knower. Unless one is a real Zen

student, one cannot understand the Master's meaning from the surface of his words. Here he means "intrinsic power," which to us, to the human being, is a mystery. As you know, all existence in the universe has its own type of reaction. The melon in a valley has a thick skin if the winter is to be a cold one, so the farmer knows if the heavy snow is coming. The fox of Greenland prepares thick fur for a heavy winter and thin fur for a mild one. If you observe nature carefully, you will find these mysteries everywhere. See how the tendril of ivy searches for the sunlight with that blind body, searching each little slit of light, pushing forward with a little hand to touch the sunlight. It may reach ten to fifteen feet to find it.

We all have this intrinsic nature innately. No one can teach us. But when we see someone struggle mentally and physically, we try to help. It is our nature to do this; we are not forced. If we are troubled by notions, jealousy, anxiety, or anger, we rush about and try to forget it. No one teaches us this. But the Buddhist can forget through meditation. This is the mystery, the *bodhi*, the wisdom that we wish to attain. Somehow we know we have the mystery in us. This is our Fourth Vow. When we become Buddhists, we decide to follow the Four Vows.

Remember, when Lin-chi uses the word "appear," he means to act or talk from this state.

"*If you come into my presence asking about nirvana, I will appear in accordance with the state of serenity.*" Nirvana, like Buddha or bodhisattva, has many meanings, but here Lin-chi means annihilation of all entanglements; *bodhi* has carried him to the other shore—nirvana. He has attained the original state of mind. One gets out of the jungle of mind-stuff.

"*Although there are manifold circumstances, there is only this one and no other.*" Pureness, compassion, mystery, serenity—the elemental circumstances. Lin-chi puts on each and uses each. But there is only THIS ONE in the universe who does this. There is no other being in the universe but God; no man, animal, or insect, just THIS ONE.

"*Therefore, this one manifests in accordance with circumstances like the moon in water.*" He transforms himself into the manifold performances of his transforming body that is called *nirmanakaya*. The true body of Buddha is like the sky. But when he appears according to circumstances, it is like the moon on the waves.

> *"Brothers, if you wish to live by the Dharma, you must have the spirit of a great man. But if you haphazardly dawdle your days away, you cannot live by the law. A cracked jug is unfit to store divine soma! To be a great vessel, one must not be deluded by others. Wherever you are, be a master, and wherever you stand is the place of truth. You need not accept every circumstance that comes along. A moment of doubt, and evil enters your mind. When even a* bodhisattva *harbors doubt, evil seizes its opportunity. When anything comes to you, illuminate. Believe in that which you are using in each actual moment; there is no other existence. In this moment, your mind begets the three worlds and in accordance with circumstances divides itself into the six senses. In this moment you enter the pure and the impure; enter into the Tower of Maitreya and into the Land of the Three Eyes. Wherever you travel, you will observe only empty names."*

SOKEI-AN SAYS:

The Buddhism in China of the eighth and ninth centuries was a very complicated philosophy, impossible of application to daily life, and entirely useless. But then it took on a new aspect, an esoteric one. The masters of the time were saying that you could realize this esoteric aspect in one's self. It wasn't necessary to talk about it, or to study it; it could be applied to daily life.

The word "esoteric" sounds a bit mysterious, but if you understand, it's not so mysterious. It is like an axiom, self-evident. You can see it and handle it; it is not necessary to dream up a metaphysical system. The great axiom of the universe is clear to us, but if we try to see it through knowledge, it is difficult to grasp.

"Brothers, if you wish to live by the Dharma, you must have the spirit of a great man." Dharma has many meanings. The subjective *Dharma* is the law written in oneself, and the objective *dharma* is all phenomena arranged by the law of the universe. You feel this law of the universe. If you eat too much you are sick; if you steal, you feel compunction. You do not know the law; you merely feel it and are not quite sure of it. Instinct, too, is written law; you feel it but are not clear about it.

To understand the law written in the self, you must be very true to your self at every moment, and you must think deeply; otherwise you cannot live in the law. You must make right judgments and act accordingly; you must have the axiom in your mind. Where do you get this axiom? Lin-chi said there is no other place to find it but within one's self. You must be a human being. Do not compromise and do not flatter. You must be clear as the blade of a sword. It is with your own wisdom that you will judge and perform. But you cannot do this unless you are what Lin-chi calls a great man. You can talk about swimming and how it is done, but how different it is when we go into the water!

To live in the law you must understand the law of the universe, the law of nature, the law of self, and you must understand the relation of yourself to the universe. Is there a great consciousness in the universe as you have consciousness within you? Does it plan and develop? Or has that great power of the universe no plan at all? Is this great flowing universe just accidental or like your dreams? This is a great question. You think if the universal law has a plan, there must be a relation between it and you, that it is not a mere accident. There must be something between this and that—like karma. All such questions must be settled before you enter into the real path of religion.

"But if you haphazardly dawdle your days away, you cannot live by the law. A cracked jug is unfit to store divine soma!" Do you know the principle of the law? If you do not, there is no use keeping commandments. Each commandment has a particular viewpoint that penetrates the law of nature and the law of the universe. Buddhism really grasps the principle of all law. You must realize it in your system, your heart and soul. Whatever you do, have no compunction and no anxiety.

If you do not know the law, you are managed by it. But if you know it, you will succeed. If you are managed by nature, you will fail; you will be conquered by nature. So, in actual daily life, practice the law and you will know compassion and love. You will manage by knowing the wonderful law that is written in you. But without light and wisdom, you cannot use the law. Buddhism emphasizes this innate wisdom, the real light. To discover this is not so easy, yet you can do it, you can use the hard to conquer the hard. To live in the law is difficult.

In the Zen school knowledge must be as clear as crystal; you must study all of life a long time to come to the point where you can drill through the wall. It is like a wood worm which, not eating, will die within the wood. Eating, however, he will finally come forth and see the outside. This "drilling through the wall" means to realize *shunyata*—clear nothingness. When the Buddha uses the terms *shunyata* and nirvana, it means coming out of the wood.

"*To be a great vessel, one must not be deluded by others.*" Do not say your Chinese teacher says this, your Hindu teacher says that, and your Japanese teacher says something else. All law is written within your self. Return to the your self and think deeply.

"*Wherever your are, be a master, and wherever you stand is the place of truth.*" If you know the law, the principle, then you can master it and come to the place where the truth will be seen from all angles. Some call it God, some call it Allah, some call it Brahma, and some call it Tao. You will see the one thing from all aspects. If you enter into real religion, you will come to that place where all is one. Christianity is the true place. Buddhism is the true place. Taoism is the true place. Find that one place in yourself.

"*You need not accept every circumstance that comes along.*" Every standpoint is the true standpoint. When screaming, drinking water, entering a temple, or bowing before a symbol, if you understand one thing, then whatever place you are in is the true place. In Lin-chi's understanding, the true place is never outside, so it is not necessary to care about circumstances.

What he is saying here about not accepting every circumstance is a dangerous bit if you swallow it as written. He abominated the idea that man must be a monk and keep himself in a cave, living only as a "soul" and abominating the "flesh." This is not real Buddhism or real religion. Lin-chi would call it filthy rubbish. There is a frog that alters its color according to circumstances—on a leaf, a rock, and so on, so no one knows its real color. It does not accept any circumstance as final. It is entirely independent. It changes its color according to its situation, its place.

Lin-chi does not mean to say that he does not agree with all existence on the outside but is pointing out that the truth is in yourself. Therefore, do not care about eating, sleeping, and whatnot. You must be entirely alone and must not accept anything that is in form or no-form wherever you are. You must not perceive anything or think anything. If you think this way, you will find yourself in a cave like the old *arhat* who thinks he is enlightened. Lin-chi does not consider this great enlightenment.

When the moon reflects upon water, the water shines until the moon vanishes. Like a mirror, the water does not hold onto the light. Yellow flowers, yellow mirror; blue flowers, blue mirror; the mirror does not keep anything at all, but changes according to circumstances. When one enters hell, one changes into a hell-being, etcetera. Consciousness enters into all circumstances but does not change its form. You are not patterned by any circumstances. But . . .

"*A moment of doubt, and evil enters your mind. When even a bodhisattva harbors doubt, evil seizes its opportunity.*" When a bodhisattva conceives a doubt about the Buddha's teaching of *prajnaparamita*, the vehicle of wisdom that reaches the other shore of nirvana, he is thinking, Is there such a thing? Is there such a shore? Is there salvation? Is there anyone to be delivered from agony? The Buddha said there is no one to be delivered—evil, the evil of mind-stuff and emotion has seized its opportunity. The bodhisattva's mission to save others from agony and to carry them into a land of peace has become in doubt. And all these doubts come finally to one point: Is this consciousness really existing or not? This is the final question. One must kill the last *alaya-consciousness* and come into *parinirvana*. This is a dreadful moment of doubt, almost impossible to settle. This is that moment of doubt when all day long the mind is not clear.

"*When anything comes to you, illuminate. Believe in that which you are using in each actual moment; there is no other existence.*" Anything—man, woman, money, food, philosophy, mind-stuff, outside, or neutral—you must reflect it with the action of the natural mind, and you must believe that this reflecting action is the real treasure. Nature is a glass reflecting God, and this reflecting action must be free. If it is bound by any idea or theory, it will not reflect because it is not true nature.

Lin-chi always emphasizes that the Master is not dependent upon anything. He is a free man. There are all kinds of men in yourself, so you can respond as the frog that adapts to its situation. In all circumstances adapt yourself. There is no other existence than that man who reflects everything upon this consciousness. In the first and second stages of *kamadhatu* and *rupadhatu*, there is consciousness, but in the third stage, that of *arupadhatu*, there is no consciousness.

Peace does not exist. To make peace, you need war. To be happy, you must know sadness. To enjoy yourself, you must weep. There is no particular joy, pain, or agony. They are not really existing. These are notions of the human being. If you observe this existence carefully, however, there is no particular existence that is like a die cast in some particular mold. There is only one existence—the man who does not depend upon anything. Real enlightenment will come upon the one who is master of all circumstances. Phenomenal existence is not an object to be analyzed in order to obtain enlightenment—one's self alone is the study to open that door.

"In this moment, your mind begets the three worlds and in accordance with circumstances divides itself into the six senses." Your mind, *this* mind, begets the three worlds, be they *kamadhatu, rupadhatu* or *arupadhatu,* past, present, and future, or desire, passion, and ignorance. But your mind is begotten in these worlds, and runs up and down like a worm. *This* mind is like a child of Great Existence. *This* mind that begets the three worlds and relates to all circumstances is the pure mind that has had no contact with the outside, like an infant in his mother's bosom. He is still in the Tushita Heaven, still in the womb of Vairocana, the bosom of God. But undergoing experience, he will slowly realize the outside world by the function of the sense perception of the six senses. The master is not in the six senses, that is, relative existence.

Of course, there is no time, space, mutability, or eternity in Mind-itself. The body of the ocean of mind, from our observation, looks eternal, but eternity is related to mutability; to deny one is logically to deny the other. So this mind is beyond all existence, and all supernatural power is in your possession. You must understand that your body is not limited in using this power, but only if you kill this separate ego and come to one with that Great Life, possessing the six supernatural powers.

All this is beyond reasoning. Your will reacts immediately. It is something like instinct. You react, you feel, you judge. If you are free from everything, you are just like this bell sitting here. You realize your adaptability. But if you have preconceived ideas, there is no adaptability. Then you must sanctify your impure mind by meditation, where nothing is lacking.

It is your own choice. If you see the world from a so-called "impure" standpoint or wish to see it from a so-called "pure" standpoint, that is your own choice. You can see the body either way. All this is your own attitude, however; no one limits your mind. You put yourself into a dungeon, binding your body and mind so that you cannot act freely. There are many that bind themselves with these views. The Buddha said the Middle Way is not outside. Search it out and you can enter into the true Dharma instantaneously, at this moment. But where is this moment, and when is it? Lin-chi is pointing out the truth directly.

"In this moment you enter the pure and the impure; enter into the Tower of Maitreya and into the Land of the Three Eyes." Do you wish to enter into the Tower of Maitreya, the bodhisattva of universal love and friendship, and meet him? How? By meditating upon your self. Then the door of your mind will open and you will enter and see that the whole world has instantly changed its aspect. And when the door closes, you will realize that the inside is empty—no form, no sound, no figure, no flower, no sun or moon. It is *shunyata*, emptiness. But suddenly you will see from every standpoint, multiplied; you will be standing in front millions of Maitreyas in worship. You can enter now, at this moment, the tower of Maitreya or the Land of the Three Eyes—*dharmakaya, sambhogakaya,* and *nirmanakaya.*

To become a bodhisattva, to manifest as a bodhisattva, giving is the first deed of every Buddhist. Giving wisdom opens your mind and opens the mind of others. Giving is the Eye of all deeds. Giving opens your wisdom, and taking does too, for giving cannot exist without taking; it is one action, for there are no two men in the world, only one. But if one does not know this and tries to take without giving, the world does not run smoothly. Giving opens the Eye of Wisdom, not only between men, but between man and a little chick. You give him care and he belongs to you, and he takes and you enter into him and he loves you.

The second deed of every Buddhist is the giving of fearlessness. This is benevolence.

The third is the giving of Dharma, religion. This opens the Eye of others to reality. If you do not grasp reality, it is just as though you went to the city of a king and did not meet him. To meet him, you must have wisdom and benevolence, must have *Dharma*. But, as Lin-chi has said many times, "Wherever you travel, you will observe only empty names."

XVII

Someone asked, "What is the Land of the Three Eyes?"
The Master said: "When together we enter the land
of excellent pureness wearing the garment of purity and

speak of Dharmakaya Buddha. When we enter the land of similitude wearing the garment of non-differentiation and speak of Sambhogakaya Buddha. When we enter the land of emancipation wearing the garment of light and speak of Nirmanakaya Buddha. The Land of the Three Eyes is nothing but mutability, a change of states. According to the scholars of the sutras and shastras, dharmakaya is the base and sambhogakaya and nirmanakaya are the use. But according to my view, dharmakaya does not comprehend my sermon. Therefore, the ancients said, 'These bodies exist only in theory, and their fields are the natural consequence of the bodies themselves.' The essential body and the essential field of Buddha are now evident; they are but systems hypothetically established, like an empty fist or a yellow leaf used to deceive a crying child. What kind of juice do you expect to get from such a dry bone? There is no Dharma on the outside, and the inside is unfathomable. So what do you seek? But everywhere you say there is something to practice and something to attain. Do not commit an error! Even if there is something to practice and attain, it is only the karma of life and death."

SOKEI-AN SAYS:

In this section Lin-chi is again speaking about the *trikaya*, the three bodies of Buddha: *dharmakaya, sambhogakaya, nirmanakaya.*

Someone asked, "What is the Land of the Three Eyes?" The explanation of the Land of the Three Eyes appears in the *Avatamsaka Sutra*, but it is entirely different from Lin-chi's interpretation. Lin-chi is interpreting this idea from his own standpoint and not that of the *sutra*. Now Lin-chi is asking himself a question, and he himself answers.

The Master said: "When together we enter the land of excellent pureness wearing the garment of purity and speak of Dharmakaya Buddha." According to Lin-chi, this state of existence, *dharmakaya*, is reality, the body of Buddha in real existence.

Dharmakaya can be translated in many ways in English— omnipresent body, essential body, essence, or body of law—but none are good translations. Buddhists speak of buddha-nature, the body of Buddha-itself. It can also be the body of God that is omnipresent, which is clearly stated in Christianity. We cannot see it, yet a Zen master will ask you, "How do you see it?" There must be an "excellent" conception about this. When Lin-chi says, "When together we enter the land of excellent pureness wearing the garment of purity and speak of Dharmakaya Buddha" he speaks with his body—his lips, his mind. How does Lin-chi speak of *dharmakaya* with his body? Can you speak by your body and mind?

In Lin-chi's teaching, this "excellent pureness," always means the absolute state of existence. We know the meaning of the word "absolute," but with the five senses we cannot prove this absolute existence. All here (the five senses) is relative existence and all these notions, visions or imaginations, which relate to our mind and our concepts of this monistic existence, also relate to our philosophical mind. Our monistic idea is nothing but pure existence of time and space, just as if you were to beget yourself in the center of the sky; you perceive nothing but time and space. That is our concept of monistic existence. But if you carefully think about it, this concept is still relative to our mind. As long as we conceive that existence, it proves there is a concept that is reflecting upon the mirror of our mind. So existence is not yet pure. It is just as two mirrors reflecting each other—pure time and space. Yet between this subjective consciousness and objective existence of pure time and space there is no absolute. The absolute is incomprehensible. We cannot conceive it. We can talk about it, but we cannot prove it. In the *Diamond Sutra* it is said that if you wish to see or hear *tathagata* from his looks or voice, you are practicing the wrong method. You cannot see *tathagata* that way.

Tathagata is a symbol for the absolute Buddha. Shakyamuni is not absolute Buddha, but one who attained buddhahood. Buddha is the infinite, or absolute. In Buddhism we do not use the word "God," we use "Buddha" instead of "God." We use the word "Buddha" in the broad sense, such as Amitabha Buddha or Vairochana Buddha. Such use is almost equivalent to "God" in Christianity. In other words, if you try to see God or to hear God, you are using the wrong device. You cannot see God with the physical, mental, or even the single eye, nor can you see *tathagata* with any of these eyes. In meditation we perceive everything upon our own consciousness, and we cannot see God. We recite mantras, try to hear through the inmost ear, but we cannot. In a koan there is a famous question: "How do you see him? By what method do you see him?" In one word—undemonstrable!

The reality of the universe is incomprehensible through words. This is really the entrance to religion. You cannot understand the true ground of religion through philosophy. You must realize it, enter it, and you will find that all religions of the world are the same. Lin-chi calls this the land of excellent pureness. However, it is not necessary to give it any name.

"*When we enter the land of similitude wearing the garment of non-differentiation and speak of Sambhogakaya Buddha.*" The "garment of non-differentiation" is seen everywhere—on the battlefield when two enemies look at one another, realize their unity, and die as friends. Leading your daily life from this standpoint is "speaking of Sambhogakaya Buddha."

Dharmakaya is the body of the ocean, of entire space, of wholeness. *Sambhogakaya* is a little different. Draw an imaginary line in this ocean of water at right angles and each square of water is *sambhogakaya*. It is not different from *dharmakaya* but is observed from the angle of a part, while *dharmakaya* is observed from the aspect of wholeness. My soul, his soul, your soul, the same soul but in a different body, the same quality. You cannot discriminate one from the other. *Sambhogakaya* differentiates but does not discriminate between *sambhogakaya* observed as separate consciousness. If you have no idea of the wholeness of *dharmakaya*, then you will be stuck in the notion of a separate soul, which we call individuality. *Sambhogakaya* is not ego. However, it is Selfhood, but it does not grasp anything as its own. *Sambhogakaya* is that union when the mind comes to the knowledge that that mind is Buddha. It is enjoyment by union when our straying soul once more reaches home.

"*When we enter the land of emancipation wearing the garment of light and speak of Nirmanakaya Buddha.*" *Nirmanakaya* is different from *sambhogakaya* as well. It is action in differentiated bodies. The ox has a big body; the mouse has a small one. But when the ego is thrown away, one lives in a transformed body, the great body of *nirmanakaya*, the "garment of light," as Lin-chi says.

You are *dharmakaya*, for your body is not different from its essence. Your body is not just this body, for your body is expanding through the universe,

From the standpoint of *dharmakaya*, there is no human being. Just one God existing that is separated into all different stages of consciousness. God enshrines in our body and takes form as a woman, a man, a farmer, a merchant, a soldier, a politician, a sparrow, a crow, insect, and dog; and all speak the existence of *nirmanakaya* by body, mind, and lips.

"The Land of the Three Eyes is nothing but mutability, a change of states." When Lin-chi enters the Land of the Three Eyes he wears the garments of *dharmakaya, sambhogakaya,* and *nirmanakaya*; and from each stage he acts. Real existence is just one existence. Where is this Land?

"According to the scholars of the sutras *and* shastras, dharmakaya *is the base and* sambhogakaya *and* nirmanakaya *are the use."* In this sentence Lin-chi is pointing to those scholars on Mount T'ien-t'ai who at that time were studying *sutras* from morning to evening and were talking nothing but philosophy. It is like talking about the menu of a restaurant and never tasting the food. Zen does not care for such Buddhists, so Lin-chi talks very severely about them.

"But according to my view, dharmakaya *does not comprehend my sermon."* When I am speaking and you are listening and apprehending my meaning, who is apprehending? Who is the one in you that does that? That Master has no name, but performs his functions vividly. Yet, when we try to acquaint ourselves with him, he disappears.

Ananda asked Mahakashyapa, "What was it that the Buddha gave you beside the robe and bowl?" Mahakashyapa called, "Ananda!" "Yes" "Put up the awning." "Ah—yes!" and he understood.

What was it that Mahakashyapa inherited from the Buddha when he held up a flower and Mahakashyapa smiled? That one is *nirmanakaya* but also *sambhogakaya* and *dharmakaya.* It is existence upon a pinpoint, but it also covers the whole universe. It has no three bodies, nor one body. Sometimes it has no body and sometimes it has manifold bodies. Why put this into a category?

In the Zen school, you will be given the question that the Sixth Patriarch put to his opponent: "Before father and mother, what were you?" You will answer this when you come to the point, grasp the reality. It is not *dharmakaya* nor *sambhogakaya* nor *nirmanakaya,* yet it covers the whole universe and stands in its center through past, present and future. It stands upon the moment, though there is no instrument that could point to that particular moment. You will realize it in that moment. This one will understand Lin-chi's sermon.

Lin-chi is brushing these terms aside and showing us True reality.

"Therefore, the ancients said, 'These bodies exist only in theory, and their fields are the natural consequence of the bodies themselves.'" That is, to cough, one must have a throat. Body must have place; without place body cannot stand. So when the Buddha speaks of *dharmakaya*, he must then invent the field that keeps the *dharmakaya* upon it.

"The essential body and the essential field of Buddha are now evident; they are but systems hypothetically established, like an empty fist or a yellow leaf used to deceive a crying child. What kind of juice do you expect to get from such a dry bone?" That is, there is nothing in it, so stop crying. *Dharmakaya, sambhogakaya, nirmanakaya*—nothing left. Yet, we do not know what it is.

Lin-chi is again saying that we try to get everything out of names, or philosophical constructions, just like one who tries to get juice out of a dry bone. Even a hungry dog cannot make anything out of it. But the foolish dog tries to get something and does not know it is his own saliva. He hurts his lips and tastes his own blood. Everyone can taste philosophy as well—it is just the juice of one's own brain.

Lin-chi strongly abuses philosophical Buddhism—kicks it all out until there is nothing left. Of course, he himSelf is untouched. That is a strange thing. He destroys everything but says nothing about himself.

When the Buddha said, "All these forty-nine years I have said nothing," he was fooling us. He was saying all the teachings of the Buddha can be compounded into this: There is nothing to say. But, of course, he did not deny himself nor affirm himself.

A monk once asked the Buddha about *Tathagata*: "Is *Tathagata* eternal or not?" The Buddha did not speak a world; his answer was SILENCE. One cannot say that there was no Zen at the Buddha's time! If the Buddha had said, "*Tathagata* is eternal," then he would have been trapped in the conception which affirms the ego. If he had said, "*Tathagata* is not eternal," then he would fall into the pit of absolute annihilation. If there is absolutely nothing in the universe, where does this body come from? Whatever you call this existence—phenomena or noumena—is this eternal or not eternal? How do you answer the koan "Before father and mother"?

It is easy to speak about everything in words. We say Buddhism is not egoism, but you cannot believe this word. When this comes to an end, it will go back to the ocean of soul. So this "I" will be entirely decomposed and amalgamated into this ocean. There is no ego, no soul to return to, the system of reincarnation is wrong. Do you believe this? Then why did the Buddha speak of reincarnation? You have to feel it. Are you eternal or not? Does the ego exist after death or not? You must feel it as Shakyamuni Buddha realized it in himself and understood it. He said many things— sometimes affirming and sometimes denying. One cannot cling to his words, for a teacher is not in his words at all. So Lin-chi is speaking from his own experience, and his words meet the Buddha's words exactly.

When I was practicing meditation, before entering deep *samadhi*, all fear dropped away, and nothing came up. But coming out of *samadhi* I was still on my chair. What was it? If you do not use your wisdom, you can meditate a million times and not be enlightened. Be enlightened—not in meditation, but in wisdom!

Huang-po said that your body will not give enlightenment to your meditation, is not the real cause of enlightenment, but wisdom is the cause of enlightenment. We talk of wisdom—here, there—but do not grasp it. When we grasp wisdom-itself, it is like a moth flying all around the air and finally entering the fire—Wisdom! Wisdom! Wisdom!

When you finally come to focus, the whole universe will shine and shout. Then you will grasp *prajna*, the last vehicle to bring you to nirvana. Everyone thinks wisdom is the last vehicle, so the conception of nirvana ends in ego, in consciousness, in a spark, in light and never knows true nirvana. Sometimes one enters into nirvana and dies never to return, so his understanding (*prajna*) is not that of the Buddha.

To those who long for nirvana (as a child wishes gold and we give him a yellow leaf, and the child believes it is gold) we give *dharmakaya*, *sambhogakaya*, *nirmanakaya*. Then, "Ah, I understand, I am enlightened; it is ISNESS!" There is no such enlightenment in the world.

Lin-chi speaks directly to destroy all such Buddhism. He throws dynamite into the philosophical system of Buddhism. It is no wonder that all were afraid of him at that time. If one asked him, "What is Buddhism?"—Bang!

"There is no Dharma on the outside, and the inside is unfathomable. So what do you seek? The outside is mutable, a vision, not true existence; and the inside is unfathomable. Can you get any dharma from the inside through meditation? Is there anything you can grasp? "Oh, this is the Dharma—it's empty!" This is all vision—all from the outside, impressed upon the brain system, as the impression of the sun in your eyes remains after looking at it. The sun and its changing colors are in your eyes, but to

your mind that shadow stays a long time and gives you that vision, gives you that dream. That is not Dharma.

In meditation you grasp nothing. If you are thinking, you are not meditating. Do not be fooled. The interior is incomprehensible. Exactly! Lin-chi is a real teacher. He is not fooling us. He tells the truth.

"*But everywhere you say there is something to practice and something to attain.*" Yes, we thought so—I am teaching so: "The law (*Dharma*) can be practiced; and in meditation and *sanzen* you realize the Dharma." You can practice Buddhism, follow the commandments, and finally attain enlightenment by meditation and by reading the *sutras*. But did you realize Buddhism really? I want to know!

"*Do not commit an error!*" Lin-chi is denying the practice of meditation, reading the *sutras*, keeping the commandments, and so forth. He has brushed them all aside.

"*Even if there is something to practice and attain, it is only the karma of life and death.*" You say that you attain by practicing. However, from his point of view, practice and attainment are but the karma of life and death. They are karma factories—reading, meditating, and so on. There is a reason for such talk. If, for example, almsgiving is performed from generation to generation without a real understanding of Buddhism, then it is only manufacturing karma.

"*You also say you must practice the sixfold paramitas and the ten thousand virtuous deeds. In my view, this is just making karma. Seeking bodhisattvahood is making karma. Reading the sutras and studying the teachings is also making karma. The Buddha and the patriarchs are those who have nothing to do. Therefore, whether their minds flow or flow not, are impelled to action or not impelled to action, their deeds are pure.*"

SOKEI-AN SAYS:

Lin-chi is also smashing the six *paramitas*—almsgiving, commandments, forbearance, exertion, meditation, and wisdom leading to enlightenment, the six methods to carry one to the other shore of nirvana. And when he says seeking the Buddha, the Dharma, and bodhisattvahood, as well as reading the *sutras* is also karma-making. It is the final dynamite!

The Buddha never told us the real point to Buddhism. It is not written in the *sutras*. But the Buddha transmitted something to Mahakashyapa when he held up the blue lotus and smiled. Some may say this is only legend, but in our transmission of the torch the teachers say, "There was nothing to transmit. We have received nothing from you." Then what is the transmission? It is marvelous Dharma that is not transmitted from the Buddha to Mahakashyapa. Excellent and marvelous, yet not transmitted!

"The Buddha and the patriarchs are those who have nothing to do." They are men of no worry. They have done all, and there is nothing left for them to do.

There are three very important principles of Buddhism to relieve us from all entanglements: First, we have to separate from wrong views (our attachments to phenomenal arrangements, such as small, large, her, him, and so on).

Second, know that there is no such thing as the outside, that it is just a conception. We destroy this wrong view by the koan: "Through the three worlds nothing is existing. Where does your soul come from?" When you have answered this koan, you will understand reality and will no longer be bothered by the external world; you will come to the conclusion that this is a transient vision. Then, with a more difficult koan, you will destroy this wrong conception as well. To save oneself from delusion is hard work. We must see that all is just conception. Does this bring us to true understanding? I should say not! But we must pass through this phase.

In the universal stage, there is no observer and no stage. All are actors, and you must know your part. So what do I do at this stage? To be a good actor you must know all of the reality or you do not know what you are doing. This is why I tell you there is no audience, all is a performance and you must know your part. Buddhism is in America, so I must take my part also.

The third principle, here, is the real performance of life. We know who is taking the part and who is the observer.

"Therefore, whether their minds flow or flow not, are impelled to action or not impelled to action, their deeds are pure." These two terms "flow or flow not" are very important in Buddhism. In Sanskrit, they are *asrava*

and *anasrava*. *Asrava* is "flowing," "leaking," "running away," "afflicting." It is nothing but the flowing motion from the soul to the external world through mind, emotion, and body. It is discharging something from the inside to the outside—like brain-stuff from the lips. It is mind-stuff flowing out from the center of mind.

Anasrava is the non-leaking mind. It is the soul that has entered the religious life, has gone back to its original home and exterminated the filth unconsciously gotten from the outside. In burning oil the impure oil produces a sound which continues until all impurities are burned away. Then comes the scarlet flame, a pure flame with no black smoke, like beaten gold—all impurities are gone. This is the sanctification of mind; you realize that pure mind innate in yourself. This is the non-leaking mind.

Lin-chi said that *all* are pure deeds. So flowing out of mind-stuff and non-flowing out of mind-stuff are both pure life. You, however, use your flowing mind for unnecessary actions, actions that are not quite natural, that are caused by impure thought or more desire than necessary. This is impelled action. In non-impelled action, all artificiality is gone, and you understand that the law of nature is pure nature, nature and man with no distinction.

Lin-chi has told his followers that all deeds called the practice of Buddhism are nothing but karma-making. He brushed aside all practices and said that all Buddha and patriarchs are men of no worry who have nothing more to do. It is like a monk who studied in a temple in Kyoto for twenty or twenty-five years, and then one day he finished everything. He returned to his small temple upon the mountain and stretched himself upon the floor and extended his arms and looked at the blue sky where the white clouds were floating—no need to practice anything. He returned to his own state of humankind. It is not necessary to imitate the Buddha which is a wooden image and not necessary to imitate the patriarchs whose biographies are in the *sutras*. He would say, "I lie down, extending my arms and feet." There is nothing to say, right or wrong. "I take a long nap and I awake. I see the sunset in my west window."

If you do not reach there you will think there is something different from this life of mankind. Here you are free from everything. Lin-chi says to you now you must brush all the methods of Zen aside. He is pointing out the real foundation of life upon which we must stand. He is teaching us to stand upon the real earth with two feet. But these lectures are for advanced students, not a lecture for beginners.

> *"There are blind baldheads who after finishing a stomachful of food sit down to contemplate tranquillity, restrain the flow of their minds, and abandon the mind's activity. They abominate noise and seek calmness, but this is heresy. A Patriarch said, 'If you restrain the mind to contemplate tranquillity, raise the mind to observe externals, hold the mind to behold serenity within, or concentrate the mind to enter trances, you must know these practices are all fictitious devices.' He who is listening now to my sermon, how can he be approached, realized, or adorned? He is not one who can be approached or adorned. But if he does adorn himself, he adorns himself with all existence. Do not commit an error!"*

SOKEI-AN SAYS:

Lin-chi has settled all questions about meditation, concentration, and so forth. He tells us this is no true Buddhism. Your common sense might ask, "Then what is the merit of sitting all day in meditation?" He will give you the answer, but you must understand that his answer is from his own standpoint as a Zen master. He is not a student. His meditation when young was a very severe one, but now he no longer needs any device.

"*There are blind baldheads who after finishing a stomachful of food sit down to contemplate tranquillity, restrain the flow of their minds, and abandon the mind's activity. They abominate noise and seek calmness, but this is heresy.*" Now he is touching all Zen monks and calls them baldheads, the unenlightened. In Zen temples, if you close your eyes in meditation, you are hit. You must have an open eye, sensitive to all that is around you. You must let your mind flow naturally.

"*A Patriarch said, 'If your restrain the mind to contemplate tranquillity, raise the mind to observe externals, hold the mind to behold serenity within, or concentrate the mind to enter trances, you must know these practices are all fictitious devices.'*" Wild fox Zen. This is a heresy, but it's a fault of all beginners. The study of Zen is dangerous without a teacher.

Whether you keep your mind contemplating calmly or raise it to observe the external, or, look into the self to keep it as the moon's reflection in the pool, all these are but devices and not true Buddhism. There is the koan: "Your soul is turning day and night like a marvelous wheel with every circumstance. How do you turn it?" When you answer this, you will realize the real standpoint of Buddhism.

In a Chinese temple there was a poem engraved upon the two doors of a gate. One side said, "The soul is so marvelous and so mysterious." The other, "It turns into all circumstances." A monk entered the temple and, meeting the abbot, said: "I read the two lines of the poem. On the one side it speaks of the mysterious soul and on the other, turning into all circumstances. I wonder, which point is the more important for us?" The abbot said, "The soul is turning like a marvelous wheel." But a patriarch of Japan, hearing this, remarked: "I do not agree. If I were to emphasize either side, I would choose, "Turning with circumstance."

"He who is listening now to my sermon, how can he be approached, realized, or adorned?" So why do you try to approach, or realize, or adorn, or prove, or ascertain, or demonstrate by evidence, by argument? He who is listening in your presence is living in yourself—buddha-nature, the Buddha. There is no other being in your self. There is just one buddha-nature in the universe, in you, in all sentient beings. I am speaking here and you are listening, but it is really one soul. There is no man, god, animal or insect, just one buddha-nature. When I say buddha-nature, you "image" a Buddha who is always meditating. It is not an image! Buddha-nature is the nature of the universe.

"He is not one who can be approached or adorned." Who? This One? [Strikes chest.] How do you approach him?

This existence is always *here*. There are no two existences in the world. Who could approach him? There is no high. There is no low. You think you are a human being. But you are God. You put a cheap value upon your own soul from your own ignorance. It is not necessary to prove that you are God. But you, of course, would say, "If I am God, I must make decisions. Yet I do not know what to do."

Well, God is still creating the universe and the creating will be endless. God has not decided anything yet. How could you decide? If you think you can decide, then you attach too much importance to yourself. If you study the Buddhist commandments, you will understand decision as a cardinal principle.

This phenomenal world is transient, mutable. It changes phase at every moment. If you make the decision to adhere to this world, that decision is violating the Buddha's commandment. You make yourself useless. Look at water and how it flows. See how the clouds change at every moment! No artist can depict the changes. If you do not understand the law of transitoriness, you do not understand Buddhism. So "He, who is listening now to my sermon" is buddha-nature. He is the one you can adorn.

"But if he does adorn himself, he adorns himself with all existence." That one adorns himself with the blue sky, the green earth, flowing water, whispering breeze, singing birds, stars and flowers. Don't you realize that he adorns himself with a universal crown—the sun and moon? Don't you know the experience of wholeness? Do you not know the moment when you enter into the universe and the universe enters into you? You are not just a human being. If you have no experience of adorning yourself, you are still outside Buddhism. So Lin-chi says, "Do not commit an error!"

Some say that Buddhism and Christianity are not very different. To me all this talking is a nuisance. There is no Christian God. There is no Buddhist or Mohammedan God. There is just one taste in the universe. But somehow we are trying to explain one thing from many different directions. We are trying to explain God or Buddha from a different angle, different experience. But, because the nature of each is the Dharma of the universe, we point to one thing. Essentially the Buddhist and the Christian are alike. We laugh. We smell the same way. Some say in the future there will be only one religion—it's foolish. Religion is just one nose in the world.

"Brothers, you adhere to the words that have issued from the mouths of some old teachers, and think them to be the true teaching. You think they are wonderful teachers, so that you with your common mind, dare not take the measure of those eminent sages. Blind idiots! You go through life holding this kind of understanding, betraying your own two eyes. Like a donkey trembling on a frozen path you say, 'I do not dare to abuse the sages for fear of making karma with my mouth.'

"Brothers, only the great sage dares to disparage the buddhas and the patriarchs; dares to pronounce the right or wrong of the world, condemn the tripitaka, damn infantile scholars, and look for a man in either favorable or unfavorable circumstances."

SOKEI-AN SAYS:

The Buddhism that was transmitted to China from India during the first century of the Christian era was metaphysical. The monks were very busy studying philosophy and had no opportunity to actually realize it, just like a student studying swimming on the floor knows the motions but has no actual experience in the water. Metaphysical Buddhism is a guide; it is not true Buddhism. However, by following the stages as outlined in Buddhist meditation, we will enter the gate. It was after five or six hundred years that the Chinese students of Buddhism slowly finished their metaphysical phase, then began to lay emphasis upon realization— that is, how to live in Buddhism. In Japan we went through the same process for a long time. It has been Buddhist now for about seventeen hundred years. First the monks came privately from China or India for about three hundred years, and later, when Buddhism was authorized by the power of the emperor, eminent monks were formally invited. It was at this time that Japan, having been in its metaphysical period for about six hundred years, came to the realization of true Buddhism. Like a huge tree, it grew slowly.

One of the emperors of the time built that huge bronze statue, You can enter the nostril with an umbrella open, and you can sleep in one of its fingers. When the emperor had it cast out of a mountain and the molten bronze poured inside, it took away a huge hill. To celebrate the occasion, the emperor invited five hundred monks from India and five hundred monks from China. Accompanied by disciples, merchants, and families, in all, about five thousand came. And they continued to come for two years, and many stayed. I have come to America to try to clear away the weeds, to sow the seed, and to bury my bones on this soil. If I succeed in this, my mission will have been accomplished.

Lin-chi's Buddhism has no philosophy in it, but points directly to the realization of Buddhism in daily life. The Buddha is no more than a human being. Bodhidharma, the founder of the Zen School, is also a human being. We are also human beings. Why must we draw a distinction? Buddha enlightened himself. Why shouldn't we also? If we return to our own body of consciousness and find the entrance into that consciousness, and through *that* become one with the universe, then this hand is mine no longer. All that we see is the power of the universe. It is easy to talk about, but difficult to realize. But students always place emphasis on theory first by reading books and listening to lectures.

When you have time to look into yourself, your first question should be: "What is my consciousness?" I wish to move my hand, and I do. If this is the power that comes from the great universe, then by using this power, I will find the universal law. After dinner, before sleeping, whenever you have the opportunity, think, What is my consciousness? Where is the center of consciousness?

The soul is the equivalent of this consciousness. But everyone thinks the soul has some form, some individual characteristic, and will stay around forever from the beginningless beginning to the endless end of the universe, that it is really created separately by God and that the cat's soul will remain a cat's soul and a man's soul will remain a man's soul throughout aeons of time. It is not so, of course. Just as a flower blooming on the tip of each branch is individual, so are we in Selfhood—but we come from one root, the root from one seed, and the seed from one flower. The root of our life is this planet, this huge tree of a planet growing in the ground of the sky. We come here as a flower. If we fall as a drop of the water into the ocean, we will disappear but not be annihilated. It is through our sight that there is space and time. But in consciousness, there is no space or time; there is no soul after death to be scattered anywhere like a drop of alcohol in water. That realm is beyond time and space and cannot be explained in words. It is part of the esoteric teaching. You can enter and realize it. It is not necessary to wait for a saint to explain the experience to you. No! You can enter yourself and you can know all. It is very simple.

"*Brothers, you adhere to the words that have issued from the mouths of some old teachers, and think them to be the true teaching.* "Inside." "Outside" "Nothing outside." Or vice versa. Lin-chi is speaking of such teachings. An *arhat* in India asked his disciple, "Is that stone in the garden inside of yourself or outside of yourself?" How would you answer this?

The whole universe is nothing but the view created by the five senses (nothing outside) all is a picture on the camera of your self. Well, the stone must be inside of yourself. But to reflect something, there must be something to reflect. Force? Quality? Maybe the reality outside has no quality. Perhaps we are only reflecting consciousness, the law of the camera. Then the stone is outside? Well . . . which is it?

There are various doctrines and schools in Buddhism. One teacher will say one thing, and any other teacher will say something else, and you will never eat real food but only smell it. Religion is something to eat and to actually digest. You may get all the information about a trip you want to take, but if you never buy a ticket or take a train you will never get anywhere. Gathering information is no good. You must get IT, practice IT, and then realize *who* is practicing it. What power in yourself is trying to get buddha-nature? Who practices buddha-nature, you or Buddha?

"You think they are wonderful teachers, so that you with your common mind dare not take the measure of those eminent sages!" All is true law. There is the real teacher. Who teaches? The buddha-nature in yourself teaches you. But you think the teacher is a sage and different from a common man. No, you must find the sage in yourself. That is what Lin-chi is pointing to.

Lin-chi is not really a domineering teacher. He is just trying to point out the real buddha-nature in yourself. Buddha-nature is the only one to open your eye and show you the law written in your body and mind. If you have that law, you need not "decide" anything. At every moment you will live it.

"Blind idiots! You go through life holding this kind of understanding, betraying your own two eyes. Like a donkey trembling on a frozen path you say, 'I do not dare to abuse the sages for fear of making karma with my mouth.' Lin-chi has denied all training according to *sutra*, all practice of deeds of the six *paramitas*, and the practice of meditation that blindly has you sitting in quietude without knowing what you are rally aiming at. Meditation is very important, of course, but first you must understand *who* is practicing, *who* in yourself is meditating. Do your toes or eyes practice meditation? Does your body, your emotions or mind? What part of you really practices meditation? You may answer, "Consciousness is my master. He practices meditation." But then Lin-chi would ask you, "Where is your consciousness?"

We all put too much importance on consciousness, not knowing that consciousness is still an attendant of the Master. It is not the Master. You would say your hand has consciousness; but if there is no touch, it does not feel. I feel my hand; it is warm, cold, and so forth. To feel my hand it is not necessary to touch anything, for I feel its existence. We call this consciousness. And while we have a body, we are quite sure that we have it; it has its own function. But without a body, how do we prove it? After death, when this consciousness is annihilated, are we not annihilated? Then how can you believe in reincarnation? If there is an absolute void after death, why doesn't it happen before birth? If there is absolutely nothing before birth, from that absolute nothingness, how can you form yourself, and by what power, by what process? Without body or mind, what is consciousness?

Lin-chi is telling you that you yourself are not a bit different from the eminent sages. If those sages could attain enlightenment, why not you? If you do not pursuee the words spoken by teachers, but rather turn your attention to yourself, you will attain enlightenment as they did. This is his viewpoint.

"Brothers, only the great sage dares to disparage the buddhas and the patriarchs, dares to pronounce the right or wrong of the world, condemn the tripitaka, damn infantile scholars, and look for a man in either favorable or unfavorable circumstances." The Record of Lin-chi does not contain many viewpoints. It pushes one point, hammering strongly, so that if you carefully follow this record, you will understand a Buddhism that is without entanglements or philosophizing. In a moment—without meditation—you may reach this point! If you are very honest, his Buddhism is easy to follow, but you must give up philosophizing and the use of all devices and truly believe in This One [striking chest]. In Western terms, you could say the "person," in the Christian sense of a personal God, is enshrined in one's self. You will realize Buddhism in yourself when you meet the Master in yourself, as well as in the universe.

All great religions are very plain and simple. But we are degraded human beings. We are so intoxicated that we cannot believe in a plain simple teaching. We go on building fantastic theories and go astray, losing ourselves in those entanglements. We are like the Chinese hermit who built a labyrinth, a maze, but before he had finished had lost himself in it. It is interesting that this story of the labyrinth can be found in all countries. In Greek mythology the hero had to kill a bull in the heart of a labyrinth, and a princess had to give him a thread so he could find his way back. If you wish to build a philosophical labyrinth, please remember to keep the thread. What thread? Zen is the thread. If you let it go, you will not come out. *Dhyana* is the thread.

So comes the great question. All of you have this question. It is the gate, the entrance to Buddhism: Is there really decision in human life? Look at nature. Water flows. Which way it is going? It makes no decision, no determination. Is there any decision in nature's course? If not, why must the human being have this decisive question? Perhaps we are wrong. This you must think out as the base of human life, or you will be like the donkey. The one who has the realization of buddha-nature has no need of Buddhism, however, for it is just a carriage. He has reached the other shore.

The Buddhist religion is a vehicle to reach somewhere. If you reach this place, which is real understanding, you do not need it. If you do not reach this place, you must live in the commandments all your life. It is like an artist who copies life and never comes to live his own. The Buddha did it and we can too. We can come to real life, which is written in ourselves. We can read everything there.

And so Lin-chi dares to disparage the Buddha and the Dharma. In his eyes, the philosophical scholars are infantile.

"For the past twelve years I've searched for karma but have found none even the size of a poppy seed. If you are like those new-bride Zen masters, you will be frightened of being driven out of your temple and starving to death. From ancient days, wherever our ancestors went, people did not believe them. Only after these true masters had been expelled did the people revere them. And if they had been accepted by these people, what good could they have done? The roar of a lion rends the brain of a fox."

SOKEI-AN SAYS:

The *Lin-chi Record* is very hard to translate, for the writer was not a scholar and often used the vernacular. We are now using this record as a mirror to reflect our own minds and to compare our understanding with that of the Master himself. It is through man that man understands something beyond himself—the power actively moving in him. Man is the entrance, and there are steps to ascend and to descend. Man is the link between *this* and *that*.

"For the past twelve years I've searched for karma but have found none even the size of a poppy seed)." The ignorant one receives karma, but the awakened one, moving naturally with the universal stream of nature, does not.

Man is originally in the state of *avidya*, the darkness of ignorance. He does not know the true law of nature and continually adds unnecessary effort to this natural force, consequently making karma. A farmer cuts down a forest, a flood comes, and the whole village is destroyed. If he repeats such actions, and a flood comes again, he will eventually understand and be enlightened and delivered out of karma. The real mind of man knows the natural force. According to the Buddha's teaching, when the mind is cleared, the indicator in the mind points as a compass to the correct road in nature. We have this indicator, but it is covered with the dust of attachment. However, the darkness of *avidya* in the world of nature is buddha-nature in us, which has not yet opened it petals. There is no such thing as a karma nature, for karma does not actually belong to any man, and karma has no needs of its own.

"If you are like those new-bride Zen masters, you will be frightened of being driven out of your temple and starving to death." A Zen master has the power to judge others' minds, but if he has a "new-bride" attitude, he will be careful not to offend for fear of being driven out by his supporters.

"From ancient days, wherever our ancestors went, people did not believe them." Like Bodhidharma when he met the emperor. They had an argument and the emperor threw him out. Only after these masters had been expelled did the people revere them.

"And if they had been accepted by these people, what good could they have done?" If they had understood Buddhism, what need would they have had of them?

"The roar of a lion rends the brain of a fox." Lin-chi's attitude is that of a lion. What is Buddhism? Bah! There is no Buddhism to be acquired. All is in yourself. The true attitude is the base of Buddhism. To return to that point and to live there, safely, without any doubt, that is enlightenment!

"Brothers, everywhere it is said there is a Way to be attained and a Dharma to be proved. Speak! What Way is there to be practiced, and what Dharma is there to be proved? At this moment, what powers are you lacking, what needs to be repaired? Our junior scholars, however, do not understand this. Believing in wild fox spirits, you permit them to bind you up when they say, 'One attains buddhahood as a result of keeping one's deeds in accordance with the truth and guarding oneself from being dissolute with the three karmas.'

"Those who speak in this fashion are as numerous as the spring rain. The ancients said, 'When you meet an adept on the Way, do not stand in the Way.' It is also said, 'If you attempt to practice the Way, the Way will not operate, and ten thousand evil circumstances will compete to raise their heads. But when the sword of wisdom comes forth, there will be nothing at all. Then you will see brightness in darkness, and in darkness, brightness.'

"Therefore, the ancients said, 'The everyday mind is the true Way.'"

SOKEI-AN SAYS:

Buddhism was transmitted from India to China in the First Century A.D. The Chinese have been Buddhists for two thousand years, the Japanese for one thousand four hundred years. It was only about one hundred years ago that an Englishman started to look into the Buddhist cannon. European scholars first studied Buddhism mainly from the Pali scriptures, which they came to call Southern Buddhism, and our form of Buddhism, that of Japan and China, they called Northern Buddhism. At first they believed that Southern, or Hinayana Buddhism, was closer to true Buddhism and that Northern, or Mahayana Buddhism, was not. Today, of course, opinion has changed. Now scholars realize one cannot actually understand Mahayana Buddhism without truly understanding Chinese. Schopenhauer came to a deep understanding of Buddhism through the study of these early European translations. I believe he said, "Of all the philosophies in the world, the Buddhist philosophy is the best." He also studied Taoism, though through very poor translations. Of course, he was a genius. The Mahayana scriptures only came to the ear of European scholars about sixty years ago.

"Brothers, everywhere it is said there is a Way to be attained and a Dharma to be proved. Speak! What Way is there to be practiced, and what Dharma is there to be proved?" As usual, Lin-chi's Buddhism has a peculiar aspect even though he is smashing it to pieces. He does not depend upon any *sutra*. He even avoids the practice of meditation. Huang-po, his teacher, said in his record that meditation is of no use to attain enlightenment, that the body will never attain enlightenment, only the mind. You can meditate for three thousand years, but if your mind is not clear, you will never open the eye of enlightenment.

So Lin-chi took Huang-po's theory as his own and did not emphasize the blind forms of meditation that were at that time being practiced in China and India. Some monks were more interested in attaining supernatural, clairvoyant, or mind-reading powers. This was achieved, they believed, by completely relaxing the mind in quietude so it would return to a Selfless state of consciousness. In this state it was believed one could read the mind of others. Of course, ignorant fishermen do this all the time, but they are not enlightened. What they have is a peculiar sense or feeling. If you practiced for about ten years, you would be able to do the same. But, of course, of what use is it?

Another form of meditation that was practiced at the time was different. Its main concern was with knowing the self, how it is related to the universe, and how it acquires its universal power or law. How does this universal power or law operate in us? To acquire this human and universal power, we meditate. And, of course, Lin-chi said no to this as well. Water must wave. If you still it, you will only create dead water, and that is of no use—no fish will live in it. But if you wish to attain a living mind, you must attain it by using it in actual conditions. Of course, he came to this after many years of meditation.

"At this moment, what powers are you lacking, what needs to be repaired?" Today we say if you have enlightened yourself, you must be tested by a teacher or some adept of the Dharma or master of Zen. He will tell you if your enlightenment is true or not. And, of course, as a Zen teacher, he will destroy that conclusion as well. Can the self be tested? Can you actually create a perfect self? No, Lin-chi says, you are *originally* perfect. There is no reason to be approved or disapproved. If you understand this, he says, you *are* a perfect one! But remember, this perfection is realized in the phenomenal world. God is still engrossed in his work of creation. Nothing is brought to perfection. So we cannot

judge the right or wrong of anything. This perfection is like a transitory dream. Waves. Clouds. We cannot grasp them. If you are looking for perfection on the outside, you will never believe in yourself. The true attitude is to *return* to your self and look into it, and in a moment! It is not necessary to meditate in darkness. Look at this box. One minute is enough. Why take five minutes?

"*Our junior scholars, however, do not understand this. Believing in wild fox spirits, you permit them to bind you up when they say, 'One attains buddhahood as a result of keeping one's deeds in accordance with the truth and guarding oneself from being dissolute with the three karmas.'*" The three karmas are those of body, speech, and mind—attachment to jealousy, hatred, or inverted views: drinking, gambling, amd so on. Transmigration is not only through your body but your mind, emotion, and mood as well. My children may be my future body, but your mind may be my future mind. There is only one sentient being living in the universe. You and I, he and she are not separate. It is through karma that all becomes dissipated.

The wild fox spirits are the so-called sages, the old Buddhist teachers. The old spirit of the fox tells you something and you believe it, and you blindly follow his command without knowing why. Lin-chi as always denounces this.

"*Those who speak in this fashion are as numerous as the spring rain. The ancients said, 'When you meet an adept on the Way, do not stand in the Way.'*" This line is very difficult. If you meet one who is really skilled in something, you stop him and you say, "Your method is wonderful, will you let me try it with you?" He will tell you to go away. The Buddhist monk will try to please you by speaking about nirvana, but he will start by asking you to please go away as well. The depths of Buddhism are not in talking about Buddhism. If I visit a Chinese man and he says, "Sit down and take tea," this sounds deep to me. nirvana, enlightenment— what use?

"*It is also said, 'If you attempt to practice the Way, the Way will not operate, and ten thousand evil circumstances will compete to raise their heads.'*" This line is very important. If you attempt to operate the natural law of the mind, you will only spoil it. I think you will realize this through your practice of any activity. In meditation you try *not* to think, that is, stop mind activity, and think you have succeeded. But this is a wrong concept; it is merely negative instead of positive. You are using your own power, so the result is the same. Your intuition can give you the same result, stopping the flow of thoughts just as well.

But, according to Lin-chi, if you take the attitude that the body is already perfect, why put more purpose into it? It is the same with mind. Mind, itself, is marvelous! You have only to use its power that is in yourself. If you do not understand its law, and spend much of your time in practice, it's of no use, and all unnatural circumstances will spring out like mushrooms after rain—unnatural art, wrong observation of nature, unnatural practice and morality.

Nearly all are enticed by doctrine. Regular life is a formula of good and evil. But it takes a real capability to observe the relationship *between* good and evil. Mere charity can really be evil in some circumstances, because by that charity you may bend the mind of men. You must penetrate this power of good and evil. This is the practice of true virtue. You must know the negative and positive, the two aspects of anything. You can use a device, but do not be used by it. Buddhism is a device to attain knowledge and enlightenment. When you attain enlightenment, you do not need Buddhism any more.

Without testifying or signifying, we live in the true light from morning to evening. That is the life of a Buddha and a bodhisattva. In other words, one attains buddhahood—one's life is a pure deed. From this standpoint, there is nothing to be abominated, all is a desire to enlighten one's self and all is pure, both physical and mental. If one comes to a real understanding of man, one will become a ruler, a master and judge of human beings. He must attain the power as the Buddha or Lin-chi did. There can be no imitation or pretension. This is forbidden in Buddhism. All must be true.

"But when the sword of wisdom comes forth, there will be nothing at all. Then you will see brightness in darkness, and in darkness, brightness." When the sword of wisdom comes forth there will be nothing at all—no enticement of any sort in the world. This sword, this diamond sword, will annihilate everything: time and space, beginning and end, true and false, good and bad. The negative and positive are aspects seen from the human angle. but from the universal angle there is just one aspect, and that is absolute. There is no negative or positive. When this sword shines alone in heaven, all is reduced to nothingness. The sword of wisdom, the absolute sword, cuts out all relative conceptions. It is in SILENCE that

one attains this sword. When you reach this view, you have the sword of wisdom! Do you have that sword in yourself?

But when you get this sword of light, do not make a mistake. It is not oneness! Oneness is also a conception, for it takes up a relationship to the many. When you disagree with many, you must abandon your conception of the one *and* the many. This is the mystery. It is from this abyss that all phenomena spring up. There is no darkness or light. The brightness holds the darkness within it, and the darkness holds the light. There is no life or death, no time or space. When you annihilate all thoughts and words from you mind, you will reach the pitch darkness of this latent consciousness. There is no name for it. When you realize this darkness, it is not dark, it is bright. You must take the sword from its scabbard and cut the dust away. Then you will see the original sword. You feel the darkness when the mind is covered by the ignorance of the past—the dust of the five senses—because you are not yet familiar with the True Law.

Well, after understanding the dark, ignorant side, we come to the real point, the sword of wisdom. In this sword of wisdom, you will realize the absolute, and so understand the relative.

"*Therefore, the ancients said, 'The everyday mind is the true Way.'*" The everyday mind of Lin-chi is the True Law, but not the mind of ignorance. If you obtain the sword of absolute wisdom—the negative factor turns into the positive—you will attain wisdom in your practice of meditation and *dhyana*, and your *samadhi* will not be a mere *samadhi*.

When I was young, my woodcarving was very much like the practice of meditation. For three years, I sharpened my tools so the steel and the surface of the wetstone would meet exactly. It was like concentrating into a koan and coming clearly to the point, and then giving the one answer to your teacher. If you learn this kind of concentration, then "everyday mind" is the true law.

What is the everyday mind? This is a koan.

"*You, good brothers, what do you search for? The one listening at this moment to my sermon depends upon nothing. He is the one who is real and vital and lacks nothing. If you*

desire not to differ from the buddhas and patriarchs, you must
observe it as it is. Do not harbor a doubt about it!

"*Your mind which differs not in attitude each moment,*
that I call the living Buddha. If your mind differs in attitude
each moment, that differentiates your performance from your
essential nature. But if your mind does not differ in attitude,
your performance will not differ from your essential nature."

SOKEI-AN SAYS:

This is really fundamental Buddhism. The word "mind" in Western terms is limited in its meaning, but for the Buddhist, mind covers all the mental activities of brain, heart, spirit, soul, nature, and so forth. You can call it universal consciousness or eternal consciousness, Buddha or God. A scientist might call it energy. Plato called it "idea."

In Chinese, mind is referred to as *hsin*. Since there is no equivalent in English, we usually translate *hsin* as "mind." But this mind is really nameless. Any description only limits its true capacity. In India the conscious mind is referred to as *citta*, considered the sun aspect of mental activity. The moon aspect, the subconscious mind, is called *hrdaya*. We can draw no clear line between these aspects of mind, as we can draw no distinction between man and nature. It is in all sentient and insentient beings. It is the power that operates the universe. The term *hsin* covers all the distinctions of this wonderful manifestation. It can be called God, universe, or consciousness.

A Zen master once said not to ask too many questions about the mind because answers will be created for the questions, but the answers will not cover all its aspects. You ask me a question from one angle, and I answer from another, and you do not understand. It is better not to ask but to understand all at once.

You cannot escape the universe. When you think about the universe, do not exclude yourself. If you watch your mind, you will find that it is different at every moment, like the surface of the ocean that is in constant motion. But no matter how agitated the surface becomes, the bottom of the ocean is always calm. So it is with the mind. It may be disturbed on the outside, but the axle of the mind is always calm and motionless. This is the true meaning of the expression "the moon in the bottomless pail." If the pail has a bottom, the water will move, of course. But if you knock the bottom out?

This bottomless mind is necessary. With it we penetrate to reality. It is not limited; it is just our own consciousness. Inspiration comes from this bottomless mind, this mysterious power. Compared with this power, our intuitional mind action is very slow. The finest philosophy and construction of logic comes in a flash by that power. It is wonderful, but not yet the axle of mind.

"*You, good brothers, what do you search for? The one listening at this moment to my sermon depends upon nothing.* He *is the one who is real and vital and lacks nothing.*" Lin-chi is warning us against searching in books, temples, and so forth, and thus forgetting our daily mind. He does not care about the things that are sought, but only the searcher. He depends upon nothing. All law is written within himself. Therefore, *he* is no different from Buddha. You have that factor in yourself, the true sword of wisdom. This is the one lacking in any capability. You have all that is requisite for your daily life.

"*If you desire not to differ from the buddhas and patriarchs, you must observe* it *as it is. Do not harbor a doubt about it!*" You will attain this "it" in the Zen room. There is no word to truly express it, so Lin-chi uses "it," or "that one." This is not a man or a woman, cosmic consciousness or selfhood. We Buddhists draw no line between the nature of man and the nature of the universe. You, however, think your power is in your mind. But when you don't think, something is still working in your brain. It has its own power that is coordinating with your personal mind. There is no distinction between them. "It" is not God, nature, or man. "It" is IT. And you must harbor no doubt about it. It is here! Why not attain it?

"*Your mind which differs not in attitude each moment, that I call the living Buddha.*" If you keep your mind calm, God will enshrine within your heart. However, consciousness is not representative of God. We in Zen say, "Do not keep the shrine in your mind. Nothing enshrines in it." In other words, do not attach to consciousness and do not think that anything will reflect it. Everyone tries to put a name to IT, but the Buddha always kept SILENCE. I will call it "nameless mind." A Zen master said to push out the bottom of the pail.

If your mind differs in attitude each moment, that differentiates your performance from your essential nature." Essential nature is the axle and performance is the mind that we try to operate. True mind action comes by training, like driving a car. This is Lin-chi's essential faith. If you do not try to operate your mind, it will be operated. Then where do we place the emphasis? On that mysterious point where man and nature meet. Yet, if nature does not give you the opportunity, you cannot reach this point.

"*But if your mind does not differ in attitude, your performance will not differ from your essential nature.*" The universal force operates through you, and you act accordingly. How do we cooperate with this universal consciousness? Do you cry? Do you sneeze? If you are in your true home, it is not necessary to ask any questions. There is nothing to ask. But if you have lost your home, you may never recognize your parents even though they pass near you. You may even meet them! You will not find your home by asking questions. In what attitude will you return? When you meet your father, you will know. Try to meet him in your lifetime.

XVIII

Someone asked the Master, "What is the attitude of mind that differs not in each moment?"

The Master said: "As soon as you question me, your mind has already differed, and that differentiates your performance from your essential nature.

"Brothers, do not commit an error. All the dharmas of either this world or of the transcendental world are without self-nature or a pervading-nature. They are but empty names, and the names themselves are also empty. But you adhere to those good-for-nothing names and think they are true. You are committing a big error! Though these names exist, they are only dependent, transient aspects of existence, aspects such as bodhi, nirvana, emancipation, the three bodies, the objective and the subjective, bodhisattvahood and buddhahood. What are you searching for in these transitory phases? All of them, from the three vehicles to the twelve divisions of the teachings, are nothing but waste scraps for cleaning away rubbish! Buddha is nothing but an ephemeral phantom, and the patriarchs, mendicant friars! Were you not born of your mother? If you pursue the Buddha, you will be in the grip of buddha-mara. If you pursue

the patriarchs, you will be bound by the mara of the patriarchs.
If you pursue anything, it will cause you anguish. Better be
peaceful."

SOKEI-AN SAYS:

To us Buddhists, Buddhism is a very simple religion. We believe
in the power that enshrines in our self. We do not worship anything
outside giving it the name of God, Buddha, Allah, or Krishna. The
performing power is here in ourselves. We feel it, know it, and we can
come to realize it. It is not ego. We give it no name, but we worship it.
This is the starting point, the foundation of religion. We need no other
evidence of its existence, for we can demonstrate it in body, mind, and
word. Through this body, we become one with the whole universe, and
through this mind we enter into SILENCE [demonstrates]. We can enter
in one moment after an action and before a new action; or we can pause
one moment after the sound of a word—Ah! Then SILENCE. This is the
starting point, the shrine and altar.

Someone asked the Master, "What is the attitude of mind that differs
not in each moment?" The Master said: "As soon as you question me, your
mind has already differed, and that differentiates your performance from
your essential nature." Lin-chi is speaking of the very axle of the wheel
of Dharma, the central figure of centripetal power. If anyone should ask,
"What is that?" I will answer, "This is IT." Or I will grunt or make some
movement. Lin-chi calls it essential nature.

"Brothers, do not commit an error. All the dharmas of either
this world or of the transcendental world are without self-nature or a
pervading-nature." This world is that of desire, attachment, and thirst.
The transcendental world is that which we are trying to experience
through the device of religion. Lin-chi tells us that throughout the two
worlds—this world and the transcendental world—all entities have no
self-nature. Therefore, nothing goes from here to there or comes from
there to here. There is no space and no time; therefore, no possession.

"They are but empty names, and the names themselves are also empty.
But you adhere to those good-for-nothing names and think they are true.
You are committing a big error!" This world and the transcendental world
are nothing but empty words.

"Though these names exist, they are only dependent, transient aspects
of existence, aspects such as bodhi, nirvana, emancipation, the three bodies,

the objective and the subjective, bodhisattvahood and buddhahood." Nothing exists objectively. All is subjective. This is the conclusion of the Lin-chi Zen school. If you do not believe in this one, and seek outside, you will never return to your home. You must give up the long-established habit of mankind to search outside, as he seeks for food.

When you live subjectively in your own shrine, not in the physical senses but in the innermost shrine of self, this is the phase of the transcendental world attained by meditation. Sometime in your religious life you may have touched it—Ah! But you cannot speak of it or you may lose it. You feel it, this correlation between your consciousness and Buddha. It is by understanding this correlation that one attains enlightenment. Buddha extends his experience into the whole world. He sees the leaf fall in the winter and the flower bloom in the spring.

"What are you searching for in these transitory phases?" Everyone is searching for peace and security and believes that religion is the only path for its attainment. Yet, we find that almost all religions have disturbed human life and brought unhappiness. For example, those who believe in one religion cannot associate with those who follow other faiths. Once a Chinese Buddhist cited this as an illustration:

There was once a man living in a valley under a mountain. He wanted to see how his home looked from the top of the mountain: how far the house was from the river, how far to the nearest village, and how small everything would look from the mountain top. So he climbed to the highest point, looked down, and understood. But, somehow, something went wrong in his head. He stayed on the mountain top, forgot to come down, and as a consequence died of starvation.

This is the point: to attempt to attain the real base of human life you must have a capacity to accommodate to circumstances, to shift into the different stages and altar your conceptions accordingly. Sometimes you must descend into the stages of *kamadhatu*, enter the stages of *rupadhatu* and its different grades, then enter into *arupadhatu*, the purely transcendental state. Having attained to the real position of the human being, you can return to your former life and find true satisfaction and make no errors. But if you stay in *arupadhatu*, existing in pure time and space, how can you live? Some human beings never return to our primary state. They are difficult to associate with. If religion is not good for human life, why enter into it? We cannot live as animals, nor as *devas*, so we have to come back to this life. We do not give it a name, but *this* is the Truth and it is all we can attain: *THIS is THAT.* From this universal standpoint, we know the whole universe. From the universal law, we observe the outside and we realize the inside. Here is the mirror that reflects all the specks of dust in detail. We see. We feel.

All the *lokas,* or higher stages of *rupa* or *arupa,* are not outside, not in interstellar space or any vacuum, but are all *here* [indicates himself]. *This One* observes all three worlds and in all their stages. It is this through which *This Master* comes and goes. Though you pass through the three worlds, if you forget *This Master,* what can you do? You must put the importance not in a place but in *This Master. He* reflects everything in the universe. *He* is the nucleus. It is through *Him* that you know every element.

Through a microscope, you will see an electron. But this universe, this self, is seen only by looking within. It tells us the design and the law of cause and result. This is natural. This is the place where we live. Why make our place so hard? All the stages, the transitory phases, the different aspects are like waves on the ocean. As Lin-chi says:

"All of them, from the three vehicles to the twelve divisions of the teachings, are nothing but waste scraps for cleaning away rubbish!" Clean that rubbish from your brain! They are all traps to catch the mind. When caught, it no longer needs them. When you trap the Master, you need no more traps.

"Buddha is nothing but an ephemeral phantom, and the patriarchs, mendicant friars!" The Buddha lived for eighty years, died, and was cremated. He was a passing phantom! We are not seeking for such a Buddha. We try to face the Buddha that exists eternally.

"Were you not born of your mother?" This is very powerful. This is the self. If you do not understand this, you will not be certain of anything. Who is first? Who is this mother? One of your first koans will be, "Before father and mother, what were you?" Before creation, before all relative existence, before space and time, what was your original face?

"If you pursue the Buddha, you will be in the grip of buddha-mara. If you pursue the patriarchs, you will be bound by the mara of the patriarchs. If you pursue anything, it will cause you anguish. Better be peaceful." If you try to find truth on the outside, you have already fallen into an evil spell. All intention to seek truth outside yourself is evil. You have the foundation in yourself. Any foundation outside yourself is an erroneous conception.

Everyone asks "What is truth?" Lin-chi gives us his answer. The truth is self. But then you might say, "This eye is not truth. This body is not truth. This mind is not truth. Where is the truth?" Well, in yourself.

The eye of which you speak is the physical eye, the ear is the physical ear, the mind is the one that flickers in your brain. They are all the objects observed by yourself. But who are you? You are a synonym of truth.

After the Buddha's death, Ananda asked a question of Mahakashyapa: "The Buddha transmitted to you something beside his robe and bowl, what was it?" Mahakashyapa called, "Ananda!" Ananda answered, "Yes?" A Zen Master will ask you this question: "When Ananda answered "Yes," who gave the answer?" And you will answer, "The non-ego of Ananda, or the ego that incarnates and transmigrates throughout the universe," and so on. But the master will not accept these answers. You must really know *who* answers.

This understanding came to Ananda later, when Mahakashyapa called his name three times. Then Mahakashyapa said, "Pull up the awning!" And in that moment, Ananda said, "Ah!"

If you grasp that one, you will understand. The truth is so clear!

"There are certain baldheads who say to students that Buddha is ultimate wisdom, that they must undergo three asamkhya kalpas of practice to achieve consummate enlightenment. Brothers, if you say Buddha is ultimate wisdom, why did the Buddha at eighty years of age lie on his side between two sala trees near Kushinagara and die? Where is Buddha now? Clearly we know that he differed in no way from our mortal life.

"If you say the thirty-two auspicious marks and the eighty secondary marks make a buddha, then you should say Cakravartin is also a tathagata. We now know they are phantoms. As the ancients said, 'The holy marks upon the body of Tathagata are distinguished so that they may conform with common conceptions. For fear people might conceive nihilistic views, the Buddha hypothesized these empty names'. We only speak of the thirty-two holy marks as an expediency. The eighty

*secondary marks are also empty names. This mortal body is not
the body of knowing; no appearance is true appearance."*

*"You say a buddha has six supernatural powers, that it is
a mystery. All devas, immortals, as well as ashuras and great
pretas, also have supernatural powers. Are they buddhas?"*

SOKEI-AN SAYS:

*"There are certain baldheads who say to students that Buddha is
ultimate wisdom, that they must undergo three asamkhya kalpas of practice
to achieve consummate enlightenment."* Asamkhya kalpas is limitless time.
The bodhisattva may say it will take many reincarnations to become
enlightened, but the Zen master speaks entirely differently: "It is at this
moment that you attain buddhahood!" This is the highest wisdom. Not
knowledge, but universal wisdom.

It is not so hard to emancipate the mind through knowledge, but
to be emancipated from everyday anguish, that is a really difficult
study, and it may take a lifetime. But in Zen, wisdom comes first and its
understanding in your mind. You have the candle, but you must kindle
the flame. Your candle of wisdom must be lighted.

Te-shan studied the *Diamond Sutra* and made a commentary on
it in eigthy volumes. He made a wooden box to contain it, and, cane in
hand, bore it on his back and traveled throughout China. He wore straw
sandals, a hat like a big umbrella, and proudly won all arguments on the
subject of the *Diamond Sutra*. This is how he entered Southern China.
One day he met an old woman selling luncheon boxes on the road. When
he requested from her some refreshment, she replied that she would give
him some refreshment if he could answer her question. If not, he had to
go away empty-handed. Then she asked: "In the *Diamond Sutra* it is said
that the past, present and future mind is impossible to grasp. What mind
do you wish to refresh?"

Te-shan at this hesitated and repeated the question to himself.
"To what mind should I point?" He pondered the question and was
dumbfounded. Then the old woman drove him out, and Te-shan realized
there was something in Zen with which he was not familiar. Later, he
became a great Zen master famous for the use of his stick. When a
student asked him, "What is Buddha?"—Bang! "If you speak, I will strike
you; and if you are silent, I will strike you!" What to do? How can you
escape from his rod? His koans were hard to answer.

The Zen school believes we can attain buddhahood immediately, that it is not necessary to wait three *kalpas*.

"*Brothers, if you say Buddha is ultimate wisdom, why did the Buddha at eighty years of age lie on his side between two Sala trees near Kushinagara and die? Where is Buddha now? Clearly we know that he differed in no way from our mortal life.*" Buddha as a human being lived in India two thousand five hundred years ago and died between two Sala trees. Where is he now? That is Lin-chi's question.

His expression is very clear. Who is *this*? I am Sokei-an, but I do not care about the name. This temporal aggregation of physical and mental organization is not the one called God or Buddha. "Sokei-an" is not the living spirit, the important one. Where is that one?

The brain is like a radio receiver, but you think this activity takes place separately someplace in your mind. If I say to you that all memory is held in the brain, you will say, "In such a small space?" If I tell you that *this* is immense space, you will look at the sky and say, "In here?" Observing philosophically, there is no space and no time. It is a mystery.

Observing with *this eye*, all is immense space. And when we turn our view upon time, where one million years is a moment, we know everything depends upon our viewpoint. Reality is wonderful, but phenomena are also wonderful!

This body is like a microcosmic eye—one copy of the universal body. If we observe our physiognomic signs, we can read all the signs of nature. If you understand this question, you will certainly free yourself from the egoistic, separate view about your own soul.

"*If you say the thirty-two auspicious marks and the eighty secondary marks make a buddha . . .*" Some of the sacred signs or marks of a buddha are that the soles of his feet are flat and smooth. His toes and fingers are very long. His hands reach below his knees. His tongue is long enough to cover the forehead. His eyelashes are as long as an ox's. And the shape of his head cannot be seen because it is always radiating mysterious rays. However, to be born with thirty-three holy marks was absolute perfection, and the Buddha, of course, had thirty-three, but the thirty-third was invisible, so Indians say he had thirty-two. In India the numbers "four" and "eight" are holy numbers: four truths, eight paths; four times eight is thirty-two, and so on.

"*Then you should say Cakravartin is also a tathagata.*" In Indian mythology, Cakravartin was a wheel-turning monarch. He occasionally appeared to rule the earth. He had the marks of Buddha, and yet was not a buddha—that is, a *tathagata*. *Tathagata*, the absolute one, means THAT or ISNESS. He came from nowhere and he goes nowhere; as reality it does not come or go. This is the *dharmakaya* view.

Do not call it by any name, whether matter, spirit, or whatever. Here it is! If you philosophize you will lose it. You must grasp it! This is the *sambhogakaya* view, and is the place of real understanding. From here, we see the *tathagata* who came as Shakyamuni Buddha and enlightened himself and attained the highest wisdom.

Then we view *tathagata* from the angle of *nirmanakaya*, the body of transformation. But you must throw away the idea of a separate soul. When the first star was created, according to the Buddhist conception, the entire power of the universe met in one place. We are also that power of the universe together in one place, and it is creating us. As you play a stringed instrument the sound comes from the one place that you touch, but sound is created by the whole string. So this self is the center of the universe; its power cannot be explained by this body. It is just the instrument to manifest that aggregation of universal power.

"*We now know they are phantoms. As the ancients said, 'The holy marks upon the body of Tathagata are distinguished so that they may conform with common conceptions. For fear people might conceive nihilistic views, the Buddha hypothesized these empty names.*'" You must not attach to any view; all is empty; all is wholeness.

"*We only speak of the thirty-two holy marks as an expediency. The eighty secondary marks are also empty names. This mortal body is not the body of knowing; no appearance is true appearance.*'" The Buddha asked, "Do you think you can see the *Tathagata* by his thirty-two and eighty signs? No, *Tathagata*, the thirty-two and eighty marks is not *Tathagata*." All marks and all consciousness are not the Buddha. Throughout them all, we cannot find Him. They are only signs. Then how do we meet *Tathagata*? If you say you cannot, you will fall into absolute non-existence. Then what about *this* consciousness? And where am I? How to meet *Tathagata* is one of the first koans.

"*You say a buddha has six supernatural powers, that it is a mystery. All devas, immortals, as well as ashuras and great pretas, also have supernatural powers. Are they buddhas?*" The three bodies, *dharmakaya*, *sambhogakaya* and *nirmanakaya* are just hypothesis. reality is not a word, but we call it emptiness—*shunyata*. By understanding emptiness with our wisdom, we reach the other shore, which is nirvana—*prajnaparamita*.

The scientist says everything consists of protons and electrons, but we say Buddha, and all sentient beings potentially exist in it. This is the person, a microcosm. When we meditate, we feel this mystery within us, so we join our hands and realize that religion is here.

"Brothers, commit no error. When Asura battled with Indra and Asura's army suffered defeat, Asura led his eighty-four thousand subordinates into the pipe of a lotus fiber. Are they buddhas? Everything I have mentioned here is but the power that resides in them from karma or from transfiguration. The six supernatural powers of a buddha are utterly unlike that. In the world of color, you are not deluded by color. In the world of sound, you are not deluded by sound. In the world of odor, you are not deluded by odor. In the world of taste, you are not deluded by taste. In the world of touch, you are not deluded by touch. And in the world of mind, you are not deluded by mind. Therefore, if you attain this, the six powers (color, sound, odor, taste, touch, and mind) are all empty appearances, and you are the one who depends upon nothing and whom nothing can entice. Though you still ooze the five skandhas, you have the mysterious power of walking on earth."

SOKEI-AN SAYS:

The lecture tonight is about the six supernatural faculties, the six mysterious powers of the Buddha. Many students of Buddhism try to attain them by meditation, not knowing the real meaning of these powers.

"Brothers, commit no error. When Asura battled with Indra and Asura's army suffered defeat, Asura led his eighty-four thousand subordinates into the pipe of a lotus fiber. Are they buddhas? Everything I have mentioned here is but the power that resides in them from karma or from transfiguration. The six supernatural powers of a buddha are utterly unlike that." They exist subjectively, not objectively. They are natural faculties. But one who clings to objective existence does not understand

these subjective faculties and so believes them to be supernatural. To the Buddha, they were as natural as a sneeze.

I remember a day when I was in Seattle, Washington and a friend of mine bought a new sailboat. We were out on a lake, and it was my friend's first experience in manipulating a sailboat and it is huge canvas sails. Finally, after the boat capsized, he said, "When I was in Japan, I had no trouble with my small boat. It's wonderful how Americans manage these huge boats. It's really mysterious!"

When you are in your concentration, you must first try to hear all that mental chatter whispering in your brain. When you have attained this, the world will vanish and the universe will become just one huge ear. This is the entrance to meditation. Should this be a mystery? From the ordinary viewpoint, all powers are mysterious, but from the enlightened viewpoint there are no mysterious power in the universe.

"In the world of color, you are not deluded by color. In the world of sound, you are not deluded by sound. In the world of odor, you are not deluded by odor. In the world of taste, you are not deluded by taste. In the world of touch, you are not deluded by touch. And in the world of mind, you are not deluded by mind." The six senses really extend through all existence to the end of the universe. One can hear all sound through past, present and future. This is not mysterious at all. But for the one who stays in his ego and sees another with that power, it is mysterious. One mind can go through all of space and time, become many and return to one, can understand the thoughts of all minds, both boundless and bounded, know both light and dark, and enter all stages of mind: *kama, rupa, arupadhatu*—all worlds. One can immediately feel in which stage each one dwells, what mind-stuff he pursues, and estimate the other's quality of mind. There is nothing mysterious about it. Everyone can do it, but you must know your own position. Are you a man, an animal, a *deva*? You can know your past and future, where you come from and where you are going. When you meditate you can hide yourself while sitting or standing. You can disappear. To some extent all Zen students do such things; there is no mystery about it. But when it is spoken about as it is written in the *sutras*, it seems wonderful.

As I've said, all these powers are subjective. If you can hide yourself in consciousness, you are a Zen student. To the ordinary mind this is a supernatural power. But to grasp *real* emptiness is to open your spiritual eye and to see from the inside rather than the outside. Then you will know that there is no mystery in viewing life and judging values in this way.

So these supernatural powers which are like the Buddha's are quite natural to us. But if you are deluded, in the world of color you may see a beautiful flower and have the desire to pick it and carry it home. In the world of sound, you may be attached to music or the cries of war. In the world of odor, you may be intoxicated by the scent of beautiful women and courtesans. (In China, they call such women "castle shakers". Kings have lost their kingdom for a smile!) In the world of taste, tea—only when the tea master hears a sound that is like "distant thunder" is it time to pour the boiling water. (Here in America, they boil any water, but they certainly make good coffee!) In the world of touch, you are deluded by soft skin and silky hair. And in the world of mind, "I love you. I hate you"—mind-stuff.

"Therefore, if you attain this, the six powers (color, sound, odor, taste, touch, and mind) are all empty appearances, and you are the one who depends upon nothing and whom nothing can entice." Nothing can entice you, and you depend upon nothing.

"Though you still ooze the five skandhas, you have the mysterious power of walking on earth." A young monk was once told by his master that he did not really understand the true law, that his law was an artificial human law of passion, anger and ignorance. The student, wishing to observe the true and natural law went into a forest for three years. Watching the trees, small and large, the sunlight, wind and rain, he observed that each element operates by its own law, but that they all come together, modifying, harmonizing, and making peace. So we humans, who also act according to our own nature, must also conciliate with others. We are all controlled by the same law, the same true law.

"Brothers, true Buddha has no figure, and true Dharma has no form. You are creating something out of ephemeral phantoms. But even if you do obtain something, it will only be the spirit of a wild fox—the idea of a heretic, not a true buddha.

"The true student pays no regard to buddhas or to bodhisattvas and arhats, or to the goodness of the three worlds.

He is beyond all, and adheres to nothing. If heaven and earth should invert, you will have no doubt. If the buddhas of manifold directions should appear, you will not care. And if the three abysses should suddenly come to light, you will have no fear. Why? As I see it, all existence is empty appearance. And the appearance consists in one's inverse view, and without it there is no appearance. The three worlds are only mind-stuff, and all existence is consciousness—phantoms, dreams, flowers in the empty sky. Why exert yourself to grasp them?"

SOKEI-AN SAYS:

Among the great Zen masters of China, Lin-chi and his teacher Huang-po showed us the truth that everyone searches for—the where and what of truth, and how one attains it. These masters showed us truth itself. If we truly understand, we cannot doubt it anymore.

From Lin-chi's standpoint, *you* are the truth. There is nothing else in the whole world. If *you* are not true, your God is not true. If *your* theory is not true, your religion is not true. *You* are the starting point in attaining truth, and you are the conclusion. It is through you and I that *this one* is truth.

Lin-chi is a Buddhist, and he destroys Buddhism! Of course, if Buddha comes again, he will destroy all that Buddhism as well. The master's attitude is the true one. He came into the field of Buddhism and destroyed it completely—and I think the Buddha would agree with him.

When the Zen student begins to look for truth, we do not teach him Buddhism. We destroy Buddhism, until finally he is in agreement with the Buddha. When the Buddha enlightened himself, he destroyed all previous religions, all preconceived notions of religion, and found the truth in himself. That is the right attitude. When we seek truth, we have to destroy all of Buddhism and throw away all our preconceived notions. As followers of the Buddha, we do exactly as he did. This is what Lin-chi did and what all Zen students must do. No one should swallow the medicine of any old doctor. We must find our *own* illusions and our *own* medicine, and we must cure ourselves.

"*Brothers, true Buddha has no figure, and true Dharma has no form.*" The Buddha that we worship has some white hairs between his eyebrows and his hands are so long that they reach to his knees. He has thirty-two marks upon his body, as well as eighty secondary marks. Where is the true Buddha? And he is not in the body of that Prince Shakyamuni from Kapilavastu either, or in a bronze statue. The true Buddha has no form, nor has the true Dharma, the true law.

The Buddhism that we study, however, has form, has the three treasures of Buddha, Dharma, and *Sangha*, the six *paramitas*, the eightfold path, and so forth. But true Buddhism is without form. If you understand that, you yourself are truth, and you will find that all is written in your mind and body, and you will need no formula. To take or not to take is your own choice. But first you must attain to the Truth. You must reach your true body once and see it, and you must reach your true mind once and see it.

"You are creating something out of ephemeral phantoms." If you merely pretend to be something, like a monk who comes to the temple and reads the *sutras*, wears a robe and carries his beads like he knows something, it's just pretense. There is no religion in it.

"But even if you do obtain something, it will only be the spirit of a wild fox—the idea of a heretic, not a true buddha." Like one who lives in a grotto and meditates through his life and never looks at another face. There is no truth in it. Lin-chi is throwing dynamite into Buddhism, and says these are the ideas of heretics and not true Buddhism.

"The true student pays no regard to buddhas or to bodhisattvas and arhats, or to the goodness of the three worlds. He is beyond all and adheres to nothing. If heaven and earth should invert, you will have no doubt. If the buddhas of manifold directions should appear, you will not care. And if the three abysses should suddenly come to light, you will have no fear." This is easy to understand. This is the true ground of religion. When you enter the true world, you will not care about any previous notion, or any teaching that some teacher has established. *This* is the beginning and the end.

"Why? As I see it, all existence is empty appearance. And the appearance consists in one's inverse view, and without it there is no appearance. The three worlds are only mind-stuff, and all existence is consciousness—phantoms, dreams, flowers in the empty sky." All existence is empty appearance, no substance, just a phantom, a dream, an inverse view, and we are living in that dream and do not know about it. If

someone asked you if you knew you were moving at six thousand miles a minute, you would probably say, "No, I don't think so. I'm sitting here."

You cannot measure this dream by your five senses because this dream is not your dream but the dream of the consciousness in which you are living. You are living in the bosom of the mother consciousness, the *alayavijnana*; and you are the child of this mother, so you cannot know it. It is because we do not know our true standpoint and are absorbed in this phenomenal changeable state that we call it an inverted view. We are standing upon this unconscious ground and blindly looking into phenomena that is nothing but instinct, like a dog or cat looking at food. We are standing on this unconscious base, and there is no understanding in it.

A Buddhist stands upon *this* [thumps table], not phenomena, not noumena. We do not call it substance or matter. We look right into the original aspect, then turn and look once again into the phenomenal state. Of course, this is seeing the inverted aspect as well, but it is the enlightened view. If you invert a telescope, look into it, and then invert it and then look into phenomena—"Ah, now I understand!"

All phenomena *is* our own phantom. In reality there is no color, no smell, no pain. So as Lin-chi says: *"Why exert yourself to grasp them?"*

We have to waste our existence before we can understand it.

"But there is one, brothers, in your presence, who is listening to my sermon, whom fire cannot consume and waters cannot drown; who enters the three hells and walks as though within a garden. Among demons and beasts, he is free from disturbance. Why? He is without disdain for any existence. [The ancients said,] 'If you favor the sacred and abhor the secular, you will find yourself in the tumultuous sea of life and death. All afflictions exist because of your mind; if you do not object to bearing them, you will be indifferent to afflictions. Do not endeavor to discriminate, to take up forms and appearances; then, it is natural you will attain the Way at any moment.'"

"If you seek to understand by running around to ask your neighbors, even after countless kalpas, you will end up in the sea of life and death. Better be peaceful. Sit down and cross your legs upon a plank of temple floor."

SOKEI-AN SAYS:

Here Lin-chi is speaking as a Zen master—there is no more philosophy. He is directly pointing to the true thing. *Here* is the one— this fire-consciousness that cannot be extinguished. Hell is just your own notion, your own aspect. If you annihilate this aspect, you will reach consummate enlightenment and have nothing to fear. No such distinctions exist. However, if you hold to them, you will never be emancipated.

"Brothers, when students come from all directions and host and guest have interviewed one another, the student puts forth a query to measure the teacher. The student selects a slippery line of words and throws them in the teacher's face, asking, 'Do you understand or not!' The master, understanding it to be an external feature, seizes it and flings it into an abyss. But the student, nevertheless, fearlessly inquires after the master's teaching. The master then demolishes the student's attitude. But then the student says, 'Superior wisdom! A Great Adept!' Shouting at the student, the master says, 'You can't even tell good from bad!'

"Another instance is a master who chooses a mass of external existence and plays with it in the presence of the student. The student, comprehending it, masters the situation and is not bewitched by the external appearance. The master at that point manifests half the body, and the student thunderously shouts. The master again enters into the way of discriminative words and struggles with the student. The student then says, 'This old baldhead can't discriminate good from bad.' The master then sighs in admiration and says, 'You are a true student!'

"Then there are those blind old teachers who, unable to discriminate right from wrong, whenever a student comes to ask about bodhi, nirvana, the three bodies, or perfect wisdom, start explaining. When he is reviled by a student, such a teacher grabs his staff and hits him, saying, 'You are without civility!' He is the one, however, who has no eye and should not be angry at others.

"Then there is another group of baldheads who, unable to tell good from bad, point to the East and point to the West, delight in clear skies and in rain, delight in lanterns and pillars. Look at how many hairs are left in their eyebrows!

"There is, however, a cause. Not understanding, the minds of these students rave. Such teachers are the spirits of wild foxes and woods and are abused by the good students. Smiling at him pitifully, they say, 'Blind old baldheads bewitching everyone under heaven!'"

SOKEI-AN SAYS:

Today Lin-chi speaks to his disciples about so-called masters and disciples. There were already such masters and disciples about a thousand years ago, and there are such in the world today. The teachers are blind and the disciples just follow. The teachers do not know what the students are talking about, and the students do not know what they are listening to. They are all just wasting time and calling it religion. Such will be the case, of course, sometime in the future, and it will be the end of Buddhism.

Today it is very hard to find a real teacher. Many are just talking about Buddhism and enlightenment from their own imaginations. They have no true foundation. Their judgment depends upon someone else's experience. How dangerous to depend upon someone else! Our daily lives are like flowing water that never flows back. You cannot repeat yesterday's law in today's life. So we must find the real principle and stand upon it and then judge daily life. Nor can human life be judged with the two faces of good and evil, not even in the courts of law. If you do not find the law written in your own heart, then you are the same as Lin-chi's baldheads who cannot discriminate between good and evil.

Once there was a young monk who wandered into a village in China, built a hut, and lived by begging from a rich layman. One day a woman, a young pilgrim, arrived at the hut and they started to live together. The following day, when the novice went to the rich man to beg for food, he was refused. The novice immediately said, "I'm trying to find the law written in my body!" "I know," said the rich man, "I give you alms to find the law written in my mind."

They argued about these two laws for awhile. Finally, they went to consult a Zen master. The Zen master drove them both out with a stick, and the people in the village who heard about the argument said, "If Buddhism is so difficult to understand, we'll have none of it!" This is fiction, of course, but that is why Lin-chi calls the monks baldheads.

It is also said you must read the *sutras* and truly absorb yourself into them, but it is not really necessary to understand them to be emancipated. Many monks are like this. All they do is read, read, read. When Americans ask questions of such monks in Japan, they get no answer. These baldheads can teach you how to worship, bow, light incense, and keep commandments, but they do not know *why* they join their hands, nor *what* they are saying when they bow before the Buddha. I observed these kinds of monks in Japan. Once on a rainy day a monk caught his sandal in a crack and injured his foot, and a young woman ran to help him. "Don't touch my body!" he shouted. And it became a big drama. Of course, he is observing the commandments.

There is another story. Two monks were traveling through the country, visiting famous teachers. One day on a country road a heavy rain had swollen the river so much that is was difficult to cross. A young girl was kneeling on the shore and weeping bitterly. The elder monk said to the younger monk, "Something must have happened. I'll ask her what the trouble is." The younger monk said, "You are a monk. You shall not speak to her."

The elder monk said nothing, but sweeping his sleeves behind him, he questioned the young woman. She said, "I'm the daughter of a farmer who lives on the other side of the river. Today I received a message saying that my mother is dying. I came running, but now the water is so deep I can't wade to the other side! Perhaps my mother will die before I reach her!"

The monk said, "I will help you," and he tucked up his robe and carried the maiden through the water, setting her down on the other shore. "Go, hurry to your mother!" he said.

That night the two monks reached a town and took lodging in a temple. As they were washing their feet before entering, the younger monk said, "You violated your commandment today!" The elder monk said, "I dropped her long ago, but you still carry her in your arms."

Then there are the monks who repeat each other's philosophy—since they have never had one of their own. Their Buddhism is like a map—here is India; here is China, and so on. We can only laugh at them. In Japan we say they are boiling the teapot of ignorance.

A great Zen Master does not talk about keeping the "lantern," that is, light, inside. What is consciousness? What is Buddha? A master would not answer such questions. He would say, "Go away! Open your eye!" Or he would just say, "The star is in heaven and the flower is in the vase. Do you understand?"

Today, every great temple in China or Japan is truly the crystallized sweat of its founder. But many of the monks who inhabit them really know nothing of Buddhism. They live by the gong and the incense stick, and, like trained actors, give a wonderful impression. And people say, "They are sages!"

A true Buddhist acts with complete simplicity. His understanding is so fundamental and deep that there is no need to act. His life is as plain as the man on the street. It is hard to find such a one. You might pass him in a garden, tending his flowers in great reverence and you might not know him. His everyday life is his Buddhism. For him, there is nothing more to talk about. He may have studied Buddhism for twenty, forty years, and in his old age he may look like a farmer, but he is a living tiger to anyone who has the eye to see him—"Ah! *This* is *That!*" You may wish to kneel before him.

"*Not understanding, the minds of these students rave. Such teachers are the spirits of wild foxes and woods and are abused by the good students.*" There are many stories about how wild foxes enchant men's mind, how these men meet with them on some old road as beautiful maidens. They go into trances, bathe, dance, and sleep, and in the morning they awaken in a rice-field where they had been sleeping all night long.

"*Smiling at him pitifully, they say, 'Blind old baldheads bewitching everyone under heaven!'*" Real students will recognize that such a religion as only "dope," just like the Russians say, "the opium of the people." But there is no opium in true Buddhism.

Lin-chi says that the masters and students of his time were like these kinds of baldheads.

"Brothers, renouncers of home must study the Way. I myself in former days fixed my mind upon the vinaya and then directed my attention to the sutras and the shastras. Later, I understood them to be remedies for relieving the world of distress. However, they are only theories put forth to have something to talk about. Thereupon I threw them away at once, went in search of the Way, and came to Zen. Then, meeting a great teacher and having acquired clear insight into the Dharma, I understood all the old teachers under the sun and could discriminate the real from the feigned. I did not have this understanding when I was born to my mother, but I realized it in myself after a long period of training."

SOKEI-AN SAYS:

In the previous lecture Lin-chi described different kinds of teachers and students, and their meetings in which they examine each other. In this lecture, he tells of his own experiences and how he searched for and found his teacher.

Before coming to Zen, Lin-chi studied all sorts of Buddhism, but when he came to Zen, he really understood the true Dharma. He understood what was the matter with himself and what was the matter with all the blind teachers of his day. Finally, he concluded that the ordinary man cannot have this attainment. One must strive to open the eye of Universal Man, of mind and body, and then he can understand the meaning of true religion. This is what Lin-chi is saying to his disciples.

There are monks who have renounced everything to open the Eye of the Universal Body, but there are also many who, though living in seclusion, keep much mind-stuff in the brain, and they are just like laymen. Keeping away from the world is not real renunciation. If it were so, those in jail would be renouncers. One must renounce the world and live. Where? In a mountain cave? In a temple? One must live somewhere! The real recluse needs to learn for a while, so he must seek out a place in which he can make his renouncement. He must learn by study, however, for he cannot buy the law.

"I myself in former days fixed my mind upon the vinaya *and then directed my attention to the* sutras *and the* shastras." The *vinaya, sutras,* and *shastras* are all there is to Buddhism. The *vinaya* is the practice of how to live correctly, the commandments or precepts. They are a ruler for the mind, a common rule of behavior, how to talk to others, observe

etiquette, and so on. If you go to a monastery you will realize that it takes a long time to learn all of this. Everything is timed to the minute, even the bowing of the monks to each other. According to Lin-chi, like all novices, he began his study here. Then after about two years of precepts, he probably took a vow to keep them. Then, according to his vow, he became a monk.

The *sutras* teach us how to meditate and understand the Buddha's life, his disciples and incidents, and all the teachings that came from his golden lips. The *abhidharma* is the commentary on the Buddha's teachings, the philosophical part of Buddhism. All three are call the *tripitaka*.

"Later, I understood them to be remedies for relieving the world of distress. However, they are only theories put forth to have something to talk about. Thereupon I threw them away at once, went in search of the Way, and came to Zen." These remedies are used as a means of counteracting any deficit of mind or body, like remedies for a malady you may have. For example, "You shall not kill." These words are like medicine, but there is no profound meaning in them. As for philosophies, they are just theories to talk about, like the Theosophist talking about his astral and etheric body. Every religion uses this to kill time, to murder time. If you attain it, okay; if you do not, it's good for nothing.

"Then, meeting a great teacher and having acquired clear insight into the Dharma, I understood all the old teachers under the sun and could discriminate the real from the feigned." He is speaking of his teacher, Huang-po. Certainly Lin-chi came to the conclusion of religion with that master.

"I did not have this understanding when I was born to my mother, but I realized it in myself after a long period of training." Self-experience is required to attain enlightenment. Reading books and listening to lectures is not sufficient. You must attain through your own body and mind, and then you will understand. Understand what? The face of the child of the Mother we speak of.

"Brothers, if you want to attain a perfect understanding of Dharma, be not bewitched by others. Whatever you confront,

inwardly or outwardly, kill it as soon as you meet it. If you
meet the Buddha, kill the Buddha! If you meet a Patriarch, kill
the Patriarch! If you meet an arhat, kill the arhat! If you meet
your father and mother, kill your father and mother! If you meet
your kinsfolk, kill your kinsfolk! Killing them, you thus attain
emancipation. Without obstruction, you freely penetrate at will."

SOKEI-AN SAYS:

The Master says that you shall not be bewitched by anybody who is not yourself. In other words, better not listen to anyone about his own enlightenment. This is the conclusion of supreme wisdom. One does not look to the Buddha, Bodhidharma, or a teacher to settle your question. It must be settled in your own mind. You must not imitate anyone in trying to find the true law. Like an artist who does not imitate another, he creates. In such way we can find truth.

"Brothers, if you want to attain a perfect understanding of Dharma, be not bewitched by others. Whatever you confront, inwardly or outwardly, kill it as soon as you meet it." Lin-chi uses a strong word here—"kill." Usually, we say "annihilate," but Lin-chi is using his big hatchet!

Lin-chi, of course, is telling you to kill your thoughts. If you meet the name only, kill it! In such a way you will realize the true law. It is not really necessary to kill mind-stuff but to kill your conceptions, as it is not necessary to make any kind of separation in the ocean.

The Buddha attained the highest truth. When Lin-chi attained to it, he looked at the Buddha and said, "Who are you? You made such and such a commandment, but I have nothing to do with it!"

"If you meet the Buddha, kill the Buddha! If you meet a Patriarch, kill the Patriarch! If you meet an arhat, kill the arhat! If you meet your father and mother, kill your father and mother! If you meet your kinsfolk, kill your kinsfolk! Killing them, you thus attain emancipation. Without obstruction, you freely penetrate at will." This Buddha Shakyamuni made great trouble for Buddhists! He existed two thousand five hundred years ago and founded this religion. How do you kill him?

As art is original, so the Buddhist is original. He leads his own life, not the Buddha's. So how does one live in this living model? The law is written in *this* body and *this* mind! That is Buddhism.

"Of those students who come from all directions, none have come from that which depends upon nothing. Therefore, I hit you in the direction from which you come. If you come forth from the hand, I will hit you on the hand. If you come forth from the mouth, I will hit you on the mouth. If you come forth from the eyes, I will hit you on the eyes. There has not been one who has come from absolute emancipation. All have come from the useless contrivances of the ancients. As for this mountain monk, I have no Dharma to give you. All I can do is cure illness and remove bondage.

"You, brothers, who come from every direction, try coming here without depending upon anything! I would like to deliberate upon this matter with you. In the last five, ten years there has not been one. All have been clinging to leaves and grasses, like the spirits of bamboo and trees. They are wild foxes chewing upon heaps of dung! Blind fools who waste their sacred alms and call themselves recluses! This is their understanding.

"I tell you, there is no Buddha, no Dharma, no practice, and no attainment. What are you searching for all over the neighborhood?

"Blind fools! You are putting another head on the head you already have. Is there anything wanting?"

SOKEI-AN SAYS:

The Buddha's Buddhism takes its own aspect once more through Master Lin-chi, just as it happened in India when the Buddha was living. Lin-chi's Buddhism is not philosophical; it is Zen. But Zen is inclusive of philosophy, which will carry your reason to the gate of Zen. Reason ends there, at the gate. We enter without reasoning. When we handle Zen, we do not analyze the reasoning; we cast it away and handle the essence. To come to New York you need direction. When you get here, at first you must walk the ground of the city—but your *life* is Zen.

It seems to me, this speech must have been given to the disciples at the time of the rainy season, the three months in the summer when all the monks come together from all directions and then, in the autumn, scatter. It's the same today. All come back to their own temple and their own master, and in the autumn, they return to their own business.

Lin-chi is speaking to new students, from various parts of China, but none are coming from "nothing." None of them are taking an independent attitude. All are dependent upon some word, some reason, some philosophy. So when Lin-chi says, you must "depend upon nothing," he means your mind must stand independently and not depend upon reason or theory. But just as a slender willow must be supported, so your mind leans upon Buddhism or Christianity. Lin-chi abominated this, however.

According to the Master, your mind and body must stand upon its own feet. Why lean upon names like "*dharmakaya*," "*sambhogakaya*," "*nirmanakaya*," and so forth? If you have not found this "nothing," you have not yet found your own mind and body, and it is a parasite upon something else. It is a disembodied spirit desiring to do mischief, waiting in the wood to enter any passerby's mind, or like a gold digger of Broadway who makes someone buy her a fur coat. When you depend upon something, you are ruled by it. It is so with those who depend upon Buddhism. So when Lin-chi says he will "hit" you, he means take your burden from you. He is offering to remove your bondage and give you emancipation. Everyone is bound like a man who walks through the woods with a spider's web wrapped about him.

Sometimes Lin-chi speaks of himself as a "mountain monk." Who is this, and in what place? When the Buddha showed his disciples a lotus flower, he did not speak a word. Te-shan answered questions with a stick. When a student asks Lin-chi a question, he hits them as well. In other words, *where did the disciple's question come from?* "What is Buddhism?" "What do *you* think?" and so forth. If the student shouts, Lin-chi hits him. No need spending time. Wipe all talk out of his mind.

Lin-chi is kicking all props out from under his students. He is saying that if Buddha comes again, he will not acknowledge him. If you conceive of a law, you cannot act according to nature. If you reason, it will not be thinking for yourself, but from some source. You can never judge at the moment yourself. If someone lives in New York, he will tell a visitor there is nothing to see, that it's a monotonous city. But the visitor from another country finds plenty to see. As we say, "A fish always living in the water never knows the taste of water."

This is how Lin-chi was living in Buddhism. His heart *was* Buddhism, his word *was* Buddhism, so he never speaks Buddhism! This is a true and natural attitude.

Someone once asked a Zen master, "What is the most priceless thing in the world?" The master said, "The head of a dead cat is the most priceless thing, for no one can name its price." We need the real thing. We do not need information. The real thing is not philosophy. In Zen, we do not handle philosophy from beginning to end. All philosophy is but a ferryboat, and that is all. You must meditate with *this* consciousness, and open the unconscious consciousness to a clear state of understanding. If you say, "I saw reality." Lin-chi would say it's a lie, and he would hit you upon that eye!

There is another story about Chao-chou when he was a young monk. Once in a temple there was a cat that was being fed by the monks in the east wing of the temple and by those in the west wing of the temple. One day, all the monks met and began to argue as to which group owned the cat. At that moment, the Zen master, Nan-ch'uan, entered. He clutched the cat's neck in his left hand, and, holding a dagger in his right, said, "Tell me which wing this cat belong to. If no one answers, I will cut off its head! Tell me! If anyone can say the word, I will spare its life. Speak!"

No one could answer, so Nan-ch'uan killed the cat.

Later Nan-ch'uan met Chao-chou, who was a young student at the time, and asked him, "If you had been present, what word would you have said?" Chao-chou put a sandal on his head and, meowing like a cat, left the room. Nan-ch'uan called after him, "Ah, if you had been there you would have saved the cat!"

Do you understand?

Lin-chi takes no attitude, Buddhist or otherwise. It is like the Buddha's Buddhism. But now he can find no student who depends upon nothing. Certainly Lin-chi was looking for someone to whom he could transmit his Dharma.

A Zen master is always looking for someone already created in his understanding—"Ah, here is a true man!" They meet eye to eye and heart to heart. That is the idea of transmission from the Buddha's time to today. All the patriarchs were prepared to receive the Dharma, like the Sixth Patriarch to whom it was transmitted in one night.

Lin-chi says, "*I tell you, there is no Buddha, no Dharma, no practice, and no attainment. What are you searching for all over the neighborhood? Blind fools! You are putting another head on the head you already have. Is there anything wanting?*" Everyone is searching for something with which to pad their minds, but this is quite different from searching for mind-itself. How can you search for the mind by the mind? The one searching for mind *is* mind. It is not necessary to search for another head. Your head is already there. Buddhism is not the search for padding. Buddhism tells you *This self* is *That*. You must find mind-itself—your foundation. And then you will return to your original state, the gate of Buddhism. If you do not enter, you will fall into a ditch! This is Zen!

"Brothers, your present activity is not different from that of the Buddha and patriarchs. As you do not believe it, you seek for it in the external world. Do not commit an error. No dharma exists externally. The internal is also unobtainable. Better be peaceful and take a rest than to take the words from my mouth. That which has already risen, do not continue; and that which has not yet arisen, set free. This is better than a ten years' pilgrimage.

"In my view, there are no problems. Live a plain, ordinary life. Put on your clothes and eat your food. Spend your time in peace. All of you who come here from every direction are holding something in your mind, so you search for Buddha, search for Dharma, search for emancipation, search for deliverance from the three worlds. Idiots! After having delivered yourself from the three worlds, where will you go? 'Buddha' and 'patriarch' are mere names of adoration. Do you wish to know the three worlds? They do not differ from the base of your present mind listening to my sermon! The thirst that occupies your mind is the world of desire. The anger that flashes across your mind is the world of form. And the ignorance that deprives you of your mind is the formless world.

They are the paraphernalia of your house. The three worlds do not call themselves 'the three worlds.' But you, brothers, obviously throwing light upon everything and forming an estimate of the world, create the names of the three worlds."

SOKEI-AN SAYS:

In the last lecture Lin-chi made some negative statements to which many people will react mistakenly: If there is nothing in the universe—no elements, and so on—then the whole universe will be annihilated, and there is no evil or virtue. Then what is *this*? If there is nothing, there is no manifestation, so there must be something.

Why does Lin-chi speak like this? He means that there is no such thing as Buddhism, Christianity, or Taoism. Before the conception of anything like these religions, there is only Truth—no Buddha, no Dharma. All of this life is Truth. Why put more onto it? Of course, it took him many years to realize this stage.

A famous fencer in Japan studied fencing all his life, and at the age of seventy he realized everything was the sword. The chopstick was the sword. The pan cover was the sword. Everything was the sword. So no sword existed for him anymore. He thought all of life is a sword!

Lin-chi's understanding is something like that, and if you understand it, you will see his dreadful face confronting you. But you must have the Eye to see him. This is true Buddhism.

"*Brothers, your present activity is not different from that of the Buddha and patriarchs. As you do not believe it, you seek for it in the external world. Do not commit an error. No dharma exists externally. The internal is also unobtainable.*" In the external world there is nothing but the green mountains and the skyscrapers of New York. But they are all shadows of your own mind—*all* is consciousness. The *alaya*-consciousness meets the outside and creates its own *vedana*, feelings and perceptions. Then do we search inside? The inside is also unpredictable and "unobtainable."

Lin-chi is bringing together *this* actuality—phenomena—and reality—noumena. Both are the same.

A young monk once asked Nan-ch'uan a question: "What is it that the Buddhas of the three worlds do not know but the badgers and foxes know?" Nan-ch'uan said, "Before the Deer Garden time, it was clear." This means before the Buddha's enlightenment, before father and mother, it was clear. This was Nan-ch'uan's answer to the question. Do you understand?

Then the monk asked, "Why do the badgers and the foxes know?" Nan-ch'uan said, "How can you doubt it?"

Very interesting koan! If you understand it, you will know this "it"— the ability of the cat and the dog. The Buddha and myself are not different from all the Buddhas. You will understand if you do not put too much padding on your mind. Just get to the pure water of mind, and pay no attention to the debris floating in the water. To grasp this is Zen.

"*Better be peaceful and take a rest than to take the words from my mouth.*" Never mind hypothesis and theory. Just get into *yourself*. Externally—green mountains! Internally—*vedana*!

"*That which has already risen do not continue; and that which has not yet arisen, set free. This is better than a ten years' pilgrimage.*" This "that" is a very simple one. It is not that which we try to express in silence, but that which you can observe in your mind—mind-stuff. You shall all know the real gate to Zen if you understand that mind and mind-stuff are two different things, and then it is not so difficult to enter.

In observing visible phenomena, you are aware of the object and the sense organs. You would say matter and consciousness are a spiritual entity. But I would say that that is the real gate of *mis*understanding. Somehow you must divide it into the subjective and the objective. You think *that* is phenomena and it exists *there*, and that *this* is spiritual and it exists *here*. But mind-stuff is semi-material, not entirely spiritual. The dreams, phantoms, and thoughts that come and go with names have their own place, but no geometrical form. They are not square, triangular, or three-dimensional. And they have no weight. But your dream is not purely spiritual either, it is mind-stuff or *klesha*, defilement, or "filth" as Buddhists say. I think your mind is really living in it just as your body is in this house.

New York is a three-dimensional form, but in your mind you call it four-dimensional. To me, these are just words, for it takes a million directions at once. China, New York, France are all in one place. You feel it but cannot grasp it. This world is entirely different from the world you can see and touch, and it takes a finer sense organ to perceive it. The sense world is just for animals. This world is really the home of Being that consists of mind and mind-stuff. It is like wood and fire. Without mind-stuff we cannot prove mind. You must grasp that mind-itself and not the stuff! This is the entrance to Zen.

The mind of which I am speaking is eternal and not destroyed by death. The mind-stuff "that has already arisen," let it go, so you can see the clear blue sky of mind. The deep part of your mind does not belong to you, but to great nature.

When Lin-chi speaks of "that which has already arisen and that which has not arisen," he is covering the whole teaching.

"*In my view, there are no problems. Live a plain, ordinary life. Put on your clothes and eat your food. Spend your time in peace.*" Calamity comes, but the mind is at peace. All states still exist, but they will be transparent to you in the real mind. There is actuality and reality, but there is peace. But today, our lives are not plain, they are very complicated, and we do not find any peace in our mind. So how can we attain this meditative attitude?

"All of you who come here from every direction are holding something in your mind, so you search for Buddha, search for Dharma, search for emancipation, search for deliverance from the three worlds. Idiots! After having delivered yourself from the three worlds, where will you go?" The three worlds are the universe, of course. By jumping out of the universe, where can you go? There is the kama, rupa, and arupadhatu. We cannot conceive of anything outside of them. How can you? So, in this stage, you must find the real stage.

It is usually some ism—the seed of the entire conflagration—that distorts the real mind. "This is the world of desire and ignorance. I must be delivered from them!" This is the usual attitude of religious students as they attempt to ascend and go beyond.

Everyone tries to understand this washing away of mind-stuff, so they say they must stop it. But this, too, is mind-stuff! How can you stop it? You are swimming in it, and you can understand it. I drop my fishing pole into the waves, and I do not care how the waves act toward it. The waves take it to and fro, but the pole is always there. You see the eternal side and the ephemeral side at once. As the *Prajnaparamita Sutra* says, phenomena *is* reality.

"'Buddha' and 'Patriarch' are mere names of adoration. Do you wish to know the three worlds? They do not differ from the base of your present mind listening to my sermon!" Yes, the mind without stuff is the transcendental world, and it is very near. Enter into it, and it is eternal. If your mind is pure, honest and zealous to enter in, you will do so; but if doubt enters, it will be a yoke.

The mind that Lin-chi talks about is a little deeper than the pure mind without mind-stuff. This mind stage belongs to yourself, but you have not yet reached the deeper layer that belongs to Great nature. And he says it is not necessary to find it by meditation. Eating and sleeping, you can be there.

"The thirst that occupies your mind is the world of desire. The anger that flashes across your mind is the world of form. And the ignorance that deprives you of your mind is the formless world. They are the paraphernalia *of your house."* He is talking about the three poisons, and he is relating them to the three worlds. It was a fundamental idea of the Buddha that our mind will enter these stages or worlds and find that it is with out ego. If you do not use them correctly, you will die. But if you use them correctly, you will live.

Desire is to keep your physical form. It is an unconscious desire, and it drives you throughout your life. Anger is trying to win against another, be superior, strong, or famous. All of them are "driving" elements. And ignorance is an unconscious, driving force as well. You eat, study and work to cure this ignorance, to bring yourself from the unconscious to the conscious stage. So he connects them to three worlds.

In *kamadhatu*, the world of desire, you live with intention, in the human state. In *rupadhatu*, the world of form, you perceive beauty without desire. *Arupadhatu*, the formless stage, is the world of an uncovered mind, nothing but sky—the mind itself. All cover is gone—no seeing, no tasting, no feeling, no consciousness. Consciousness is proved by objective existence—no objective existence; no subjective existence, they prove one another; neither mind nor no mind—terrible philosophy! But our minds are always covered by color and form—that which we see. And so it is with ear, nose, and tongue. They are always covered. But when you have awakened to the "coverless" stage of Mind-itself, you have attained buddhahood.

Lin-chi does not regard these stages as really important. He is giving his own attitude. They are all like the implements of your home.

"The three worlds do not call themselves 'the three worlds.' But you, brothers, obviously throwing light upon everything and forming an estimate of the world, create the names of the three worlds." You create the names, and you throw the light on everything. Then, what is really in these names? Well, *you*—here, there, everywhere.

Lin-chi's style of Zen is like a thunderbolt—swift and clear. Zen is the conclusion of Buddhism. To demonstrate Zen, you do not need a word, and to speak about Zen is impossible. But there are Zen "records," which, of course, are not Zen itself. It is through them, however, that you can be informed about it.

"Good brothers, the visible body which consists of the four great elements is transient. The spleen, stomach, liver and gallbladder, the hair, nails and teeth prove that all visible existence is empty phenomena. The place where your mind ceases from acting is called a bodhi tree; the place where your mind does not cease from acting is called a tree of ignorance. Ignorance occupies no place and has neither beginning nor end. If your mind cannot cease from acting, it will go up the tree of ignorance and enter into the six realms of existence and the four modes of birth, put fur on your body and horns on your head. If, however, your mind ceases from acting, that is the pure body. Not harboring a thought in mind, you are up the bodhi tree— you transfigure yourself and unfold the three worlds, incarnating your body as you please. There is joy; there is delight; effulgence abides within you. When you want a garment, there will be a thousand folds of brocade; when you want food, you will be provided with hundreds of delicacies; and there will be no illness of any kind. Bodhi has no place to abide. Therefore, nothing can be attained.

"Brothers, if you are a true man, what is there to doubt? Who is the one whom you are using in your present activity? Seize and use, but do not name. This is the fundamental of Zen. If you observe this, there is nothing that is abominable. The ancients said, 'The mind turns according to circumstances, and this turning is mysterious. When you recognize your nature in its course, there is neither anguish nor joy.'"

SOKEI-AN SAYS:

Lin-chi says that a man who lives for his physical body alone is merely trying to gather empty phenomena. This is the usual view of Buddhism. I think it is not necessary to speak at this point about the transience of the body. To the eye of the Buddhist, *this* phenomena is one body. I am aware of my existence with my consciousness, and the phenomena on the outside is produced by this consciousness, so all is the production of this one consciousness.

In a Buddhist story the God Brahma made sentient beings within one consciousness so that he could communicate with all of them without speaking. I think you know about telepathy. God was very proud of his creation. Then, one day, Yama (the first man) grew ill and, therefore, all grew ill. Yama died and all died. So God thought that this was not a good way after all—he would have to separate this consciousness. He recreated man so that each one could express itself. His first experiment was with a plant: all the stems grew up from the root. But when one stem died, all died, and then the root itself died. So he made one trunk which separated into two boughs with many branches. Each branch had a separate degree of consciousness, but all were controlled by one conscious power—became one system. So all those bodies that constitute this consciousness are arranged in the universe and all are within one consciousness, and their bodies consist of the four great elements. Today, we count many elements, but in ancient days there were six. The first two are *akasha* and *vijnana*—ether and consciousness. The Buddha put consciousness into the material side, for if there is no material you cannot prove consciousness. So consciousness comes between matter and spirit, but the Buddhist puts it on the side of matter.

This transience is an important element in Buddhism. If all is transient, upon what we can depend? "All manifestation is transient," said the Buddha. Like steam from a kettle, these words could be gone forever, but Lin-chi brings them into detail. Man works all his life long, and after—death, the tombstone! That is his production, really. If he works for himself, what does he get in the afterlife?—the tombstone. One will say not to work for self but for children; and after the children have gone, what is left?—a pile of bones, a memento of all human effort.

Lin-chi takes this pessimistic view—that if we work for the physical body, the outcome is nothing! The clouds, waves, the dream exist, manifest for a certain time, and vanish. You cannot stamp anything upon the physical body. This is not *the* reality. Someone will say, "Well, we do something for the mind and body. That is the real body in which the human being lives." So we eat mind food: read, hear, think. And we chew the cud of mind-stuff. This is what we feed to children called education. So will they live forever? "I teach morality to my children. My words will live in their minds." This may be true, but from the Buddhist standpoint, you are only creating the cause of karma. All karma exists in this mind and body. It is but waves in this ocean of Mind and cannot exist without consciousness. The waves of the ocean have nothing to do with the water; we cannot stand upon them. It is not a real base on which we can build our lives. It is the changeable aspect of substance, not substance itself. The rainbow has colors, but they are not the rainbow. The real substance of the rainbow is not in this color that our mind produces. This transient karma is not reality. It is very dangerous to build your life on this transience. As time passes and circumstances change, the colors fade away, and then you must change your standpoint.

"The place where your mind ceases from acting is called a bodhi tree." Under the Bodhi Tree, the Buddha became enlightened. The moon and the morning star sparked in his mind, which included heaven and earth. At such a moment—"Ah, *this* is *that!*" This will not come to the sleeping mind; there must be no concept of any kind. If you keep eternity, God, Buddha, or Zen as a cover for your mind, you will never realize what you are. After three or four months of meditation, such conceptions should drop off like dry leaves. Perhaps one word, "this," will remain; then "this" will drop off as well. Then one day—*"This is that!"*

All sentient beings possess this buddha-nature, so the Bodhi Tree is a symbol of enlightenment for us. The Buddha said, "If one attains buddhahood, all nature shines." You must realize this omnipresent body. This is the Bodhi Tree and the entrance to all religion. This is the ceasing mind. Do not fear to become foolish. Try it!

"The place where your mind does not cease from acting is called a tree of ignorance. Ignorance occupies no place and has neither beginning nor end." Action, movement goes with the mind that is transitory. You may change your faith many times, you may cover your face in meditation to hide the dirty world, but how can you cover against conception?

The Bodhi Tree is rootless and opens its petals against the moon. It is the inmost man who has no root, and spreads to the end of the universe. But this *avidya* tree has a root—in the darkness, and we are living upon this root. It is called ignorance. You can prove it from your own experience. You came from your mother's womb, and you experienced the embryo stage. You did not know time or space, sweet or bitter, your mother or yourself; you do not remember, but you were there existing. You cannot say you were not you; you were not aware of your own existence. Then somehow you start to move. Realization comes of duration in time and space—motion. These are the first realizations of infancy. This is the elemental stage. We call it *samskara*, our impulses. Then *vijnana*, consciousness, making contact. In Buddhism, this unconscious existence is called *avidya*. The Buddha gave us the theory of the twelve chains of causation, but the origin of causation is *avidya*. From the darkness of *avidya*, you never find your own home. How many times do you pass the gate of your own house, but never enter because no one calls you from inside? How will you find your foundation of life? This human life has many stages of consciousness opening one by one. Then, perhaps, in the end—that star, and we see reality!

"*If your mind cannot cease from acting, it will go up the tree of ignorance and enter into the six realms of existence and the four modes of birth, put fur on your body and horns on your head.*" The six realms are the six evil ways. The four "modes of birth" means man may become a *deva* in mind and body, but he still has to go through these stages—fur and horns—because he has never returned to the original state of mind

"*If, however, your mind ceases from acting, that is the pure body. Not harboring a thought in mind, you are up the bodhi tree—you transfigure yourself and unfold the three worlds, incarnating your body as you please.*" Let the waves and the debris go, and come to eternal consciousness. That water is you, and that water is Buddha. Here is the foundation of your life.

Lin-chi is speaking here one of the most important theories of Buddhism, empty-mindedness. The mind must be clear, like water in a glass, so that one can concentrate into the object directly; the flower is red, the willow is green—all phenomena is clear to the five senses—yet no stuff in the mind! That we call emptiness, *shunyata*. When you realize this, be very careful; in that moment you may seize reality!

Reasoning will not open the veil to reality. It can only take you to its entrance. You must burst into reality! If your mind is clear—*this* is *that*. Without a conception in the mind, the veil is torn down and reality is disclosed. You are in it, and you will climb to the top of the Bodhi Tree. This is transfiguration, which is being done at every moment. Subjective reality and objective reality are one. And, while keeping the physical body, you transfigure into different mind-bodies. You enter the three worlds of *kama*, *rupa*, and *arupadhatu*, yet you are always in that body which is omnipresent. To incarnate the mind is the same thing.

"*There is joy; there is delight; effulgence abides within you. When you want a garment, there will be a thousand folds of brocade; when you want food you will be provided with hundreds of delicacies; and there will be no illness of any kind.*" Garments—not clothes for the physical body but for the consciousness body. The physical body needs food that is palpable to the five senses (eggs need hen's feathers). In human life, this is connected with our emotions. The mental food is ideas and philosophy, but the consciousness food is religion. Without religion, we cannot realize this consciousness, and without consciousness, we are not living.

If your mind is not clear, you are a slave to the garments on your mind and cannot change at will. But when you understand *shunyata* and nirvana, you enter at will. You must first realize this IT, which eats food and wears garments. IT is always healthy! So, attain IT before you speak of mental cures.

"Bodhi *has no place to abide. Therefore, nothing can be attained.*" A good line! Wisdom abides in a pinpoint and in the whole universe. Therefore, it is a paradox to say that there is no time and no space. A broadcast can cover the whole world, yet it is in no place, and no one can grasp it. The word "eternity" is a trap, it limits the conception, and the name is dangerous—"I am a Christian"; "I am a Buddhist." These are just garments. You are independent, so form no conception of attainment or no-attainment. When you enter into real attainment, you cannot say a word. How to enter is the problem.

Nothingness, emptiness, and so forth., can be looked at in two ways. In the mother's womb there is no space, time, conception, or awareness. In *bodhi*, phenomena is only the vibration of energy: the five senses make contact with the outside and the blue color of the sky appears in our eye. This is not the sky, it is just manifestation upon our body, like a dream, and if we attach to it, we are trapped. To realize this emptiness, you must render all this phenomena into the pure substance, ether, so *avidya* and enlightenment are the same thing. In Japan the persimmon is a crude and astringent fruit. You cannot eat it. But if you dry it, it becomes very sweet. It is the same with *avidya* and enlightenment.

"*Brothers, if you are a true man, what is there to doubt? Who is the one whom you are using in your present activity? Seize and use, but do not name, this is the fundamental of Zen. Thus, if you observe this, there is nothing that is abominable.*" You have it! Why think? Before you think, that thinker is the One. However, this is not like Rodin's "The Thinker"!

Who is this "presence"? Is it man? God? Who? Is it necessary to "seize it"? It is always yours. And is it even necessary to "use it"? It is always moving. This is the fundamental of Zen.

"*The ancients said, 'The mind turns according to circumstances, and this turning is mysterious.*" The mind turns" is a Chinese expression. Mind extends, enters into, expands, as water enters every place there is. The mind will, like water, rush through the eye of a needle. There is every shade of mind-stuff. As the uplifting power in water creates myriad forms of waves, so the expanding mind creates many words and objects. If the Buddha should appear once more, I think he would destroy this old style of Buddhism—but knowing this old type, we understand how to create new life.

Think of all the shades of mind in word "mysterious"—conceptions, feelings, and so on. Certainly we feel the mystery in it.

Here again we must differentiate between mind and mind-stuff.

In the early days of Japan, Daito Kokushi, a Japanese Zen Master of the thirteenth century, went to China and brought Zen to Japan. In China, he went to a mountain temple and saw two inscriptions on either side of the entrance. On one side, "The mind turns according to all circumstances." And on the other, "The whereabouts of its turning is mysterious."

Meeting a novice in the temple, Daito asked a question: Could you tell me upon which side (inscription) the master of this temple lays emphasis?" The novice answered. "He places emphasis on the side which has the word "mysterious."

After Daito returned to Japan, he told this to one of his disciples, who asked, "Do you agree?" "No" said Daito. "Then on which side would you place the emphasis?" "On the side of the turning mind."

Why?

The "mysterious" is the subjective aspect of mind, and the "turning" is the mind activity, the rolling shell. But if you realize what this mind activity is, you will find that they are the same. If you lay the emphasis on the shell, you will discriminate between evil and virtue; and if you lay the emphasis on the activity, there is neither evil nor virtue.

"*When you recognize your nature in its course, there is neither anguish nor joy.*" Many Zen students cherish this line like a ministering deity. Some are emancipated by it. I lived for six years in objective nature. Then I came to the realization of the great current rolling in my heart and mind. Then I understood how to grasp it and use it. When we find harmony between ourselves and nature, that is religion. No other religion exists.

You know, Lin-chi's Zen is like a thunderbolt. It is like a screen made of crystal. No one can put a finger on it, because it is nothing but reality. He does not speak much theory. What he really does is to demonstrate reality-itself, discloses it strikingly without a word. It is like the Buddha's

Buddhism that was handed down by Ananda and Mahakashyapa. Ananda remembered every word spoken by the Buddha, and Mahakashyapa accepted *dhyana*—the unspeakable mind of Buddhism from the Buddha. *Dhyana* is Zen. Bodhidharma transmitted *dhyana* to China and became the First Patriarch of Zen in China. Bodhidharma had two eminent disciples and Zen swept through China from that time.

Lin-chi is one of the most eminent of Masters. There were five schools of Zen: Lin-chi, Ts'ao-tung, Fa-yen, Wei-yang and Yun-men Wen-yen. Today, in Japan, there are but two Rinzai (Lin-chi) and Soto (Ts'ao-tung), which include the other three.

"Brothers! In the Zen school, life and death advance conditionally. The student of Zen must examine this. When host and guest meet each other, they enter into conversation. They may transform themselves into objects, or unveil their wholeness. Sometimes they may struggle in anger or in joy with each other's devices; or they may unveil half of the body, ride on a lion or on an elephant. The true student roars like thunder and holds out a sticky lacquer tray. If the master does not apprehend this as an outward circumstance, he climbs upon it and assumes an attitude. The student roars again, but the master is unwilling to relinquish his position. The student roars again, but the master is unwilling to relinquish his position. The student shows his true substance, but the teacher holds his assumption. Such a teacher claims to be an adept, but a true teacher makes no assumption. This is a disease that has reached the marrow and is incurable. I call this, 'student examines master.'

"Sometimes the master offers nothing, depriving the student of all his questions. The student, having been deprived of questions, clings to them until the end. This I call, 'master examines student.'

"Then there is the student who presents himself before the master in a state of purity. The master, apprehending the circumstance, removes it and casts it into a deep pit. The student says, 'Fine!' The master says, 'Bah! You don't know the difference

between good and evil!' The student then pays homage and bows low. This I call 'master examines master.'

"There is still another type of student who presents himself before the master fettered and handcuffed. The master puts the student in an additional noose. The student enjoys it. They do not know what they are doing. This I call 'student examines student.' Good brothers, I disclose these instances so you will be able to discriminate the evil and false from the real."

SOKEI-AN SAYS:

To speak about Zen is not an easy task. To recognize your own buddha-nature is the object of Zen. It flows from the universal current that is life and death. The student must come to terms with these so-called opposites. Then there is neither joy nor anguish.

"Brothers! In the Zen school, life and death advance conditionally. The student of Zen must examine this." In Zen, at first, you may think you have killed the ego and entered into oneness, when you have not yet thrust forth your foot or your hand. When you enter the first gate, you take the negative attitude. It is like dawn before the sunrise, but you feel your heart palpitate with a universal rhythm. You are still motionless, then you slowly understand how to move out from it, how to dance and sing in it. After you enter the first gate, there are many stages. Bodhidharma said there are three great and nine minor stages.

"When host and guest meet each other, they enter into conversation. They may transform themselves into objects, or unveil their wholeness." Lin-chi is talking about how a master (the host) and student (guest) meet and struggle together. For example:

Master: "What is the *dharmakaya* which cannot be destroyed?"

Student: "The blossom of the mountain blooms like brocade, and the deep pool in the dale is clear as lapis lazuli."

Master: "This shows only half. Show me the whole."

"Sometimes they may struggle in anger or in joy with each other's devices; or they may unveil half of the body, ride on a lion or on an elephant." The lion is *Bodhisattva* Manjushri, and the elephant is *Bodhisattva* Samantabhadra. The lion means intrinsic wisdom and the elephant means complete unity. In Zen this can be manifested!

"The true student roars like thunder . . ." When you study Lin-chi's Zen, you will often come across this expression. When a true student

meets a master who is not true, he gives him a shout. But my teacher said not to give the usual, terrible shout, but only "Humph!" There is a little derision here, and that is enough. There are many impostors in Zen, monks who are not teachers but who assume that position. There were many during the later Tang Dynasty, as well.

"*And holds out a sticky lacquer tray.*" A pitched tray, sticky like flypaper, is a word that traps the mind and its conceptions. If you are trapped, like all systems of philosophy, it is hard to get out. A "pitched tray" is an expression peculiar to Buddhism. The "pitched tray" comes from the use of a Chinese lacquer tray which, when not yet dry, was very sticky and trapped insects. Some later Mahayana and Hindu teachers said that many *sutras* of the *tripitaka* were nothing but traps, pitched trays. If you become trapped in a particular school of Buddhism, you are lost, and will never come out again; like a fly in syrup, you struggle but cannot fly, cannot realize emancipation. Not only the *tripitaka* but all that exists in the universe is a pitched tray. If you fear this pitched tray, you may commit suicide.

I would like to say a little more about this tray. It is said in Buddhism and other religions that one must lead one's life free of attachment, that attachment is not good. But detachment is not a good way either. If you emphasize detachment, you must deny this existence and go to the summit of a mountain, drink from leaves, eat acorns and, perhaps, die there. But if you attach to your desire, your anger, and idleness, you will enter the syrup sea like a fly. Then what do you do? You do not know. If you detach, you suffer because you find some space between subject and object; you cannot enter into oneness. You are not emancipated. Then what shall you do? The answer is like what happens when a moth enters a flame—suddenly no moth and no flame. You have entered oneness. If you are afraid of the fire, you must keep away, but you will never find emancipation. If you stay outside a koan, you will never answer it. You must enter into it. And if you stand outside and look at the universe, how can you enter in? This is the pitched tray!

"*If the master does not apprehend this as an outward circumstance, he climbs upon it and assumes an attitude. The student roars again, but the master is unwilling to relinquish his position. The student shows his true substance, but the teacher holds his assumption. Such a teacher claims to be an adept, but a true teacher makes no assumption.*" He has not recognized the trap so he tries to answer the student's question: "How can I become one with the universe?" or "Is there such a thing as oneness?" He is asking to find out if this is a true master, and he watches the answer. Perhaps the teacher will give a lengthy answer; perhaps his mind is still in a cloud of abstract thinking!

"This is a disease that has reached the marrow and is incurable. I call this, 'student examines master.'" Such a master had better be cremated! If sickness of mind gets into such a condition, better not try to study religion.

"Sometimes the master offers nothing, depriving the student of all his questions. The student, having been deprived of questions, clings to them until the end. This I call, 'master examines student.'" This is the true master. If asked a question, "Will you have a cup of tea?" He gives the student true substance and explains nothing. If the student does not understand, he is blind and clings to conceptions—"ego," "non-ego," and so on. He is caught in the pitched tray and will never realize emancipation. The master cuts off all questions at the root.

"Sometimes the master offers nothing, depriving the student of all his questions." *"Then there is the student who presents himself before the master in a state of purity. The master, apprehending the circumstance, removes it and casts it into a deep pit. The student says, 'Fine!' The master says, 'Bah! You don't know the difference between good and evil!' The student then pays homage and bows low."* He is manifesting himself in a purified mental stage. Such a type of student is very dangerous. It is an external state. If a student is a true one, he does not take any state, so that in reality he takes all circumstances. To take no state is to take all states—terrible paradox! If his attainment is perfect, he does not attach any posture of mind or senses. He enters into all postures. One student may say, "I attained *dharmakaya*, I attained the omnipresent body, so I will not enter into any physical body." If he speaks like this, you feel that his attainment is dubious; if he understands, he will not speak about "entering", but will just take tea. So to the student that presents himself by taking a sort of purified circumstance, such as, "I entered *dharmakaya*," I can only say, "Humph!" This is very, very dangerous! Or, the student of which Lin-chi is speaking about here may have presented himself with, "I, Heaven and Earth are of the same origin." This would manifest the pure elemental stage. Therefore, we say that the seven-colored three-dimensional phenomenal existence is impure, not elemental. Such purity and impurity has no moral meaning, but is elemental and phenomenal.

Nan-ch'uan gave a beautiful answer to this statement, "I, Heaven and Earth and all nature are of the same origin." Pointing to a peony in the garden, Nan-ch'uan replied: "Men of today at this moment are looking at this flower, and they all feel as though they were dreaming."

When the master takes it off and casts it away into a pit, the master does not fall into the trap, this philosophical, hypothetical pit. The master sees through the mind of the student and answers in reality itself. If someone asks you, "What is God?" much the same as the question to Nan-ch'uan, and you explain, God is this or God is that, then God is a hypothesis, a mere conception. Human beings created this image in the past, an image that must have six senses like themselves, a personal God. Our idea is different. We view all ideas about the nature of God as a hypothesis created by our own minds. We do not care to talk about these things. We wish to look into reality. Certainly [banging table] this is important; it has value if you really understand.

If the Master understands that the student has set a trap for him, he grasps the trap and throws it away.

Student: "What is God?"

Master: "Did you ask a question?"

Student: "Yes."

Master: "Well, what are *you*?"

If you do not understand this, you cannot understand God.

"This I call 'master examines master.'" There are many stories about Lin-chi and P'u-hua where we see this kind of meeting.

"There is still another type of student who presents himself before the master fettered and handcuffed." Fettering (philosophy) and handcuffing (metaphysics, mantra, faith, superstition). Such a student will say, "I observed the commandments these twenty-five years. To me the universe is such and such." But you must know this fourth-dimensional world with its fetters and handcuffs. You must see that it is nothing but mind-stuff, see your inverted view. Analyzing this mind-stuff is like looking into a glass of impure water.

"The master puts the student in an additional noose. The student enjoys it. They do not know what they are doing." The master puts more stuff on the mind-stuff of the student, which he enjoys!

"This I call 'student examines student.'" They are parasites on religion, they are eating religion—the blind leading the blind, and both fall into the ditch.

I cannot help laughing. They are parroting a great teacher's teaching.

"Good brothers, I disclose these instances so you will be able to discriminate the evil and false from the real." We associate this with the hangers-on, the parasites and dependents who scarcely care to ask for more. We pity them. But the religious parasite is very bold.

Lin-chi teaches real mind activity as distinguished from mind-stuff.

"Brothers, sincerity is rare and Buddha's Dharma is profound, but to those who understand, it is plain. I unveil it for you all day long, but you are not aware of it. You step across it a thousand, ten thousand times, but for you it is a night of darkness. It is without appearance, yet it is clear as light. But students, unable to have faith in it, rely on the meaning of words. Their ages having reached to half a hundred, they drag their dead bodies about and run to their neighbors bearing baskets of books on their backs. Someday, payment for their sandals will be claimed."

SOKEI-AN SAYS:

Lin-chi has been speaking about the four kinds of masters and students, how they meet and demonstrate their understanding with each other. Lin-chi wishes to discriminate between true and false teachers and students. I think if one understands these four combinations of student and master, that one can understand the four positions of host and guest, a very important idea in Lin-chi Zen. Many advanced koans point to these four positions. Sometimes the master is blind but his guest has the eye. Sometimes the guest has the eye and the Master is blind. Sometimes both have the eye. And sometimes both are blind. If you elect an inferior man as president and he makes a mess of the country, he is a guest in the master's place. But if he is a man with personality and mind, he is master in the master's place. In koan study, such discriminations between master and guest are part of our psychological understanding.

"Brothers, sincerity is rare and Buddha's Dharma is profound, but to those who understand, it is plain." Lin-chi confessed how hard it is to find a sincere student, a man who has both heart and brain is very rare.

The Buddha's Dharma is Zen. Chao-chou said, "The whole universe is reduced to a poppy seed, but looking for it, you cannot see it." Buddhism emphasizes law, the Dharma, to get rid of hypothesis and get into nirvana or absolute emancipation, which is reality. When you realize reality, it is plain to see that hypothesis makes many unnecessary anxieties and efforts. Look at history, at the symbols. We have made all hypotheses. Today's economy is also hypothesis. We think there is real value in it and we try to rule human life by that scale. Someday we must open the eye to reality, and upon that we must build our lives!

"I unveil it for you all day long, but you are not aware of it." It is covered by your notions—conceptions are a cover. Because you cannot see the true, you make many false types of religion, and all the hypotheses fight one another like the horse, mouse, and mole.

"You step across it a thousand, ten thousand times, but for you it is a night of darkness. It is without appearance, yet it is clear as light." Step across [strikes self and table]. The Zen master demonstrates with his staff.

Someone asks Yun-men, "What is Buddha?" Yun-men shows his staff. Quite so, it is as clear as light! Lin-chi speaks too much. I think if Hakuin were there, he would slap Lin-chi's face! But "no appearance" can be said. From the essential aspect, there is no appearance. On all of Broadway, nothing has happened! All are silver waves scraping the infinite sky.

"But students, unable to have faith in it, rely on the meaning of words. Their ages having reached to half a hundred, they drag their dead bodies about and run to their neighbors bearing baskets of books on their backs." The students read the *sutras* and try to get the meaning. Lin-chi says there is no spirit in their bodies.

"Someday, payment for their sandals will be claimed." They will have to pay the penalty.

"Good brothers, if I say there is no Dharma on the outside, you do not understand and assume that it will be on the inside. So you place your back against a wall, place your tongue upon the roof of your mouth and remain motionless. You take that to be the Buddhism of the school of Bodhidharma. A great error!

If you recognize motionlessness and purity as correct, you must thereby recognize the darkness of ignorance as the master principle. The ancients said, 'Truly frightening is the dark and bottomless pit!' This was said to warn you of your error.

"But if you accept motion as the principle, the natural motion of the plant must surely be the Way. Is it not so? Motion is the air element, and motionlessness is the earth element. Motion and motionlessness alike are without selfhood. If you try to grasp it within motion, it will elude you in motionlessness. If you try to grasp it within motionlessness, it will elude you in motion. Like a fish hiding in a pool, it leaps throbbingly from the water! Good brothers, motion and motionlessness are different circumstances. In reality, he who depends upon nothing utilizes the motion of motionlessness.

"When students come here from every quarter, I divide them into three classes according to their potential. If one with a medium to inferior potential comes here, I deprive him of his surroundings, but do not exclude him from attainment. If one with a medium to superior potential comes here, I deprive him of his surroundings and also of attainment. If one with an excellent to superior potential comes here, I do not deprive him of his surroundings, his attainment, or of himself. But if one with a transcendental potential comes here, I act toward him from wholeness and do not classify him to any degree. Good brothers, when a student reaches here, his attainment is so immeasurable and vast, no wind can enter. It is as instantaneous as a spark or a flash of lightning. If you so much as move an eye, there is no relation between you and it. Attend to it, and you miss it. Shift the mind, and it is opposed.*

SOKEI-AN SAYS:

In the last lecture, Lin-chi says that the student who tries to attain reality will search for something on the outside, will discover that it is nothing but phenomena, and then turn to the inside, thinking that deep meditation will lead him to reality. Lin-chi says this is erroneous because the one who denies the outside must also deny the inside. The inside exists relative to the outside and vice versa. The hypothesis of outside and inside will lead you nowhere. Lin-chi thought that enlightenment is at any moment. It is not necessary to wait a long, long time. If you understand, you can grasp reality in one second. So he denies all conceptions and all words that express something. Bodhidharma said Zen does not use a word.

It is not necessary to ask where the mind is; it is everywhere. It is here before you ask about it; it is self-evident. But the human being tries to put a name on it—"This is my mind. It is nature's action or the instrument of God." This only covers it, like putting on a hat. In Zen we do not call it by any name.

The Buddha's Buddhism is the same as Bodhidharma's. Shakyamuni denied all the hypotheses existing in India. He studied with three great teachers and accepted all the teaching as theory, for he did not accept their attainment. Then he struggled to attain reality by himself through meditation. He attained enlightenment and called it nirvana.

If you open the record of the famous Chinese sage Lao-tzu, you will read in the first line: "The Tao which is called Tao is not the true Tao." And we say: God, Buddha, reality, anything conceived as a name is not true. A Zen master said, "Wipe all images from this mirror." The student assented. "Now," said the master, "destroy the mirror." Wipe everything from the slate and destroy the slate; that is Buddha's Buddhism.

This is Lin-chi's discourse. He is talking like an old mother who is too kind to her children!

"When students come here from every quarter . . ." This is how the "here" to which students come was once expressed: "A three-foot sword cuts the lightning in the spring breeze." This is a terrible "here"!

"I divide them into three classes according to their potential." Of course everyone who is in the way of enlightenment still has some conceptions and philosophy in mind, so Lin-chi made three classes.

"If one with a medium to inferior potential comes here, I deprive him of his surroundings, but do not exclude him from attainment." All the circumstances, mountains, river, sky, earth, color, sound. Lin-chi will destroy all phenomenal existence for him. Today we say all this is not objective existence, but phenomena produced by the five senses.

Then the student thinks, "Well, if we destroy phenomena, there is still essential existence, or non-existence, something called reality." That is so-called attainment. So he makes conceptions.

There is no past, present, or future in reality. Therefore it is infinite, pure ether, transparent. We cannot be aware of that existence so we call it non-existence. Noumena, reality, wholeness, *dharmakaya*—all this is attainment, but it is not the real, clear ground.

I think Lin-chi was very kind to his students who could not accept more than this. "Well, let him attain so much!" Such are medium-inferior; he does not speak of the inferior class at all.

"*If one with a medium to superior potential comes here, I deprive him of his surroundings and also of attainment.*" Destroy phenomena and noumena, wipe the slate clean and destroy the slate. What is left? Would you be afraid at this stage? As long as we have consciousness, it is impossible to destroy it. But consciousness is relative, not absolute existence, not reality. The scientist can prove that consciousness appears when the tissue of one protoplasm contacts another. It appears between them. Yet, almost all religions build upon consciousness, and fall into error. How would you call the stage that is not consciousness? Unconsciousness? This is really the vital point of Buddhism. Some say that this stage of consciousness is unconscious, but how to prove it?

For this medium-superior type, Lin-chi destroyed both phenomena and noumena. This is a good student to whom he could really speak.

A Zen student in China went to see Nan-ch'uan and found him standing upon a stepladder and plastering a wall. (Great Zen masters, according to the records, are always working at the time the stories are told. They are not sitting in a golden robe; they are cutting wood, digging in the fields, and such.)

The student said, "A word or no-word is like wisteria twining around a tree. When the tree falls, where do these words or no-words go?" (Word is surrounding; no-word is attainment; the two, wisteria. The tree is neither noumena nor phenomena. Wisteria is both noumena and phenomena.)

Nan-ch'uan threw the plaster on the student's head, laughed, and returned to his room. That was his answer; no explanation.

I think this is a clear discourse. It has a good feeling.

"*If one with an excellent to superior potential comes here, I do not deprive him of his surroundings, his attainment, or of himself.*" What does he do with such a type? "Do you like tea or coffee?" A good turnip is living in the field!

"*But if one with a transcendental potential comes here, I act toward him from wholeness and do not classify him to any degree.*" Ah, this action is terrible! Wholeness, what is it?

"Good brothers, when a student reaches here, his attainment is so immeasurable and vast, no wind can enter." How measure him? *This* cannot be measured by space, time, phenomena, or noumena.

"*It is as instantaneous as a spark or a flash of lightning. If you so much as move an eye, there is no relation between you and it. Attend to it, and you miss it. Shift the mind, and it is opposed.*" No space to peep in.

When the Buddha entered nirvana, all the *devas* tried to offer him flowers, but they could not find him. How do you explain this?

"*Good brothers, you bear your bowl-sack and your dung-tub [the body] and run around the neighborhood asking for Buddha and the Dharma. Do you know the one running around searching? He is active but he has no root. He cannot be gathered in, nor can he be dispersed. If you search for him, he recedes farther and farther. When you stop searching, he appears in your presence, his mysterious voice resonating in your ears. If you do not believe this, you are wasting your hundred years of labor.*

"*Brothers, at this very moment you enter the world of the Lotus Treasury, the land of Vairocana, the land of deliverance, the land of freedom, the land of purity, and the Dharma world; enter the pure and the impure, the sacred and the secular, the realm of hungry demons and of beasts. No matter where you search, you will never see birth and death, only empty names. They are phantoms, dreams, flowers in the empty sky. Why exert yourself to grasp them? Gain and loss, right and wrong, get rid of them all at once!*"

SOKEI-AN SAYS:

In the last lecture, Lin-chi tells his disciples that enlightenment is instantaneous, that it is not necessary to wait a thousand years, not necessary to practice intense meditation or to follow after philosophical systems. He says when the time comes you will enter into it suddenly. But if you are sleeping, the time will never come even though you meditate for ten years. If you sleep in meditation, you will never awaken.

Lin-chi describes the moment when you enter into That which has no name. IT is THAT. If you give it a name, you will fall into hypothesis. If you call it "personality," you will look at it from the human standpoint. The pronoun IT is perhaps the best. It is intersticeless, spaceless, cannot be measured. It is not narrow like a pinpoint, not broad like the universe. No wind can blow in. It is instantaneous as a spark, like lightning. As the Buddha said, "I run after the arrow and catch it before it falls." However, if you try to look at it, you will only see it from your experience in the three-dimensional world.

In the above passage Lin-chi is talking about reality, essential existence, and that there is no reality outside. *This* is all phenomena, not external existence. It is like a cloud in the sky. If phenomena are the shadows of our senses, the truth cannot be outside. Then it must be inside. Thus one enters meditation. Lin-chi, of course, is speaking about the attitude of the student who searches outside himself: He studies page after page, goes to temple after temple, neighborhood after neighborhood. Once a famous Zen poet of China wrote a poem:

My soul is like a moon
Reflecting upon the clear water of autumn.
It is so bright and clear—
Nothing can compare with it.

Well, it's no good to think about it. Before you do, here it is! If you say, "here," you have already missed it. "Here" is a conception relating to "there." Relative existence cannot grasp the absolute. You may say, "It enshrines in my heart," but "heart" is a hypothesis. Are you trying to "mind" it in your heart? Then you say, "Well, I will not mind it," and you abandon your mind. But if you grasp it, it goes nowhere, Grasp what? Heart? Brain? All these words are nonsense. These lines of Lin-chi say nothing! Of course they go nowhere. If you don't point, then it doesn't exist. But the human being must point somewhere; it's a habit.

"Good brothers, you bear your bowl-sack and your dung-tub [the body] and run around the neighborhood asking for Buddha and the Dharma." All life long, we drag around this digestive system. If I do not know IT, how can I close my eyes in peace? In Japan old people climb mountains, go from temple to temple searching for a comfortable death, and so students

run from teacher to teacher. They seek for the Buddha in the Three Refuges, and so on.

"Do you know the one running around searching?" Who is he? Man, angel, devil? Who is the one running around and calling, "Buddha, Bodhidharma where are you?" Who is searching for you now, at this moment?

"He is active but he has no root." Now Lin-chi talks about IT. This consciousness is so active. Where does consciousness come from? We know that it comes only with contact, and the absolute has no contact, for in the absolute there are no two things. Consciousness cannot prove its original form; therefore, it has no roots. It is like holding golden sand in water: it slips out and you cannot gather it.

"He cannot be gathered in, nor can he be dispersed. If you search for him, he recedes farther and farther." Just like a shadow, you cannot catch it. If you try to catch it in *rupa*, it will enter *vedana*. It enters all five shadows and you can never grasp it.

"When you stop searching, he appears in your presence, his mysterious voice resonating in your ears. If you do not believe this, you are wasting your hundred years of labor." A cat sometimes does not wish to answer your call. If you forget about soul, it is here! The mysterious universal voice has no sound, like Hakuin's universal hand.

Lin-chi is telling us again where not to look for your own self. Wash your hands and come back to your own quilt and fold your legs. When you abandon all measures and return, you will find this place.

Lin-chi, as usual, is trying to destroy all your preconceived ideas and notions and bring you into the ground of pureness. If you try to seek something in your mind, analyzing your notions and conceptions, you will find no master there. The one who is seeking, he is the master; he is the important one. Where is that knower? You think you know, you see and hear, but when asleep, you dream yourself. In the dream you walk and talk. Which is really your self, the true one? Is it this one, or so-called nature? When you realize emptiness, you realize your own spirit. In a green bottle, the water is green, but the water itself has no color. When you realize reality, you can enter all. There is no difference between life and death, sacred and secular, unless you name it. Reality-itself is always pure and never changes its light or force. From the Zen standpoint, you shall not grasp father or mother. Before you try to grasp them there is something.

Zen is a little different from other teachings because the others always speak of going upward, while our way is from inside to the outside. The Zen student must invert this habit from outside to inside. So you must be like the moth that flies around a flame and finally enters the flame. Then there will be no moth and no fire. Everyone knows that there is something we can enter into. If you faithfully follow Zen, you will enter.

"Brothers, my buddhadharma has been directly transmitted from generation to generation, from Ma-yu, Tan-hsia, Ma-tsu, Lu-shan, and Shih-kung. It has been widely disseminated on earth, yet no one believes in it, and everyone speaks ill of it.

"Master Ma-tsu's actualization of Zen was pure and unadulterated. All of his three to five hundred students failed to understand him. Master Lu-shan's Zen was spontaneous and genuine. Whether his actualization with them was natural or adversarial, none of his students could measure the limit of his mind; all would stare in blank dismay. Master Tan-hsia played with the pearl of wisdom, concealing and revealing it; all who came before him were refused. As to Master Ma-yu's actualization, it was bitter as bitter herbs no one could approach him. Master Shih-kung's actualization was to seek out a man with the point of his arrow; all who came before him were in fear.

"As for my actualization today, it is true creation and destruction, a play of miraculous transformation. Entering into all kinds of surroundings, I am peaceful. My surroundings cannot alter me."

SOKEI-AN SAYS:
One by one, I have been translating and lecturing on the discourses of Lin-chi. We are now nearing its end. Next will come his biography and the record of his Zen battles with other masters. If you do not understand his discourses, you will find it difficult to understand the rest of this record.

"Brothers, my buddhadharma has been directly transmitted from generation to generation, from Ma-yu, Tan-hsia, Ma-tsu, Lu-shan, and

Shih-kung. It has been widely disseminated on earth, yet no one believes in it, and everyone speaks ill of it." That is because Zen is transmitted face to face, eye to eye, soul to soul.

Lin-chi has given us the names of his descendants, the patriarchs of Zen before him. After the Fifth Patriarch, Hung-jen, Zen separated into two branches, the Northern and the Southern schools. The Sixth Patriarch belonged to the Southern school; the Northern Zen lineage discontinued after five generations. Today, we say Zen came from the Sixth Patriarch, the Southern School. Under him, two branches were formed, that of his disciples Ch'ing-yuan [*n.d.*] and Nan-yueh Huai-jang [677-744]. Nan-yueh was a direct disciple of the Sixth Patriarch, and Ma-tsu of Huai-jang. Pai-chang Huai-hai [720-814] was a disciple of Ma-tsu and Huang-po of Huai-hai. Lin-chi was a disciple of Huang-po. After twenty-seven generations in China, the teaching came to Japan transmitted from one flame to another. One flame stretched from India to America!

Ma-yu, Tan-hsia T'ien-jan [738-823], Ma-tsu, Lu-shan Chih-ch'ang [*n.d.*], and Shih-kung Hui-tsang [*n.d.*] all came from one jar! Ma-yu was a disciple of Ma-tsu. The later part of this record will describe him. He came to ask Lin-chi a question. Tan-hsia (no one knew from where he came) was a politician.

Ma-tsu was the greatest master in Zen history. One hundred and thirty disciples attained enlightenment under him. But he did not become a master until he was 80 years old, at which time he was proclaimed throughout China.

Po-chang Huai-hai, one of his disciples, entered the temple as a very little child, and became a wonderful master. One day, on a journey with Ma-tsu—the child carrying his master's bundles upon his back—some geese in a field abruptly took flight. Ma-tsu asked, "What is it?" This is a dangerous question! "Geese." "Geese, hey? Where have they gone?" "Well—" Ma-tsu pinched his nose and he howled. [Sokei-an honked like a goose] "Why don't you go?" Ah—at that moment Po-chang understood!

Shih-kung Hui-tsang (n.d.) was also a famous disciple of Ma-tsu. One day he was hunting a deer, pursuing it up a mountain. Coming down, he came close to a monk meditating under a tree. It was Ma-tsu. The hunter asked, "Have you seen a deer passing in this direction?" "Direction?" "Yes, which direction?" "What are you?" "A hunter?" "Ah, a hunter—then I will ask you a question: 'With one arrow, how many deer can you get?'"

"What a foolish question! One." "And you call yourself a hunter?" "And you—how many can you get?" "One million" answered Ma-tsu.

But this hunter was not stupid. He stopped hunting and became a disciple of Ma-tsu, transmitting his Zen. Shih-kung dealt with his disciples with his bow and arrow. For twelve years all his disciples ran away. One returned, called San-p'ing I-chung (781-872). Shih-kung started to draw the bowstring, when San-p'ing bared his breast and said, "Shoot the arrow! This is not a joke." Shih-kung broke the bow and threw it away, crying, "Today I cut down one half of a stupid saint!" That was Shih-kung's transmission.

"It has been widely disseminated on earth, yet no one believes in it, and everyone speaks ill of it." It was so in Lin-chi's time and it is so today!

"Master Ma-tsu's actualization of Zen was pure and unadulterated. All of his three to five hundred students failed to understand him." If Zen is not actualized, it is not worth studying! Actualization is most important; it is every-day life. The Zen student has a mind like a thief. He is quietly trying to strike the real chord of life in all circumstances.

I have met many Zen masters; some are like singers—hoarse in every-day speech but great on stage. My own teacher, Shaku Soyen, was always spontaneous. He was a great teacher from Kyoto. He practiced a pure and unadulterated Zen. Such Zen is rare today. "I wish to know what is Buddhism." "Oh, I am glad you came upon the mountain!"

"Master Lu-shan's Zen was spontaneous and genuine. Whether his actualization with them was natural or adversarial, none of his students could measure the limit of his mind; all would stare in blank dismay." No measure can apply to such a mind. "Are you a Zen master?" "I am quite sure you believe in my ivory head!" Just like a snake.

To think about something takes much time, and each question must pass through the mental categories. When you become stupid, you are a good Zen student.

In Japan, there was a beggar with a nasty disease. He could not work, so he beat a little gong and begged on the streets. All who saw him wished to give and pass quickly. Then a doctor came and took pity on him. "If I operate, you can be cured in three weeks. Will you come to the hospital?" The beggar answered, "Thank you, but this happened in my youth, and I have always made my bread and butter by begging. How would I live if I were cured?"

There is theory Buddhism, and then there is Zen. In Zen, all relative existence is reduced to nothing. What is nothing? The question is theory; the actualization is Zen. Everyone creates the idea first, and when it comes to applying it to life, they do not carry it through.

"Master Tan-hsia played with the pearl of wisdom, concealing and revealing it; all who came before him were refused." No one could stay with him. If asked a question, he would laugh and say, "A foolish question! Why ask me? Do you not belong to Zen? Zen is mind and you have mind—get out of here!"

This "pearl of wisdom" is *prajna*, for which there is no good English translation. *This* present consciousness is the pearl of wisdom, the consciousness of the enlightened one. In this universal light, he sees the appearance and the reality, the existence not related to the five senses.

"As to Master Ma-yu's actualization, it was bitter as bitter herbs; no one could approach him." When a student came to see him, Ma-yu would ask, "Where do you come from?" Dreadful question! (The "before father and mother" koan), The student would fear to answer and the master would grow angry and shout, "Blind one! When I question you, you always take it as Buddhism! Go away!" The mind always makes a hypothesis and never sees true existence. Ma-yu would say, "This monk is a five-year-old bamboo trying to compare himself with this million-year-old pine tree." He was not speaking of himself, but of the whole of existence.

"Master Shih-kung's actualization was to seek out a man with the point of his arrow; all who came before him were in fear." There is one arrow that kills and another that brings life! For thirty years he taught with bow and arrow, but no one could stand against this arrow—all ran away. Then San-p'ing came to him, bared his breast, and asked, "Is it the arrow that kills or brings life?" The same arrow has two different functions: creation and destruction; all the universe has it. For answer, Shih-kung broke his bow and arrow, and throwing them away, said, "After thirty years, I have shot half a saint!"

"As for my actualization today, it is true creation and destruction, a play of miraculous transformation." Lin-chi now confesses his own attitude toward the student: he sometimes takes away the student's notion, and he sometimes animates it through creation or destruction. In "miraculous transformation," he stands upon all the different stages of consciousness—now a materialist, now a spiritualist. Freedom of actualization!

"*Entering into all kinds of surroundings, I am peaceful. My surroundings cannot alter me.*" The root, the trunk, bough and leaf—all are the same.

"*When anyone comes to see me, I come out and see him, but he does not know me. When I change my robes, he forms a meaning from this and falls into my words. It is mortifying. The blind baldhead has no eye [to see reality]. He only sees blue, yellow, red, or white, according to the robe I put on. If I take off the robe and enter the state of purity, he looks at me and is joyously aroused. If I remove the state of purity, he is stupefied and runs amok, raving, 'The master is naked!' If I ask him whether he knows the one who wears the robes or not, he abruptly turns round and sees it's me!*

"*Good brothers, do not declare the robe to be the true man! The robe cannot change the man who puts on the robe. There is the robe of purity, the robe of non-existence, the robe of bodhi, the robe of nirvana, the robe of the patriarchs, the robe of the Buddha. Good Brothers, they are nothing but words, just changes of robe! Whipping up air from your abdominal sea, you rattle your teeth and make meanings. It is clear they are only phantoms.*

"*Good brothers, in the outer world you display the works of speech; in the inner world you manifest the mind's place. Mind exhibits itself with thoughts; therefore, they are only robes. If you acknowledge the robe that you put on to be true understanding, though you pass through kalpas of time, you are only a man of robes and will transmigrate through life and death in the three worlds. Better to be peaceful. Meeting him, I am not aware of him. Conversing with him, I do not know his name.*

"*Students of today cannot attain because their understanding is based on names. They write the words of some dead, old man upon the pages of a big book, enfold it in four or five layers of cloth and allow no one to see it. They declare, "This is the mystery!" and carefully attend to it. This is a great error.*

Blind idiots! What kind of juice do you expect to get from such a dry bone!

"Then there are those who, unable to discriminate good from bad, conjecture and speculate on the Buddha's teachings and haphazardly set up meanings. It is like putting a lump of dung into your mouth and transferring it to another. They are like people playing word games, spending a lifetime for nothing. They say they are renouncers of home, yet they cannot answer a question when asked about the Buddha's Dharma. In their dismay, their eyes stare like black-lacquered beads, and their mouths bend like carrying poles. Even at the advent of Maitreya [they will not meet him], but will transmigrate to another world and suffer the torments of hell."

SOKEI-AN SAYS:

Zen is very plain, but it is the eye of wisdom. All Buddhists, while they are studying so-called Buddhism, get caught in devices and forget the goal. A device is necessary to get somewhere, but before you start to practice the device, the real thing is there. You have your own truth, so before you step out, you must first step *back* and find your *self.*

When a student comes to see Lin-chi, however, all the student speaks about is mind-stuff; he never shows him mind-itself. Today, it is exactly the same. When I ask what is a cherry blossom, you will tell me the color, number of petals, fragrance, and so forth. If I do not see the cherry blossom with the naked eye, in whatever way I am informed about it, I will not see it. But if you bring a blossom and show it to me directly—"Oh, I understand!" If I ask your mind, you try to explain. But if I ask your eye, do you explain? I think you will point to it and show me. So in Zen, you must show it.

Real Dharma is not so easy to attain. One certainly must struggle. One who also tries to teach Dharma is really risking his life. It is no pasttime or amusement! One who fishes in a goldfish pond may enjoy himself, but the one who tries to get a whale is risking his life. It may look easy because he is not running amok, but such a one must have a "copper forehead and iron guts." He must throw away all hopes and desires and try to keep the torch of Shakyamuni Buddha and Bodhidharma alive. This is not easy. The student takes pains to attain such a Dharma. All the previous masters struggled for a lifetime to get one or two good students.

But when they, the students, realize that this teaching has existed through twenty-five hundred years, they realize the value of it.

"*When anyone comes to see me, I come out and see him, but he does not know me.*" The master understands the student's stage, but the student cannot see the Master.

"*When I change my robes, he forms a meaning from this and falls into my words.*" "Robes" means mental attitude. When Lin-chi tells a student that he must understand "oneness," the student harps upon it in his mind.

"*It is mortifying. The blind baldhead has no eye [to see reality]. He only sees blue, yellow, red, or white, according to the robe I put on.*" Lin-chi is speaking of the robes of *dharmakaya, sambhogakaya, nirmanakaya*; the robes of purity and the robes of impurity, of *manas*-consciousness, *vedana*, and *prajna*. All are robes. Each robe is for a different state of consciousness. Is there anyone who puts on these robes? You must find the real body that puts them on. It is not difficult to find. You can grasp the robe, but if you really grasp the body, that is the end of Buddhism! No need to study Zen. But whatever a student grasps in his hand, "Ah, *This* is *That!*" That is a robe, not the real body.

Every monk puts on some kind of robe over his body of reality. You can see it in their attitude, in some display of manner of every kind—lovely, kind, and so forth. Such things are not religion. These blind baldheads call themselves monks and are supported by good laymen and laywomen. They have nothing to give because they are blind. Their eyes are just like the eyes of ordinary men and women. Their eyes do not penetrate through phenomena to reality. Such monks are of no use, and there are many. In Zen we abuse them to warn them to be careful.

Everyone speaks about reality. If you study the philosophical books of Kant and Hegel, this word is big. If you do not know the meaning of these philosophical terms, you do not understand what I am speaking about. We can say that reality is this cup, but a picture or a description of it is not reality. We are not students of metaphysics; we say reality is the real body of the universe. You can see it with the eye, but when you *talk* about reality it is not the real body of the universe. You can see it with the eye, but a picture or a description of it is not reality. We in the Zen school are not students of metaphysics; we say reality is the real body of the universe. You can see it with the eye, but when you talk about reality, you cannot demonstrate it. Only he who knows reality will understand. "In the pitch dark of night the wooden man sings and the stone woman dances." If you understand this koan, you will know what I am speaking about. "Before father and mother, what was your original aspect?" All these koans are pointing to reality.

"*If I take off the robe and enter the state of purity, he looks at me and is joyously aroused. If I remove the state of purity, he is stupefied and runs amok, raving, 'The Master is naked!'*" Lin-chi takes off all robes, all garments and enters into the pure state of *dharmakaya*. Then all say, "Ah, Lin-chi is a saint! He is in the transcendental body!" The student then tries to enter in. Again, Lin-chi takes off that absolute state of consciousness; and they all say, "Ah, Lin-chi has no robe on him!"

To put on the pure garment of *dharmakaya* is easy, but to take it off and show the real body, how do you see it? Without knowing this, you cannot have the real ground of life. *Dharmakaya* is like a pure white or colored glass: all colors will reflect upon it except the same color. When absolutely pure (no color), every color will reflect, but there is no ego. From the egoless state you observe all existing states of phenomena, and everything will reflect upon your body so that you can understand all circumstances. One can come into that pureness by concentrating into one's self, but without abandoning the ego. This is not a real Buddhist. He must drop the ego on entering and he must not take it up when he comes out. Such a one is a real being. You may call him, if you wish, the Son of God; he is the child of the real father; he observes all circumstances and adjusts himself to them. If you carry some previous notion in your mind, you cannot adjust to circumstances.

From the Buddhist standpoint, there is no real "matter" in the universe The four great elements are the *alaya*-consciousness; this body is *manas*-consciousness and the semi-material mind-stuff. All is spiritual, not material. We see the root through all stages of consciousness, all circumstances. This is the foundation upon which we build our lives. From this standpoint, the Buddhist is a pure materialist. But from the standpoint of real existence, are there such things as spirit and matter? Do such names exist? According to country, time and place—the actual circumstances—you must adjust yourself. Lin-chi takes this naked attitude and has no robe.

"*If I ask him whether he knows the one who wears the robes or not, he abruptly turns round and sees it's me!*" "You, yourself?" Ha! Lin-chi has nothing to do with it! The one who puts on the robe is not a human being, and he is not Lin-chi. You must meet him, meet him with your naked eye, with your real hand you must touch him!

"*Good brothers, do not declare the robe to be the true man!*" Lin-chi has put on many garments, and he asks his disciples, "Who is the one who puts on and takes off these garments?" But the student does not see the real one, just Lin-chi himself. The Buddhist attitude toward the true man is different from that of cults like Theosophy, and so on. In the *trikaya*, *dharmakaya* is *sambhogakaya* and *sambhogakaya* is *nirmanakaya*. This [indicating self] is the True Man. That man is True Man. But usually the student will see this or that man and not see the True Man.

In my experience of giving *sanzen* to Western students, I find that they do not know so-called *samadhi*, that is, concentration. Our attitude of meditation: *This*—the self—is a microcosm of the universe. We unite with the universe, casting aside our usual notions. Immediately we enter into the universe and the universe enters into us. An athlete has this concentration; his function is really actuated by universal power. Such an actualization should come to the student in *sanzen*, but he does not have the concentration and fails. He should enter the Zen room from this center of concentration. The word is the last thing, the period, absolute oneness. Before that must be the foundation. Then that last touch will come. But realization must come with your heart, your body, and the whole universe. All three must be in it! This elf is the true man when he is absorbed into the universe.

"*The robe cannot change the man who puts on the robe.*" The robe is the attitude. We can create logical structures according to the nature of the brain, like monism, dualism or pluralism, but they have nothing to do with reality. You can observe reality from any standpoint, but reality itself is always the same; all the rest is just mental play, intellectual enjoyment—nonsense!

"*There is the robe of purity, the robe of non-existence, the robe of* bodhi, *the robe of nirvana, the robe of the patriarchs, the robe of the Buddha.*" Pureness is the *dharmakaya* aspect. Non-existence is non-actualization: it exists as essence but not as phenomena. In *sambhogakaya*, there are many vestures. In Zen, we say the vestures of Buddha and Bodhidharma. These are included in *nirmanakaya*. But from the angle of the true man, there is no *dharmakaya*, *sambhogakaya*, *nirmanakaya*, no non-existence and no pureness.

Dharmakaya is essential existence, the power that produces nature as a dog, a cat, or a man. The power is the same. In the auto factory the same power produces all its different parts, and in the universe this power is *dharmakaya* entering into all the different shapes. The *dharmakaya* is the invisible manifestation, and *nirmanakaya* is the visible. But there is a quality that equalizes everything as consciousness, the same link as between the three *kayas*.

"Good Brothers, they are nothing but words, just changes of robe! Whipping up air from your abdominal sea, you rattle your teeth and make meanings. It is clear they are only phantoms." The karma of speech creates them. Philosophy is created by words.

"Good brothers, in the outer world you display the works of speech; in the inner world you manifest the mind's place." We say that the depth of concentration in meditation is *alaya*-consciousness, and so on through the eight consciousnesses. We call this the stage of mind. Mind and mind-place are different.

"Mind exhibits itself with thoughts; therefore, they are only robes." Without place and without thoughts you cannot prove your mind. If mind does not incarnate into bird, animal, man, but always keeps the essential form, there is no way of comparison and you cannot prove mind.

These robes or garments are thoughts and conceptions, different angles from which to observe reality. But all philosophy has been spoken in the past ages. It leads to the gate, but there you must come to the conclusion of philosophy and enter Zen.

Zen permits no hypothesis of any system. Zen is mind itself, mind activity itself. It does not emphasize how to take care of mind-stuff. The Buddha returned to his own mind activity and discovered the universal law in his mind. That was truly the religion of the buddha. Mind, of course, is not this ego, but something that animates all sentient beings.

This mind activity manifests itself with mind matter, just as fire exists with wood and coal. Without material there is no fire. Thoughts are the record of outside experience; we cannot create any thoughts without the experience of our sense perceptions. These thoughts dragged in from the outside we call mind-stuff. It is not entirely spiritual, nor is it entirely material existence. We call it semi-material because it has a place which is not three-dimensional.

You will realize this in observing your own thoughts. With these thoughts, we can prove our mind activity; without thoughts, though it exists, we cannot prove it. So if you place too much importance upon the mind-stuff, it is exactly like a garment of the body. The mind handles mind-stuff.

"Robes" is almost like a technical term in the *Record of Lin-chi*. It means mind-stuff. Mind-stuff is not a new idea; in the East it is quite old. Today Westerners speaks of this semi-material quantity as a four-dimensional quantity existing between matter and spirit. So they think of the universe as divided into matter and spirit. This is really a very rough scale of analysis! But now they divide it into three parts: matter, semi-matter, and spiritual. This spirit has place but no weight. It is just like a dream. You know where it is but you cannot grasp it. A dream is mind-stuff, called by Lin-chi a robe. Some of the philosophical systems are beautiful, but they are, after all, but a robe. All creations, conceptions, or words, are but robes. But there is something behind the robe, controlling it. Everyone attaches to the robe and forgets about the One which is not the ego, not yourself. It is manifesting itself in yourself.

"If you acknowledge the robe that you put on to be true understanding, though you pass through kalpas of time, you are only a man of robes and will transmigrate through life and death in the three worlds." The true one has neither birth nor death. There is coming and going, but there is no mutability, no death. *This one* does not go through any sort of transmigration. But one who attaches to some kind of dream, he will go through all the stages of existence, for robes go through many kalpas, changing color and texture. So if one attaches to robes, he will go through this transmigration; he cannot realize any sort of manifestation, never sees the external existence. Buddhism teaches how to free oneself from this transmigration.

That one has no name, but they do not know him so they call him by many names: We say, *bhutatathata*, meaning "IT is THAT." What is it? In Alice in Wonderland, the Mad Hatter and Alice see IT. But the student places emphasis upon the robe, as true understanding, and calls it Allah or God, thinking it exists outside somewhere in the sky! He forgets the one who is really acting in himself, so he pursues the outside. They study this or that religion, study this or that philosophy, but they are only tailors tailoring their robes.

Lin-chi said this is a misunderstanding.

"Better to be peaceful. Meeting him, I am not aware of him. Conversing with him, I do not know his name." You really meet him at every moment, day and night. Though you may be in a fathomless sleep, you are with him, but you do not know him. He has no name, though he is noumenal. You are always speaking with him and listen to his whispering. If you would stop disputing, you would hear him. You attach to your egotistic thoughts, and even though you sometimes hear his voice, you do not know the difference. So Lin-chi says it is no use searching if you are blind, but some day you will see him.

"Students of today cannot attain because their understanding is based on names." It is impossible to attain while you attach to empty names. This universal consciousness has one name; a personal God has one name; oversoul has one name. Thus you dispute over these empty names and believe it to be true understanding.

"They write the words of some dead, old man upon the pages of a big book, enfold it in four or five layers of cloth and allow no one to see it." Lin-chi is being very sarcastic and mischievous! The "dead old man" means Shakyamuni Buddha or those teachers before him, and their teachings.

"They declare, 'This is the mystery!' and carefully attend to it. This is a great error." You must keep this one [strikes chest], which you can feel, which you can realize working in yourself. *This One* you must worship, not the visible one. All reflections are One if you attain to this real self.

Zen is the Buddha's Buddhism. It represents primitive Buddhism, the attitude of the Buddha toward truth. But the real teaching of the Buddha is written in the soul of everyone; on the heart of all human beings everywhere. You must watch your own soul, your own mind. That is the nearest way to reach the truth.

These lines are not very important, but you will understand Lin-chi's attitude toward esoteric Buddhism. He places the whole emphasis on self-realization and debases the attitude of the student who follows an ordinary teacher.

When we meditate upon our soul, our heart, our own nature, we will meet the Father because he is living there. You will not recognize him by looking at a photograph! Buddha-nature is enshrined in your heart, your mind. So if you meditate upon it, you will find it. This is the attitude of the Zen Buddhist.

Mind, heart, and soul are not three different elements existing in our self; they are one. You ask about life after death. Some believe that souls are separated by the creator from beginning to end. The Buddhist does not believe in such a soul; he believes in non-ego. My soul is not mine. Your soul is not yours!

"Blind idiots! What kind of juice do you expect to get from such a dry bone!" In China and Japan monks write words on paper and you pay one yen and bring it home, cover it with brocade and worship it. It is to those kinds of monks that Lin-chi gives this abuse, and then he turns his abuse upon the teachers who are teaching such nonsense.

"Then there are those who, unable to discriminate good from bad, conjecture and speculate on the Buddha's teachings and haphazardly set up meanings. It is like putting a lump of dung into your mouth and transferring it to another. They are like people playing word games, spending a lifetime for nothing. They say they are renouncers of home, yet they cannot answer a question when asked about the Buddha's Dharma. In their dismay, their eyes stare like black-lacquered beads, and their mouths bend like carrying poles. Even at the advent of Maitreya [they will not meet him], but will transmigrate to another world and suffer the torments of hell." Because he has no meditation in himself. Meditation is hard work, but without any experience in it, they cannot call themselves teachers. A parrot can call for tea, but when he gets it, he does not know what it is.

Lin-chi is referring to the Buddhist descriptions in the *sutras*: The Buddha said, "I am seated and hidden, but when I suddenly appear in the center of the sky and smile, the whole universe sees the effulgence." The teachers would explain it thus: "Seat" means latent consciousness; "smile" means enlightenment and "sky" means realization. Realization is the base of Buddhism. Some say faith. What is faith?

When the Sixth Patriarch received the torch of Dharma from Hung-jen, the Fifth Patriarch, he had to flee the temple to save his life. He had reached the southern border when he heard a voice calling him. He turned and saw a strong and savage dragon, the monk Hui-ming pursuing him. The Sixth Patriarch placed the robe and the bowl upon a rock and hid himself. Ming tried to lift the bowl and the robe but could not. The Sixth Patriarch appeared and said, "This bowl and this robe are the symbol of my faith. You can have them if you can lift them from this rock." Ming tried again, but they were as heavy as a mountain. Then he realized that they belonged to the Sixth Patriarch. All of nature had given him permission. This is a koan: What is this faith?

> "Good brothers, what are you searching for so restlessly, running about everywhere until the soles of your feet become flat? There is no Buddha, no Way, no Dharma to seek! If you pursue the Buddha of visible form, he is not similar to yourself. If you wish to know your soul, it is neither within nor apart from your attention.
>
> "Brothers, the true Buddha is without form; the true Way is without body; the true Dharma is without signs. These three are one and in one place. If you are unable to understand this, you will be called a being of karmic-consciousness."

SSOKEI-AN SAYS:

The monks' feet become flat because they are searching in the semi-visible sphere of mind-stuff and the fires of emotion. There they reach the highest peaks of suffering as they seek the truth from temple to temple and from teacher to teacher. What are they searching for? On the peaks of emotion there is only doubt (reasoning, mind-stuff), so it is not the way to open the door to Buddhism. Buddhism is within yourself!

These monks Lin-chi is talking about are flying around like *devas* in the sky among mountain peaks sharp as the point of a sword. So if your mind is living in passion or anger, every one of those peaks of emotion has the power to destroy your mind. Anger, ambition, and such, can kill you at any time. They are strong, natural powers, the powers of nature herself—and our life is based upon that nature. The *Lotus Sutra* says the world is a house afire. It animates us and gives us food. But if we do not know how to take care of ourselves, it will take care of us! Every power within us has the power to kill. So if you run around upon the peaks of emotion, you will get nowhere. That is why meditation is so important; it has the power to keep us quiet. Tranquillity is the gate to entering Buddhism. But many monks fail here and perish because of this searching desire, this doubt, this reasoning. So they cannot keep themselves quiet in this house that is afire. You know about the fisherman, don't you, who gave away his net and followed Christ?

"There is no Buddha, no Way, no Dharma to seek! There is no such thing. This is the famous hammer with which Lin-chi destroys all hypotheses and all contrivances. The Buddha destroyed all previous religions, as well, gave up his philosophical research and sat in meditation under the Bodhi Tree; and there he entered into *samadhi*. When you enter *samadhi*, you must give up all affectations and just sit and act like a good baby! In such a psychological moment there is no Way and no Buddha. Nothing is better than the mind when it takes a real, honest attitude. Is there anything more beautiful than that? At such a moment, there is no Buddha to search for; Mind-itself is Buddha. For the Way and the Law, there is no need to seek outside this Mind. Mind does not exist in your brain, in your heart or body. If I as this Mind create the human word, certainly I will call all parts of the body and all exterior objects Mind, as well. So the fire that is burning in the sky is Mind, too—and the silver moonlight.

"If you pursue the Buddha of visible form, he is not similar to yourself." The Buddha of visible form is the Buddha that is characterized by eighty signs of nobility; you can see these signs on carved statutes of him. This is the visible form, and not similar to you. But in the *sutras* it is said the Buddha's first words were, "In heaven and on the earth, I am the only one to be revered!" This "only one" is *here*. [Points to self].

"If you wish to know your soul, it is neither within nor apart from your attention." What is this attention? Can you see your own eye? If you cannot see nor handle your own soul, how do you attend to it? It's like a bird: if you pay too much attention to it, it will not sing. If you don't, it does. When you are given the koan, "Where is your soul at this moment? Show it to me," how will you answer?

"Brothers, the true Buddha is without form; the true Way is without body; the true Dharma is without signs." That is, no place.

"These three are one and in one place. If you are unable to understand this, you will be called a being of karmic-consciousness." A being of karmic-consciousness is an unawakened soul traveling through mountain peaks of fire, not knowing its place or what it is. You may see it while still

sleeping. You are traveling through the peaks blindly, and you may fall below.

(No commentaries survived for Sokei-an's first translation of Discourses XIX through XXI. They are presented as is. ed)

XIX

Someone asked the Master, "What is the true Buddha, the true Dharma, the true Way? Please reveal their significance."

The Master said: "Buddha is purity of mind; Dharma is effulgence of mind; the Way is the light of mind that is without hindrance wherever it penetrates. These three are one, yet they are empty names and have no true substance. With the true man of the Way, every moment of mind is without interruption.

"When Bodhidharma came from the West, he searched for one who would not be enticed by anyone's views. Later, when he met the Second Patriarch, he understood him in one word and realized he was exhausting himself in fruitless efforts.

"The view I hold today is not at variance with that of the Buddha. He who attains it at the first word will become the master of Buddha. He who attains it at the second word will become the master of men and devas. But he who attains it at the third word, cannot even save himself."

XX

Someone asked the Master, "What is the significance of Bodhidharma's coming from the West?"

The master said, "If it had any significance, he would not have saved even himself."

Someone asked, "Since there is no significance, how did the Second Patriarch obtain the Dharma?"

The Master said, "To obtain means to not obtain."

Someone asked, "If it is not to obtain, what's the significance of not obtaining?

The Master said, "Our minds never cease to run about. Therefore, a Patriarch said, 'Superior men! You search for your head with your own head!' When you turn your illumination back upon itself, you will realize that your body and mind are not different from those of Buddha and that you have nothing more to do. This is what is called 'obtaining the Dharma.'

"Good brothers, today out of necessity, I have had to resort to words of desecration. Do not commit an error! In my view there is nothing to reason about. If you are disposed to use it, use it. If you are not, take a rest.

"Everywhere people are talking about the six paramitas and the ten-thousand deeds as constituting Buddha's Dharma. I say such deeds are the sublimity of Buddhism and its application, but they are not Buddha's Dharma itself. Those who have observed the precepts with the intensity of one holding a vase of oil, not wanting to spill a drop, will some day have to pay their debts. Their Dharma-eye being unopened, they will be asked to recompense the cost of their portion of rice! Why is it so? The ancients said, 'He converted to the Dharma, but he did not acquire realization, so he returned to the flesh to pay for the alms that he had received. When the wealthy man reaches eighty-one, the tree will no longer produce the fungus!'

"Those who live upon isolated peaks, eat once at noon, sit upright without lying down, or practice good deeds, are all men creating nothing but karma. And those who give everything away as alms, their heads and eyes, land and abodes, their wives and children, all their treasures—will have no deliverance. Better to be peaceful, be simple and uncomplicated.

"Even the bodhisattva who has attained the tenth stage cannot find any trace of the follower of the Way. Hence it is said, 'All the devas rejoice and the gods of earth clasp his feet in adoration. Of all the buddhas in manifold directions, there is none that does not praise him.' Why? Because the one at this moment listening to my sermon leaves no trace of his activity."

XXI

Someone asked the master, "It is said the Great Supernatural Supermundane Buddha sat for ten kalpas in a shrine of meditation but no buddhadharma was disclosed, so he was unable to obtain the Buddha Way." I wonder what this signifies? I beg the master for elucidation."

The Master said: "'Great Supernatural' denotes your penetration everywhere into the state where all entities are without self-nature or form of their own; therefore this buddha is called Great Supernatural. 'Supermundane' denotes your not entertaining a single doubt anywhere and never acquiring a thing; therefore the name 'Supermundane.' 'Buddha' denotes the pure light of your soul which penetrates throughout the cosmos; therefore 'Buddha.' 'Sat for ten kalpas in a shrine of meditation' means one's conformity with the ten paramitas. 'But no buddhadharma was disclosed,' means that Buddha was not born and Dharma cannot be destroyed. So how can this revelation be disclosed? 'So he was unable to obtain the Buddha Way,' means that Buddha does not attain Buddhahood again. The ancients said, 'Buddha lives in the world but is not stained by the dharmas of the world.'

"Brothers, if you are disposed to attain buddhahood, do not conform to the ten-thousand things. The ancients said, 'When the mind appears, all dharmas appear. When the mind disappears, all dharmas disappear. When no mind arises, all dharmas are free from blame.'

"Neither in this world, nor in the transcendental world do Buddha or Dharma exist; neither do they veil nor unveil themselves. If anything did exist, it would merely be a name, a remedy for a child. A name of itself has no characteristic. Instead, it is the one who is bright and clear, who sees and hears and throws light upon everything that establishes the name.

XXII

"Good brothers! Commit the five nefarious crimes that cause you to fall into the torment of hell, and then you will attain emancipation!"

Someone asked the Master: "What are the five nefarious crimes?"

The Master said, "To kill the father, to kill the mother, to shed the blood of a Buddha, to destroy the harmony of the sangha, to burn the images and holy books. This is committing the five nefarious crimes that cause you to fall into the torment of hell."

Someone asked, "What is the father?"

The Master said, "Ignorance is the father. When for a moment you try to find the place where your mind arises or where it sets, and you cannot find it, like a sound echoing through the sky—this is called 'to kill the father.'"

Someone asked, "What is the mother?"

The Master said, "Greed is the mother. When for a moment in your mind you enter the world of desire pursuing greed, and see that all entities are empty phenomena and you are without adherence to any circumstance—this is called 'to kill the mother.'"

Someone asked, "What is it to shed the blood of a buddha?"

The Master said, "In the pure essential world, where you have not created a single conception and everything is dark and black—this is called 'shedding the blood of a buddha.'"

SOKEI-AN SAYS:

In the last lecture, Lin-chi said, "Good brothers! Commit the five nefarious crimes that cause you to fall into the torment of hell, and then you will attain emancipation!" This hell is uninterrupted torment. It has no space, no time, no cause, and no result. Yet, if you commit the five nefarious crimes and fall into the hell, you will attain emancipation. This is very strange. Lin-chi is using the five nefarious crimes in an odd way, so that he is not easily understood. In this lecture he will begin to explain his words.

Someone asked, "What is the father?" The Master said, "Ignorance is the father. When for a moment you try to find the place where your mind arises or where it sets, and you cannot find it, like a sound echoing through the sky—this is called 'to kill the father.'" You cannot find such a place because your mind appears and disappears. You realize this in meditation when you suddenly enter and come out of non-existence. You call this the "shelf of consciousness." It's like the surface of water: you plunge into it and emerge from it. In your meditation you might strive to find that surface but you cannot because there is no line between the conscious and the unconscious. When you enter, you do not know it; but when you come out, you realize you were in it. So you cannot find that horizon in your mind, that from which it arises and into which it sets.

The sound vibrates to the corners of the universe without hindrance. This is the essential stage, *dharmakaya*. In the stage of phenomena, *nirmanakaya*, it does not [strikes gong]. Its echo resounds back and forth, here and there, but it does not vibrate throughout the universe. But in the essential stage it is like a radio; it goes in all directions without hindrance. The sound of man's mind is the same. It reaches myriad directions at once. This is not a three dimensional existence. It is all directions at once. It is like myriad buddhas all surrounding the self. This law operates at once through the sky, the ocean, everywhere. In the East, all those buddha statues that you see symbolize their manifestation—many hands and feet, and thousands of heads. The monstrous *Avalokiteshvara* is the symbol of this stage.

So Lin-chi says this is the Father. But it is really *sambhogakaya*. When it operates outwardly it is also operating inwardly. This is the condition of one's soul, like Plato's Ideal or perfect flower. In the *Tao Te Ching* this is clearly described as the negative and positive, the *yin* and *yang*. Every unit of universal existence has this, and you feel it in your mind. The infant has a wonderful expression because that freedom is not yet limited in its body, not yet ruled by this material law.

The *sambhogakaya*, the second body, is the Father. Now you understand this law and try to grasp it in your mind but cannot see it. This is killing. You know it but you cannot grasp it. But Lin-chi says it reaches whatever direction it wills without hindrance. It comes back to the same point—but there is no point. If you try to find a center of consciousness in yourself, you cannot. But it exists. Strange, isn't it?

Someone asked, "What is the mother?" The Master said, "Greed is the mother. When for a moment in your mind you enter the world of desire pursuing greed, and see that all entities are empty phenomena and you are

without adherence to any circumstance—this is called 'to kill the mother.'"
This is the third body, *nirmanakaya*. It operates in only one direction.
So the second law operates in ten thousand directions at once and the
third operates in only one, as phenomena. There are myriad forms in this
nirmanakaya—this world of transformation. We have this second law,
sambhogakaya, but we live in the third, the accidental law, *nirmanakaya*;
therefore we suffer, trying to enter *sambhogakaya*. If we must use a stone
to make a spark for fire, this is the way we must operate, the way to realize
freedom. We must give up the idea of a fourth-dimensional law and enter
into the natural law of the accidental. The great man does not oppose
the natural law, while the small man opposes it and fights it. As a unit of
the whole, you cannot fight it; you must go with it, like a cloud. But you
should not go blindly—you must know the second law and use the third.
This theory is clearly shown in the *Tao Te Ching*.

*Someone asked, "What is it to shed the blood of a buddha?" The
Master said, "In the pure essential world, where you have not created a
single conception and everything is dark and black—this is called 'shedding
the blood of a buddha.'"* This is the first law and the hardest point of
Buddhism. If you try to understand it, it will come down to the second
or third law. The pure essential world—Isness, in Sanskrit—is the
dharmadhatu. It is the same as the "before father and mother" koan.

"Dark and black" is not good; no such thing exists in that stage. If you
say black, then you postulate white, and there is no negative and positive;
so this is not a true description. Lin-chi must have been up against it to
use this poor expression.

This first law is the entrance to Zen. In the pitch dark, the wooden
man sings and the stone woman dances. When you have entered this gate,
you will understand the second and third laws; and then your teacher will
take you back to the first. The second time it is hard to grasp, and many
students fail here.

*Someone asked, "What is it to destroy the harmony of the
sangha?"*
*The Master said, "When for a moment in your mind you
truly realize that all afflictions are void like the sky and that*

there is nothing to rely upon—this is 'destroying the harmony of the sangha.'"

Someone asked, "What is it to burn images and holy books?"

The Master said, "When you observe that cause and relation are empty and that mind and phenomena are empty, you come to the determination to transcend all existence and to become peaceful—this is 'to burn images and holy books.'"

"Good brothers, attain this and you will be free from the obstruction of such names as 'holy' or 'profane.' Your mind at this moment is creating meaning with an empty fist, kneading dough out of your senses and circumstances.

"Attaching little importance to yourself, you say, 'I am a commoner; he is the saint!'

"Bald Idiots! Why are you so busy wrapping yourself in lions' skins and crying out like jackals? You are great men who do not breathe like great men. Unable to believe in that which is in your own house, you only look outside and establish yourselves upon the useless words of the ancients. Relying on the negative and wandering over the positive, you are unable to reach the goal. When you are in contact with a circumstance, you join with it. When you are in contact with some dust, you adhere to it. Wherever you are, you harbor doubt. You have no standard of judgment.

SOKEI-AN SAYS:

Lin-chi is speaking of the five cardinal sins, but his meaning is entirely different from the usual meaning. Here he is speaking about the unnecessary superstructure of the human mind. And, according to Lin-chi, we will attain the true ground by destroying these unnecessary superstructures. Your mind is living in the bushes of mind-stuff. Cut off the bushes and then you will understand how the bushes of mind-stuff grow out of your mind. You will really find the religious ground—the real home of mind, body, and life. Buddhism is very simple if you truly grasp its essential doctrine.

Someone asked, "What is it to destroy the harmony of the sangha?" The *sangha* of the Buddha can not be destroyed but the *sangha* of your mind must be destroyed. In Buddha's *sangha* are many monks keeping harmony within themselves. In this temple there are many monks making a *sangha* of many thoughts. Each thought is a monk, and these thoughts are like a rainbow in the sky. The rainbow is floating, and that bridge has no ground on which to depend. These thoughts also have no ground to depend upon. If there are no thoughts, there will be no afflictions to intertwine. If you understand the real ground of mind, it is like the sky that has no clouds and no rainbow. You annihilate this *sangha* from your mind in order to see the real ground of mind and realize it. So destroying this *sangha* is necessary to attain real religion.

The Master said, "When for a moment in your mind you truly realize that all afflictions are void like the sky and that there is nothing to rely upon—this is 'destroying the harmony of the sangha.'" You must have an empty mind.

Someone asked, "What is it to burn images and holy books?" The Master said, "When you observe that cause and relation are empty and that mind and phenomena are empty, you come to the determination to transcend all existence and to become peaceful—this is 'to burn images and holy books.'" So you do not need temples in the mind, nor books, nor symbols, nor words. Burn them in the fire so you can find the real ground of mind.

"Good brothers, attain this and you will be free from the obstruction of such names as 'holy' or 'profane.'" "Holy" is only a word that you speak before you see reality.

"Your mind at this moment is creating meaning with an empty fist, kneading dough out of your senses and circumstances." So much outside, so many sense impressions that you knead dough out of it. The circumferences are the five sense organs with the seven different colors, sounds, and so forth, this three-dimensional existence.

Without this outside, your sense organs do not exist, just as phenomena do not exist without the sense organs which create them. You take this seriously, and knead the dough all day when it is unessential. In one moment, you see *tathagata*—Ah! Wash off all mind-stuff and use the brain like lightning. It has material movement without words. Without such a brain you cannot use Zen in your daily life.

"Attaching little importance to yourself, you say, 'I am a commoner; he is the saint!'" If you know your real importance, it's not necessary to knead dough! You are bored, however, for you do not know what to do, because you cannot grasp the true meaning of life. You say, "Well, I am just a common man after all, and he's a Saint Francis. We are not the same."

That is your conclusion. From the real standpoint, there is no buddha and no common man.

"Bald Idiots! Why are you so busy wrapping yourself in lions' skins and crying out like jackals?" What is the pressing matter from morning to evening? You are running after something to find yourself, running after your own shadow, your own reasoning. Your brain is smarter than you are. Without reasoning it understands the answer. Before you construct a logical system, your brain has already grasped the answer.

In God's skin you make a human cry! When you realize this wonderful power to know, you will understand that it is the one treasure in the world. Earth is wonderful, but it has no power to know. The human is smart, but he has very little power of knowing himself. But God is wonderful and has complete power to know and has always known. So we say that Shakyamuni Buddha attained enlightenment under the Bodhi Tree, but he had already attained it in the remotest past incarnation.

We have this power to know, but the power is not the human being. We use a little of it, but with many hindrances and ill-fated conditions, we cannot use its full power. That is why we make a fox-cry in the lion's skin.

"You are great men who do not breathe like great men. Unable to believe in that which is in your own house, you only look outside and establish yourselves upon the useless words of the ancients." You search outside for this wonderful power, not believing that you have it. It is inherent and you do not know it.

When a foreigner comes to Japan, he cries, "What wonderful art! These wood-prints—no other country has these." Then the old Japanese grandfather will dig up all the old prints from the wastebasket. The foreigner will buy them for a large sum. "Ah, these must be good!" You never believe your own is good. You search in books and you meditate—foolish! The heavenly drum is in yourself.

Well, the ancients used a million words to express themselves, but words are utensils like a glass; you can make the utensil, but there is nothing to put in it.

"Relying on the negative and wandering over the positive, you are unable to reach the goal." In the *Tao Te Ching*, positive and negative are called *yin* and *yang*. All opposites are a product of mind,. No such things exist. Before father and mother (positive and negative) what were you? Before creation, after creation—nonsense!

"When you are in contact with a circumstance, you join with it." It becomes your mental attitude; you become one with the circumstance.

"When you are in contact with some dust, you adhere to it." All phenomena are the circumference (the cherry blossom, the great ocean)—Ah! You adhere to everything without knowing your own inherent nature.

"Wherever you are you harbor doubt. You have no standard of judgment." You are always puzzling. You have doubt at every moment because you have no standard of judgment. To have judgment you must have the real earth as ground for judgment. The field is the criterion of the farmer: he sows the seed and the field gives him the answer. Of course he must enrich his ground.

The Zen student must take pride in his own ground of mind. But if it is like a desert and has no life in it, he must cultivate that ground and make it beautiful. It is the foundation of his life; it has the law in it. To find this ground and to use it is the way of religion. Philosophy and art can grow on that ground, but the religious student must stand upon it, and then he can enjoy everything that grows out of it.

"Brothers, don't be taken in by my exposition. Why? Because expositions are not the foundation itself. They are drawings on the void, symbols represented by a painting or carving.

"Brothers, don't take Buddha as the absolute. In my view he's a dung pit. Both the bodhisattva and the arhat are stocks that confine one. This is the reason Manjushri decided to kill Gautama with his sword and why Angulimalya attempted to harm Shakyamuni with his dagger.

"Brothers, no buddha can be acquired. Even the three vehicles, the five natures, and the teachings of enlightenment are but medicines to cure particular illnesses. There is no essential way. Even if there were something, it would only be a likeness, an arrangement of letters on a poster—like what I am saying now.

"Brothers, then there are the usual baldheads who endeavor within to attain the transcendental. They have also committed an error. If one seeks Buddha, one misses the Buddha. If one

seeks the Way, one misses the Way. If one seeks the patriarchs, one misses the patriarchs."

SOKEI-AN SAYS:

Lin-chi tells his disciples not to be taken in by his words. Following the words of the ancients is only drifting around pursuing rainbows. They are not real. Words are not reality. For example, when people think of a forest, they only think about the trees and bushes, they forget the ground, the foundation itself. But without the ground, there is no forest. It is the same when a man tries to grasp the reality of his own nature; he always searches for words and for conceptions, and so forth. He only has bushes. So when he gets entangled, and forgets the ground of his own nature, how can he grasp reality? The farmer must have a field or there will be no vegetables. If you keep all your groceries of knowledge in your brain, you are just a farmer of groceries, not a real farmer of wisdom.

That is why Lin-chi says it is like a Chinese painting on the sky. The sky is empty and the picture is but a phantom; it has no real existence, no power of existence. Red, blue, and so on, exist only as phenomena. Phenomena depend upon the five senses. Everyone attempts to find truth from this phenomenal world, but one who knows it is a mirage would rather look into empty space, the real ground of all phenomena.

"Brothers, don't take Buddha as the absolute. "This Buddha is not Shakyamuni Buddha. Buddha in Sanskrit means the Knower, *bodhi*, to know. Shakyamuni Buddha is only the representation of this great Knower.

"In my view he's a dung pit." Lin-chi always uses this type of expression. Though he says this, make no mistake. He has no intention of destroying morality. It is just that purity or impurity do not exist or have any reality.

"Both the bodhisattva and the *arhat* are stocks that confine one." If you observe nature very clearly, nature has no *atman*; we have *atman*. The true *atman* feels karma, judges the sin, commits the sin, receives the punishment and reward.

"This is the reason Manjushri decided to kill Gautama with his sword and why Angulimalya attempted to harm Shakyamuni with his dagger." Shakyamuni is the one who enshrined this power of knowing in his flesh. The real knower is the principle that we try to attain. We all have this

sword. So decide everything in everyday life without puzzling. You call it intuition.

"*Brothers, no buddha can be acquired.*" When you believe that you have grasped buddha-nature, this is only the ego action of mind. When it is truly attained, there is no sign of its acquirement. When you enter *samadhi*, as in meditation, there is no sign of *samadhi*; you do not think to yourself, "I am now in meditation, I am now in *samadhi*." To grasp Buddha is just the same. This is the real sign of attaining Buddha.

"*Even the three vehicles, the five natures, and the teachings of enlightenment are but medicines to cure particular illnesses—there is no essential way. Even if there were something, it would only be a likeness, an arrangement of letters on a poster—like what I am saying now!*

The three vehicles are the *shravakayana, pratyekabuddhayana,* and *bodhisattvayana.* The *shravakayana* can be translated as the "vehicle of the listener." The *shravaka* listens to the Buddha when he speaks the law according to the Four Noble Truths and the Eightfold Path. He annihilates his afflictions and attains the state of an *arhat.* He stands upon the ground of nirvana and observes the operation of the law of causation—the blooming of the flower in the spring, the falling of the leaf in the autumn—and he realizes the mysterious law of the universe. He has the seed of buddhahood in himself. He will realize emptiness in himself, and he lives his daily life in tranquillity.

He who practices in the *pratyekabuddhayana* is the "solitary one," the one who lives without relating to any other. He observes the twelve stages of causation in existence, but he himself remains outside. He comes to an understanding of nature and the universe. His goal is to save himself.

The *bodhisattvayana* takes the standpoint of compassion, working for the salvation of all sentient beings. He understands Buddhism directly and immediately; he enters the life of a human being and promulgates the law.

These three types are the three foundations of Buddhism. Judging by these natures, the teacher knows whether or not the listener is able to attain enlightenment or not. His attitude is not the same toward all students; he changes according to the five kinds of natures of the listeners. But Lin-chi says that all ways of understanding, all types of Buddhism or of students, are just medicine for the cure of illnesses according to their type. You talk about reality but it is not reality itself; it is like an advertisement. All three types are just different types of posters.

"*Brothers, then there are the usual baldheads who endeavor within to attain the transcendental. They have also committed an error.*" Aha! If Lin-chi says nothing, he must mean something! In Chinese music there are eight sounds. Silence is the first sound. It is like zero—you must count it as a number—so silence is a good zero. The monks listen to the words, but they cannot grasp buddhahood, which goes contrary to the word.

"*If one seeks Buddha, one misses the Buddha. If one seeks the Way, one misses the Way. If one seeks the patriarchs, one misses the patriarchs.*" So where is Buddha? It is like asking a cat to come to you! The cat will come of itself. So, when you forget about it, suddenly you will realize Buddha. And when you think about *bodhi* and the Dharma, you are trying to catch a shadow.

I hope you will all have the opportunity to meet Buddha!

"*Good brothers, do not commit an error. I do not care if you are well informed about the sutras and shastras. I do not care if you are a king or a minister. I do not care if you are as eloquent as a river, or if you are sagacious and intelligent. I only want you to have true understanding.*"

"*Brothers! Even if you master a hundred* sutras *and the* shastras, *it is better than to be one who does nothing. If you master them, you will only regard others with contempt, like the battles of asuras and the egotism of humans that increases the karma of hell. Even Sunaksatra bikshu, who obtained the knowledge of the twelve divisions of the teachings, fell into hell alive—the earth would not pardon him. Better be peaceful and take a rest. I eat when I am hungry, and I close my eyes when I am drowsy. The idiot laughs at me, but the wise man understands.*"

SOKEI-AN SAYS:

Last time Lin-chi said that if you seek Buddha, you will miss Buddha. If you seek *bodhi*, you will miss *bodhi*. And if you seek Dharma, you will miss the Dharma. Why? Buddhism is your own mind. Where is your mind?

Lin-chi has a clear view of true Buddhism. He knows that a true understanding of the universe has nothing to do with the intellect. If it bothers your brain it has no value; it is of no use in any predicament. So he tells us that he doesn't care about our knowledge, no matter how good our understanding is of the *sutras* and *shastras*. He says he doesn't care a fig for it. Perhaps you are a *maharajah*; he doesn't care as well.

Lin-chi is abusing all of the virtuous abilities of the human being and his precious position in the world because he is placing emphasis upon *this* mind. He prefers only your true understanding. This true understanding is the important thing. It is not so easy to grasp! If I ask you, "What is this glass?" it is not easy to answer. In China, a Zen master pointed to a wooden water pot and said to his disciples, "If you do not call this a water pot, what is it?" One by one the disciples gave various answers, like "universe," "reality," "infinite," "piece of wood," and so forth. The Master did not approve any answer. Then a disciple, the cook, kicked it across the floor and left the room. The teacher approved. It is easy to speak of noumena, phenomena, or reality; but if I ask you what reality is, you will try to explain with another word. It is like driving another nail in to drive the first nail out. So you do not have true understanding. If you cannot understand this glass, you will not attain true understanding of everything. And if you do not find this understanding, your life is not a true life; you come like a dream and go like a mirage. We must not be content with such dreaming! We must have something that is true in our life.

You know, in English, you always speak of I, I, I. It seems to me like a tall telegraph pole standing in the center. When we Japanese write a letter, we prefer not to use this I-ness. On some occasions we are compelled to do so, so I always write it into the margin or some unostentatious place. When we know we are existing relatively, we cannot take the egotistic attitude any longer. The karma we thus create is bad enough. But Lin-chi calls it "hell karma." And if you are like Sunaksatra who obtained the knowledge of the twelve divisions of the Buddha teachings but then fell into hell, you are in a dangerous pit. This *bikshu*, which means monk, came to the end of existence, and then returned—he had realized emptiness—but it was only a conception. Emptiness is not a conception of the human being. It is real emptiness.

Many students fall into this pit and do not come back. At this point, you must open your mind, humbly, and take it as it exists. It is not easy!

You must make a door out of it—break through—and then you will get it. So Lin-chi says—

"*Better be peaceful and take a rest.*" Being peaceful means attaining true understanding. Then you have nothing more to do. You eat lettuce and peas, and speak nothing. You have reached the goal.

> "*Brothers, do not seek in letters. When you use the mind you will only be fatigued. Inhaling cold air is of no use. It is better to abide where no mind arises and to go beyond the bodhisattvas who depend upon the pseudo teachings of the three vehicles.*
>
> "*Good brothers, do not spend your days haphazardly. In the past, when I had no understanding, the world was pitch black, but I knew that I could not pass my time in vain. So with a boiling abdomen and a bewildered heart, I ran around and sought the Dharma. Finally, I obtained assistance, so now I can talk with you like this. I advise you, brothers, not to strive only for your livelihood. Life in this world passes swiftly, and meeting a real teacher seldom comes to pass—as seldom as the blooming of the udumbara tree.*"

SOKEI-AN SAYS:

In the last lecture, Lin-chi tells us that gathering information about Buddhism is not Zen, nor even the practice of meditation. If Buddhism is just the study of something, it is better to study the arts. They are a real help to one's life. If you study Zen, you must live in it. In everyday life, one should feel and do Zen at every moment. If you feel it every moment, the law that is written in your heart, you will understand this attitude. The cherry blossom comes with the spring. The maple is rouged in the autumn. The wheat field becomes a palate of silver when the sun sets. It is hard to take this attitude, however. Confucius said, "At twenty I began my study. At thirty I studied the way of life, and at forty I puzzled no more. At fifty I understood my fate, my destiny—and whatever I have, I affirm, taking no opposition. I act and speak according to this decision, and always go with the law of great nature."

We must not wait till we are seventy. We must realize THAT earlier!

"Brothers, do not seek in letters. When you use the mind you will only be fatigued." Particularly, you cannot get it from books. You must get it from the experience of every moment—you will see the evidence in daily action, that which is *written* in books. Watch your own feeling and the reaction of others, this is more like Zen than the koan you are working on. But you use your mind to understand the meaning of Buddhism, and what do you get?

"Inhaling cold air is of no use." And vomiting hot fire is no use either (this comes from a *sutra*). It is very tedious. You go somewhere and get abused by vulgar people and you feel disgust. The great teacher goes to meet another in simple garb. A true man does not show his success,. He has humility. You must realize Zen in such a way.

"It is better to abide where no mind arises and to go beyond the bodhisattvas who depend upon the pseudo teachings of the three vehicles." This "no mind arises" is important. I have experienced it in the middle of the battlefield—a shriek. But no mind arises! In daily life, you smile, you grow angry in abuse—but no mind arises.

You must find that particular spot, the point in your mind that is absolutely vacant, purely empty. When you find that point, you are not bothered by any words and you do not fall into causality; you take a plain, simple attitude, which is the true center of mind. Seeing your teacher, you put off the golden robe and put on the cotton robe. True feeling comes naturally. That is the place where no-mind arises. All is the flowing tide of nature.

"Good brothers, do not spend your days haphazardly." Buddhist today and Christian tomorrow! In this way you will get nothing in a whole lifetime.

"In the past, when I had no understanding, the world was pitch black." Lin-chi confesses. All was just one monotonous dharmakaya—pitch black—like a black ox sleeping in the dark, or the crow in the blackness without a sound. How can you realize the ox and the crow?

"But I knew that I could not pass my time in vain." Day and night you must be watchful.

"So with a boiling abdomen and a bewildered heart, I ran around and sought the Dharma. Finally, I obtained assistance, so now I can talk with you like this." Such a day did not come suddenly for him. With his yearning heart and boiling abdomen he attained it. Everyone talks about

the law written in the book, but it is very hard to realize it in one's self and still harder to perform it in daily life.

We can usually measure how far we have succeeded in performing the law written within ourselves. *Sanzen* is one of the measures; it is not the practice of pursuing a hypothesis or a philosophical conclusion. But with the help of a teacher, the disciple struggles to operate his own law, and the teacher also struggles with the disciple's manifestation of it. However, both student and teacher must be good!

Sometimes when a teacher takes drastic action, measures the pupil, the pupil will think, "Perhaps I have not paid enough money." When this happens the teacher cannot struggle with the student with full force, he cannot use him kindly, cannot use his hand—he keeps it in his pocket. With such a pupil, the teacher is always very much disappointed.

"I advise you, brothers, not to strive only for your livelihood." This was said by the Buddha and is often repeated. Your livelihood is in Dharma; *Dharma* is not your livelihood. Your food, your roof, your clothes, your everyday equipment, is in the Dharma Mind of yourself, and Dharma Mind is not in these.

When I came to America the last time and was staying in a layman's house for eight months, my teacher wrote me a letter, "Your daily provision is in your Dharma Mind." But I had lost it and had to seek for it again. His words were true; it was in my *Dharma* Mind. We believe Buddha does not feed us—our link is in our *Dharma* Mind and not vice versa. *Dharma* Mind is the first thing that we have to uphold. There is deep significance underlying this word, which is somehow the heart of Buddhism. We cannot reach there by philosophy. The Zen student is not a philosopher. He must have deep faith—in a real predicament he has some little moment in which he can smile.

"Life in this world passes swiftly, and meeting a real teacher seldom comes to pass—as seldom as the blooming of the udumbara tree." I don't think there is a need to explain this. I entered the monastery when I was twenty; now I am over fifty. It could have been but a few days ago! My commandment teacher wrote me, "Your future is universal like the ocean." I should say that my evening has already come. But my way is far to reach.

It is not hard to find a teacher who will talk about this and that, or who will read to you from a cookbook—you can even have a good time in argument. But it is a rare opportunity when you find a teacher who will take every notion, every hypothesis, from your brain and give you some understanding of the truth. It is the same in Japan today: hundreds of students go to this or that temple that have different schools of thought— or even this and that temple of Zen—yet, they seldom find a truly enlightened teacher. An authentic teacher is so simple that the students cannot believe it; they say things like, "Is he really enlightened?" or "We saw him swimming in some pool!" They think he should have long silvery whiskers, a bent backbone and a glaring eye. Should they see such a real teacher at the movies—"Oh!"

The udumbara tree when it blooms is a rare thing, and like the cherry blossom, it is a sign of the advent of Buddha. When Buddha comes, the udumbara blooms, but it blooms in your own mind. Though you are ignorant, occasionally a flash comes across your mind; you may open your eye and change your view entirely—"Perhaps the one I saw swimming is a real teacher!"

But the udumbara does not bloom often; the mind is usually covered up by conventions that are not your own thoughts. These thoughts of yours are like suits of clothes made in a store, and you buy them. But they were not made for you, so they are not like your own.

"Everywhere you hear of this old fellow Lin-chi, so you come here with your queries to shut him up so he cannot answer. However, overwhelmed by this mountain monk's actualization of wholeness, you vacantly stare and cannot move your mouths, and you do not know how to answer me. Then, of course, I say to you, 'An ass can't endure being trampled on by a dragon elephant.'

"You are always hitting your chests and sticking out your ribs, saying, 'I understand Zen! I understand the Way!' But let two or three of you come here and you don't know what to do. Idiots! Everywhere you go with your body and mind you go fanning your lips, bewitching villages and towns, but someday you will get a beating with iron rods! You are not renouncers of home. You will all be sent to the world of the asuras!

"The way of the ultimate is not the sort of thing that can be obtained by controversy, nor is it the noisy refuting of heretics. In the transmission of the buddhas and patriarchs, there is nothing special. Although there are teachings such as the three vehicles, the five natures, and the cause and effect that leads to the rebirths of men and devas, they all fall into the sphere of seeming truth. But in the teachings of perfect enlightenment, it is not so. Sudhana did not stop at any of these!

"Good brothers, do not use your mind falsely. Be like the great sea that keeps no corpse. But you run about under heaven bearing loads. You yourself raise obstructions that hinder your minds. When the sun ascends, the clouds vanish into the blue. When you have no mist in your eyes, there are no flowers in the sky.

SOKEI-AN SAYS:

In this lecture we are nearing the end of Lin-chi's discourse. Lin-chi is speaking in this section of the students who come to him and cannot do anything. Under his iron rod, one by one, they cannot meet him. They are all standing upon notions, conceptions, mind, matter. They do not know that their feet are really standing upon the earth, so they think this actual existence has nothing to do with Zen. Such an attitude toward Zen is no use; it is insignificant in real life.

"Everywhere you hear of this old fellow Lin-chi, so you come here with your queries to shut him up so he cannot answer." From Southern China, from Northern China, from everywhere you hear of Lin-chi, but have you seen him? No? You must go! So I will go; I will give him a question and make him shut up! This is the attitude of the half-baked Buddhist student. In Lin-chi's time, there was a real struggle between teacher and disciple.

"However, overwhelmed by this mountain monk's actualization of wholeness, you vacantly stare and cannot move your mouths, and you do not know how to answer me." When Chao-chou asked Lin-chi, "What is Buddhism?" Lin-chi grasped his chest and returned the question. Chao-chou was puzzled. Lin-chi slapped him and pushed him back. Chao-chou staggered; his eye vacant. A monk who had observed this interview, asked Chao-chou, "Why not bow to the teacher?" Chao-chou realized that he had been absentminded in this respect. He went

to Lin-chi and bowed, and in that moment—Aha! He entered into enlightenment. At such a moment, he entered wholeness. Nakedly he came into true reality. Such a one is marvelous!

When there is nothing in the mind, this is the precious moment that you will receive the light. But usually the brain is all stocked up with the sawdust of conceptions, philosophy, and whatnot, so it cannot be a conductor of light. But occasionally the veil drops and consciousness and phenomena make real contact, and you realize the whole universe within yourself.

Today, the human brain is more complicated than in the time of Lin-chi, and therefore the teacher uses a more complicated method.

"Then, of course, I say to you, 'An ass can't endure being trampled on by a dragon elephant.'" Most Buddhist teachers speak like phonographs, repeating sentences from sutras, and such. Lin-chi does not speak thus; he stamps upon the student and squashes him!

A Western psychologist went to visit a monk. He vomited thunder (spoke about psychology) for a couple of hours. At the end, the monk asked, "Will you have some tea?" He really stamped upon that blind ass!

A student once observed: "One should feel fear when a master offers tea." A Zen master's action in carrying out the Dharma is very clear, but it is very hard to observe it.

"You are always hitting your chests and sticking out your ribs, saying, 'I understand Zen! I understand the Way!' But let two or three of you come here and you don't know what to do. Idiots! Like mice entering a small tube—they cannot come through or go back—a rat trap. Because their Zen is all notion and theory, they just act out a drama. Real Zen is not a drama, not theory; it is not on the street corner. One could say, the real drama by William Shakespeare is on the street corner, not on Broadway. But Zen is not on the street corner!

"Everywhere you go with your body and mind you go fanning your lips, bewitching villages and towns, but someday you will get a beating with iron rods! That will happen when you enter the dominion of Yama, the God of death. He will give you strokes with his iron rod. Lin-chi is being sarcastic.

"You are not renouncers of home. You will all be sent to the world of the asuras! "You think you are renouncing the world, but you are still disputing, arguing and fighting. The real renouncer is not such a one. The one who is free from the clamor of all mind-stuff—he is the renouncer.

He does not stand upon the conception of reality, but upon new ground, upon reality itself. Such is the real monk. In both China and Japan today, such monks are disappearing.

"The way of the ultimate is not the sort of thing that can be obtained by controversy, nor is it the noisy refuting of heretics." There is nothing to dispute about—spirit and matter, time and space, reality and manifestation. No such things exist in Zen.

In India during a learned dispute, they assembled people by beating drums. Lin-chi must use some word—so he says, "the law of the ultimate." What is this? What is the true ultimate of the Dharma—the goal of attainment? One teacher will say the goal is your own consciousness. So think consciousness is in your body—that you are meditating upon consciousness. Nonsense—you are just keeping quiet! When you close your eyes, you cannot reach consciousness—and when you open your eyes, you cannot catch it. Though you reach your hand to the corner of the universe, you cannot grasp consciousness.

From the noumenal standpoint, reality is a mass of *akasha*, the pure, essential essence constituting the universe. So the koan asks, "The three worlds are empty. Where does your soul (consciousness) come from?" It is not a difficult one.

Ma-tsu gave this koan to Huang-po, who answered: "Buddha is my consciousness." Ma-tsu said, "Buddha is not your consciousness." But Huang-po really understood and replied, "No matter what is said—Buddha is consciousness." A very good answer—but his answer is not in the words. It does not come from the lips of a prescription monk—Huang-po had reached there.

"In the transmission of the buddhas and patriarchs, there is nothing special." From the Buddha to Mahakashyapa to Ananda, and so on—many torches. The flame expires but the fire is maintained—not word to word, but from soul to soul; face to face, this fire is transmitted. This is Zen.

"Although there are teachings such as the three vehicles, the five natures, and the cause and effect that leads to the rebirths of men and devas, they all fall into the sphere of seeming truth." Pseudo Buddhism—beautiful to read, but now degenerated into secondary hypothesis.

"But in the teachings of perfect enlightenment, it is not so." That is, there is nothing to talk about. You must demonstrate directly. Hakuin asked his disciples to show him the sound of one hand. Through such a

koan, one can immediately enter in. It is like the Buddha holding up the blue lotus flower and smiling at Mahakashyapa. He was the only one in the multitude who understood. Zen is begotten here! The Buddha spoke no word, but the torch was handed to Mahakashyapa who "smiled."

"Sudhana did not stop at any of these!" Sudhana, a young priest of India who appears in the *Avatamsaka Sutra,* did not attach to any place or any viewpoint. Because he was a true student he did not remain in the outward pretense of any doctrine, the nonsense of mind-stuff. The real thing you can grasp. But not to grasp anything is not Buddhism! But in Mahayana Buddhism there are many rules—outward pretenses.

"Good brothers, do not use your mind falsely. Be like the great sea that keeps no corpse." If you are the Great Sea, do not keep any dead body in your mind. Do not pursue with the mind the vagaries of truth in the inner or the outer worlds. Do not even keep that lotus flower or the hand of Hakuin. Do not keep one word of the Buddha in your mind. Throw it out! Return to pure activity of mind.

"But you run about under heaven bearing loads. You yourself raise obstructions that hinder your minds." You try to find your soul on the outside—how ridiculous! Analyzing and talking is a way of looking at the soul from the outside. What you call introspection by meditation is also looking from the outside. Many students make this foolish endeavor. Such meditation is of no use. The soul must look at itself—that is the real attitude. If you are a fire, do not observe the bottom of the fire from the top; you must place yourself at the bottom—this is real meditation.

"When the sun ascends, the clouds vanish into the blue." This is the real experience of meditation; forgetting everything, you gaze into the soul; you are born in it. From here you can rise up. Here a real teacher is required; if misled at this point, one may never rise up from the bottom of the soul: This "sun" ascends just as true fire "into the blue." This "blue" is a beautiful word—all mind-stuff vanishes. Then you come into real *shunyata*—emptiness. Emptiness is a dangerous word. If you misunderstand this word, you can fall into nothingness. Nothingness and emptiness are very different.

"When you have no mist in your eyes, there are no flowers in the sky!" Conceptions are like flowers in the sky. If you see a universe made out of your own conceptions, you are not living in the Dharma.

"Brothers, if you wish to live precisely in the Dharma, all you need to do is not harbor doubts. When it expands, it extends throughout the cosmos. When it contracts, there is not a hair's breath to stand upon. It is clear and bright. It has never been lacking. No one has seen it, and no one has heard it. So what do you call it? The ancients said, 'To talk of it does not hit the mark.' Seek it only in yourselves! Is there anything that exists?

"There will be no end to this discourse. You, yourselves must strive! Farewell!"

SOKEI-AN SAYS:

How do you grasp this "it"? In philosophy, reality is discussed, but one must *know* this reality must *realize* it. Pure Dharma is reality. Noumena and phenomena are just terms, philosophical terms, used to discuss reality and non-reality, that is all. You can carry mind-matter and convictions with you as the outcome of your philosophy, that which is merely a prescription for medicine or a menu for food; but no matter how much you think and read about it, after all, it is just a prescription, just a menu for food. You do not get a *real* dose of medicine or a *real* dinner. A teacher will say to you, "reality exists as pure subjectivity, pure essential body. But all that you can feel or taste, and so forth, is subjective, since all that you perceive (receive from perception) is the shadow of reality. reality itself is incomprehensible; that is, we cannot see it or hear it. It is not white or black or transparent. It is not space, nor is it time, nor waves of electricity. So when you think you understand reality, and someone asks you, "What is this glass of water?" you are puzzled. You can talk about it, but you cannot grasp it and do not realize it.

The relative view, noumena and phenomena, raises a fence between *this* and *that*, so you cannot grasp it. If you cannot understand this reality in the beginning of religious experience, you cannot enter into the gate of religion. Philosophy *talks* about reality (this is the first chapter), but in religion you must *realize* it. Inside this reality, the mystery of the world will be revealed; outside you will never understand this mystery. Today, we use many avenues to enter—optics, dynamics, and so forth; but through the experience of these sense organs, you cannot enter this reality. The ancients, those who lived two or three thousand years ago, strove to enter in a different way. In Sanskrit, Brahma Dharma signifies that reality. Some call it noumena, but I prefer the word reality.

"Brothers, if you wish to live precisely in the Dharma, all you need to do is not harbor doubts." Dharma is the law, the reality, the actuality (picks up glass), the body and the action: With this body and this action. You must live precisely in this universal Dharma where man and the universe are one, or no man and no universe. If you are with the law itself, the Dharma, you are truly a religious man. You will not conceive any questions. Lin-chi said that if you have no doubt, you are enlightened. It is hard to realize this attitude of mind.

"When it expands, it extends throughout the cosmos." We call "it" by many names: God, Allah, Brahma, reality, *tathagata*, or noumena and phenomena, but they are just names. There is no end to the universe. Einstein said space has an end, but is boundless. Time has a beginning and end, but is limitless. If you have long, long hands stretching into space, you realize that your fingertips must extend throughout the *dharmadhatu*.

"When it contracts, there is not a hair's breadth to stand upon. In centripetal constriction, you will find no center and no point upon which even a pinpoint could stand.

"It is clear and bright. It has never been lacking. No one has seen it, and no one has heard it." These statements really indicate the deepest point of Buddhism. There are no descriptions of God—if you have no mist in your eyes. Some claim to have seen him and met him face to face, and it is very interesting: "I saw half of his body," says one. Another says, "I have never seen him."

These experiences are *all* true descriptions of the meeting: "I am confronting Him." "I can see Him, hear Him, and touch Him." These are all true descriptions. Seeing "half of His body" and "I have never seen Him" are also true descriptions. If you have the real experience, you will understand all these statements and prove your experience of meeting Him.

"No one has seen it and no one has heard it" is having one wedge to drive the other out. The last word is "no." How do you take this "no" away? You cannot do so if you must express it in words. A Zen teacher will ask you, "What is the *dharmakaya*?" The student starts to make an answer, but the teacher quickly closes the student's mouth. Then—"Ah!" The student understands.

"So what do you call it? The ancients said, 'To talk of it does not hit the mark.' Seek it only in yourselves!" You cannot explain it by metaphor or

allegory; no word strikes home. This "in yourselves" is misleading. You can meditate for a hundred years on something within yourself, and if you say "I saw something in myself," that is a lie.

"Is there anything that exists?" If you wash everything away, even the blue of the clear sky, what happens then?

"There will be no end to this discourse. You, yourselves must strive! Farewell!" Here Lin-chi ends his discourse and says, "Farewell!"

Examinations

I

One day, when Huang-po had an occasion to enter the kitchen, he casually questioned the head cook, "What are you doing?"

The head cook said, "I am sorting the rice for the monks."

Huang-po asked, "How much do they eat in a day?"

The monk said, "About three bushels."

Huang-po asked, "Isn't that too much?"

The monk said, "My fear is that it is not enough."

Huang-po struck him.

Later the cook related the incident to the Master. The Master said, "I will test that old fellow about this for you."

When the Master went and stood beside Huang-po, Huang-po told him about his conversation.

Then the Master asked, "Isn't that too much?"

Huang-po said, "Why not reply, 'Tomorrow we ought to have another dose?'"

The Master said, "Why must it be tomorrow? Take it now!"

Thereupon the Master slapped Huang-po in the face.

Huang-po said, "This lunatic has come again to pull the tiger's whiskers!"

The Master thundered, "HO!" and left the room.

Later, Kuei-shan asked Yang-shan, "What was the two venerable ones' intention?

Yang-shan asked, "What do you think?"

Kuei-shan said, "Fostering a child one knows the love of a father."

Yang-shan said, "I do not agree with you."

Kuei-shan asked, "Then what do you think about it?"

> *Yang-shan said, "It's something like this: keeping a thief in
> the home damages the home."*

SOKEI-AN SAYS:

I shall try to elucidate this first examination for you. Lin-chi died in
866, so he was about 30 years of age at the time. Huang-po, Lin-chi's teacher
(who was about seven feet high), was a disciple of Po-chang Huai-hai,
whose teacher was Ma-tsu Tao-i. Ma-tsu was a disciple of Nan-yueh
Huai-jang, and Huai-jang's teacher was Hui-neng, the Sixth Patriarch.

*One day, when Huang-po had an occasion to enter the kitchen, he
casually questioned the head cook."* Usually the abbot and Zen Master will
not enter the kitchen. Something is about to happen!

"What are you doing?" The head cook is not a young monk, of course.
He has been training for a while. He probably had an enlightened eye.
Who this monk was is not clear in the record. So it is not an idle question.

The head cook said, "I am sorting the rice for the monks." Before
polishing the rice, he must sort out the yellow kernels and small pebbles,
which is not an easy task in such large quantities. On this occasion, the
reality of the Universe is in the state of the monk and in his action. When
one comes to this state of understanding, life becomes precious at every
moment. Such a one is not living blindly.

The cook's answer was good, but Huang-po wished to test his
enlightenment.

*Huang-po asked, "How much do they eat in a day?" The monk said,
"About three bushels." Huang-po asked, "Isn't that too much?"* Too much
or too little! Dangerous words! In observing from the real standpoint is
there anything *too* much or *too* little? Huang-po has poison in his mind,
trying to test this cook.

The monk said, "My fear is that it is not enough." Ha! The cook did
not understand clearly enough Huang-po's question. He fell into the trap
of "more or less." Before that, Huang-po had asked the "quantity" eaten
in a day. We do not really know what he was speaking about, rice or
something else. There was nothing wrong in the cook's answer here, but it
was a ticklish moment.

Huang-po struck him. I am quite sure he struck him with his staff.
Huang-po, an old Zen master, would have a long staff. The poor cook must
give in; he doesn't understand why Huang-po hit him, and to hit, in Zen, is to
show him the *actualization*. Out of compassion, Huang-po tried to show him.

Later the cook related the incident to the Master. The Master said, "I will test that old fellow about this for you." Lin-chi would find out what his teacher really thinks.

When the Master went and stood beside Huang-po. In a Zen temple, when the Master is seated cross-legged upon a big square stool, the disciples come in, join their hands, and usually stand on his left side, their hands folded upon the breast until noticed by the teacher. If there is no word from him after about ten or fifteen minutes, the disciples will bow and turn away. So Lin-chi stood beside his teacher. That day Huang-po must have been in a good humor, so he told the story. He was sure Lin-chi was trying to sniff out something and Huang-po wanted to test him. And Lin-chi was also trying to fish something out of Huang-po. Both famous fishers looking for trouble. Something must happen. Lin-chi asked the question in a special way. Perhaps Lin-chi thought that Huang-po might say a word that the cook should have said.

Huang-po told him about his conversation. Then the Master asked, "Isn't that too much?" Lin-chi repeated Huang-po's question. Then, unexpectedly and softly, Huang-po said—

"Why not reply, 'Tomorrow we ought to have another dose?'" Another bushel, but in the record it is written "another dose, like a dose of medicine, or of abuse, or a dose of the fist! Huang-po is inviting trouble. He knows Lin-chi's nature.

The Master said, "Why must it be tomorrow? Take it now!" Thereupon the Master slapped Huang-po in the face. That was expected. He gave Huang-po a dose, and Huang-po was really tickled to death. "Ah, my disciple thinks this way!" Had Lin-chi paused to think it over, Huang-po would have driven him out!

Huang-po said, "This lunatic has come again to pull the tiger's whiskers!" Huang-po is pretending to be angry, but in his heart he is so very glad. Lin-chi had slapped him before, of course. Some old reverend, a missionary in China, said, "Lin-chi had the power to pull whiskers and pass through the blade of a sword." I do not understand what he meant by that, but I shall not criticize him, he's a dead man. But had I met him, I certainly would have said something good!

The Master thundered, "HO!" and left the room. This is a good passage of arms.

Later, Kuei-shan asked Yang-shan, "What was the two venerable ones' intention? Yang-shan asked, "What do you think?" Kuei-shan said,

"*Fostering a child one knows the love of a father.*" Kuei-shan Ling-yu's [771-853] style of Zen is different from Lin-chi's. The Zen between Huang-po and Lin-chi is like lightning. Here it is like a good father and a good child. Kuei-shan felt the joy of Huang-po at having such a wonderful disciple. He showed his heart to his disciple Yang-shan Hui-chi [807-883]. But Yang-shan did not say, "Yes, father," he tried to challenge his teacher.

Yang-shan said, "I do not agree with you." Kuei-shan asked, "Then what do you think about it?" Yang-shan said, "It's something like this: keeping a thief in the home damages the home." Huang-po in keeping such a thief as Lin-chi will have his house overturned.

Kuei-shan acknowledges Lin-chi's actuality and sympathizes with Huang-po's delight. Although there was a distance of two or three hundred miles between the temples of Huang-po and Kuei-shan, there was a heart-to-heart understanding between them.

II

The Master asked a monk, "Where do you come from?"
The monk gave a HO!
The Master asked him to be seated. The monk hesitated.
The Master struck him.
The Master saw another monk coming. The Master raised his flywhisk. The monk bowed low. The Master struck him.
Yet another monk approached. Again the Master raised his flywhisk. The monk paid no attention. The Master struck him as well.

SOKEI-AN SAYS:

This is a Zen dialogue as expressed during the ninth century of the Tang Dynasty. Our Zen in comparison with this period is greatly developed. Of course the shortcoming of Zen today is that students do not think their life *itself* is Zen. They think Zen practice is something entirely different from their daily lives. In the Tang Dynasty the Zen student practiced Zen at every moment and on all occasions—in bed, talking, walking, eating. It was a living Zen. Of course Zen still exists in this fashion today, but the teacher and student do not quite reveal the sharp points of their swords. We, today, express Zen in daily life in a much more subtle way so that the ordinary eye cannot see it.

These dialogues are Lin-chi's style of Zen. Swift as lightning, ferocious as thunder. There is no time to reason or philosophize. In one moment, the cosmos turns like a whirlpool. Reasoning, observation, and action are simultaneous.

The Master asked a monk, "Where do you come from?" This is a universal question. Lin-chi is hiding the point of his sword.

The monk gave a HO! This "HO!" is a peculiar expression. It is a tremendous shout. Three generations before Lin-chi, Ma-tsu thundered "HO!" to his disciple Huai-hai. It was said that Huai-hai could not hear for three days and three nights. Of course, it wasn't his physical ear that couldn't hear but his Zen ear that really became deaf after such a terrible "Ho!" With this sound all the cosmos was swept away, crushed to powder. There was nothing left. Such is the power of the sound. Usually when a Zen student comes to the Zen room with a HO! The teacher laughs. This HO! is correctly pronounced like "Caw!" deep in the throat. So Lin-chi's school is sometimes referred to as the "crow school".

The Master asked him to be seated. This was a good student. Lin-chi was asking him from what part of the cosmos he had come. What part of time? What part of space? Is there space and time? The student's answer, "HO!" was not bad, but Lin-chi wanted to see deeper. He wanted to examine with a second stroke. At the first stroke, the student had parried quite well, so Lin-chi changed his attitude and asked him to be seated.

The monk hesitated. The Master struck him. His hesitation was not so bad. There is no space to blow a breath in, no crack to push a line of hair in. Lin-chi will not wait for even such a fine hesitation; so he hit him. This is how one must act in Zen discourse. The whole cosmos was moving back and forth between the master and his disciple. This strike by the Zen master is different from the strike that is performed out of anger; it is a good strike.

The Master saw another monk coming. The Master raised his flywhisk. Lin-chi was seated cross-legged in the monastery. The monk came from outside of the temple and made obeisance to Lin-chi. Lin-chi is not dramatizing. He lifted his *hossu*, his flywhisk, and looked at the monk. He is at attention. War has been declared already!

The monk bowed low. The Master struck him. Guest and Master! A beautiful interview! All the monks of that time who had visited many masters came in the end to visit Lin-chi. They knew about his ferocious and thunderous "HO!" and his lightning hand. So this monk, seeing Lin-chi raise the *hossu*, spread his mat and bowed low, expecting the blow. This is a good guest in the guest position and a good master in the master's position. The monk had come to attention after the blow.

Yet another monk approached. Again the Master raised his flywhisk. The monk paid no attention. The Master struck him as well. I'm sure Lin-chi had interviewed this monk on the previous day, and he had not come to attention and bowed after the blow, so Lin-chi hit him again. The second hit was a real hit, for this was not a real monk. Lin-chi was using all his power as a master.

III

One day the Master and P'u-hua went to a patron's home to dine. The Master asked a question: "A thread of hair swallows the ocean, and a grain of poppy seed contains Mt. Sumeru. Is this a profound mystery, or is it the primary itself?"

P'u-hua kicked the table over.

The Master said, "What coarseness!"

P'u-hua said, "What do you know! Talking about what is coarse or what is fine!"

The next day the Master again returned with P'u-hua to dine at the patron's home and asked, "How do you compare today's dinner to yesterday's?"

P'u-hua kicked the table over.

The Master said, "You caught it accurately, but it's too coarse!"

P'u-hua said, "Blind fool! In Buddhism, there is no reason to
talk about what is coarse or what is fine!"
The Master poked out his tongue.

SOKEI-AN SAYS:

One day the Master and P'u-hua went to a patron's home to dine. P'u-hua [n.d.] was an elder Zen master living in a town near the Yellow River. His teacher was a disciple of Ma-tsu. Mat-tsu was from an entirely different school than Lin-chi's. So, as soon as they met, they begin to fight in the usual Zen fashion. But they have a good relationship. Perhaps P'u-hua had introduced Lin-chi to the patron, a rich layman who loved to support the monks, so he invited them every day for the noon meal.

The Master asked a question: "A thread of hair swallows the ocean, and a grain of poppy seed contains Mt. Sumeru. *Is this a profound mystery, or is it the primary itself?*" Is this some mysterious power, some occult or supernatural power? Or is this reality itself? Today we call this primary "reality" in philosophical terms and "noumena" in scientific terms. From the viewpoint of the primary body, this koan presented by Lin-chi is not so hard. When Christ broke bread and called it his "flesh," it has the same meaning.

P'u-hua kicked the table over. The Master said, "What coarseness!" Very good! If Lin-chi had been asked such a question by P'u-hua, what would have been his answer? Perhaps he would have vomited out a "HO!" while striking P'u-hua at the same time. But P'u-hua kicked the table over. Alas, the poor patron's table crashed to the floor. The utensils rolled about the courtyard, and the food spattered all over the pavement.

P'u-hua said, "What do you know! Talking about what is coarse or what is fine!" From his standpoint, there is no such relative standpoint as "coarse or fine"—it's the viewpoint of an infant. Lin-chi is a young monk, but looking at P'u-hua he is not so sure of the old monk's enlightenment. He wishes the opportunity to examine him further. They do not yet understand one another. So—

The next day the Master again returned with P'u-hua to dine at the patron's home and asked, "How do you compare today's dinner to yesterday's?" And just like the day before—

P'u-hua kicked the table over. P'u-hua's standpoint has not changed. It is the same as yesterday's, today's, or a million years in the future. There is only one standpoint. But Lin-chi did not wish to miss the opportunity of examining him further. So he says—

"You caught it accurately, but it's too coarse!" You got it, and you understand, but your understanding is too primitive!

P'u-hua said, "Blind fool! In Buddhism, there is no reason to talk about what is coarse or what is fine!" The Master poked out his tongue. There are much finer phases in understanding! Why take such a coarse and crude attitude? But P'u-hua's Zen is actualization, and therefore Lin-chi "poked out his tongue." He understood the drastic measure taken by P'u-hua. He liked the clear action of Zen without philosophy or discussion in it. This is the active actualization of Zen.

IV

> One day the Master was sitting in the company of the elders Ho-yang and Mu-t'a by a fireplace in the monks' hall. Someone said, "Everyday P'u-hua behaves in the streets like one possessed. Who can tell whether he's a commoner or a holy man?"
>
> While they were talking, P'u-hua entered the room and joined the group. Lin-chi asked P'u-hua, "Are you a commoner or a holy man?"
>
> P'u-hua said, "You tell me whether I am common or holy."
>
> The Master shouted, "HO!"
>
> P'u-hua pointed his finger at them and said, "Ho-yang is a new bride. Mu-t'a is a grandmother, and Lin-chi is a running boy, but he has the eye!"
>
> The Master said, "What a thief!"
>
> P'u-hua cried out, "Thief! Thief!" and left.

SOKEI-AN SAYS:

This temple was not Lin-chi's temple; we do not know whose temple it was, but it had been a temple of old Zen masters who had been interred in the town. In the East sometimes an old temple is kept in town without an abbot or master, and then a new monk comes along and takes over the temple and becomes the abbot.

One day the Master was sitting in the company of the elders Ho-yang and Mu-t'a by a fireplace in the monks' hall. Lin-chi was sitting in a circle with two Zen masters around a fireplace. A fireplace in a Chinese temple is different from a Western fireplace. It is placed in the center of a paved area so one can take a seat upon it when it is cold.

At this time, Lin-chi was quite young, about thirty-seven or thirty-eight, while the others were about fifty or sixty. He was at this temple and was mingling with some old Zen masters. Lin-chi was a newcomer, not fully accepted by the town. Just as I, when I came to New York, was not accepted. To be accepted, you must stay quite awhile. He was not accepted for four years, but took to them right away. To be accepted as a monk takes about eight to ten years because a Zen master must have prestige. Not just be someone's son!

The pedigrees of Ho-yang and Mu-t'a are not clear in the records. They are recorded here as Zen masters, but not in any other record. In Zen, if a master's pedigree is not clear, we do not pay much attention to him. All Zen students must have a teacher at whose ordination there are least one hundred witnesses. His name recorded, and his lineage established. It is quite different here. If someone should come to this country from the Gobi desert and say, "I am a Zen Master!" I would not pay too much attention to him. He must be introduced by his teacher—"I send him to you, please accept him."

Someone said, "Everyday P'u-hua behaves in the streets like one possessed." Every day P'u-hua ran amuck all over town. Why will be explained in the next chapter, the next lecture. He is different from other Zen masters. He went through the streets of the town, bell in hand, ringing continuously and reciting continuously something like "A-s-s-s-ghi-ghi", with his long staff in the right hand and [Sokei-an rings his bell] the bell in the left. If anyone questioned him, he hit the questioner with his staff. Such stuff! He appeared crazy!

"Who can tell whether he's a commoner or a holy man?" A saint or an ordinary man? We have had such Zen masters in Japan, too. In China they have Hotei. He is often reproduced on chinaware with a big abdomen, a loose gown and a large knapsack on his back and big staff behind him. He walked on the streets tapping rich men on the back. When the man turned around in surprise, Hotei would laugh and say,

"Give me a penny." If anyone wished to know about the weather, whether it would rain or be clear, they would ask him. He was always meditating on the breeze. If it was to be clear, he would put on his straw sandals, and if it was going to rain, he wore his wooden clogs. So everyone watched to see what he was wearing to know what the weather would be that day. But no one really knew what he was doing. Such a Zen master is not so kind; he teaches very little to anyone. He just enjoys Zen life and then he dies. Who could tell whether he's a commoner or a holy man?"

While they were talking, P'u-hua entered the room and joined the group. Lin-chi asked P'u-hua, *"Are you a commoner or a holy man?"* A very good question! When a Zen question is put in this relative way, it is always dangerous. Are you holy or common?

P'u-hua said, "You tell me whether I am common or holy." The Master shouted, "HO!" Good! Good! With one HO! he shouts down both sides, the holy and the crazy. Lin-chi is like a great archer: he kills two birds with one arrow.

P'u-hua pointed his finger at them and said, "Ho-yang is a new bride. Mu-t'a is a grandmother, and Lin-chi is a running boy, but he has the eye!" Now P'u-hua calmly points his finger and replies to Lin-chi's thunder. He points out that Ho-yang's Zen is like a new bride that lives with a new family. She talks more to her brother-and sister-in-laws than to her own husband. "Is the soup all right?" She cannot act too freely. She must take care of the father and mother more than her husband. She must stay in the background and not speak. It's like a new Zen master coming to a new temple. The new abbot and the old monks. The new abbot is taking the old master's position, but he must take a new bride's attitude.

Then there is grandmother Zen: "Oh, poor child, your answer is good, but a little is missing. Your understanding is not good. You should think in this way . . ."

This is very bad, and it disturbs the disciples. No disciple likes it. But P'u-hua understands these two attitudes. He says that Lin-chi is like a messenger boy just come to town. He is young and he is running around like a stable kid, but he has the third eye. But Zen must have a servant.

The Master said, "What a thief!" In this Zen dialogue if you wish to pay someone a compliment, you call him a thief!

P'u-hua cried out, "Thief! Thief!" and left. Just as you say on the street when someone snatches your pocketbook, "Thief, thief!" Of course, P'u-hua's statement is a compliment. Lin-chi knows he understands him.

It's fifty-fifty. And P'u-hua leaves as quick as lightening without showing his shadow.

When you understand Zen, you will understand this. I shall not be a grandmother to you!

V

> One day, P'u-hua was eating some raw vegetables in front of the monastery. The Master looked at him and said, "You are an ass!"
>
> P'u-hua brayed like an ass. The Master said, "What a thief!"
>
> P'u-hua cried out, "Thief! Thief!" and left.

SOKEI-AN SAYS:

To eat raw vegetables is not a queer thing in this country, but in China and Japan it is very queer. All vegetables are cooked before being eaten and served with some sauce. If you go to a Chinese restaurant, you will never see any fresh vegetables. So it was quite queer to see anyone eating fresh vegetables.

One day, P'u-hua was eating some raw vegetables in front of the monastery. There are usually staircases made of wood or stone in front of monasteries. Perhaps he was sitting on the stairs and was eating fresh vegetables.

The Master looked at him and said, "You are an ass!" Just like a donkey, eating raw vegetables! He is testing P'u-hua with fire. So Lin-chi showered him with abuse.

P'u-hua brayed like an ass. He showed his bare heart. Scalped out his guts and showed his great nature to Lin-chi like pure sky. Sometimes thunder roars like this.

Some people take his braying like an ass as P'u-hua's humor, but it is not shallow; it is deeper than humor. You are like an ass! Hee-haw! From the Zen standpoint, the insult and the reply are exactly balanced, have the same weight and value. But if your mind is full of "stuff" you cannot see this.

The Master said, "What a thief!" This "What a thief!" was used in another discourse, so there is not much to explain here.

P'u-hua cried out, "Thief! Thief!" and left. P'u-hua offers a compliment to Lin-chi: "You are a great master. I am a donkey!" So Lin-chi replies, "Ha! You're trying to get into my mind, you flatterer!"

This conversation is really so lofty, so high, so wonderful! It is as if a donkey looks into a well and the well looks back at the donkey. If you grasp this, you are a real Zen student. There are many people who have associated with a Zen monk or student, who say, "Those people have a sense of humor!" Zen students are not always humorous. Their action comes from their detachment from the world, which appears to the worldly as humor.

Ikkyu was a great humorist and a good Zen master of Japan. Every morning of the New Year, he held a skeleton on a staff and visited from door to door. Of course, everyone was saying, "We hope you live long! Congratulations!" But Ikkyu used to say, "Well, we are within a mile of hell! Are you enjoying it?" He was a child of the Zen temple. In those early days the language of the Zen masters was really wonderful!

VI

In the town streets, P'u-hua was always ringing his bell and loudly crying out: "Come out of a bright quarter, and I will hit you upon that brightness! Come out of a dark quarter, and I will hit you upon that darkness! Come out of the four quarters and the eight directions, and I will hit you like a cyclone! Come out of the empty sky, and I will hit you like a flail!"

The Master told his attendant to go to P'u-hua, and when he heard P'u-hua say this, seize him by the chest and ask: "If one should come out of that which is entirely different from what you have just said, what would you do?"

[His attendant went and did exactly as he was directed.] P'u-hua pushed the attendant away and said, "Tomorrow there will be a feast in Ta-pei-yuan!"

The attendant returned and told the Master what had
happened.
The Master said, "To think I always doubted that fellow!"

SOKEI-AN SAYS:

Usually Zen students of today would like to find some meaning in P'u-hua's "quarters." And the students of that day did the same. Quarters? What is the meaning? Humph . . . Dark side? Bright side? From all quarters of the sky? There must be some meaning. I will explain the meaning, if you like.

What is the "bright quarter"? It is the whole universe reflecting on *this* consciousness. What is the "dark quarter"? It is the *dharmadhatu*, Original reality. reality with no dust in it. No sun shines there. No earth supports it. If you stand upon it, there is no ground beneath your feet and no heaven above your head. There is nothing!

In the town streets, P'u-hua was always ringing his bell and loudly crying out: "Come out of a bright quarter, and I will hit you upon that brightness!" I'll crush the whole universe with one blow!

"Come out of a dark quarter, and I will hit you upon that darkness!" I will annihilate that nothingness. Nothingness is bad enough, but P'u-hua says he will annihilate even that. Then what will happen?

"Come out of the four quarters and the eight directions, and I will hit you like a cyclone!" This means everywhere. It is like the effulgence of the Buddha in meditation.

"Come out of the empty sky, and I will hit you like a flail!" A flail is used to hit grain, to take the bean out of the shell.

Strange! If you come out of the empty sky—not darkness, not brightness, not one, not zero—*all* is annihilated. I hope you grasp this. If you grasp it, it is really not nothing. If you come from this real nothingness, there is nothing to be smitten. No one can say a word. But P'u-hua said, of course, "I will strike you with a machine gun!"

He was crying this out every day, but nobody said a word. There were many students of the Zen school around, but no one said anything. He is alone, like a king in a desert calling every day. But Lin-chi understood. "Well, I will test him once again."

The Master told his attendant to go to P'u-hua, and when he heard P'u-hua say this, seize him by the chest and ask: "If one should come out of that which is entirely different from what you have just said, what would you do?" [His attendant went and did exactly as he was directed.] The attendant went outside and waited for P'u-hua to come along. P'u-hua came as usual calling aloud. The attendant seized him by the chest (in Chinese, "choked him up") and started shouting loudly what Lin-chi had told him to say.

P'u-hua pushed the attendant away and said, "Tomorrow there will be a feast in Ta-pei-yuan!" Humph! Not exciting at all. He only said he had Zen business and had been invited. This is his answer. If you do not come from any of the places P'u-hua had mentioned, there is no explanation. So if you meet an enlightened one on *your* way, what do you say? If you meet the Buddha, do you ask him, "What is Buddhism?" What do you say? Such koans elucidate this place. If you pass such a koan, you will have some understanding of this dialogue. But you will know it without reason, and you will know the mind of P'u-hua.

The attendant returned and told the Master what had happened. The Master said, "To think I always doubted that fellow!" Lin-chi, with a deep breath said, "Aha, I see. Now I know he's really enlightened!" There is no way to interpret this. You must grasp it through your own experience.

VII

An old monk came to see the Master. Before exchanging the greetings of the season, the old monk put a question to him: "Should I bow or should I not bow?"

The Master shouted, "HO!"

The monk bowed low. The Master said, "What a petty, sneaky thief!"

The monk cried out, "Thief! Thief!" and left.

The Master said, "You must not say, 'When nothing happens, that's the best!'"

The head monk came and stood beside the Master. Seizing the opportunity, the Master said, "Was there any error?"

The head monk said, "There was."

> The Master said, "Who committed the error, the guest or the host?"
>
> The monk said, "Both committed the error."
>
> The Master asked, "Where was the error?"
>
> The monk left.
>
> The Master said, "You must not say, 'When nothing happens, that's the best!'"
>
> Afterwards, a monk told the story to Nan-ch'uan. Nan-ch'uan said, "Proud horses trample one another."

SOKEI-AN SAYS:

This kind of Zen literature—dialogues between masters and disciples (hosts and guests)—is impossible to explain. The whole cosmos is moving with their minds and actions. If you think about it philosophically, you will speak volumes. In this type of dialogue the brain moves like a cyclone. There is no moment to measure the thought, no moment to build a philosophical monument. Everything must be handled in that moment as real as substance itself.

An old monk came to see the Master. We are not told who this old monk was, but from his attitude he must have been an old Zen master. He was older than Lin-chi, so we can assume that at that period Lin-chi was not so very old, perhaps around fifty.

Before exchanging the greetings of the season. As is customary the newcomer will introduce himself to the master: "I've come from such and such a temple and was studying Zen under such and such a master, a disciple of so-and-so." And then he will pay a compliment: "Ah, the garden of this temple is very beautiful." And then gradually they will enter into a dialogue. While they are talking and exchanging greetings, the master and the guest will fathom the depth of each other's understanding.

For example, in the question, Where do you come from? the "where" has a deep meaning. This "where" means before creation—reality. It has no relation to the five senses; it also means time and space. How do you answer such a question? You could say, "When I left Chin-shu it was late spring." Such an answer, which has nothing to do with philosophy or religion, might be the answer to show some understanding. It has nothing to do with you, and yet it is the answer.

Zen is like brocade. It has a beautiful rich surface. Perhaps there's a dragon or some wisteria on its face. But when you turn it over, you see all the entanglement of thread. So when a Zen master says, "How do you do? And the student says, "It's a beautiful day," there is meaning inside his words. "How far have you gone today?" "Well, I went quite far." In such a dialogue each, master and disciple, host and guest, is watching his opponent and trying to understand. But this old monk put a question to Lin-chi before exchanging the greetings of the season—an unusual proceeding.

The old monk put a question to him: "Should I bow or should I not bow?" When the old monk came into the temple he raised his mat from his arm and asked, "Should I bow or not bow?" Usually a monk would spread his mat on the pavement and kneel to pay homage to the master. But this monk stood holding his mat and asked a direct question! He was expecting something to happen. He asked his question knowing all along that the Master's Zen is like lightning.

The Master shouted, "HO!" This is Lin-chi's usual expression, of course, a strong guttural sound coming from the chest. Ho-o-o-o! But in real circumstances, "Should I bow or not bow?" Ho-o-o-o!—in Japanese, *Katsu!* I couldn't make much noise here because this is a small apartment. It comes from here [points] and comes quickly. Almost like a kkkkkkKKKK!

The monk bowed low. In Japan sometimes when the teacher explains this part, he says too much. But perhaps you are not getting the important point, so I will explain some more.

The monk was making two points when he asked Lin-chi, "Should I bow or not bow?" They are yes and no; black and white; sour and sweet; nothing and something; life and death. The monk was asking about these alternatives. He had used the bow merely to carry out this question. To bow seems simple. In Zen sometimes it's a fan, sometimes a mat, and sometimes the hand. This old monk used the bow. "Should I bow or should I not bow?" In Zen we seize whatever circumstance there is at hand to express our particular point. Shakyamuni held up a blue flower.

The monk's question had dualism, relativity, in it, so Lin-chi struck both sides at once with his "Ho!" With one arrow he shot two geese at once. The old monk understood his attitude and bowed low. In this bow there is no relativity. It is the answer to Lin-chi's "Ho!" The bow and the exclamation correspond one to another. In the beginning it was like these two hands of mine, but now the position has shifted. In the psychological moment, the two hands become one. You could say when I express it in this degree, there is no more Zen. The real essence vanishes from the explanation. But if I had to draw you a picture to explain it, I would explain it thus.

The Master said, "What a petty, sneaky thief!" The monk cried out, "Thief! Thief!" and left. With his exclamation he matched Lin-chi's HO! They have the same value. This is the Zen way. This is Zen during the Tang dynasty. Today, Zen is handled differently.

Lin-chi saw him go, then muttered to himself—

"You must not say, 'When nothing happens, that's the best!'" This is like saying, "okay" when someone asks you how you're doing. But when Zen students say something like this in a conversation, it has an unusual meaning. In spring the cherry blossoms; in summer we go fishing; in autumn all the leaves dry and fall; in winter the earth is covered with snow. All this is from a phenomenal viewpoint. But from the viewpoint of reality, nothing happened—no earth was ever created; no universe was ever destroyed; no radio wave ever vibrated; no space or time. Hmm, nothing has happened. Translated into English you could say it's event-less. You must not say, however, that "event-lessness" is best.

When P'u-hua in an earlier section said, "Thief! Thief!" as he went out, Lin-chi agreed, but when this old monk did the same, Lin-chi was not entirely satisfied. But he did not wish to disturb the circumstances too much. What was Lin-chi expecting? Maybe he was expecting the old monk to kick a chair or throw him to the pavement!

The head monk came and stood beside the Master. Seizing the opportunity, the Master said, "Was there any error?" The head monk said, "There was." It's like basketball. "Was that a foul?"

The head monk said there was an error. He must please Lin-chi, of course. So he said there was an error. The head monk was not making the situation so peaceful. He knew if he said no, Lin-chi would hit him.

The Master said, "Who committed the error, the guest or the host?" He's setting a trap! He thinks the disciple might answer, "This one," or "That one." Then, of course, he would hit him for taking a dualistic attitude. The disciple, knowing this, said,

"Both committed the error." He does not fall into the trap.

The Master asked, "Where was the error?" The monk left. He swept his sleeves back and abruptly left. Lin-chi is left alone before he had the time to give a HO! or to hit his disciple. This monk had hopped from disaster!

The Master said, "You must not say, 'When nothing happens, that's the best!'" This disciple, like the old monk, met Lin-chi's attitude exactly. If you compare the two, both attitudes were the same.

Afterwards, a monk told the story to Nan-ch'uan. Nan-ch'uan was old at the time. He was a famous teacher and we have many difficult koans from him.

Nan-ch'uan said, "Proud horses trample one another." This is Nan-ch'uan's answer to Lin-chi's statement: peace is best; we need not fight at all. Hmm, I think there is some deeper meaning. There is something more in the cosmos than this egoistic view. Nan-ch'uan's statement is like taking an entirely impersonal view, like observing. the trees of Central Park as they bow to each other during a storm. There is something more than just the peace that we can observe.

VIII

> One day the Master entered an encampment where he had been invited to a feast. At the gate he saw an officer. Pointing his finger at a pillar, he asked the officer a question: "Is this common or holy?"
>
> The officer did not say a word. The Master struck the pillar with his staff and said, "Though this one has answered my question, it is merely a wooden pile," and he entered.

SOKEI-AN SAYS:

I'm sure this was the encampment of Ma Fang, Lin-chi's Patron. In those days the patrons of Chinese monks were all warriors or in governmental service. Many officials studied Zen from the monks. Lin-chi was invited, so he went to the feast.

At the gate he saw an officer. Pointing his finger at a pillar, he asked the officer a question: "Is this common or holy?" This man was standing guard at the gate as you see doormen of this country standing impersonally like puppets at the entrance to apartment buildings. This amused Lin-chi, and he put his question to the guard so that his disciples following him should be tested as to their understanding.

The officer did not say a word. The Master struck the pillar with his staff and said, "Though this one has answered my question, it is merely a wooden pile," and he entered. Of course the guard paid no attention to what Lin-chi had said. He was only a puppet. Lin-chi looked at the guard and understood his psychology. He probably didn't even hear the question as it had nothing to do with his business. To Lin-chi, however, this puppet's attitude was very interesting—like some sort of Zen answer. So he acted out the part of the master as he would put a koan to a student—"Before Father and Mother, what was your original countenance?" The student, standing still, seems to be answering the question. But this is not enough, so the Master strikes him. Bang! Lin-chi strikes the column with his staff and says, "Though this one has answered my question, it is merely a wooden pile." Humph! This "wooden pile" has nothing to do with Zen!

I recollect something that once happened with Dr. Goddard while I was with him in Vermont. He had three hundred acres of land and in the center of the field there was a big tree that died quite sometime before. He said to me, "I always come here and sit beneath this tree and meditate." So I said: "Oh, you do? Then you must really know this tree, and this wood." And I hit it, the big tree—BANG! But my question did not penetrate into his mind. He looked at the sky and answered, "Yes, the tree died a long time ago. I observe individual meditation, not tree meditation." Even if he came a million years to sit and meditate under that tree he would never understand the tree or observe the depth of its meditation! Does the tree understand this meditation? The erroneous one can be measured immediately with this question. If one is truly a Zen student, then of course the tree understands this meditation. Perhaps it will hit my face. "Hey, I'm dead a long time. Do you feel like conversing with me?" In such a conversation, and at any moment, the Zen mind can testify for you. Hmmm.

Lin-chi strikes the column. "It is just a wooden pile," and enters.

A long time ago I made a poem when I saw a huge stone on Mt. Rainier. Looking up, I could hardly see the sky for this huge boulder blocking it out.

How long is this stone meditating?
From the begininglessness of the universe.
What is meditating?
The stone does not meditate.
I meditate, but I understand the stone's meditation.

So silence is not the answer in Zen. Motion is not the answer in Zen. You must understand what the answer is.

IX

The Master said to the director of temple affairs, "Where have you been?"

The monk said, "I have come from selling the yellow rice in the province."

The Master asked, "Have you sold all of it?"

The monk said, "Yes, I have."

The Master then drew a line with his staff in front of him and asked, "Can you sell this?"

The monk shouted, "HO!"

The Master struck him.

The head cook came in, and the Master told him about the conversation. The cook said, "The director did not understand the Master's point of view."

The Master asked, "So how do you understand my point of view?"

The head cook bowed low. The Master struck him as well.

SOKEI-AN SAYS:

These discourses of Zen in the Tang Dynasty are very interesting!

The Master said to the director of temple affairs . . . The director of temple affairs is the boss of the temple. The Zen master has nothing to do with temple business. *"Where have you been?"* A very dangerous question! "You've been so busy bustling about, I've not seen you this morning!"

The monk said, "I have come from selling the yellow rice in the province." When the black rice gets old, it turns yellowish, dries and crumbles. Before this happens, they must sell it and buy new rice or carry it away and exchange it for something else. This is the business of the director—the monks are supported like a regiment. But Lin-chi's question goes deeper, of course—

The Master asked, "Have you sold all of it?" Ha! There's some poison in his mind! Lin-chi is trying to catch his tail. This "all" has some meaning in it. The director knows there is something in the Master's mind—

The monk said, "Yes, I have." But Lin-chi must test still further.

The Master then drew a line with his staff in front of him and asked, "Can you sell this?" What does Lin-chi mean by "this"? In the old style of dialogue, the master sometimes made this circle, this delineation with his staff. Lin-chi was looking for trouble with the director.

The monk shouted, "HO!" So he's a true disciple after all—he thundered! The whole cosmos rolled out with the sound. Everything was annihilated.

The Master struck him. Good master and good disciple—good host and guest! Lin-chi took the opportunity to show this.

Every master would wish to have such a disciple—"HOOO!" Beautiful. But if the director had taken the staff of Lin-chi and hit him, instead of giving the HO!, what would have happened? It would have been more interesting I'm sure. Being hit, the director kept his position. Hitting, Lin-chi kept his position—both good. Good student and good master.

The head cook came in, and the Master told him about the conversation. The head cook is also an important official in the temple. He is not just a cook, however. I'm sure he wanted to test Lin-chi. So he quietly entered and stood beside the Master, and the Master told him about the conversation. But Lin-chi knew that he was looking for trouble. Then the cook said:

"The director did not understand the Master's point of view." I wonder if the director really understood Lin-chi's point of view. Even if he had, he had not "disposed of everything" in matching Lin-chi's point of view.

The Master asked, "So how do you understand my point of view?" In Buddha's Jetavana Garden there was a bell tower that had a crystal bell at its very center and a bell of silver at each of its four corners. The silver bells murmured in the breeze, and, of course, when there was no breeze they were silent. But the crystal bell was always murmuring as if it were reciting sutras—with the breeze, without the breeze, it murmured always. After the Buddha passed into nirvana, the crystal bell disappeared. Men, *devas*, and demons searched the universe, throughout heaven and hell, but they never found it. This story points to something important in Buddhism. How do you find this bell? All schools of Buddhism have this particular point. Of course, Lin-chi is showing it directly to the head cook. This point of view is very important.

It is said the Buddha transmitted no Dharma to Mahakashyapa. Then what were all those patriarchs from generation to generation transmitting?

The head cook bowed low. The Master struck him as well. The head cook was very good. Lin-chi did not miss the opportunity of giving him a blow. He was like thunder! But what if the head cook had swept his sleeves back and hopped out, giving Lin-chi no opportunity to strike him, what would Lin-chi have done?

Many koans point to this particular part. I cannot give any philosophical explanation for it. A Zen student's mind must be more like lightning. It has a natural movement without words. Without such a brain, you cannot use this in daily life.

X

One day a distinguished lecturer came to have an interview with the Master. The Master asked the lecturer, "On what sutra do you lecture?"

The lecturer said, "I have made a study of the Treatise of One Hundred Dharmas."

The Master said, "Suppose there was one who had no comprehension of the three vehicles and the twelve divisions of the teachings, and there was another who had perfect comprehension of the three vehicles and the twelve divisions of the teachings. Would there be a distinction between them, or would they be exactly alike?"

The lecturer said, "To one who has attained comprehension, both are the same. But to one who has not attained comprehension, they appear different."

At that time, Lo-p'u was the personal attendant of the Master. Standing behind the Master, Lo-p'u said, "Sir, what kind of place do you think this is, discussing whether they are the 'same' or 'different!'"

Turning his head, the Master questioned the attendant, "What do you think about it?"

The attendant roared, "HO!"

When the Master came back from seeing the lecturer off, he asked his attendant, "Did you roar at me?"

Lo-p'u said, "Yes."

The Master struck him.

SOKEI-AN SAYS:

The lecturer is probably a member of the philosophical T'ien-t'ai school of Buddhism "T'ien" means "heaven" and "t'ai" means platform. So it's the Heavenly Platform School of Buddhism.

One day a distinguished lecturer came to have an interview with the Master. I'm sure the lecturer was a stranger to the Zen school. Perhaps he wished to know something about the Bodhidharma School, and having heard of the famous Lin-chi, he wanted to question him. Such an interview is called *shoken* in Japanese. It is the first interview with a newcomer. The master will evaluate the newcomer and decide to take him or not as a student. This is an important task!.

The Master asked the lecturer, "On what sutra do you lecture?" You will notice that Lin-chi's attitude is different here. When he meets a Zen monk, he will draw a line with his staff from side to side, or raise the *hossu*, or abruptly ask a question: "Where do you come from?" But here he is speaking in the lecturer's terms.

The lecturer said, "I have made a study of the Treatise of One Hundred Dharmas." The answer is very humble. He did not take an overweening attitude. He was very modest. He lectures on enlightenment.

The Master said, "Suppose there was one who had no comprehension of the three vehicles and the twelve divisions of the teachings . . ." With the three vehicles and the twelve divisions of the Buddha's teaching we have the whole of Buddhism—the same as the one hundred Dharmas.

"*. . . and there was another who had perfect comprehension of the three vehicles and the twelve divisions of the teachings. Would there be a distinction between them, or would they be exactly alike?*" Lin-chi comes down to play with the baby! Funny question, wasn't it? Here one knows nothing of Buddhism and here one has an entire knowledge of it, and Lin-chi asks if it is the same or different.

The lecturer said, "To one who has attained comprehension, both are the same. But to one who has not attained comprehension, they appear different." Not a bad answer. It is true. To the one who has not yet studied Buddhism, they are entirely different, but to the adept they are the same. Not bad. His brain is clear.

At that time, Lo-p'u was the personal attendant of the Master. Standing behind the Master, Lo-p'u said, "Sir, what kind of place do you think this is, discussing whether they are the 'same' or 'different!'" This is important. When Lo-p'u Yuan-an [834-898] says, "What kind of place?" he does not mean Lin-chi's temple. So I ask you, what do you think this "place" is?

I don't think Lin-chi's attendant understood what Lin-chi was actually doing. There is a poem in Zen: If you meet a fencer offer the sword / If he is not a poet, do not offer your poem. So if I meet a butcher, I ask him the price of pork chops. If he's not a poet, I do not recite my poem. A Zen student always talks in accordance with whom he is speaking. It is the usual attitude of a Zen man.

Turning his head, the Master questioned the attendant, "What do you think about it?" The attendant roared, "HO!" Too lofty. I am sure the lecturer must have jumped from his cushion! Perhaps the conversation continued until the lecturer took his leave.

When the Master came back from seeing the lecturer off, he asked his attendant, "Did you roar at me?" Lo-p'u said, "Yes." The Master struck him. Now Lin-chi hooks the fish! Lo-p'u was not a poor student, but he was trapped. He really understood, yet he was not yet able to give a true HO!

XI

The Master had heard that Te-shan always said, "Whether you can utter a word or cannot utter a word, I will administer thirty blows!"

The Master told Lo-p'u to go to Te-shan's and put this question to him: "Why should you administer thirty blows to one who can utter a word?" Then the Master said, "When he hits you with his staff, seize it with your hand and shove him with it. Then watch what he does."

Lo-p'u went to see Te-shan and questioned him as he had been instructed. When Te-shan hit him, Lo-p'u seized his staff and shoved him with it. Te-shan went back to his quarters. Lo-p'u returned and related the incident to the Master. The Master said, "To think I always doubted that fellow! However, do you understand him or not?"

Lo-p'u was disconcerted. The Master struck him.

SOKEI-AN SAYS:

This is a famous dialogue of the *Record*. Te-shan Hsuan-chien [780/2-865] was a well-known Zen master of the day and older than Lin-chi. When he was young he had made a commentary on the *Diamond Sutra* of which he was very proud, and it had given him a big head. Of course at that time there were no small printings, so he wrote it upon scrolls and bore the many volumes on his back. In this manner he had traveled from the Western part of China to the Southern part, where he had heard there was a new school of Buddhism called Zen. This school declared that one could attain buddhahood immediately, while with the *sutras* it was the result of hard practice. So Te-shan thought he would go to the South and meet this Zen sect and crush it. After traveling on foot for many days and nights, he arrived in the South and found Zen everywhere. One day he stopped by a roadside for lunch at a little hut where an old woman was serving tea and food to travelers. Pointing a finger at a cracker, he said, "I'll take that."

The old woman said to him, "Pray be seated. May I ask you a question, venerable sir?"

Te-shan felt queer looking down at this old woman. "Of course, you can ask me any question."

The old woman asked, "Well then answer me this: what's all that on your shoulders?"

Hmm, the question was strange! Te-shan said, "My commentary on the *Diamond Sutra*."

The old woman said, "Oh! That must be precious. You know, I've heard a famous line from that *sutra*: "The past soul is impossible to point out, the present soul is impossible to point out; and the future soul is impossible to point out. What soul do you wish to point out? If you can answer this, I will offer you my cracker. If not, you must go and get your lunch elsewhere."

"To point out the soul" is idiomatic in Chinese. It also means "cracker." The old woman used this word to ask her question.

Te-shan looked at the old woman's face, dumbfounded. This is his greatness. If he had been just an ordinary monk, he would have probably spoken philosophically. But his greatness prevented the words from slipping from his lips. He had merely made an interpretation of the line when he made his commentary. But at this moment he was confounded, so he said, "You are not a usual old woman. What are you, my great sister?"

The old woman answered, "A lay woman of the Zen school." Ah, this was Te-shan's first opportunity to meet such a one!

"Then there must be a famous Zen master around here." The old woman pointed to the roof of a big temple seen through the trees and said, "You'd better go there and see the teacher Lung-t'an."

Te-shan, who had come from the West to the South of China with the great hope of crushing Zen, began to feel a little uneasy. When he went to the temple and met Lung-t'an, they had an interesting conversation, but it is too long for tonight. The following morning, Te-shan set fire to the volumes of his work, reducing them to ashes. He then became a Zen student.

Te-shan died in the Tang Dynasty at the age of 86. He used a long rod to express his Zen.

The Master had heard that Te-shan always said, "Whether you can utter a word or cannot utter a word, I will administer thirty blows!" In last Saturday's lecture on Buddhism a heretic asked the Buddha a question: "Neither speaking a word nor no word, show me your true Dharma." The Buddha's answer was SILENCE. In some schools of Buddhism, to utter a million words and to utter one word is the same thing, and in other schools, one utters no word.

The Master told Lo-p'u to go to Te-shan's and put this question to him: "Why should you administer thirty blows to one who can utter a word?" Then the Master said, "When he hits you with his staff, seize it with your hand and shove him with it. Then watch what he does." A diamond cuts a diamond, poison cures poison, but it is not a *nirmanakaya* law; it is a *sambhogakaya* law. In this law, everything radiates from one central point in all directions, while in the third law of *nirmanakaya*, one point marches in one direction only. It is within this physical human law, *nirmanakaya*, that we act. But in the disembodied second law of *sambhogakaya*, everything is directed from one point, a point that reaches the corners of the universe—a million different directions.

Lin-chi is pointing to *sambhogakaya*. It is here that the Zen student takes the fifty-fifty attitude.

When I give explanations like this, it is only a philosophical illustration. But as a Zen student, Lo-p'u understood.

Lo-p'u went to see Te-shan and questioned him as he had been instructed. Te-shan hit him, Lo-p'u seized his staff and shoved him with it. Te-shan went back to his quarters. This is a beautiful! Why didn't Te-shan say a word? I'm sure he was staggering as he withdrew.

Lo-p'u returned and related the incident to the Master. The Master said, "To think I always doubted that fellow! However, do you understand him or not?" Lo-p'u was disconcerted. He was dumbfounded. He had gone there and acted like a puppet.

The Master struck him. He did not see the *real* Te-shan! But Lin-chi understood.

It is not easy to understand Zen Master Te-shan's attitude. It is easy, however, to observe his first admonition. But to retire without a word when pushed? That is difficult!

XII

> *One day, Counselor Wang paid a visit to the Master. Meeting the Master in front of the monastery, he questioned him: "Do the monks read the sutras?"*
>
> *The Master said, "No, they do not read the sutras."*
>
> *Wang asked, "Do they study Zen?"*
>
> *The Master said, "No, they do not study Zen."*
>
> *Wang then asked, "If they do not read the sutras or study Zen, what are they doing?"*
>
> *The Master said, "I only make them buddhas and patriarchs."*
>
> *Wang said, "Man worships gold dust, but if it falls into the eye, it is a problem for the eye. How do you understand this?"*
>
> *The Master said, "I always thought you were a commoner."*

SOKEI-AN SAYS:

In this small temple perhaps thirty or forty monks studied under Lin-chi's direction.

One day, Counselor Wang paid a visit to the Master. Meeting the Master in front of the monastery, he questioned him: "Do the monks read the sutras?" The Master said, "No, they do not read the sutras." Lin-chi's monks do not care a fig for the *sutras.* Each studies Buddhism from his own mind. All is written in yourself, in your own mind and body. The key to the mystery of the cosmos is already in your possession; so you must read this self first, find the law in this self before opening the records of the ancients. So in a Zen monastery, reading the *sutras* is not so much emphasized; but reading one's own mind in meditation is. This self is a microcosm, and if you read it carefully, all the laws of the macrocosm can be found there within you. Introspection is emphasized in Zen, but if you take the word "inside" literally, you are in error. What is mind? Where is it? Inside? Outside?

We usually blame the outside for our difficulties, but nothing exists outside. It is merely phenomena, a vision of the eye and a delusion of the mind. True existence is the reality that has no color, smell, or sound. Today it is called noumenon. Everything is this same substance, but when you perceive it with your five senses, you take it as phenomena. So nothing exists outside. The outside is reflecting upon consciousness and consciousness is keeping the impressions as mind-stuff. Some deny outside and affirm inside, but this is illogical because the inside exists only relative to the outside. So you must know this first when you observe the inside. You must observe your mind as a gardener observes a seed under a cover of soil in wintertime. This one will be an iris and that one a lily. There are many seeds in the mind and the gardener cannot always tell which ones will sprout. If in the spring, you find a strange one latent in your mind, you must observe it as it sprouts and opens into a flower. After awhile you will suddenly recognize the observer of all this mind-stuff. It has no name. It is different from that which it observes. This observer is not your self. So who is this observer? Who is observing your mind action? The Knower; He is the gate; He is the Master. But you will not find this Master in all the beautifully written records. He is enshrined within your self.

Here you have already touched something that is important in entering *dharmakaya*—there is no other gate by which to enter Buddhism. You must find this nameless one!

Wang asked, "Do they study Zen?" The Master said, "No, they do not study Zen." Wang must have long been a student of Zen before coming to Lin-chi. But Lin-chi's answer was rather queer for a teacher of Zen. In fact you cannot study Zen. You can study philosophy, mathematics, and science, but not Zen. Zen is already written in yourself. There is no way to study it. An infant cries, "Wahhhh!" but no infant studies how to cry. The dog barks, "Bow wow!" but it has not learned how to bark. True law is written in body and mind, but you forget about it because you are always looking outside—looking in books, looking through microscopes. You even study the psyche by reading! We in the Zen school, however, learn about the psyche through meditation, looking for the law in mind action. It is like a monkey eating a chestnut: he tears open the prickly burr and breaks the hard shell to find the fruit inside. So you must take off the dirt that is covering your Zen and find out what has been existing there from beginningless beginning and what will last till the endless end of the cosmos.

Hakuin said studying Zen is like peeling an onion layer after layer until there is nothing left. So the Zen student must peel off his philosophy, his notions, even the discovery of his own psyche. And when he has lost everything, he enters the second gate of Zen, the real *shunyata*, the real nothingness. True Zen is daily life from morning to evening. To study in a temple is like learning to swim in a swimming pool. True Zen is like swimming in the ocean, in daily life. But no one studies daily life.

Wang then asked, "If they do not read the sutras or study Zen, what are they doing?" The Master said, "I only make them buddhas and patriarchs." He is testing Counselor Wang to see how deeply he understands.

Wang said, "Man worships gold dust, but if it falls into the eye, it is a problem for the eye. How do you understand this?" Gold is valuable, but it is a nuisance in the eye. Attaining buddhahood and becoming a Bodhidharma is wonderful, but it will be a nuisance to one who really understands the cosmos.

The Master said, "I always thought you were a commoner." In other words, I always thought you were a philistine. However, Lin-chi is not abusing Counselor Wang. He is treating him like a real Zen student.

There are two points of view here. One says to study Buddhism, reach nirvana, you must practice the commandments, meditate, and read the *sutras*. It is through these kinds of practices that one attains buddhahood—that is, realizes the *dharmakaya*, the body of the infinite of all potentiality.

The other view says, "After all, why make the effort to climb the mountain? Nirvana is a nuisance." Such a person really has no religion; daily life is all that matters. We call this a "flat" observation, nihilism, and it leads to hedonism: All laws of morality are for convenience sake; there is no original law of the universe; we can only work upon the surface of things, for no one can see the back of the wall. Therefore, when Lin-chi uses the word "commoner," he means those who hold these views.

In the previous lecture between Lin-chi and Te-shan, we saw the equivalent viewpoint to one presented here: both masters have clean, washed, bottomless minds as they meet each other. These conversations give us a feeling of the men who have no egotism in their hearts, no mind-stuff or theory in their minds. They are living Zen students and masters, not like the ones who nibble at the cheese of Buddhism! If you do not understand this last part, you must find it for yourself. It is an important "seal" to be attained in *sanzen*.

XIII

The Master questioned Hsing-shan, "What is the white ox on the bare ground?"
Hsing-shan said, "Moo, moo!"
The Master said, "A mute, eh?"
Hsing-shan asked, "What do you think, elder?"
The Master said, "What a beast!"

XIV

The Master questioned Lo-p'u, "Suppose there were two masters: whenever one administered a blow with his staff, the other would give a HO; which one is more familiar to you?"
Lo-p'u said, "Neither of them are familiar to me."
The Master said, "So what is more familiar to you?"
Lo-p'u roared, "HO!"
The Master struck him.

XV

The Master, seeing a monk approach his quarters, opened both his hands wide. The monk did not utter a word. The Master asked, "Do you understand?"
The monk said, "No, I do not."
The Master said, "Hun-lun is impossible to rend asunder. I shall give you two pennies."

SOKEI-AN SAYS:
Such strange conversations! I'm sure this type of talk is new to Westerners. Even for Easterners it is difficult to understand the meaning behind these words. Now in this first dialogue, the Master questions Hsing-shan—

"What is the white ox on the bare ground?" Hsing-shan Chen-hung [n.d.] was a disciple of Yuan-yen in the ninth century. They were the forefathers of the Soto school in Japan of today. I belong to the Rinzai, or

Lin-chi school in Chinese. So Hsing-shan came from a different school to interview the Master.

The question about the White Ox and the bare ground is a story found in the *Lotus Sutra*. In this story a king realizes his castle is on fire and sees that his children are playing within it but are not aware of the danger. The king's dilemma is like the mother who sees her child standing on a windowsill. If she screams, the child may fall, so she approaches slowly and tries to grab the child before it falls. So what the king does in the *sutra* is offer them four carts: a goat cart, a horse cart, a white ox cart and a white elephant cart. "I have made you a beautiful cart, drawn by a white ox with many beautiful things inside! Come quickly!" In this way he hopes to get them to leave the palace.

This story about children playing in a fire is about you. If I say that you are in danger, you might say, "Never mind, it's warm here; it's a cozy place and I'm amusing myself." But while you amuse yourself in this worldly life, the fire comes and wipes you out. So this *sutra* appears on earth to give you comfort and understanding and not to scare you. Slowly it takes you from this world and carries you into the transcendental world. The white ox means the dynamic, powerful energy of Great Nature; it removes you slowly from the fire of this world to eternal peace, from desire to eternal rest.

Lin-chi used this quotation from the *sutra* as a test. If your mind is like a library of words and notations, holding many conceptions and all the systems of philosophy, East and West, you will certainly take this question seriously and try to give an answer from that secondary conception. But Lin-chi uses the quotation in an entirely different way, though I cannot express this point in words. It is like opening a book like Mother Goose and finding this question: "What are little girls made of?" You can hardly get the meaning of it. Do you understand? If you ask, "What are you thinking about?" "Oh, I don't know," it's the same. Lin-chi is expressing this attitude with his question: "What is the white ox on the bare ground?" This is not a joke. There is something which is impossible to express, but Lin-chi expresses that point with that question. And Hsing-shan wasn't a foolish monk. Hsing-shan replied—but not philosophically—

"*Moo, moo!*" Just as the Hatter asked Alice at his tea party, "What is 'it'?" and she says, "You know what it is." Perhaps the writer of *Alice in Wonderland* knows *it*. He was a teacher of mathematics, and I think he understood *it*. And children understand *it* while adults do not. But Lin-chi does not give in; he tests him once more:

The Master said, "A mute, eh?" This question is poison. I can picture and experience that moment with Lin-chi, but I cannot explain his answer.

Hsing-shan asked, *"What do you think, elder?"* He took the upper hand.

The Master said, "What a beast!" I cannot explain anymore except to say that it is like the gate of a beautiful shrine in Japan. At the gate are two pillars of the same size and same design, but the lion carved on one side has an open mouth, and on the other side, a closed mouth. So Lin-chi is using this natural law. He is seizing an opportunity to give the monk a dose of abuse—"What a beast!" At this moment, it is of fifty-fifty value. You must understand this law: in weight, the balance is fifty-fifty, but when one gains the other loses. You must study such things in the practice of Zen.

The Master questioned Lo-p'u, "Suppose there were two masters: whenever one administered a blow with his staff, the other would give a HO!; which one is more familiar to you?" When a Zen master "demonstrates" by striking with his staff, the power of the entire universe is in it. We do not explain the staff in these terms, of course, but we use this power. "What is Buddha?"—strike! This is the way of Zen teaching. But today we do not use the blow or the HO! This room is too small. I'm not able to use this HO! here. This HO! is a very big roar. So, the blow or the HO!—"which is more familiar to you?" Lin-chi certainly uses funny words. What he means is, which master is nearest the truth?

Lo-p'u said, "Neither of them are familiar to me." Neither blow nor HO! is familiar. He denied both at once. In other words, we try to find our selves in time and in space, but we must find time and space within ourselves. Do you understand? Today we find time and space in one truth and affirm both at once. This is Lo-p'u's attitude toward the rod and the HO!

The Master said, "So what is more familiar to you?" Lo-p'u roared, "HO!" The Master struck him. Had I been Lo-p'u, I would have hopped out of sight *before* the blow! I don't have the words to explain this any more deeply.

The Master, seeing a monk approach his quarters, opened both his hands wide. The monk did not utter a word. The Master asked, "Do you understand?" This opening of the hands is a particular expression of the Zen school and many masters do it. For example: When a student asks, "What is the highest Dharma?" the teacher says, "If you help me in my rice field today and work hard, I will give you the true answer tonight."

That evening in the cloister the student repeats the question, and the master opens both his hands—the highest Dharma.

There are many silences in Zen. Sometimes the silence is the word. The master does not wish the meaning to be adulterated by words. But this monk was dumbfounded by Lin-chi's gesture. So Lin-chi put the question; "Do you understand?"

The monk said, "No, I do not." This kind of monk is no good.

The Master said, "Hun-lun is impossible to rend asunder. I shall give you two pennies." Lin-chi is referring to a big mountain on the border of Tibet and Turkestan, running parallel with a Himalaya range running to the west. This mountain, called Hun-lun, is impossible to tear apart. The bolt of thunder may make a purple rift, but the mountain stands. The lightning may kill all angels of heaven and the demons in the sea, but the mountain remains. No more could Lin-chi open the mind of this monk: "Here's two cents. Go somewhere else. You are hopeless!"

XVI

When Ta-chueh arrived to pay homage to the Master, the Master raised his flywhisk. Ta-chueh spread his mat. The Master flung away his flywhisk. Ta-chueh folded up his mat and entered the monks' hall. A crowd of monks said, "That monk must be a kinsman of the Master. He didn't bow or get a dose of the Master's staff."

The Master heard of this and sent for Ta-chueh. Ta-chueh came before the Master. The Master said, "The crowd is grumbling that you have not yet bowed to this elder."

Ta-chueh said, "How are you?" and returned to the assembly.

SOKEI-AN SAYS:

Through this dialogue you will grasp a real element of Zen.

The Buddha said that the common mind is based upon its conceptions and does not see true existence. But once the common mind is enlightened it is based upon . . . there is no word, I am afraid to say anything here. It is very difficult to say a word in this place . . . You see, I cannot use any word here. It is based upon something that is not your mind-stuff. It is based upon the function that is bestowed by the cosmos. The enlightened mind is comfortably based upon this function and performs this function and uses this function as a carpenter uses his tools, as a doctor uses medicine, as an artist uses tubes of colors. This is the attitude of enlightenment, but the unenlightened attitude is based upon the tube. The tube is his base and he pushes color out of his brain and with this color smears the cosmos. No wonder he cannot see anything straight. The mind is an overcoat. Sometimes when I see somebody, if necessary I put on this overcoat. Otherwise, if I think it is not necessary, I just look at him and do not speak. When he says something, I say, "How do you do." If he says nothing and suddenly boxes my ears, I kick him. The cat and dog are like this; they growl, they spit, and slap. But the human being hears the growl and thinks, "Oh, how terrible, I'm afraid! What shall I do?" The thing to do is speak original stuff first, then think. That is the Zen attitude. So when I ask a Zen student, before father and mother, what were you? in answer the student must bring the entire cosmos, bring the universe, and not bring his mind. Then, in that moment, there is no mind or mind-stuff. Just bring me the whole universe. Then everything is finished.

When you read this dialogue between Ta-chueh [n.d.] and Lin-chi you will see that no action comes from mind-stuff. They are clear Zen students reflecting each other with clear mirrors.

When Ta-chueh arrived to pay homage to the Master, the Master raised his flywhisk. This is a very nice view of the Master's mind and enormous vision—a clear sky creating the black cloud of a hurricane.

Ta-chueh spread his mat. He spread his mat but didn't bow—as a fisherman quickly puts down his sail when he sees a black cloud on the horizon. So when Ta-chueh saw Lin-chi raise his *hossu*, he spread his rug. Is there any mind-stuff in Ta-chueh's brain?

The Master flung away his flywhisk. Ta-chueh folded up his mat and entered the monks' hall. It's the same view. The fisherman hoists his sail when the thunder fades away. Are you not doing this in *zazen*?

Hakuin asked about the sound of your single hand? How do you answer? If you are thinking about the symbol of the hand, that it must be some sort of esoteric, mysterious sound, you are using mind-stuff, and you cannot enter Zen.

A crowd of monks said, "That monk must be a kinsman of the Master. He didn't bow or get a dose of the Master's staff." I am quite sure Lin-chi was discouraged having heard this grumbling. What mind-stuff is this? Where is Zen? Where is the teaching?

The Master heard of this and sent for Ta-chueh. Ta-chueh came before the Master. The Master said, "The crowd is grumbling that you have not yet bowed to this elder." Hungry elders! When Ta-chueh came back all the monks came with him of course.

Ta-chueh said, "How are you?" and returned to the assembly. Ta-chueh and Lin-chi, spreading the mat and holding the *hossu*. They made a very deep connection. Lin-chi recognized Ta-chueh's great homage to him; he knew Ta-chueh, but he was testing his disciples to see if they had any understanding of his teaching.

Ta-chueh came up and said: "How are you?" He did not bow low; just leaned forward, because he was a kinsman of Lin-chi by his attitude— not by blood but through the Dharma, through understanding. In the Chinese idiom, one could say, Ta-chueh licked the whole crowd as a cat licks the whole plate. In American slang, Ta-chueh made a fool out of them.

This discourse illustrates both the one who acts directly from his clear soul without using mind-stuff and the one who doesn't. Being not involved with mind-stuff he performs his function while the other makes nothing but mice. When the monks said—*"That monk must be a kinsman of the Master. He didn't bow or get a dose of the Master's staff"*—it's just street-corner gossip.

XVII

Chao-chou while on a pilgrimage came to see the Master, whom he unexpectedly found washing his feet. Chao-chou questioned him, "What was the purpose in the Patriarch's coming from the West?"

The Master said, "I was just washing my feet."

Chao-chou approached the Master and gestured as if listening.

The Master asked him, "Do you wish to have a second dipper of muddy water thrown on your head?"

Chao-chou left.

SOKEI-AN SAYS:

Six generations from Bodhidharma was the Sixth Patriarch, Hui-neng. Under the Sixth Patriarch were two great disciples, Nan-yueh Huai-jang and Ch'ing-yuan Hsing-szu. The next generation after Nan-yueh was the famous Ma-tsu Tao-i. The third generation from Nan-yueh was Nan-ch'uan Pu-yuan, a famous Zen master, and Chao-chou was his disciple. He lived to be one hundred and twenty years old. He was a wanderer and in his old age had visited many Zen masters in his pilgrimages all over China. He is a great figure in Chinese Zen. Lin-chi and Chao-chou were contemporaries of that period, the Tang dynasty.

Once Chao-chou was asked by a monk, "What is Chao-chou?" (This is the same as asking the Buddha, "What is Buddha?") Chao-chou said, "East gate; west gate; south gate and north gate."

That was his answer. That was his style of Zen. Another story: Chao-chou's hometown, called Chao-chou, was famous for a great stone bridge. A monk on his way to see Chao-chou came to the bridge and was surprised to see just a wooden plank bridge. There must have been a stone bridge in the olden days. So when the monk met Chao-chou he asked him about it. "I heard of the famous great stone bridge of Chao-chou, but all I saw was a wooden plank bridge." (He is a little sarcastic.) That is: "I heard of the great master, Chao-chou, but now I only see a poor old monk!" Chao-chou said: "You only saw a wooden plank bridge, you did not see the great stone bridge of Chao-chou." (Chao-chou is, of course, talking about the great cosmos, the great universe.) The monk asked, "What is the great stone bridge of Chao-chou?"

Chao-chou said, "A donkey and also a mule will go through."

His words seem flat and insignificant, but his Zen is quite lofty and not so easy to understand. He was a very great Zen master. And of course, there is the koan MU. Once a monk asked Chao-chou: "Has a dog Buddha nature?" Chao-chou answered: "MU!"—NO! This is a wonderful koan. Anyone who has this koan spends about a couple of years on it. With this koan we clean up the bottom of our minds.

Chao-chou while on a pilgrimage came to see the Master, whom he unexpectedly found washing his feet. Like a tiger coming to see a dragon, Chao-chou entered the temple from the backyard, not from the front gate. He did not enter the temple as a great Zen master but as a beggar. It was probably the dusk of evening, and Lin-chi was washing his feet. Perhaps he had been working in the garden all that day long with the young monks and now in the evening was on the veranda cleaning up. Here Chao-chou walked in like a wolf—he was older than Lin-chi—and the Master looked at him. The great Zen Master Chao-chou then asked him a question, a wonderful question, before greeting him. What does it mean?

"What was the purpose in the Patriarch's coming from the West?" How do you observe this koan? Why do we study Zen thirty or forty years and as a result get nothing. You give up your home, your wife, your children, and as a result, you get nothing? For what purpose had Bodhidharma carried this doctrine to China? What was the purpose of this Zen Father coming from the West? This question, of course, means, What is the cardinal principle of Buddhism?

The Master said, "I was just washing my feet." What is the cardinal principle? I am washing my feet. *That* is the cardinal principle.

Chao-chou approached the Master and gestured as if listening. Five or six steps. He was inviting some trouble. Great courage, great man.

The Master asked him, "Do you wish to have a second dipper of muddy water thrown on your head?" The "second dipper" is quite interesting. At the first question, this first dipper was not thrown, but answered. Now, in this second question, he says: "Do you wish to have the second dipper of this muddy water thrown at your head?"

Chao-chou left. Chao-chou disappeared very quickly into the dusk of evening, and he never came back. That was the first meeting and the last. He didn't stick around. They were great contemporaries. Once in a lifetime they saw each other face to face. Chao-chou realized Lin-chi's sharpness. Lin-chi realized the common, flat style of Chao-chou. I like this. It's like someone coming to see me and finding me opening my letter-box in my overalls and asking, "Where is he?" and I answer, "He's not here."

XVIII

When Shang-tso Ting visited the Master to pay homage,
he asked a question: "What is the fundamental principle of
Buddhism?"
The Master descended from his seat. Seizing Ting by the
chest, he gave him a slap and shoved him back. Ting, recovering
his balance, stood fast. A monk who was looking on said, "Ting,
why don't you bow?"
As he bowed, enlightenment burst upon him.

SOKEI-AN SAYS:

When Shang-tso Ting visited the Master to pay homage, he asked a
question: "What is the fundamental principle of Buddhism?" This was the
formula for asking a question in those days—just get to the big point.

The Master descended from his seat. Seizing Ting by the chest, he gave
him a slap and shoved him back. You see this in Japan. I wish I could do
this in your country, but you come to my Zen room with philosophy. I
should slap you and see what you would do!

Ting, recovering his balance, stood fast. A monk who was looking
on said, "Ting, why don't you bow?"—when you get such wonderful
instruction. He was slapped, almost lost his balance and stood still. If he
hadn't been clean-hearted he would not have been able to bow.

As he bowed, enlightenment burst upon him. I cannot say much about
this, but there is a story about Ting when he was on a pilgrimage. One
day on a bridge at some river he met a young Zen monk going to see
Lin-chi. Ting asked him, "Where are you going?" They are strangers, but
they are Zen students and they recognize each other.

"I'm going to see Lin-chi."

"Sorry but he has entered nirvana."

"Oh, I've lost my opportunity in seeing him. Did you come from
there?

"Yes."

"Then I'll ask *you* a question, "What is the depth of this Zen river?"

Ting seized him and threw him in the water. There he will realize its
depth!

XIX

Ma-yu arrived at the monastery to pay homage to the Master. Spreading his mat, Ma-yu questioned him, "Which of the twelve faces of Kuan-yin is the main face?"

Descending from his seat, the Master seized the mat in one hand and grasped Ma-yu with the other and asked, "Where has the twelve-faced Kuan-yin gone?"

Ma-yu pulled himself free and attempted to sit on the mat. Raising his staff, the Master gave him a blow. Ma-yu seized the staff in both hands. Holding the staff between them, they entered the Master's chamber.

SOKEI-AN SAYS:

In this record Ma-yu is mentioned twice. Ma-yu is the name of a mountain in Southern China.

Ma-yu arrived at the monastery to pay homage to the Master. Spreading his mat, Ma-yu questioned him. This was unusual. He didn't bow. To ask something of a master, you must bow first then ask your question. Sometimes in abbreviating this ritual the monk just stands and opens the mat. Among friends, the brotherhood, we do that; we open a corner and it means salutation.

"Which of the twelve faces of Kuan-yin is the main face?" An interesting and unusual question. I think everyone knows Kuan-yin very well. You call her the Goddess of Mercy. This has nothing to do with the Goddess of Mercy, however. In Sanskrit, she is male, and her name is Avalokitesvara, the "Looking-down Lord." He looks down upon us with compassion. Avalokitesvara is a figure that represents the three great powers of wisdom, compassion, and courage. Avalokitesvara is represented in many ways. There is one that has a thousand arms that each grasps a different instrument. In this figure the entire occupation of sentient life is symbolized.

However, Ma-yu is asking about the twelve-faced Kuan-yin. Which of the twelve faces is the main face. We don't need to discuss how many—ten, twelve, or fourteen, it's not important. It's like asking which of Avalokitesvara's arms is the main arm. It's the same thing. Here it is, Kuan-yin. Which is the main face?

Descending from his seat, the Master seized the mat in one hand and grasped Ma-yu with the other and asked, "Where has the twelve-faced Kuan-yin gone?" Where has she gone? I wish to make an understanding with her. In the Zen school there is no discussion or philosophy. All is realized in body and soul. Lin-chi came down and took the mat in his hand. This indicates his transformation into Ma-yu. He seized him and asked, "Where is the twelve-faced Kuan-yin? Where has she gone?" There is no moment to take a breath. There is no Kuan-yin!

Ma-yu pulled himself free and attempted to sit on the mat. Lin-chi came down and took the Zen of Ma-yu. The matted floor is not so high. They exchanged their positions. Which is the main face now, Lin-chi or Ma-yu?

Raising his staff, the Master gave him a blow. They are not acting. The rod is painful if it falls upon your head!

Ma-yu seized the staff in both hands. Lin-chi took hold of one end of the rod and Ma-yu took hold of the other, pushing and pulling Which is the main face of Kuan-yin? In that moment, who is the king of the world?

Some Chinese monks criticize this part. They are like nervous tailors. They do not wish to make a wrinkle in the even cloth of Zen. If there is some wrinkle, they don't know the cause. If two pull evenly, there is no disturbance of ground. I think the Goddess of Mercy is not a good tailor making wrinkles. Like the human being, we are pulling the rod from both ends. Who is the master, you or I? Which is I? Which is you? Everyone talks about capitalism, communism, socialism, many isms, but which is the main face of Kuan-yin?

Holding the staff between them, they entered the Master's chamber. Kuan-yin is a good illustration of the whole community of the world, and Ma-yu and Lin-chi, without speaking any theory demonstrated all society. Pulling and pushing they understood each other and so holding to each other went out to Lin-chi's own chamber. Their battle was neither of words nor thoughts. They fought a fifty-fifty battle. They were both great Zen masters.

To understand this dialogue, you must understand that the Avalokiteshvara Bodhisattva of a thousand arms is a symbol of wholeness. We are the hands of Avalokiteshvara, and we have instruments in these hands. Avalokiteshvara is a plain picture of the whole cosmos—the unity of all sentient beings, the whole *and* parts. Usually in the West, the creator creates all individuals separately, but in the East Avalokiteshvara is a symbol of no-creation. He exists from the beginningless beginning to endless end and has only *one* body. Avalokiteshvara is beyond the Western imagination. The Western God has two arms, but Avalokiteshvara has one thousand arms and one thousand faces. This conception illustrates the wholeness of the universe and the relation between its parts. Each part will become the master and the subject. When one becomes the host, the rest will be the guests. Host and guest are interchangeable as Ma-yu and Lin-chi demonstrated. This happened in one moment and it took my tongue fifteen minutes to talk about it!

This disclosure is very easy to understand as a Zen discourse. There is no secret. When you attain Zen every day and every moment, this demonstration must be in your own daily life or else there is no value.

XX

The Master questioned a monk: "In certain circumstances, my shout is like the jeweled sword of the Diamond King. In some circumstances, my shout is like a golden-haired lion squatting on the earth. In other circumstances, my shout is like a pole that drives out fish, or like a cluster of weeds thrown upon a river to gather fish under its shade. And in yet other circumstances, my shout has no effect. How do you understand this?"

The monk was confounded. The Master shouted, "HO!"

SOKEI-AN SAYS:

Lin-chi is talking about the principle behind his four kinds of HO! The monks of the Tang Dynasty used it everywhere. Today it is sometimes used in *sanzen* and not at any other times. Lin-chi is asking us if we understand his shouts. It is the main point of the lecture tonight. There is no other place in this record that he explains it. Sometimes the HO! is used to scold, to upbraid, or to blame, but Zen students use it as an expression of their understanding of the manifold dimensions of the universe, Occasionally a Zen master will shout to scold someone, but it is very rare.

The Master questioned a monk: "In certain circumstances, my shout is like the jeweled sword of the Diamond King." It is the hardest of all diamonds. In this circumstance his shout is like the thunder of the Diamond Sword; all phenomena of the cosmos crash into pieces and disappear. With the blow of the diamond sword, all the cosmos takes a tumble and hangs upside down in the sky. When Lin-chi shouts HO! all the necks of all the devas of the Brahmaloka roll out from their bodies and their blood floods the universe. Brahmaloka is this [indicates head]. "Brahma" means pure place, or head. "Loka" means world. You may think this world is small because you always observe yourself with your physical eye. When you look up at the sky and see a shining star you feel it does not belong to you. You do not know that the distance to that star which reflects into your eye is a part of your physical extension. When the shining star reaches your eye, this million-years traveling of light is *your* physical extension; that is, it is your cosmos, your world, and no one else's. When we talk about this scientifically, you agree, but when we talk about this religiously, you don't agree. In the Christian sense, you think perhaps God in guarding you, gives you your ability to manage your life. But in the Zen sense, all this cosmos is yourself. God is not guarding you; you are guarding yourself. In Zen, when I say "I," I include you. So when you say "I" you include me, too. So when Lin-chi shouts HO! which is the diamond sword, all this cosmos hangs topsy-turvy in the sky. One shout and all disappears. And if you go to Lin-chi and ask him, "What is Buddhism, and how does it differ from the Buddha's?" Lin-chi would shout HO! which is the diamond sword. Thus your small question is blown from your brain. He wipes the slate and destroys it. This is his diamond sword shout.

"In some circumstances, my shout is like a golden-haired lion squatting on the earth." It squats like a sitting lion. When Lin-chi shouts this HO! all those wild foxes—wild spirits—meditating in caves, deep in fundamental meditation, will shake awake, and trembling in their fear, disappear. And not only wild foxes. Those meditating monks who say, "I am a highly esteemed ascetic and have come from a cheap and dirty world," will also have their dreams scatter and awake from their hypothetical meditation— charlatan Zen master and student alike. But when the empty sky—the golden-haired lion—hears it, it will smile. But how can the sky of the Sitting Lion smile? As Mahakashyapa smiled when the Buddha held out

the blue lotus. That is how. If you have really destroyed all notions, you will smile when you hear this HO!

I do not want to explain too much more, but I will give you a hint concerning the two shouts of Lin-chi so far. In the shout of the Diamond Sword, all existing notions are destroyed—all phenomena and those identified with appearances. In the shout of the golden-haired lion, all false meditation, assumed tranquillity, and all conceptions of nothingness will be destroyed. The third one is easy to understand.

In other circumstances, my shout is like a pole that drives out fish, or like a cluster of weeds thrown upon a river to gather fish under its shade." This is Zen idiom. It is the bamboo pole with which you poke fish out of water. On a hot day a fisherman throws a cluster of weeds on the water and the fish go into the net. This is the ancient way of fishing. I think American fish are too smart and it may not work here!

One who hears this shout drops all masks and shows his real face. If a thief were to hear this shout, he would drop his loot, run, and disappear. It is the same when a Zen students enters the room of his Zen master. Before he can even ask a question the student is sometimes received with a shout. One HO shows everything the Master has in mind. Everything comes out. The fourth one is dreadful.

"And in yet other circumstances, my shout has no effect. How do you understand this?" The student receives this shout with no effect, but answers HO! just the same. You hear this most dreadful HO! and you awake from the dream of spring under the cherry blossoms; you open your eyes and you realize that all your comrades are sleeping, that all the world is sleeping. When I was in my regiment on the battlefield of Manchuria, I awoke on a snowy night and thought, "These bodies around me are deeply sleeping, but their minds are still active, still fighting. It is the same with all this Buddhist talk. All the disputations of the teachers are nothing but sleep-talk. But when you hear the HO! that has no effect you will awaken. When you hear HO! you wake up and see that all exposition, all eloquence, all discourse is nothing but sleep-talk.

The monk was confounded. The Master shouted, "HO!" Lin-chi suddenly turned his weapon on the pupil, and the student was startled. When the monk was confounded, Lin-chi smote him with a Diamond HO!

XXI

The Master questioned a nun, "Is this a good visit or a bad visit?"

The nun gave a HO!

Brandishing his staff, the Master said, "Once more! Once more!"

Again the nun gave a HO! The Master struck her.

SOKEI-AN SAYS:

Lin-chi asked this nun a dualistic question: Is this a good visit or a bad visit? In an Indian Buddhist temple, one would as a salutation say, "Welcome, this is a good visit." So Lin-chi asks the nun, is it or not? In this question is good or bad, this or that. Is this a good morning for you or a bad morning for you? When the nun gave a HO what sort of HO was it? Is it the Diamond Sword HO? Is it the Sitting Lion HO? The air is choking. Brandishing his staff, Lin-chi says, "Once more!" How do you observe this? Was she affirming one and denying the other, falling in with Lin-chi's dualism? This is a good morning. It's not necessary to ask if it is bad. To test her once more, Lin-chi asked her to shout again. Her second HO was affirming the "good morning." Lin-chi understood that her understanding of the universe was realistic. She was suddenly driven into a corner, so Lin-chi hit her. He must hit her; there was no other way in this case. Certainly no other way for Lin-chi, and certainly no other way for the nun except HO. But this type of elucidation will spoil you. It is not a *real* understanding of this conversation.

This is a beautiful fight and the nun certainly acted wonderfully,

XXII

Lung-ya questioned the Master, "What was the Patriarch's purpose in coming from the West?"

The Master said, "Hand me that back rest."

Lung-ya put the back rest in his hand. The Master struck him with it.

Lung-ya said, "I submit myself to your blow, but there was no purpose in the Patriarch's coming from the West."

Later, when Lung-ya went to see Ts'ui-wei. Lung-ya questioned him, "What was the Patriarch's purpose in coming from the West?"

Ts'ui-wei said, "Hand me that mat."

Lung-ya handed him the mat. Ts'ui-wei hit him with it. Lung-ya said, "I submit myself to your blow, but there was no purpose in the Patriarch's coming from the West."

After Lung-ya had become the master of a temple, a monk entered his room and asked for an explanation, "We heard that when your Reverence was a wanderer, you went to visit two elders. Do you acknowledge their authority or not?"

Lung-ya said, "I deeply acknowledge their authority, but there was no purpose in the Patriarch's coming from the West."

SOKEI-AN SAYS:

The koan, "What was the Patriarch's purpose in coming from the West?" is also found in the famous Zen koan collection *Blue Cliff Record*. In this dialogue, the magnanimous Lin-chi couldn't say a word in reply to Lung-ya, and Lin-chi and Ts'ui-wei couldn't use their rods on Lung-ya.

Lung-ya questioned the Master, "What was the Patriarch's purpose in coming from the West?" That is, what is the basic principle of Buddhism? The Patriarch is Bodhidharma.

The Master said, "Hand me that back rest." Lung-ya knew—of course he knew—if he handed him the backrest what he would do.

Lung-ya put the backrest in his hand. The Master struck him with it. This is the basic principle of Buddhism—a funny principle. Do you understand? It's the same as your mother asking you for her yardstick, and when you give it to her, she strikes you with it. Is this the basic principle of Zen? Yes, it is the principle. It is so very plain to me, but so very difficult to explain.

Lung-ya said, "I submit myself to your blow, but there was no purpose in the Patriarch's coming from the West." Later, when Lung-ya went to see Ts'ui-wei. Lung-ya questioned him, "What was the Patriarch's purpose in coming from the West?" Ts'ui-wei said, "Hand me that mat." Lung-ya handed him the mat. Ts'ui-wei hit him with it. Lung-ya said, "I submit myself to your blow, but there was no purpose in the Patriarch's coming from the West." It's as though Lin-chi and Ts'ui-wei had used television or the telephone—had talked to each other before Lung-ya arrived at the temple. They acted exactly the same way.

If you were hanging from the top branch of a tree by your teeth and your hands and feet were not free and someone asks you, "What was the Patriarch's purpose in coming from the West?" how would you answer? If you say a word, you will fall. If you do not, you cannot answer the question. What do you do? Somehow you smile!

When Lung-ya said, *"I submit myself to your blow, but there was no purpose in the Patriarch's coming from the West,"* there was no Buddhism. "All right, hit me if you want to." In New York the answer would be "Oh yeah?"

If you study art, you might begin to study from plaster forms—from plaster hands and feet, torsos and busts. Then you might try to make a copy of the statue Venus de Milo, or copy the sculptures of Michelangelo or study Chinese and Japanese art, then come to a life model. You cannot see the beauty of nature at first in a life model—study first, and then see Great Nature. You cannot make everything, of course, but of what real use is clay? Living nature is the best art. The painter will throw away his canvas; the dramatist will climb down from the stage to the street corner and will see real drama in daily life. "There is no Zen, Ts'ui-wei. Hit me if you will. I submit to your blows as a chief actor." This is Lung-ya's viewpoint. Everyone will come to this at least once—every artist.

There was a famous poet in China who when he turned eighty all of a sudden evoked a poem from Great Nature. The human word wasn't good enough for him, so he stopped making poems. Everybody in the village saw him pushing a baby cart. That was his work. Many artists come to this point and die there, however. You must really come to this point by your own experience. Here, there is no Zen, no Buddhism. But if you die there you die on a flat, plain surface of earth. Someone said that not many die before enlightenment, but many die on the flat surface of earth after attaining enlightenment.

After Lung-ya had become the master of a temple, a monk entered his room and asked for an explanation, "We heard that when your Reverence was a wanderer, you went to visit two elders. Do you acknowledge their authority or not?" Lung-ya said, "I deeply acknowledge their authority." I agree with Lin-chi, and I agree with Ts'ui-wei. This is wonderful. He did not die on the flat surface of earth.

"... *but there was no purpose in the Patriarch's coming from the West.*" He is repeating the same words, but the position from which he repeats them is entirely different from the position when he was with Lin-chi and Ts'ui-wei.

With Lin-chi and Ts'ui-wei the words came from his lips—no art, no Zen, no Buddhism. In this last part he says no art, no Zen, no Buddhism. The same words, but he is persistently repeating this as his sign of his religion—used the same words and same attitude as his slogan. So he understood his standpoint.

If I had died on that flat surface of earth after all my Zen, I would not have put my robes on. I would not have come to America. I would be living in Japan with the artists. I would have put on certain clothes and taken a conventional attitude. Why must I make myself so conspicuous? For art? When you come down to the flat surface of nature you throw away your palate; you know you cannot make good enough poetry. Daily conversations are good enough. After three or four years you pick up your pen and write and it is so remote—only one line, but it says everything. Noble sculpture—some day you will find beauty in that broken arm of Venus de Milo. You must reach there. But first you must come down to the flat surface. However, if you are on that flat surface now, it is not good. After enlightenment you must come down once more.

When Lung-ya said, "*I deeply acknowledge their authority, but there was no purpose in the Patriarch's coming from the West,*" the words corresponded exactly to the blows of Lin-chi and Ts'ui-wei. I cannot say any more about this. It is the hardest part of Zen to observe. All teachers will really take the time to help the student understand this point. Some day you will come to it. If you are an artist, you will understand after you have thrown away your palettes and broken your brushes. After four or five years in silence you will find art in the fir trees of a Japanese forest—then you will survive in your art.

So in Zen, too, everyone must come to this flat life. If you die there, you are enlightened, but you cannot be a Buddhist. The same with Christianity. You cannot be a Christian. It is a new viewpoint on life.

XXIII

Five hundred monks were staying in Ching-shan's temple,
but few questioned him about Zen. Huang-po urged the Master
to go to the temple, then asked the Master, "What will you do
when you get there?"

The Master said, "I will naturally know what to do."

When the Master arrived at the temple, without removing
his traveling clothes he entered the Dharma Hall and looked at
Ching-shan. When Ching-shan raised his head, the Master gave
a HO! As Ching-shan was about to utter a word, the Master left,
sweeping his sleeves behind him.

Later, a monk questioned Ching-shan, "At that time,
reverend, what did you say that the monk gave you a HO!?"

Ching-shan said, "He came from Huang-po's group. If you
desire to know, you had better ask him."

More than half of the five hundred monks dispersed.

SOKEI-AN SAYS:

Ching-shan temple was one of the famous temples in the Tang
Dynasty. Today it is one of China's sacred places. To go to T'ien-t'ai
Mountain one must pass through Ching-shan. It is a mountain of
passages, a transient mountain. There was a famous Ching-shan the
First, and a Ching-shan the Second; but we are not quite sure which
this one was. Ching-shan the First was quite an old monk. He was not
a contemporary to Huang-po; he was a contemporary to Pai-chang,
Huang-po's teacher. Therefore, this Ching-shan is not Ching-shan the
First. This Ching-shan wrote letters to Huang-po; therefore, we can
surmise that this Ching-shan was a friend of Huang-po's.

Five hundred monks were staying in Ching-shan's temple, but few
questioned him about Zen. They were probably followers of the Pure
Land School, but they were Zen monks. This was the beginning of
Amitabha Buddha worship in China in the Tang dynasty. In every Zen
temple in China the monks chanted Amitabha's name besides practicing
meditation. Of course this chanting is not important. In Zen we just
worship according to the Buddhism of our temple.

Huang-po urged the Master to go to the temple, then asked the Master, "What will you do when you get there?" Huang-po is testing Lin-chi. His question is very simple but very sharp.

The Master said, "I will naturally know what to do." It's as you say here in America, "I'll know when I get there." It's the same, and it is the attitude of a Buddhist. We do not make preparations or make preliminary plans. We do not keep such unnecessary furniture in our brains. Lin-chi did not say, "Well, master, I'll say so-and-so." We just observe the conditions and then we decide what to say or do. There is a funny Japanese story about this:

A young novice, that is, a boy between ten and thirteen years old, was responsible for sweeping the street in front of his temple. There were temples on both sides of the street for about eight blocks, so it was known as Temple Street. It was the duty of this young novice to sweep the street every morning. Sometimes the Zen master of the temple at the end of the street would pass through as he was sweeping. The novice felt that he ought to take advantage of this opportunity and ask the master a question, but he couldn't think of any, so he asked his own master what question to ask the master. His master said, "Why don't you ask him where he is going?" This kind of question in Zen is never simple; it's a very deep question. The master told the novice to seize the passing master's sleeve and observe how he answered. One morning about six o'clock, as the novice was sweeping the street as usual, the Zen master from the end of the street appeared. The novice seized his sleeve and asked him, "Where are you going?"

The Zen master replied, "I go at the mercy of the wind."

The novice could not utter another word. He reported back to his own master and told him what had been said. Then he asked: "What should I say now?"

The master said: "Well, that wind he goes at the mercy of is no good. You must get rid of that wind. Next time say, "If there is no wind, what will you do?"

There is a saying in Japan: nature will take care of it. It's the same. But if nature doesn't take care of you, what will you do? If there is a typhoon or earthquake, nature will not take care of you. If there is no wind, what will you do?

The novice said, "All right," and went back to his work. But though he swept the street every morning as before, he never saw the master from the end of the street again.

About a month later, another Zen master came by as the novice was sweeping in the morning. The novice thought, "Oh what a wonderful opportunity! I'll ask *him* the questions."

So he asked the Zen master: "Where are you going?"

The Zen maser said, "I'm going to a funeral service."

The boy was quick with his second question: "If there is no wind, what will you do?"

The master said, "I do not need the wind for a funeral service."

This is like the story of a Japanese man who was invited to see President Taft. The Japanese man had prepared a list of three hundred questions he might be asked by the president. But when he went to the White House and met him, the president didn't ask him any of the three hundred questions, so he couldn't say a word.

Lin-chi's attitude was different. "When I arrive there I shall naturally know what to do."

When the Master arrived at the temple, without removing his traveling clothes, he entered the Dharma Hall and looked at Ching-shan. He came up unexpectedly and looked at the Master. The Zen monk puts on a very big umbrella hat made of weeds which half covers his back. His sandals are straw and he carries his *kesa*, an apron-like vestment, in a knapsack that he fastens around his waist. Lin-chi came up into the temple in his sandals, holding his hat in his hand,

When Ching-shan raised his head, the Master gave a HO! In that precise moment he vomited a HO! upon Ching-shan.

As Ching-shan was about to utter a word, the Master left, sweeping his sleeves behind him. He turned his back and left. The distance from Mount Huang-po to Mount Ching (Ching-shan) is about that from Chicago to St. Louis. Lin-chi came all that way just for this. A very strange Zen dialogue.

Later, a monk questioned Ching-shan, "At that time, reverend, what did you say that the monk gave you a HO!?" It would have been a disgrace for a Zen monk to ask such a question after Lin-chi had left. We call this "the medicine bottle after the coffin." It was like offering medicine after the patient has died, or like making a rope after the thief is gone. Do you know what thoughts were in Lin-chi's mind? If Lin-chi had any thoughts in his mind, he would not have come from Huang-po to Ching-shan. This Ching-shan was not a bad Zen master, but he was timid.

Ching-shan said, "He came from Huang-po's group. If you desire to know, you had better ask him." The master's answer was good. But if anyone were to ask Lin-chi what thoughts were in his mind, he'd better stuff cotton in his ears first!

More than half of the five hundred monks dispersed. They went to Huang-po's, and Ching-shan's temple was emptied. This was Zen in the time of the Tang Dynasty. No lectures, no discourses. Lin-chi came, said HO!, and turned on his heel before five hundred monks. I hope such a time will come again. We do not need words. If you talk about truth, there is no truth.

XXIV

One day P'u-hua was in the streets of town begging everyone he met for a one-piece robe. Everyone offered him one, but he did not accept any. Hearing about it, the Master ordered the head monk to purchase a coffin. When P'u-hua arrived at the monastery, the Master said to him, "I have provided you with a one-piece robe."

Whereupon P'u-hua carried the coffin on his shoulder and strolled along the streets of the town, crying aloud, "Lin-chi has provided me with a one-piece robe! I shall pass away at the eastern gate!"

The people of the town scrambled after him, but then P'u-hua said, "No, I cannot do it today. However, tomorrow I shall pass away at the southern gate."

Thus postponing his passing for three days, no one believed him. On the fourth day, when no one was following him, P'u-hua went beyond the town wall alone.

P'u-hua then got into the coffin and asked a passerby to nail it up. After the passerby spread the news, the townspeople

*gathered by the coffin and opened it, but P'u-hua was not
there. In the sky, however, they heard the ringing of his bell as it
gradually faded away.*

SSOKEI-AN SAYS:

This was the end of poor P'u-hua, and it is a mysterious story. I think no Hindu magician goes this way! But we must not forget there is a viewpoint to observe in this story. The morning that Christ's disciples went to the sepulcher and looked in, two angels stood there, but no Christ. Perhaps if you understand this you will understand P'u-hua's death. A terrible, beautiful death for poor P'u-hua!

One day P'u-hua was in the streets of town begging everyone he met for a one-piece robe. When the Indian monks came to China, the emperor ordered them to cover their shoulders and arms, too, so they sewed their shirt and shoulder pieces together, and then sleeves were added, and this completed the monk's robe as it is used today.

Everyone offered him one, but he did not accept any. He refused everyone. He wanted a special kind of robe.

Hearing about it, the Master ordered the head monk to purchase a coffin. When P'u-hua arrived at the monastery, the Master said to him, "I have provided you with a one-piece robe." Lin-chi provided him with a coffin. When one dies in China, friends come and bend the dead man's joints into a smaller shape. Sometimes you hear a crunch. I have heard it for myself, and it is not a pleasant sound!

Whereupon P'u-hua carried the coffin on his shoulder and strolled along the streets of the town, crying aloud, "Lin-chi has provided me with a one-piece robe! I shall pass away at the eastern gate!" The people of the town scrambled after him, but then P'u-hua said, "No, I cannot do it today. However, tomorrow I shall pass away at the southern gate." That town had four gates as is usual in Chinese towns, a wall and four gates, one for each direction of the compass. Sometimes there is more city outside these walls than there is inside, but there are always walls. The Japanese, however, dig ditches to protect themselves, and then they build a bridge to pass over them. When Japanese people meet a stranger they say: "I hope this makes a bridge between us." The Chinese say: "We hope you will break in."

Thus postponing his passing for three days, no one believed him. On the fourth day, when no one was following him, P'u-hua went beyond the town wall alone. P'u-hua then got into the coffin and asked a passerby to nail it up. After the passerby spread the news, the townspeople gathered by the coffin and opened it, but P'u-hua was not there. All the people came and broke into the coffin. They looked in and found no one. It was very simple. When I was a young monk I thought this might be a trick—a coffin trick. It is the same in Christianity. The disciples of Christ came the third day and found nothing. How do you explain it? How do you understand it?

In the sky, however, they heard the ringing of his bell as it gradually faded away. P'u-hua was always ringing his bell in the street so all would hear. He died a most beautiful death. He asked for a robe made of wood, but we always put on the robe of flesh. When we die, we die in this coffin. And if one opens this coffin, we will not be seen. When I die and you come to view me, I am sure that I will not be found, for I am not here. If you understand that, you understand this story.

Pilgrimages (a)

I

In the beginning, Lin-chi was one of the multitude under Huang-po. His deeds were pure and single-minded. The head monk commended him, saying, "Though he is a youth, he is different from the others." So he questioned Lin-chi, "How long have you been here?"

Lin-chi said, "For three years."

The head monk asked, "Have you asked the master any questions?"

Lin-chi said, "Not yet. I do not know what to ask."

The head monk asked, "Why don't you go and see the reverend who heads the temple and ask him about the fundamental principle of Buddhism?"

Thereupon Lin-chi went and questioned Huang-po. But before he had even uttered a word, Huang-po hit him.

Lin-chi came back. The head monk asked, "What happened in your questioning?"

Lin-chi said, "Before I had even uttered a word the master hit me. I do not understand."

The head monk said, "Go again and question him."

So Lin-chi went to question Huang-po again, and again Huang-po hit him. Thus Lin-chi questioned him three times, and was hit three times.

Lin-chi came back to the head monk and said, "Fortunately in your benevolence you permitted me to question the master. Three times I questioned him and three times I was hit. I regret that there must be some obstruction in my mind that hinders my *understanding of his profound meaning. I shall be withdrawing for a time."*

The head monk said, "If you withdraw, you must first take leave of the master."

Lin-chi bowed low and retired.

The head monk went to the master's quarters beforehand and said, "The youth who questioned you is the very essence of the Dharma. If he comes to ask your permission to leave, be gracious. A huge tree could be carved from him that someday will offer cool shade for all souls under heaven."

Lin-chi went and asked Huang-po's permission to leave. Huang-po said, "You must not go to any other place but Ta-yu's in Kao-an. He will teach you."

When Lin-chi arrived at Ta-yu's temple, Ta-yu asked, "Where have you come from?"

Lin-chi said, "From Huang-po."

Ta-yu asked, "What did he say?"

Lin-chi said, "I questioned him three times about the fundamental principle of Buddhism, and three times I was hit. I do not understand whether I was at fault or not."

Ta-yu said, "Huang-po, like a good grandmother, was utterly kind to you! Why have you come here asking whether you are at fault or not?"

At this, enlightenment burst upon Lin-chi, who exclaimed, "From the beginning, there has been nothing to Huang-po's Buddhism!"

Ta-yu grabbed Lin-chi by the chest and said, "You bed-wetting little devil! A moment ago you were asking whether you were at fault or not, and now you say there is nothing to Huang-po's Buddhism! What have you seen? Speak! Speak!"

Lin-chi struck Ta-yu in the ribs three times. Ta-yu thrust him away and said, "Huang-po is your teacher! I will have nothing to do with you!"

Lin-chi left Ta-yu and returned to Huang-po. Huang-po saw him coming and said, "You, young fellow! Coming and going like this you will find no end to it!"

Lin-chi said, "I came back because of your grandmotherly kindness." Lin-chi paid homage to Huang-po and stood beside him.

Huang-po questioned him, "Where have you been?"

Lin-chi said, "It was but the other day that, obeying your kind instructions, I went to see Ta-yu."

Huang-po asked, "What did he say?"

Lin-chi related the story. Huang-po said, "Wait till he comes here, and I'll give him a painful dose!"

Lin-chi said, "Why wait? Take the dose right now!"

Then he slapped Huang-po.

Huang-po said, "You lunatic! You have come to pull the tiger's whiskers!"

Lin-chi thundered, "HO!"

Huang-po said, "Attendant! Drag this lunatic out of here! Drive him into the monks' hall!"

SOKEI-AN SAYS:

At that time, Lin-chi was quite young—about seventeen years of age; some say twenty. He had studied the *vinaya* and the T'ien-t'ai and Avatamsaka Schools of Buddhism, which at that time were the dominant schools of Buddhism in China. When he arrived at Huang-po's temple, there were about five hundred monks living there. In the mornings he worked with the other students in the fields. In the afternoons he was in the meditation hall. And in the evening he helped prepare the bath for the elder monks, the food in the kitchen, and the tables in the eating hall. For three years he worked hard, exactly like the other students. He was just one of the crowd, like one out of five hundred students at a university. When the *Record* says, "His deeds were pure and single-minded," the idiom used in Chinese means "pure gold." The characters are "gold" and "oneness." There was no mixture of elements in his mind—in other words, no alloys.

It is very hard to be like that. When you are drinking water, you are drinking water. When you are eating, you are eating. When you are in meditation, you are in meditation. You are not thinking of this and that all at the same time. When you are looking at a flower or listening to music, you are doing just that and nothing more. If you think this is easy to come to, you do not understand. Usually we do not use our minds independently and do not respond naturally to circumstances that arise—we are always depending upon something. This realization came to Hui-neng, the Sixth Patriarch, when he heard a voice chanting the *Diamond Sutra* while he was selling kindling wood in the streets of his native town. (I, too, sold kindling wood in the streets for six months out West.) Hearing the words "Depending upon nothing, use your mind"— that is, use your mind independently—he suddenly awoke. It was the beginning of his enlightenment.

If you say you will do so-and-so because you are a Socialist, a Zen Buddhist, or a Christian, you are not as pure and single-minded as Lin-chi. There are many people who cannot associate with others because of their religion. It limits them if they depend on it in this way.

Seeing this about Lin-chi-chi the head monk must have said to himself, *"Though he is a youth he is different from the others."*

Lin-chi was an honest student. He had studied the *vinaya* and the *Avatamsaka Sutra* and now he was in a Zen temple. He was not stupid. He had worked faithfully and meditated sincerely. He had no questions. Why would he go to question the great master, head of five hundred monks?

So Ch'en Tsun-su questioned Lin-chi, *"How long have you been here?"*
Lin-chi said, "For three years."
The head monk asked, "Have you asked the master any questions?"
Lin-chi said, "Not yet, I do not know what to ask."

The head monk then asked him, *"Why don't you go and see the reverend who heads the temple and ask him about the fundamental principle of Buddhism?"*—that is, that which was handed down from generation to generation. But when Lin-chi stood before Huang-po and asked about the fundamental principle of Buddhism, Huang-po hit him with his six-foot rod. It was like being hit by the whole universe!

Lin-chi had questioned Huang-po three times and was hit three times. If he were an American, he would say, "Good gracious, he must be crazy to beat me like that! I'm going to Wall Street to get a job!" But Lin-chi realized there was some obstruction in his mind that prevented his understanding of the master's meaning in beating him. "I shall go away," he thought. "I have been eating the food of Buddha and partaking of Buddha's shelter. It is not right for me to continue doing this. I shall beg door-to-door for my subsistence. Perhaps I shall never come back here again. I'll go out into the world and travel, straighten myself out, and experience the hard life. Being supported in Huang-po's temple is too good for me. I'm ashamed of myself."

Well, when he told Ch'en Tsun-su about his decision, Ch'en Tsun-su reminded him that he must first take leave of the master. But before Lin-chi could get to Huang-po, Ch'en Tsun-su visited the master and told him how he had been observing Lin-chi for the last three years and had always found him to be a diligent student. Then he said to Huang-po, *"If he comes to ask your permission to leave, be gracious. A huge tree could be carved from him that someday will offer cool shade for all souls under heaven."*

Lin-chi thought over what Ch'en Tsun-su had told him. So he went to Huang-po to ask permission to leave. Lin-chi was a very young monk and Huang-po was a giant with curly white hair. Huang-po didn't have a weak character. He didn't just say all right to Lin-chi's request; he commanded him to go to Ta-yu. *Huang-po said, "You must not go to any other place but Ta-yu's in Kao-an. He will teach you."* He will show you what I meant.

Ta-yu's temple was three hundred miles to the northwest of Huang-po's temple. Ta-yu was a disciple of a Zen master who was a descendant of Ma-tsu. The trip proposed by Huang-po was no easy journey. A monk carries no provisions on such a trip; he is given about fifteen pennies to start off with.

When Lin-chi arrived at Ta-yu's temple, there was the usual conversation whenever a new monk comes to a temple. Ta-yu asked him where he had come from. Upon learning it was from Huang-po, Ta-yu inquired what Huang-po had said to him when he had left. Discouraged, Lin-chi just told the truth, and Ta-yu looked at him.

In China, whenever a master is indulgent with young monks, he is said to be like a grandmother. So when Lin-chi told Ta-yu how Huang-po had beaten him three times when he asked him about the fundamental principle of Buddhism and whether he was at fault or not, Ta-yu said, *"Huang-po, like a good grandmother, was utterly kind to you! Why have you come here asking whether you are at fault or not?"*

At Ta-yu's words, enlightenment burst upon him—Ah, I see what I did not see before! Then Lin-chi said, *"From the beginning, there has been nothing to Huang-po's Buddhism!"*

He had been three years in Huang-po's temple without asking anything, and now he realized his master's kindness—Ah, that was it!

Lin-chi's face and voice penetrated Ta-yu's heart. I'm sure Ta-yu thought, "This is unusual; I must test him." So Ta-yu grabbed Lin-chi and shouted, "*You bed-wetting little devil! A moment ago you were asking whether you were at fault or not, and now you say there is nothing to Huang-po's Buddhism! What have you seen? Speak! Speak!*" "Say it! Spit it out!"

I think Lin-chi was already a huge tree that would shelter future generations of Zen students.

Lin-chi poked Ta-yu in the ribs three times. Ta-yu thrust him off, saying, "Huang-po is your teacher! I will have nothing to do with you!" Lin-chi had suddenly opened his Eye to the true Dharma. He had seen an entirely different world. He had come out of the usual topsy-turvydom. Now he saw reality—he was really born as a man. Before this he was just like an animal—he had eyes and ears, but he was not using them as his own. Now that he had opened his Eye, he used it as his own faculty.

Here I must draw the distinction between instinct and intuition. You may see a little dog on the street, kicking and scratching at the sidewalk without realizing what it is doing. The dog is acting out of instinct. If you clearly observe the human being, you will see he is doing the same thing, just performing a function bestowed upon him by nature.

When Lin-chi got back to Huang-po's temple, Huang-po was in his own quarters. When Lin-chi entered Huang-po's room, Huang-po was ready for him: "*You, young fellow! Coming and going like this you will find no end to it!*" In other words, "You oaf! What's all this coming and going? You'll never get anywhere this way!"

So Lin-chi said, "You're so kind, just like my old grandmother. That's why I've come back."

Lin-chi is quite changed in his attitude as he repeats Ta-yu's words. Lin-chi paid homage to Huang-po and stood beside him.

In China, when a disciple wished to stay with a teacher, he would stand beside him, his hands on his chest, and would not utter a word until the teacher spoke.

Huang-po asked, "*Where have you been?*"

Had Huang-po forgotten the instructions he had given to Lin-chi? No, he didn't forget. He was trying him out, finding out what he attained.

Lin-chi said, "It was but the other day that, obeying your kind instructions, I went to see Ta-yu."

Lin-chi answered in a straightforward manner, with no affectation of any kind. Very often when a disciple comes to see a Zen teacher and is asked, "Where have you been?" or some such question, the disciple makes a dramatic answer—"I came as the wind." Or he might exaggerate what he had been through to reach the master. But Lin-chi was an honest and sincere young man.

Lin-chi told the master exactly what had happened. It might have been five or six months before and a long journey away, but he did not mention it.

Then Huang-po said, "Wait till Ta-yu comes here. I'll give it to him!"

Lin-chi said, "Why wait for him to come here? Have it now!"

Saying this, Lin-chi-chi slapped Huang-po.

This is a simple point to understand. Once, a monk who had passed Hakuin's koan, the sound of the single hand, met a nun seated on a stone outside the monk's hall. "I understand you passed Hakuin's hand koan?" she said.

"Yes," he told her.

"Now," she demanded, "without using your hand, make this nun stand up."

He was very puzzled, so the nun laughed. "You passed nothing," she said.

Everything must be observed from the *dharmakaya* point of view. This is the first sign in the understanding of reality.

Lin-chi said to Huang-po, "Why wait for Ta-yu to come here? Have it now!"

Lin-chi was already a lion, wasn't he? From that very first day he was a lion. His career as a Zen master started with his three blows to Ta-yu. Now, for the second time, he manifested his enlightenment. Huang-po was really tickled to death. But as a Zen master, he tried to preserve a dignified attitude.

"A madman!" he shouted. "He's come back to pull the tiger's whiskers!"

Lin-chi thundered, "HO!"

Where had he learned this?

You must take an objective attitude when you ask a question of a Zen master and the master's answer is a shout. It is the sword of the Diamond King. And this Diamond King is not Mr. So-and-so who has a lot of diamonds! This Diamond King is the wonderful sword of indestructible *vajraprajna*, that is, diamond wisdom.

Lin-chi's shout can be observed from several angles. Sometimes, it is like a sword that cuts away your mind, all your entanglements, and you become, not empty, but solid ivory. Sometimes it is like the roar of a lion that destroys that solid ivory. Sometimes it is a test. Other times it is to carry out the truth. The Buddha, however, expressed this Diamond Wisdom in absolute SILENCE. When the Buddha was asked if he was mortal or immortal, the Buddha's answer was SILENCE. But this silence is very different from what we know as ordinary silence. The Buddha's answer is not ordinary silence. With his SILENCE he spoke volumes.

Emperor Tai-tsung of the Tang Dynasty asked the National Teacher Hui-chung, "After your death, what can I do to honor your memory?"

The National Teacher replied, "Build a seamless tower for me."

"In what style?" asked the emperor.

National Teacher Hui-chung was silent for a moment, then asked, "Do you understand?"

"No, I do not," replied the emperor.

"Better ask my disciple Tan-yuan after I'm gone."

After the National Teacher's death, the emperor questioned Tan-yuan about his earlier conversation with the National Teacher. Tan-yuan was silent for a while, then asked, "Do you understand?"

"No, I do not," replied the emperor.

Tan-yuan then recited a poem:

> South of the Hsiang and north of the T'an
> Is the country abounding in gold.
> Under a shadowless tree a ferryboat.
> In the Emerald Pavilion, no one who knows.

The Zen student does not express his understanding by the use of philosophical terms. Zen is very different from the usual type of Buddhist expression. Today even monks in Zen temples have brought the expression of Zen "views" into something like ordinary argument, having forgotten their ancestors' Zen spirit. Zen students must not forget the essential state of Zen. When you observe your mind and find that it is boundless as the sky, an endless universe, and that your present state—this moment—is *here* [striking desk with *hossu*], that is all. I did not bring "talking"—yak, yak, yak—to this country. I brought Buddhism to this country. When you have to express yourself by words, it is not Zen. Do not misunderstand. And you must not blend Buddha's Dharma with other stuff, as well.

After Lin-chi shouted his HO! Huang-po said, *"Attendant! Drag this lunatic out of here! Drive him into the monks' hall!"*

Huang-po did not say "out of the temple," however, he said, "into the monk's hall." So he is keeping this madman, because Lin-chi is a wonderful madman.

Later, Kuei-shan told Yang-shan about the incident and asked, "What do you think? Did Lin-chi attain it through Ta-yu or did he attain it through Huang-po?"

Yang-shan said, "He not only mounted the tiger's head, he grasped its tail."

Kuei-shan and Yang-shan were disciples of Huai-hai, whose teacher was Ma-tsu, another famous master. Kuei-shan was asking who Lin-chi's real teacher was. However, Huang-po and Ta-yu were not two men. From this angle, Ta-yu was the head of the tiger and Huang-po its tail. What a huge tiger! Three hundred miles long!

II

Once when Lin-chi was planting pine trees, Huang-po questioned him: "What is your purpose in planting so many trees in these deep mountains?"

Lin-chi said, "First, to add elegance to the appearance of the temple gates, and second, to make a directional post for later guests."

Thereupon Lin-chi took his hoe and struck the ground three times. Huang-po said, "You are right. However, you have already tasted thirty blows of my stick."

*Lin-chi again struck the ground three times and spewed out
a great sigh. Huang-po said, "With you, my sect will flourish in
the world."*

SOKEI-AN SAYS:
This happened when Lin-chi was still quite young. The old Zen
monks were laborers, but there were also sects that were associated with
the aristocracy. An emperor of China was a patron of that sect. Today it's
called the Hua-yen sect. The Zen sect at that time, the later part of the
Tang dynasty, was different. It wasn't protected by the emperor. The Zen
monks protected themselves by their own labor. Huang-po made straw
sandals and Lin-chi planted pine trees deep in the mountains. Huang-po's
temple was in the southern part of China, so there weren't many pine
trees there. So Huang-po questioned him about it.

"What is your purpose in planting so many trees in these deep
mountains?" Huang-po was not asking about the pine trees, of course.
There's a Zen aspect here. Can you grasp the point? Supposed I were to
ask you, "Why sell water by a river?" What would you answer?

All life is the life of nature. From the standpoint of the human being,
there is nothing to do. *I* don't see, but my eye sees. *I* do not digest my
food, but my stomach does. *My* eye is not my own, not my self. *My* ear is
not my self, *my* nose or *my* body. Where am I, then?

From this angle, there is no human being, so why make a law in this
great performance of nature and call it religion, explain this and explain
that, and push it? Can the great performance of nature be pushed?
Yun-men said, "When the Buddha was born, he pointed to heaven and
earth with his finger and said, 'Between heaven and earth, there is only
one who is precious.' The only Buddha between heaven and earth! Alas,
if I had met the Buddha at that time, I would have beat him to death and
given him to the dogs perhaps we wouldn't have had so much trouble
after his death."

Many Zen students have said after their first study of Zen that there is
no more religion. Life on earth is religion itself. Why add to it? Well, it's a
logical conclusion, isn't it?

Huang-po is pushing this point, and I think you understand. He is
testing Lin-chi.

So Lin-chi said, *"First, to add elegance to the appearance of the temple
gates, and second, to make a directional post for later guests."* The first

reason is true, of course, and quite natural, but why must churches have a Gothic style or monks put robes on their shoulders? You might say it's necessary. Well, it's not necessary. You can worship God in Central Park. Why spend so much money and build such magnificent buildings? It's clear isn't it? Man needs a striking church.

The second reason is for posterity. What is that "directional post"? The symbol everyone will look up to—"Oh! There's a temple! Look at the tall pine trees!" The pine trees have nothing to do with Lin-chi's remark, even if they are the "directional posts." What is Lin-chi's purpose?

Huang-po labors day and night making straw sandals; Lin-chi plants pine trees. Monks work just like everyone else. My teacher, Sokatsu Shaku, makes flowers and sells them to flower shops. I carve wood. No monk should fold his arms and spend his day for nothing. This labor is the true guidepost. Lecturing or going to *sanzen* is not the true guidepost. True living from morning to evening is the true guidepost.

Thereupon, Lin-chi took his hoe and struck the ground three times. Huang-po said, "You are right." If you recall, when Lin-chi went to question Huang-po, he questioned three times and was hit three times. In this passage Lin-chi strikes the ground three times. What is this? Huang-po says Lin-chi is right, but then he says—

"However, you have already tasted thirty blows of my stick." Now it seems Huang-po doesn't agree, but Lin-chi understands his viewpoint exactly as his own, so—

Lin-chi again struck the ground three times and then spewed out a great sigh. This is funny, Lin-chi would usually give a HO! but here he just spits. This is also a Zen expression.

Humph! This is very queer. From a true observation you will call it evolution or devolution. There is some purpose in the life of the universe, or there is no purpose in the life or in the universe.

I have a friend, Soen, who is 49 years old. He saved a lot of money, and he had life insurance. Yesterday he committed suicide. He left $1000 to the Japanese government, and he did the same for his friends. He also left $100 for his funeral service. He said, "Well, this life is just [Sokei-an spits]." Many people take life so. "This is life!"

Lin-chi's answer sounds the same as my friend's, but I hope you don't make such an erroneous judgement.

III

> When Lin-chi was attending Lung-kuang, Lung-kuang said, "Today, I am fatigued."
>
> Lin-chi asked, "Old fellow, what is the use in talking nonsense?"
>
> Lung-kuang struck him. Lin-chi kicked Lung-kuang over in his chair. Lung-kuang ceased any further attempt.

SOKEI-AN SAYS:

There are three gates to enter Buddhism. Those gates are mind, thoughts, and body. I am speaking of the activity or essence of mind. This has nothing to do with the thoughts in the brain. If you analyze thoughts, you will find that they consist of many mind-pictures, words, or visions; the dreaming mind itself has no stuff in it. Mind is like pure paper, and thoughts are the paper upon which are printed the many characters.

Zen in this period was at the height of its distinctiveness. Students did not study Zen merely by taking *sanzen* but by practicing it in daily life. Today we study Zen as one would learn to swim in a pool, but in Lin-chi's time it was like swimming in the ocean. Both teacher and student expressed Zen at each moment of their day's tasks. The mountain they looked at was a koan; the sky into which they gazed was a koan. Anything and anyone they confronted was a koan. You must take this attitude in Zen. Do not think it is something different from your daily life. Daily life is the *real koan*. Zen as practiced in *sanzen* is like learning to swim in a pool. A Buddhism that only explains things is only preparation for swimming on the floor; it is just theory. How well we swim on the floor! But in the water it is something else.

At that time Lin-chi was in Lung-kuang's temple. Lung-kuang was very adept with his rod, or *hossu*. He always used one when he was asking questions of his disciples. Once he said, "Whether you utter a word or do not utter a word, I will give you thirty blows!" No disciple could answer him. What a master!

As an attendant, Lin-chi was always standing beside Lung-kuang as was the custom of the day. When Lung-kuang said, *"Today, I am fatigued,"* Lin-chi said to him, *"Old fellow, what is the use in talking nonsense?"* What a terrible thing for a young monk to say to such a famous old master!

Then Lung-kuang struck him. There is no other way to answer such words. When Lung-kuang used his rod, the whole universe rolled forth from it. The whole cosmos split into two halves.

When Hakuin showed his hand, the universe appeared from the empty sky. You must not think that Lung-kuang was angry. He was not a common man. When a Zen master uses the rod or his hand, or shouts, there is no personal feeling in it. It is a demonstration of the master's understanding.

When I hold this cup, it is the same as Lung-kuang 's rod or Hakuin's hand. So as Lin-chi questions, all is manifested completely. No need for further questions. If you do ask, you are adding something to it. It is already complete. Nothing can be added to the universe, nor can anything be taken away.

And when Lung-kuang fell from his chair, I am quite sure that Lung-kuang was tickled to death. So with a genial shrug of the shoulders, Lung-kuang said, "Hmmph! This infant knows something!"

Zen is clear; no one could express anything more clearly than this. If you give me water, I take it. Is there any question here? In this human life, if you fail to find an answer, it is your own error.

IV

Once when Lin-chi was plowing the fields with the other monks, he saw Huang-po coming, so he stopped and leaned on his hoe. Huang-po asked, "You, young fellow, are you tired already?"

Lin-chi said, "I have yet to lift my hoe. How can I be tired?"

Huang-po struck him. Lin-chi seized Huang-po's stick, punched him with it, and pushed him over. Huang-po called the field director and said, "Help me up!"

The monk came running to help him up and said, "Reverend, how can you pardon this lunatic for such impropriety!"

Huang-po was no sooner on his feet than he struck the monk. Lin-chi, digging the ground said, "Everywhere else the dead are cremated, but here I bury them alive!"

SOKEI-AN SAYS:

As a rule all the monks of a temple work together to clean up the grounds—pulling weeds, hoeing, or planting vegetables. At the time of this episode the temple grounds were not small, about a hundred acres, like a farmland. In Huang-po's temple there were about five hundred monks who worked all day.

Lin-chi was using a hoe when he saw Huang-po coming. Huang-po was more than seventy at this time and walked slowly, stick in hand. The monk in charge of work was following him.

Lin-chi took an easy pose, his arms resting on the handle of the hoe. Hearing Huang-po's words, he considered: He must not think that there was nothing behind those words, nor must he think that something was behind them. How should he answer, yes or no? It is as if a thunderbolt flashes over your head. You are puzzled: which way do you run? It's as though you were to see a great boulder rolling down a cliff at you, and you haven't a moment to think. Huang-po was testing Lin-chi's mind, and Lin-chi maintained his questioning attitude: "What is it?"

Lin-chi said, *"I have yet to lift my hoe. How can I be tired?"* Strange isn't it?

Lin-chi had been working hard since the early morning, but he said he was not tired. How can you make any sense out of that? It's the same as if I say, "I have been living for fifty-three years, but I haven't done a thing." Or, as a general coming from a battlefield where a hundred men had been killed might say, "There was no battle." Do you understand?

We Buddhists say that throughout all the eons of the manifestations of this magnificent solar system, throughout the three worlds of desire, visibility (form), and invisibility (formlessness), nothing has happened.

The *Record* says *Huang-po struck him. Lin-chi seized Huang-po's stick, punched him with it, and pushed him over.* But Huang-po did not strike Lin-chi. Did he use a stick? No one received the blow. In such a way we must observe this incident.

The old man fell to the ground. At such an opportunity the disciple must not miss; he must show his whole strength to the teacher; there must be no hesitation. He gives the teacher, who is glad to receive it, a full dose. If he thinks, Well, I could do something, but I must not hurt him, it's no good.

Huang-po called the field director and said, "Help me up!"

The monk Huang-po called on to help him was not good. He was just a blind, ordinary man with no monk's acquirement at all. There are many religious teachers like this, with no "eye" with which to observe reality. Such a one should not leave home to become a recluse. He'd do better to stay home and sell wine or cut up pork chops.

As soon as Huang-po was on his feet, he hit the monk. Of course he must hit him. Lin-chi knocks the monk down and the monk who helps him to his feet gets the stick! From the ordinary point of view this is not understandable, but from the Zen angle you can see clearly what went on with the three men.

Lin-chi paid no attention to the interaction between Huang-po and the monk. Hoeing the ground he might as well have been saying in a loud voice: "It is not necessary to kill these living, dead people. Just dig a hole in the ground and cover them with earth. That's all."

If you do not understand this point, you are one of the living dead. Are you sure you understand?

Later, Kuei-shan asked Yang-shan, "What was Huang-po's idea in hitting the monk?"

Yang-shan said, "When the real thief runs, the guard gets the stick."

Kuei-shan was like a cousin to Lin-chi, about thirty at this time. Anything that happened, he discussed with Yang-shan, who was of an age to be his father.

If you try to reason out the answer to his question, *"What was Huang-po's idea in hitting the monk?"* you will be in the same boat as the monk. From the absolute standpoint, there is no difference between being enlightened and being unenlightened. On this ground, there is no answer, but these two are testing one another.

Yang-shan said, *"When the real thief runs, the guard gets the stick."* In the pitch dark people are yelling, "Thief! Thief!" The wrong person is hit. "I am not a thief," he says. The policeman asks him, "Then who was the thief?" The thief had got away. Was the monk the policeman? You should not take Yang-shan's answer lightly. There is something deeper here. The real thief gets away, and the one running after him gets the stick. This part is beautiful!

V

One day Lin-chi was practicing meditation in front of the monks' hall. Seeing Huang-po approach, he closed his eyes. Huang-po, making a gesture of fright, returned to his quarters. Lin-chi followed him in and bowed low. Huang-po said to the head monk, who was in attendance, "Though he is young, he knows this thing."

The head monk said, "Old man, your own heels aren't touching the ground. Forget about giving recognition to that young fellow."

Huang-po slapped his own mouth. The head monk said, "If you know it, you can have it!"

SOKEI-AN SAYS:

In front of the monk's hall was an unusual place to practice meditation. Lin-chi must have had something in mind to be sitting there when Huang-po came slowly toward him.

In real meditation, we do not close our eyes. One must train the muscles, give strength around the top of the head so that the muscles pull the skin taut from the eyes and the eyes do not tire; we do not use the muscles around the eyes.

In New York, when you hear the noise of the elevated train, you concentrate into it; if you hear a dog bark you concentrate into that sound. You must be like a mirror—all of New York is in you; you reflect everything. The elevated is not running outside of you, it is running through you. While New York is in your mind, your body extends to cover the whole city: all its sounds are in you. This is real meditation. So for Lin-chi to close his eyes before his teacher was very peculiar.

Huang-po observed this and drew back, pretending fear. It was as if a baby had a stick in its hand and says, "Mama, I'm going to hit you!" and Mama pretends to be afraid.

Lin-chi had his eyes closed, but he was aware of Huang-po's gesture. He had made a fence around himself. He kept himself alone in communication with the outside. Just as a child starts a fight and comes home and says, "Wasn't I brave?" This is not too easy to understand, but if you are a Zen student, you will understand the point here.

When, entering Huang-po's quarters, to which he had followed him, Lin-chi bowed low to Huang-po. It was to say, "Thank you very much for your acknowledgment of my meditation." When Huang-po had come where Lin-chi was, Lin-chi had closed his eyes, an unusual thing. Ordinarily he would have stood up and bowed. But he closed his eyes and was now thanking him. What acknowledgment had Huang-po given him? He had just made a gesture of fear.

The head monk, who was standing beside Huang-po in his quarters, was a powerful person in the monastery, the head of perhaps five hundred monks.

Huang-po said to him, *"Though he is young, he knows this thing."* He is speaking about esoteric Buddhism. They understood each other without a word—we do not give it a name. Zen transmission is from mind to mind, soul to soul. This is what Lin-chi knew.

The head monk was Huang-po's disciple, but he was taking the peculiarly Zen attitude of abusing him. *"Old man, your own heels aren't touching the ground."*

He had taken the upper hand.

Huang-po's response was to slap his own mouth. Wonderful teacher of five hundred monks! He took the attitude of having made a big mistake. Today everyone takes an independent attitude, trying to demonstrate that they are masters. Huang-po placed himself in a secondary position. This powerful wild tiger took the attitude of a goat.

The head monk said, *"If you know it, you can have it!"* This is the way a master speaks, but here the monk says it. It is in you, you have it, but if you do not know, though it is in you, you do not have it. *This* is IT.

Lin-chi understood *this*, and Huang-po knew this. The head monk, by speaking these words, demonstrated that *he* knew this also.

What is this IT? How do you understand it, and what do you call it? As a conception in human thought it has no value. But if you can get it without conceptualizing, then you have truly grasped IT.

VI

One day, Lin-chi was sleeping in the meditation hall. Huang-po entered and saw him. Huang-po struck the front of the sitting platform with his staff. Lin-chi raised his head. Seeing Huang-po, he went back to sleep. Huang-po struck the platform once again and went to the upper section of the hall. Finding the head monk there also meditating, he said to him, "While the young monk in the lower section is meditating, what good is your sitting here creating useless mind-stuff?"

The head monk asked, "What are you up to old fellow?

Huang-po struck the platform and left.

SOKEI-AN SAYS:

This is a very important part in the *Record*. Two important principles of Zen are presented here. It is not easy to understand when your viewpoint is not quite matured. But for the future I will explain these two viewpoints. If your Zen observation is matured, you will naturally observe them.

The Zen masters of this period firmly established the attitude of Zen monks: they detested conversation in the form of philosophy and philosophy in the form of religion. These incidents in the meditation hall show us that Lin-chi's understanding was maturing at this time.

It was not permitted to sleep in the meditation hall, but Lin-chi dared to keep on sleeping there. Of course, Lin-chi was not sleeping lying down upon the floor, but in the posture of mediation, legs crossed and palms upon the lap. Real meditation is in a waking condition; if one closes the eyes, it is inaccurate. The images of Buddha show the eyes slightly open. If you open the eyes wide, the outside will disturb you; if you close the eyes, inside visions will haunt you. Keep the eyes slightly open. Some Zen students open their eyes wide, however.

But Lin-chi had closed his eyes and was sleeping. He was not following the conventional attitude of meditation. He had reached a point where he was taking the attitude of sleep as a phase of Zen, and boldly slept in the meditation hall. He was trying out this new phase to find out its true value. All Zen students come to such phases—there are many phases in Zen meditation. The abbot of a monastery with five hundred monks would never come into the meditation hall; it is strange to see him there. The Zen master keeps to his own quarters. But Huang-po came down. I can picture Huang-po Mountain, the seat of the monastery of this master. The cloister would be on top, the meditation hall near the foot. It is often so in China and Japan: the cloister on the mountaintop and the sleeping quarters or library at the foot.

Now [in 1935] Mount Huang-po has not preserved the sleeping quarters of the period described. The usual shape of a meditation hall in China and Japan is one oblong building with raised platforms on two sides and an aisle in the center. Each meditator has about four square feet. A guard, or watchman, walks along the center, long stick in hand, to hit sleeping monks.

When Huang-po saw Lin-chi sleeping, he may have thought, "Well, I understand his attitude these days; he must be attaining some progress in Zen. I must observe it." Perhaps someone had told him, "That young monk is always sleeping in the meditation hall."

Huang-po came in and made a clatter. He saw Lin-chi and realized he wasn't just sleeping. Lin-chi looked at Huang-po's face. If a mere monk is sleeping, and the osho of the mountain comes with a big clatter, he will jump and open his eyes wide. But Lin-chi, after looking at Huang-po, went to sleep again. His attitude shows his faith in his own phase of practice: My meditation is real. I do not care who criticizes it or how. I don't give a fig for Huang-po's criticism.

From the Zen standpoint, sleeping is a true phase of Zen. In sleep we go back to the bosom of the mother, of earth and of time and space; we go back where we came from. Sleep is sacred. The Zen student meditates before going to bed, for now he will really experience a moment in the bosom of the mother. This is the Tushita Heaven. All animals come from that kingdom.

There is a koan: "If anyone comes into your deep sleep and asks you, 'What is the deepest principle of Buddhism?' how do you answer?" In the answer you realize this principle. It is not necessary to say a word, to think philosophically, to divide phenomena and noumena. In real life, phenomena and noumena are one. In the day we eat and work. At night we sleep. When your day is over, go to bed. This is the true view, true religion. Who would wish to find more truth than this? What fools would seek for more religion that this? But we always try to find something more "real." In Zen there is no such foolishness. In the day we work, at night we sleep. That is all. This was Lin-chi's mind, was it not?

Before Huang-po left the hall he struck the front of the platform, then went to the upper section of the hall, which was the section occupied by older students. Huang-po said not one word, just struck the front of the platform. Doing this he gave his recognition of Lin-chi's attitude. The lower section was for young students. Meanwhile the head monk was meditating with dignity, not sleeping, but with his eyes open.

Huang-po said to the head monk, *"While the young monk in the lower section is meditating, what good is your sitting here creating useless mind-stuff?"* Huang-po gave recognition to Lin-chi who was sleeping and denied recognition to the head monk who was really meditating. Had Huang-po reached his dotage or was he trying to teach something?

The head monk said, *"What are you up to, old fellow?"* Why is he talking this way? He must be crazy.

Huang-po struck the front of the platform and went off. The head monk had used strong words. Usually the master would strike or give a HO! Here Huang-po gave recognition to the head monk, too. There was some decision in the monk's answer; it was not puzzled or hesitant. He did not harbor doubt because of Huang-po's criticism. He was quite sure. When you realize that sleep in meditation is a real phase of Zen and that meditation in a waking condition is also a real phase of Zen, then realizing these two phases, you will not take meditation as a dream, wishing to go up to heaven or down to hell, which is just imagination.

The monk meditates, the carpenter hammers, the musician plays, the cat meows, and the dog barks. This is religion. If you can meditate with a sober mind, true faith and real sincerity, what more do you want? Plain meditation is the deepest meditation. Meditation having an affected attitude is like a dung-pot. The head monk had the right attitude: "Do not disturb my meditation."

Later, Kuei-shan asked Yang-shan, "When Huang-po entered the meditation hall, did he have a purpose?"
Yang-shan said, "Two faces of the die are one."

Sometime after this, when Yang-shan questioned Kuei-shan about Huang-po's purpose in entering the meditation hall, it was the same as when Bodhidharma came from India to China. Someone had brought the story from Huang-po's temple to Yang-shan's temple.

Later, Kuei-shan questioned Yang-shan, *"When Huang-po entered the meditation hall, did he have a purpose?"* Purpose? This question is like a big hook. He who swallows it will be fished out of the water. If he has an "artificial" purpose, he is not a true religious teacher.

But Kuei-shan didn't bite. Yang-shan was not concerned with Huang-po's "purpose." He wanted to know how Kuei-shan understood the two phases of meditation.

Yang-shan said, *"Two faces of the die are one."*

That was how Kuei-shan expressed his observation.

These Zen students had a clear conception, no dream, no philosophy, no superstitions. Their minds were clear as a mirror without affectation. It would be impossible for Buddhism as a philosophical religion to produce fruits such as these.

VII

One day, when everyone in the temple was engaged in garden work, Lin-chi was following Huang-po. Huang-po looked behind him, and seeing Lin-chi empty-handed, asked, "Where is your hoe?"

Lin-chi said, "Someone took it from me."

Huang-po said, "Come here, I want to talk to you about something."

Lin-chi approached him. Huang-po raised his hoe, saying, "Just this no one in the world can uphold!"

Lin-chi seized the hoe from Huang-po's grasp and held it high, saying, "Then why is this now in my hand?"

Huang-po said, "Today, we have a man who has engaged in garden work!" and he returned to the monastery.

SOKEI-AN SAYS:

Outdoor work might include taking weeds from the temple yard or laying out new paths. Everyone at the temple took part, including its head.

Huang-po had a hoe in his hand and was walking ahead of everyone. Lin-chi was next after Huang-po, and then everyone followed him. Huang-po looked back at Lin-chi, who had nothing in his hand.

"Where is your hoe?" he asked.

Lin-chi said, "Someone took it from me." Lin-chi had become prominent in the temple. Everyone was paying him great respect. To become prominent in a temple, one cannot impose upon the others, cannot act as if he is more important than the other disciples. His prominence comes to him naturally as spring comes into summer. "Look at Lin-chi," someone says, "carrying a hoe. He doesn't have to do that now. Go take it away from him." So a student would go and ask him for the hoe." "Oh, you need it? All right." And the student would take it away.

Lin-chi would have understood the monk's intentions, that the one who came to him to get the hoe was suggesting he was not supposed to do the work himself. Lin-chi knowing this would let him take it.

The old master, holding a hoe in his hand, resting it on his shoulder, turned and said, "Oh, you have no hoe." He was saying Lin-chi's time has come. He must take his place as leader. No one had come to take away the old man's hoe. Here he was, an aged giant, bending forward and bearing his hoe on this shoulder, leading everyone. He was too powerful for anyone to come so close to say, "Old teacher, let me take the hoe." Lin-chi, they could ask, but not Huang-po. Huang-po understood this.

When he called to Lin-chi to come to him, holding his big hoe in his hand (something like a spade with the handle of a plough), he was asking, "Do you understand?"

Lin-chi raised the hoe. "Just this no one in the world can uphold!" This thing nobody in the world can take from him. In Zen, any object that is in your hand is "just this." If you have a glass in your hand, you say "just this." Or if you have a big hoe in your hand you say "just this." The

Buddha raised a golden lotus and was saying, "just this." Chu-chih raised one finger and said "just this." What is "just this"? Just *this* nobody in the world can uphold, sustain, or support. Of course, you must understand that Huang-po was not talking about the hoe, but that in his conversation "this" was not outside the hoe, but not always comprised in the hoe either.

When Hakuin showed his hand, that particular point is not outside the hand, but it is not always in that particular hand, either. Where is it? This one thing nobody can take. It is deep, very deep.

There are two sorts of Buddhism. One (in Japanese) is *tariki*—depending upon the power of others; the other is *jiriki*—depending upon one's own power. In Zen, one depends upon his own power. Christianity depends upon the power of God.

When Huang-po is talking about his hoe, saying, "*Just this no one in the world can uphold!*" he is holding his hoe up. But truly speaking, *he himself* is not holding it up. It is the same when we say so-and-so is holding the office of the president of the United States. The United States makes him hold it, you say, but the United States cannot make him uphold it either. Then who is holding the office of the president? The emperor of Japan is upholding the empire, but truly *he* cannot. The whole nation is doing it? No? Then who is doing it?

I am supporting my life, but I am not supporting it. You cannot make me support it. Then who is supporting my life? I say, I am. But you can say that I am not doing this. On this particular point you cannot say that I am one who is depending upon my own power or on the power of others. They are just two ideas. Nobody in the world can hold *this* up. You cannot offend my "oshoship"—I am the *osho*. There is some such sound in words spoken by Huang-po. Was Lin-chi afraid? Oh no—"I would not say anything to offend my osho." No, he did not say this.

Why? Lin-chi took it with his own strength. Some Zen master gave a commentary here and said that Lin-chi did not take the hoe from Huang-po's hand but seized that hand with the hoe so on one handle there were four hands! I think this is not a good commentary. Lin-chi took it and holding it up said, "*Then why is this now in my hand?*" "Why" is the important word here.

I am in New York, and I open my Zen school. Sokei-an is not doing this. New York is not doing this. After 2,500 years, from Japan, across 7,000 miles, this is the first time the seed of Buddhism has been translated into the soil of the eastern part of America. Who is doing this? Someone will imitate this, will open his own temple of Buddhism. Will he, like Lin-chi, take the hoe from my hand? If he is in the right climate and season and circumstances, he will, but he will not be doing it. In religious work, the time, place and condition are different from hanging a painting on a wall or placing an advertisement in a newspaper. A growing seed is a precious thing.

Why is "just this" in my hand? Lin-chi clearly understood Huang-po's point of view. This was not entire enlightenment day for Lin-chi, who already understood the power that seized the power of religion. Lin-chi seized the hoe and asked, *"Then why is this now in my hand?"*

Huang-po said, *"Today, we have a man who has engaged in garden work!"* It is not necessary for me to stay here any longer. I will return to my quarters. Huang-po is giving a hint to Lin-chi. "You will manage everything now. I will go back home. You are all right"—good enough. Huang-po could not say this in so many words, but he was hinting it.

"Today, we have a man who has engaged in garden work!"—I see I have a good man here. I can go home. My disciple will uphold the torch. Until that day, Huang-po could not go home—stop working, die.

This is the end of the dialogue between Huang-po and Lin-chi.

Later, Kuei-shan asked Yang-shan, "Why was the hoe that was in Huang-po's hand taken by Lin-chi?"

Yang-shan said, "The thief is a dull man but more sagacious than the superior man."

As usual, this story was brought to Yang-shan's temple. Yang-shan questioned his *Dharma*-child, Kuei-shan: *"Why was the hoe that was in Huang-po's hand taken by Lin-chi?"*

Yang-shan understood Lin-chi and hoped his own *Dharma*-child would grasp the point as Lin-chi had, so he asked, "Why?" This is the deepest question. Why was I born, why am I living, why have a moon, why are you twenty-three and I fifty-seven? Why is Mount Fuji in Japan and the Rocky Mountains in America? The answer is difficult. Kuei-shan's answer is singular: *"The thief is a dull man but more sagacious than the superior man."*

Kuei-shan sang his answer out carelessly. Do you think that Lin-chi was a thief and Huang-po a superior man? Oh, no. Why was the hoe that was in Huang-po's hand taken by Lin-chi? Kuei-shan certainly understood the word "why." If you understand this word you will not be sorry though you are penniless. If you understand this "why" you will not be proud though you have millions. Why am I a man and why are you a woman? This part of Zen you must know. No one can talk about or give any commentary upon it, or add any word of explanation. You must understand. But Kuei-shan's answer was beautiful. Sometime, in a koan you will understand this place.

When the Sixth Patriarch, Hui-neng, was handed the torch by the Fifth Patriarch, Hung-jen, he ran away from the temple. Another disciple of the Fifth Patriarch, Hui-ming, pursued him in chagrin that a mere laborer took the torch. Everyone was angry, and this one ran after the Sixth Patriarch and overtook him on a mountaintop. So the Sixth Patriarch placed his bowl and the robe handed down to him by his teacher upon a rock and hid himself behind another rock.

Hui-ming came and found the robe and bowl, but, of course, he was not able to take them for they did not belong to him—"I will take these back to the temple." But the bowl was heavy as a mountain; he could not lift it up. This is a koan. Why was it heavy as a mountain?

Later, this bowl was handed down from the Sixth Patriarch, and in two hundred years it came into the hands of the Chinese emperor. One day the Emperor, holding it in his palm, asked his prime minister, "Hui-ming could not lift this bowl up from the rock, why is it now in the palm of my hand?" The Prime Minister could not answer. Why was this in the emperor's palm? Can you answer? This is also a koan.

VIII

Bearing a letter from Huang-po, Lin-chi went running to deliver it to Kuei-shan. Yang-shan, who at that time was in charge of receiving guests, caught hold of him, took the letter, and said, "This letter is from Huang-po. Is there something that will come from you?" Lin-chi slapped him. Seizing Lin-chi by the chest, Yang-shan said, "My dear brother, since you know something of this, no more questions." Then they went to see Kuei-shan.

Kuei-shan questioned Lin-chi, "How many pupils are at my honorable brother's place?"

Lin-chi said, "Seven hundred pupils."

Kuei-shan asked, "Who is their leader?

Lin-chi said, "He has handed you the letter already."

Then Lin-chi questioned Kuei-shan, "Reverend, how many pupils are here?"

Kuei-shan said, "A thousand five hundred."

Lin-chi said, "That is a great many."

Kuei-shan said, "My brother Huang-po also has no less."

Lin-chi left Kuei-shan. Yang-shan, following to see him off, said, "Later, if you go north, you will find a place to live."

Lin-chi asked, "How can that be?"

Yang-shan said, "Just go. Later there will be one who will assist you. This one has a head but no tail, a beginning but no end."

Some time later, when Lin-chi settled in Chin Province, he found that P'u-hua was already there. When Lin-chi became known, P'u-hua befriended him. But P'u-hua entirely vanished before Lin-chi had been there long.

SOKEI-AN SAYS:

Huang-po had ordered Lin-chi to bear a letter to Kuei-shan. He wished to introduce Lin-chi to him. For a Zen student to act as messenger is an important task, especially when he goes to a great Zen master. One must expect something to happen.

Yang-shan said, *"This letter is from Huang-po. Is there something that will come from you?"* Something greater than a letter is meant here, of course. Yang-shan is fishing. But Lin-chi is like lightning. Ha!

Lin-chi slapped him. Seizing Lin-chi by the chest, Yang-shan said, "My dear brother, since you know something of this, no more questions." Then they went to see Kuei-shan. He is a disciple of Kuei-shan and so he would handle this entirely differently—in the fashion of Kuei-shan. Lin-chi, a disciple of Huang-po, handled it in his own fashion. These two are in the same Zen school, but the manner of handling Zen is different.

In answer to Yang-shan's question, Lin-chi didn't say a word, but BANG! Yang-shan did not slap back, but holding him by the chest, he spoke in a soft and relaxed manner. He did not mind if he received two or three more slaps in the face.

Lin-chi is like lightning, and Yang-shan is like a spring breeze.

Then they went to see Kuei-shan. Kuei-shan's Zen is like the spring ocean, and Yang-shan is his disciple. Huang-po's Zen is like a bursting volcano, so Lin-chi's Zen was like lightning. These two disciples had come from different teachers, but they made contact. Their understanding of Zen tallied, so they went together to see the master.

Kuei-shan had been staying on this mountain for ten years before he met anyone. He was directed to the mountain by his teacher to stay for ten years, bathing in the dew, eating fruit from the trees, and sleeping on weeds. He thought, "I have been waiting here for years and no one knows me. I will go to the foot of the mountain and give myself to a hungry tiger." So he descended the mountain and met a monk, who said, "I heard that my elder brother has been on the mountain for about ten years. I've come to assist you." The monk opened a tea hut at the foot of the mountain. There he served tea and talked about Kuei-shan. Suddenly Kuei-shan became known.

The true Zen master tries to spread the teaching in an entirely different way from those who advertise and travel with a brass band. There is one word to precisely express our religion, and that word is faith. This is different from faith in God. For faith and God are not two different things.

Kuei-shan was not a fat, old man with an enormous heart.

Kuei-shan questioned Lin-chi, "How many pupils are at my honorable brother's place?" How did Rinzai answer? Did he give a HO!? Humm, he didn't. He knew his place and felt the pressure of Kuei-shan. No space was permitted him to vomit a HO! He took the attitude of an ordinary man. Ha! Something will happen!

Lin-chi said, *"Seven hundred pupils."*

Kuei-shan asked, *"Who is their leader?* This "who" is a big word! Would Lin-chi answer? Would he say the leader is myself or would he say the leader is someone else?

Lin-chi says, *"He has handed you the letter already."* The leader is this "He," but He is nobody. Lin-chi did not show Kuei-shan his tail. He took the weapon and asked Kuei-shan—

"*Reverend, how many pupils are here?*" Kuei-shan said, "*A thousand five hundred.*" Lin-chi said, "*That is a great many.*" He vomited the words as though to please Kuei-shan.

Kuei-shan then said, "*My brother Huang-po also has no less.*" Kuei-shan will not swallow that hook! A good game—no error. Lin-chi was playing fifty-fifty with Kuei-shan. A great monk and a small monk holding a conversation with no error in it—two swords touching point to point with no space between.

Lin-chi left Kuei-shan. Yang-shan, following to see him off, said, "*Later, if you go north, you will find a place to live.*" Lin-chi's message to Kuei-shan was completed. Yang-shan had led Lin-chi to the mountain path.

Lin-chi asked," How can that be?" Yang-shan said, "*Just go. Later there will be one who will assist you. This one has a head but no tail, a beginning but no end.*" This was a prediction.

Some time later, when Lin-chi settled in Chin Province, he found that P'u-hua was already there. Do you remember the story of the coffin and the four gates?

When Lin-chi became known, P'u-hua befriended him. Finally P'u-hua entirely vanished before Lin-chi had been there long.

IX

Later, Lin-chi came up to Huang-po's for the summer
session, which was already half over. Seeing the Master reciting
a sutra, he said, "I always thought you were a man, but now all I
see is a black-bean-cramming old monk!"

Lin-chi stayed for a few days and then began to take his
leave. Huang-po said, "You came in violation of the rules of the
summer session, and now you are leaving without completing it."

Lin-chi said, "I only came to pay homage to my master."

Indignantly, Huang-po struck him and drove him out.
After he had left and had gone a few miles, Lin-chi pondered
the matter, turned on his heels, and went back to the temple to

complete the summer session. On the day Lin-chi was to take leave of the master, Huang-po questioned him, "So where are you going?"

Lin-chi said, "If I do not go south of the river, I shall go north of the river."

Huang-po struck him. Lin-chi seized him and repaid him with a slap. Bursting into laughter, Huang-po called to his attendant, saying, "Bring the chin support and the back rest that belonged to my late master Po-chang!"

Lin-chi said, "Attendant, some fire!"

Huang-po said, "Well said, but just take them away with you. With them, in the future you can sit upon the tongue of any man under heaven."

SOKEI-AN SAYS:

This part of this evening's lecture is an important part of the *Record*. There are many students who really opened their eyes in observing this part of the *Record of Lin-chi* as a koan. There are many discourses between Lin-chi-chi and Huang-po, but this one reaches the summit.

This summer session originated in India in the Buddha's time. There, everything is growing at this season, so the monks do not go out lest they crush insects and little animals underfoot. Besides it is awkward to travel about the country, so they stayed in one place for three months. We keep the same tradition in Japan, but usually it takes place in July and August, for two months, and we have one month in the spring, February.

From this record, we see that Lin-chi was not in Huang-po's temple at this time but was staying somewhere not far from Mount Huang-po. He had finished his study and left the temple, perhaps living alone to contemplate what he had accomplished. Buddhist monks would do this after having been fifteen or twenty years in the temple. Having no more to study, they would go out and observe the teaching from beginning to end. In this way they would pass three or four years before being ordained by the teacher as master. They would pass the time alone in the city, mountains, or a cave according to their own natures, but would come back to the temple for the session.

Something was in Lin-chi's mind to come for the summer session when it was half over. In China this season begins in July and ends in September, but Lin-chi came to Mount Huang-po in the middle of

August. This was not according to regulation. Everyone must come to the temple on the first, or anyway before the fifth day. Lin-chi arrived when the session was half over, but he was an accomplished student, so no one said anything to him. Even Huang-po didn't complain.

As usual, Huang-po was reading a *sutra* in the early morning. While all the students were meditating in the hall, the master was reading the *sutra* in a loud voice in the Zen room. Occasionally in the morning we take *sanzen* while the teacher is reading. He will stop, turn his face to listen, then resume reading. But in Lin-chi's time, there was no such training in this fashion as there is today. They met the teacher morning or evening at a general session. There was no particular koan, but there was always something to talk about through which the teacher could measure the attainment of the students.

When Lin-chi said to Huang-po, *"I always thought you were a man, but now all I see is a black-bean-cramming old monk!"* I would imagine there were many students there and that Lin-chi spoke loudly before them. He was humble and modest usually, so they wondered at his effrontery, shouting at Huang-po before everyone as if to indicate he was no master or patriarch, but just an old monk. They must have thought that there was something on Lin-chi's mind, or that he must be crazy. Zen students sometimes come with a notion such as, "I am as good as the teacher and as good as Shakyamuni Buddha. We are all just human beings." There are many pitfalls in Zen. This kind is called "the pitfall on the summit."

However, Huang-po said nothing at the time. Usually on such an occasion he would hit the student. Now he was calm and quiet as a forest. What was in Huang-po's mind? He was certainly taking the matter very gravely. He wanted to know what was really on Lin-chi's mind. Lin-chi was a favorite, was expected to be his heir. Now Lin-chi took this haughty attitude and Huang-po said nothing. Lin-chi remained for a few days then took his leave. Surely *now* Huang-po will say something! This is a real test, not the usual interview between teacher and disciple.

Huang-po said, *"You came in violation of the rules of the summer session, and now you are leaving without completing it."* Now Lin-chi must show his real guts. And Huang-po will find out what's on his mind.

Lin-chi said, *"I only came to pay homage to my Master."* Lin-chi-chi has reached the summit. He says that Huang-po is merely a man, and that he, Li-chi, is equal to his teacher: "There is no Buddha, no *bodhisattva*, no heaven or earth, no master, no disciple, no monks' precepts. I just came to see you and now go. Goodbye."

He had been with Huang-po for a long time. There have been many monks like this. After long training and hardship comes the summary: I am a plain man, a fishmonger, and my teacher is just the same, just a man.

Huang-po seems to be in a rage. Who is this Lin-chi? He gives the order to drive him out. Why would Huang-po do this? Why drive him out instead of acknowledging him? There must be something going on here.

Having gone about two or three miles from the temple, Lin-chi must have pondered the matter: "I studied a long time, and truly attained. Now I see that the monks are just following a formula. We are all essentially human beings. Why did he drive me out instead of acknowledging me?" Lin-chi turned on his heel, went back and completed the summer session. He did not count it as a humiliation to return in the cause of truth. If you doubt, find the root and take the doubt out of it. Don't mention the doubt until you have rooted it out.

This is the wonderful part of Lin-chi. He is a sincere man, living in faith. If he were just an ordinary man, he would say, "Well, I touched the truth. The truth hurt, and he drove me out. I'm a better *bodhisattva* than he is. I shall go and teach."

This is the attitude of the ordinary man. The religious man has one thing different—that is faith. Without faith one cannot be a religious person. He will excuse the other's error, but not his own. He will examine himself. If he harbors any doubt, he will not give up but will think it over and over, day and night. If one thing in his mind is not clear, he will lose his upright position, and his life will have no meaning. If his foundation is not true, all of the superstructure is nothing. Lin-chi was not only sincere, he was brave. Just an hour ago he had been thrown out of the gate, and now he goes back. For the truth, he accepts the humiliation.

He went back to the temple and completed the summer session, and the day came to take leave of the master. After the first of September the monks repair their robes, then scatter. Huang-po questioned Lin-chi, *"So where are you going?"*

Huang-po had been watching him, and now this was his last question. It is a simple question, but it has a deep meaning.

Lin-chi replied, *"If I do not go south of the river, I shall go north of the river."* In other words, "I shall go at the mercy of the wind like the dandelion down before the breeze, with Great Nature." This is what he meant.

What a difference! Had he changed his attitude or his philosophy? Huang-po struck him. Now, if Lin-chi is not a student with real attainment, he must give in.

He seized Huang-po and gave him a slap. If you understand this, you will be able to live freely in the world, and yet not offend the order of God. This is an important point: to live sincerely as a human being you must understand this.

Bursting into laughter, Huang-po ordered the attendant to bring him two objects that had belonged to Huang-po's master and been given to him. He was saying, "I thought he was stupid, but he really understands."

When Lin-chi told the attendant to bring him fire, he was saying: "I don't want such things. I'll burn them up! My Zen is my own. Why do I need a teacher's permission?"

It is not as before. Lin-chi and Huang-po were the same human beings as you and I. But when one passes the threshold of real enlightenment, one is different.

So Huang-po said to him, "*Well said, but just take them away with you. With them, in the future you can sit upon the tongue of any man under heaven.*" Huang-po is using an old Chinese idiom: "Now no one can say your knowledge of Zen is false." My teacher gave me the robe that was my teacher's teacher's robe: three generations to prove the Zen lineage. With this I prove my transmission of the torch of Zen.

When my teacher granted that I had finished Zen, ordained me, and sent me to New York, I had passed all the important koans. But later my teacher found from a letter I sent him that there was something not right in the foundation of my Zen, something I had not attained, and he sent for me to come back seven thousand miles. Lin-chi went back several miles. I went back seven thousand! When I asked my teacher for money to go back, he answered: "There is no such stupid question in the history of Zen!" So for eight months I worked in a factory, then returned, to spend two more years.

Keep this sincere faith, and Zen will exist in the world. Lose this faith, and Zen will perish from the earth. If you have doubt, do not give up. Find the root of it and get this root out.

Later, Kuei-shan questioned Yang-shan, "Did Lin-chi act contrary to the wishes of his teacher?"

Yang-shan said, "No."

Kuei-shan asked, "Then what is your view?"

Yang-shan said, "One who owes a debt of gratitude must know how to repay it."

Kuei-shan asked, "Was there ever such a one among the ancients?"

Yang-shan said, "There was, but he was so long ago I prefer not to say, reverend."

Kuei-shan said, "Well said! However, I, too, would like to know who he was. Just tell me."

Yang-shan said, "At the council of Shurangama, Ananda sat in adoration before Buddha and said, 'With deep fidelity I shall devote myself to all beings throughout the myriad worlds in recompense for Buddha's beneficence.' Is this not an example of payment for a debt of gratitude?"

Kuei-shan said, "It is! It is! But one's whose view is the same as his teacher's will receive only half the esteem that was accorded his teacher. Only when one's view surpasses that of his teacher is he worthy to be his successor."

After leaving Huang-po Lin-chi went to the north shore of the Yellow River to begin his teaching. In those days, a disciple took leave of his master and went somewhere far away from the teacher's temple. He might have no chance to see his teacher again in his lifetime. Today [1935], though I came seven thousand miles to America, I can go back to see my teacher. But in that day it was impossible.

In his conversation with Yang-shan, Kuei-shan was saying: "It looks to me as if Lin-chi did not obey his teacher. Yang-shan said no.

Lin-chi had left his teacher behind him. Because Kuei-shan and Yang-shan were like father and son and stayed together all their lives, their handling of Zen is like father and son talking business. I am handling Zen with you in this country in the same way. This was not my teacher's attitude.

"Then what is your view?" Kuei-shan asked. Yang-shan said, *"One who owes a debt of gratitude must know how to repay it."* This is routine business in human society. When someone invites you, you must invite back.

In Buddhism, the debt the student owes must be repaid. The student is taught by the teacher, and then the teacher sends his disciple away from the temple. The disciple will not return but will go to another place and build up his own teaching. All Buddhists since the time of the Buddha received the milk of Dharma from the teacher and repay the debt by teaching their disciples. I received my teaching; I give it to my disciples. If you receive the Dharma, you must pass it on to someone else. Buddha transmitted his essential teaching to Mahakashyapa, holding the lotus stem in his hand. Mahakashyapa looked at it and smiled. That was all. In that time man's mind was very simple, so the transmission was also very simple. Zen was such a simple thing in those old days. Mahakashyapa handed Ananda the robe and bowl, and Ananda said, "Beside the robe and bowl. Buddha transmitted something else to you. What was it?"

Mahakashyapa said, "Ananda."

Ananda said, "Yes?"

"Put down the awning."

Ananda stood and said, "Oh!"

And in that moment he understood what Buddha had handed to Mahakashyapa. That was Zen.

You observe this as a koan. Perhaps it seems insignificant to you because you do not believe very plain things. Truth is a simple, plain thing, not a complicated matter. Ananda said he would pay the debt with his fidelity. What is the fidelity of a Buddhist? Although you describe Buddhism in a thousand different ways, if you do not have this fidelity, you are not a Buddhist. To attain enlightenment for yourself and to give enlightenment to all sentient beings is the fidelity of the Buddhist. It is called recompense for Buddha's beneficence, the thanks for the milk of Dharma. It is comparatively easy to attain enlightenment, but to repay this debt is very difficult.

I spent from the time I was twenty until I was forty-seven in study. Then I came here to this country to try to repay my debt. I have worked barely five years and what have I done? Can I repay this debt in my lifetime? I am not materially rich. I cannot repay you for your support materially, but when you offer something to the temple, you are paying for what I give, and I accept this for Dharma's sake. As you know, I do not spend anything for myself. Bacon and eggs are enough!

Kuei-shan said, *"But one whose view is the same as his teacher's will receive only half the esteem that was accorded his teacher. Only when one's view surpasses that of his teacher is he worthy to be his successor."* This is the iron rule in the Zen school. So while from the time of the

Buddha other schools have perished one by one, Zen still exists. This is the measure by which the teacher chooses his inheritor. The world is progressing according to the law of evolution. If a teacher hands the Dharma down to a pupil who is inferior to him, the Dharma will disappear in five hundred years. If the teacher picks a pupil whose view is just the same as his, Buddhism will go down while we watch. In the Zen school we must show some progress to our teacher. We must show him that we have something he doesn't, and we must beat him down. Then the teacher gladly hands us the Dharma. It is never for so-called love or because you have been so good. No! When a Zen teacher transmits his Dharma it is a championship fight—the disciple must knocks him down, shows him his attainment, knowledge, and new information. Zen is still existing because of this iron rule.

Before the female hawk will copulate with the male, she flies for three days through the sky with the male pursuing her; only one who can overtake her can have her. The Zen master is like the female hawk, and the disciple is like the male. You must not forget this law.

X

Lin-chi arrived at Bodhidharma's commemorative pagoda. The master of the pagoda asked Lin-chi, "Venerable elder, will you first pay homage to Buddha or to Bodhidharma?"

Lin-chi said, "I will not pay homage to either Buddha or Bodhidharma."

The master of the pagoda asked, "Venerable elder, what is the nature of your animosity towards the Buddha and patriarch?"

Lin-chi swept his sleeves behind him and left.

SOKEI-AN SAYS:

I am speaking from the *Record of Lin-chi*, a Zen master who lived in the Tang dynasty. I have been translating it for three years, and it will soon be finished this summer or this autumn.

As I always say when I open my lectures, there are basically two kinds of religion in the world: one based on prayer, the other based on meditation. One believes that God is up there [points upward]. The other believes God is here [touches heart]. This God is a word used in Christianity. I do not use this term particularly to talk about our God, for our God has no name, so we cannot call it by any name. The Zen sect is that sect which depends upon *this* existence [touches heart]. It is not the body, it is not the mind, but it is existence in the condition of reality. We do not call this matter or spirit, which means something from our own angle. Before we began to use words to mean something these two views were not two but were only one existence. In the Zen school there is no philosophical discussion because Zen depends upon that which is very pure, or mind-itself, that which is not padded with mind-stuff. So we do not discuss anything. Our discussion is by the attitude we show each other.

In this passage Lin-chi has been on a pilgrimage after having left Huang-po's monastery. After visiting the Zen masters of the time one after another, Lin-chi-chi arrived at Bodhidharma's commemorative pagoda. The tower is no longer there. It was destroyed a long time ago, but the temple remains. When Lin-chi arrived, the master of the pagoda asked him a question:

"*Venerable elder, will you first pay homage to Buddha or to Bodhidharma?*" Lin-chi was probably looking at the images of the Buddha and Bodhidharma as if he were looking at sculpture. All the other monks would bow, burn incense, and recite *sutras*, but Lin-chi entered, took off his big umbrella hat, put it under his arm, and just looked. From his attitude you can see that he felt nothing for the Buddha and Bodhidharma in these wooden images, so he did not make his customary bow before them. The master of the pagoda must have been an ordinary monk or layman. Why else would he ask such a foolish question?

Lin-chi said, "I will not pay homage to either Buddha or Bodhidharma." Lin-chi was reacting to the stupidity of the monk. Then the monk asked Lin-chi something that proves he was nothing but a robe carrier:

"*Venerable elder, what is the nature of your animosity towards the Buddha and Patriarch?*" But Lin-chi-chi just—

Swept his sleeves behind him and left.

XI

Once when Lin-chi was a pilgrim visiting masters one after another, he arrived at Lung-kuang's temple. Lung-kuang appeared in the Dharma Hall and took his seat. Lin-chi presented himself before Lung-kuang and asked him a question: "Without projecting a spear, how do you win the battle?"

Lung-kuang remained motionless upon his seat. Lin-chi said, "My virtuous adept! There must be some way to make me see it!"

Lung-kuang gazed at Lin-chi and said, "Hyaaa!"

Lin-chi, pointing his finger at Lung-kuang, said, "My dear fellow, you are defeated today."

SOKEI-AN SAYS:

The master must have been an eminent monk, so when he appeared he naturally took his seat in the center of the Dharma hall, which was surrounded by many monks while the gong was sounded and incense was burned.

Lin-chi presented himself before the master. He was a stranger to the temple. No one knew where he had come from, but Lin-chi had asked the attendant of the temple for an interview with the master, so Lin-chi put on his formal robe and entered slowly before Lung-kuang, bowed, and asked a question:

"*Without projecting a spear, how do you win the battle?*" In those days if a student asked such a question, the master would not engage in discussion but would answer from the Zen standpoint. This is very important point of this passage.

It was a good question. This Great Nature as it is, is the truth itself. There is no part that a human being can indicate or can add or give expression to; it explains itself. The human being has nothing to do with this truth. We call it eternity, but time and space, God or Buddha, nature or consciousness, happiness or disaster, true or false have nothing to do with it. Monism, dualism, pluralism are all human hypotheses. That which exists here has nothing to do with the human being. From this point of view, none of us can say a word. But without words, no one will understand. This was Lin-chi's point.

When the master took his seat in a grand manner, Lin-chi asked his question, but the master remained motionless. Then Lin-chi said,

"My virtuous adept! There must be some way to make me see it!" Lin-chi knew the fundamental attitude of meditation in the universe and the universe within, but he tried to find out a little more, so he made believe he didn't know.

Lin-chi didn't say, Make me understand or grasp it. He said, Make me see it. If Lung-kuang's eye had been sharp he would not have been ensnared. Lung-kuang was a monk, and he understood the great SILENCE. That's all. He knew how to stop the visible sailing boat and how to stop the audible gong, but he did not know how to stop the invisible boat and the inaudible gong, so he was trapped by Lin-chi.

Lung-kuang gazed at Lin-chi and said, "Hyaaa!" Lin-chi, pointing his finger at Lung-kuang, said, "My dear fellow, you are defeated today." Lung-kuang was defeated by Lin-chi. What would you do if you were in profound meditation and Lin-chi questioned *you*?

XII

Lin-chi arrived at San-feng. P'ing Ho-shang questioned him, "Where have you come from?"

Lin-chi said, "I have come from Huang-po."

P'ing asked, "What does Huang-po say?"

Lin-chi said, "Catastrophe befell an ox of gold last night, and no one has seen a trace of it yet."

P'ing said, "The autumn wind has blown the jade flute. There must be someone who comprehends the meaning of the tune."

Lin-chi said, "He has gone instantly through myriad barriers and does not rest within the serenity of the evening sky."

P'ing said, "Your statement is much too lofty."

Lin-chi said, "A dragon bore the chick of a phoenix and has dashed through the blue."

P'ing said, "Take a seat and have a cup of tea."

Again P'ing questioned him, "Where have you been recently?"

Lin-chi said, "I have been at Lung-kuang's."

P'ing said, "And how is Lung-kuang these days?"

Lin-chi left.

SOKEI-AN SAYS:

In philosophy, the philosopher tries to come to a conclusion by reasoning. So philosophy is the "way" of reasoning to find a conclusion, which they believe is truth. In Buddhism there was the conclusion *from the beginning*. Then how does one speak of this conclusion in Buddhism? We created a philosophy. Naturally there is the question. Without reasoning how can one find a conclusion? The Buddhist answer is that we use our reasoning, but reasoning is not sufficient. We reach through without reasoning. We enter directly without using our minds, without moving our minds, because before we use our minds we understand what is mind. Before we use our intellect we come to the realization of what the intellect is; and when we embody the intellect itself, we find the truth there. In the beginning we come to the point that everyone is searching for, and when we come to the conclusion, we realize we must speak about it, and to speak about it, we create a philosophy.

There is a mother. She makes a garb for her baby before he is born. And there is another mother. She makes the garb after she has borne it. A rich mother always makes the garb for the baby before it arrives, but the poor mother makes the garb for the baby after its birth. Buddhism is like the poor mother who makes the garb for the baby after its birth, so we change the garb many times according to the baby's growth. The Zen school, of which I am speaking now, is the baby itself, without garb—the conclusion of Buddhism without philosophy. This moment is Zen. We do not need to talk about it. So Buddha's *Dharma* says that without speaking a word, pointing out the soul of man, we attain enlightenment.

This conversation between P'ing and Lin-chi-chi is one of the most mysterious in all of the *Record*. From this conversation we understand that when good masters meet each other they speak nothing but nonsense because there is nothing to speak about. When good boxers meet each other, there is no boxing; they drink liquor. When good artists meet each other there is no smell of art in the conversation. When good Buddhists meet each other, there is no smell of Buddhism,

P'ing's question to Lin-chi was a good one. When I ask you where you come from, you answer, "From One-hundred-and-tenth Street."

"And before that?"

"Japan."

"And before you became a human being?"

"God knows."

"If God knows, why not ask Him?"

"Well . . . I don't know Him."

The question is very simple, but the meaning is very deep.

Lin-chi said he came from Huang-po. He described true phenomena, that which is seen and heard—material, physical, and objective. "Well I came from Huang-po." Huang-po was the mountain on which Huang-po had been living.

P'ing's question was but the first arrow.

In archery before an archer sends the actual arrow, he sends what is called a flute arrow. As it cuts through the air, it cries "e-e-e-e-e-eeeeee." By the sound it makes the archer knows the speed and direction of the wind. So when he sends the true arrow, he will know in what direction he should send his true arrow as it drives its course through the wind and hits his enemy. P'ing understands this. He is probably thinking, "This is a true one. He is not answering me philosophically or making lofty answers. His feet are on the ground. Well, I'll send the next one."

P'ing then asked, *"What does Huang-po say?* Lin-chi understands. So he says—

"Catastrophe befell an ox of gold last night, and no one has seen a trace of it yet." Huang-po did not say, "Catastrophe befell an ox of gold last night, and no one has seen a trace of it yet." These are not his words. They are the words of Lin-chi. The words have nothing to do with the meaning of his answer.

P'ing said, *"The autumn wind has blown the jade flute! There must be someone who comprehends the meaning of the tune."* Good answer.

As you know, I am always talking about the silence of Zen. The still strings of a guitar can also be considered silence—the silence which the Zen school prefers, a silence free from grasping. A flute free from human hands hanging from a wall will make a sound like "eu-u-u-u-u-u-u-u." It's very nice. This silence is the silence of meditation. When we meditate, it must be with a free mind.

There was once a wonderful musician in China who had but one listener. When he played his harp, he would play the wind blowing in the dale and the streams flowing in the rivers. It was all in his tune and in the strings of his harp, and the listener understood. When he thought of the great ocean there was surf and ripples, and the listener understood and heard it all. When the great musician's only listener died, he cut the strings of his harp and never played again.

Lin-chi said, *"He has gone instantly through myriad barriers and does not rest within the serenity of the evening sky."* Ah, gone, not staying here, because P'ing was hinting, "You are the wonderful student of Huang-po." Lin-chi was a smart man not to be caught in this snare!

The abbot said, *"Your statement is much too lofty.* He is still treating Lin-chi like a little monk. All that you said is wonderful and so beautiful and poetic.

Lin-chi said, *"A dragon bore the chick of a phoenix and has dashed through the blue."* Now, what is this? I hope Lin-chi understands.

P'ing then said, *"Take a seat and have a cup of tea."* That's enough. The abbot surrendered. This monk was tough; he couldn't handle him with words. So tea was served. But the abbot tried to catch his tail.

Again P'ing questioned him, "Where have you been recently?" Lin-chi said, *"I have been at Lung-kuang's."* P'ing said, *"And how is Lung-kuang these days?"* Lin-chi left. That is, he hopped out. This is the answer to the question.

I think the Abbot was satisfied. He would have nothing to do with Lin-chi anymore, not with Lung-kuang, nor Zen.

Lin-chi knows there cannot be transmission from one to another, that even Buddha cannot transmit. Lin-chi knows something that we do not know, but the badger and the fox know.

XIII

Lin-chi arrived at Ta-tz'u temple. Ta-tz'u was sitting in his quarters. Lin-chi asked him, "Why are you so solemnly sitting in your quarters?"

Ta-tz'u said, "The verdure of the pine lasts through the winters of a thousand years. When an old rustic in the wild picks a flower, the spring visits myriad lands."

Lin-chi said, "Beyond present and past, the body of perfect wisdom exists, but the Three Mountains are obstructed by manifold barriers."

Ta-tz'u shouted, "HO!"

Lin-chi also shouted, "HO!"

Ta-tz'u asked, "What?"

Lin-chi swung his sleeves and left.

SOKEI-AN SAYS:

Ta-tz'u is not only the name of the abbot of the temple but the name of the town. Lin-chi carries the name of his little temple on the shore of a creek. "Lin-chi" means "peeping over the creek." Perhaps in the future I will be called "Manhattan!"

From ancient days monks lived in small rooms much like Vimalakirti's room that was a ten-foot-square room where he received Manjushri and his followers numbering five thousand. Vimalakirti made room for them all. After the 5,000 guests took their seats, there were many seats left unoccupied. How was this possible? This is a koan.

Lin-chi asked Ta-tz'u why he was sitting in his quarters so solemnly. Hmmph! This is just like the samurai standing in a dark corner, who suddenly cuts a pedestrian down with his sword. The one attacked has no opportunity for thought—not a moment. In my grandfather's day, samurai in Japan were warriors, quite useful in war but in times of peace a nuisance! When a samurai would get a new sword and had no opportunity to test it—the sword was weeping for blood! He would stand in a dark corner, and when an innocent man would come by singing along, the samurai would cut him down. But what Lin-chi carried was a wonderful sword. His question to the abbot was such a testing blade. And Ta-tz'u answered with a poem.

Ta-tz'u said, "The verdure of the pine lasts through the winters of a thousand years. When an old rustic in the wild picks a flower, the spring visits myriad lands." What is this! Do you know?

Everything changes is aspect in color and form. The beautiful flower will dry up, and the tree will scatter its autumn leaves. Nothing stays in the freezing winter but the pine tree, standing alone without change. You can sense that Ta-tz'u is talking about *dharmakaya*. His sitting alone in his quarters is like the everlasting pine tree. He indicates the *dharmakaya* with these words. Then suddenly he swings the words to the other side—from the latent, invisible world to the visible world that is seen by the light of consciousness. When the candle of consciousness is lit here [indicates self], the *trikaya* appears.

A lady may pick a flower because she thinks it looks like her; but the old rustic picks it up with a smile just because it is beautiful. In this moment the spring visits a myriad of lands, as in deep meditation—Ah! *This is that!* Spring has come all at once. This is the attitude of Ta-tz'u in his quarters. The ten-foot-square room means nothing to him. He is sitting upon the cosmos.

Now Lin-chi changes his attitude. Ha! This is a poet, not a fencer. Well, I too will speak in poetry. Then he imitates a little novice—that is, talks nonsense. You will be disappointed at this from Lin-chi. He is expecting a HO! instead.

Lin-chi said, "Beyond present and past, the body of perfect wisdom exists, but the Three Mountains are obstructed by manifold barriers." The "three mountains" of which he speaks are *dharmakaya*, *sambhogakaya* and *nirmanakaya*. They look at everyone out of the long Chinese wall, and no one can come in. They speak about the three *kayas*, but they can hardly get in. How can they get over the peaks of the three mountains? Now he is meeting *Ta-tz'u's* poem. But Ta-tz'u shouted, HO! He couldn't wait while Lin-chi spouted nonsense. Then Lin-chi also shouted, "HO!" "What?" asked Ta-tz'u. *Lin-chi swung his sleeves and left,* hopped out, vanished like lightning. Ta-tz'u's HO! was beautiful, the first exclamation even before Lin-chi's poem had come to an end. But Lin-chi was not intimidated, his HO! came like a flash of lightning after thunder. After Lin-chi left, Ta-tz'u would not be able to find him hereafter in heaven or in hell. Zen is like this.

XIV

Lin-chi arrived at Hua-yen's temple in Hsiang-chou. Hua-yen was leaning on his staff feigning slumber. Lin-chi said, "Old master! Why are you sleeping so soundly?"

Hua-yen said, "You are certainly a Zen adept and decidedly different from the others!"

Lin-chi said, "Attendant, bring a cup of tea for the master."

Hua-yen called for the director of the monastery and said, "Place this honorable monk in the third seat."

SOKEI-AN SAYS:

Hua-yen, the master of the temple, was leaning on his staff, probably taking a little rest. He was an old monk and Lin-chi was a young one. In comes Lin-chi-chi and abruptly says—

"Old master! Why are you sleeping so soundly?" Lin-chi's tongue was like poison. He didn't hesitate to heap abuse upon an old monk. Hua-yen opened his eyes and said—

"You are certainly a Zen adept and decidedly different from the others." Had Lin-chi been blind and come with such a remark, Hua-yen would have shrugged and gone back to his quarters, but he was pleased with him. It was the same feeling Huang-po had when Lin-chi slapped his face.

Lin-chi said, *"Attendant, bring a cup of tea for the master."* Then Hua-yen called for the director of the monastery and said—

"Place this honorable monk in the third seat." In the center of the meditation hall is the statue of Manjushri, the Bodhisattva of Wisdom, sitting in a shrine. The floor is raised from the tiled floor on which the monk takes his position. This is the first row, or first seat. The master and the head monk sit there. The western side of the statue is the second seat. The entrance and back of the hall on the eastern side is the third row. At dinnertime, the first row is called out first, returns for a little meditation, then the second and third rows. Lin-chi was given the third seat.

Hua-yen understands Lin-chi; both are adept—something like what a good carpenter might say to a good plasterer.

"Oh, there's a little bit of plaster on the tip of your nose!" says the carpenter.

"Oh . . . Take it off with your axe." says the plasterer.

"Aha! You *are* a good plasterer. Today, I will show you how *I* manage my axe!"

Swinging his axe vigorously, the carpenter removes the little bit of plaster from the plasterer's face without skinning his nose.

When two adepts meet, they perform a wonderful Zen drama.

XV

Lin-chi arrived at Ts'ui-feng's temple. Ts'ui-feng questioned him, "Where have you come from?"

Lin-chi said, "I have come from Huang-po."

Ts'ui-feng asked, "With what words is it his custom to address people?"

Lin-chi said, "Huang-po has nothing to say."

Ts'ui-feng asked, "How is it that he has nothing to say?"

Lin-chi said, "Even if he had something to say, there would be no place for it."

Ts'ui-feng said, "Just hint at what it is; I shall see."

Lin-chi said, "An arrow flew across the Western sky.

SOKEI-AN SAYS:

When Lin-chi arrived at Ts'ui-feng's place, Ts'ui-feng questioned him.

"Where have you come from?" This is the usual Zen question, the bread and butter of Zen.

Lin-chi said, "I have come from Huang-po." The fencer receives the blow straight on his head. Lin-chi withdraws.

Ts'ui-feng asked, "With what words is it his custom to address people?" Lin-chi said, "Huang-po has nothing to say." That is, he does not use words.

Ts'ui-feng asked, "How is it that he has nothing to say?" He's trying to catch Lin-chi's tail.

Lin-chi said, "Even if he had something to say, there would be no place for it." In other words, in this boundless universe there is no place for it. Why? This is a stick of incense; it's called "incense," and this is called "glass"— everything has a name; there is no other place to put another word in.

Ts'ui-feng said, "Just hint at what it is; I shall see." Poor old Zen master!

Lin-chi said, "An arrow flew across the Western sky." The Western sky is India. The flying arrow is phenomena; no one can see anything more. Indeed, Lin-chi is giving a true "hint," but it is so fast! He had already hinted, but Ts'ui-feng had not seen it.

Once a monk was asked, "What is the simplest unit in the universe?" Striking a tray, the monk said, "This." His answer was too late! The arrow is so swift that before you look, the question is answered.

If Lin-chi were to ask you, "Without projecting an arrow, how can you win a battle?" and you say, "Sheeeeeeeee!" Lin-chi would say, "You are defeated today." Too late, the real unit exists before you can make any sound. This is the foundation of everything. As a Zen student, you must grasp it, but if you grasp it, it is too late. It exists before that. It is like a moon print on the water. When you grasp it, it is not in your hand, but it is always there.

To this point, you must return again and again. Then the Buddha's blue lotus, Chu-chih's finger, Hakuin's hand, and Yun-men's staff are all in your hand.

Do not make yourself melancholy because you cannot grasp the moon in your hand. If you try, the moon will not rest in your hand. But if you leave your hand, it is there. If you want to understand Zen, you must grasp it immediately.

XVI

Lin-chi arrived at Hsiang-t'ien's temple and questioned him: "I ask you about neither sacred nor profane. Say something."

Hsiang-t'ien said, "I am no one but myself."

Lin-chi shouted, "HO!" and said, "Bald heads! What kind of wooden bowl [chow] are you looking for here?"

SOKEI-AN SAYS:

After Lin-chi finished his study in Huang-po's temple, he left Huang-po's mountain and went around the country to meet Zen masters one after another on a pilgrimage. And as usual, whenever Lin-chi met a master he would ask a question:

"I ask you about neither sacred nor profane. Say something."

These two words, "sacred" and "profane," are very important words in the religious life of man, very important in Buddhism. "Sacred" means transcendental, "profane" means ordinary or secular. They are the two phases of existence. If I ask you, "What is this [holds up glass]?" and you say, "It has no particular name—you can call it "heaven" or "earth," "truth" or "reality"—the Buddhist would say that you are taking a transcendental attitude. But if you answer, "It's a glass of water," the Buddhist would say you are taking the ordinary or secular point of view. These two views are like the two sides of a hand. Lin-chi said, "I am not asking you about the sacred view or the ordinary view. Say something without concerning yourself with either of these two phases of existence."

How would you answer if I asked you not to observe this question from either the sacred or the profane standpoint? Without calling this reality or a glass of water, what would you call this? What would you say?

Hsiang-t'ien said, "I am no one but myself." It sounds good, doesn't it? Well, Hsiang-t'ien was saying, "This is this."

If I say to you, "Do not call it reality, and do not call it a glass of water," what would you say? This is this?

Lin-chi shouted, "HO!" and said, "Bald heads! What kind of wooden bowl [chow] are you looking for here?" "Wooden bowl" is a Chinese idiom. It means "establishment or "furniture." To live you need furniture, and the monk in the temple needs a wooden bowl—it is the only furniture he has. So Lin-chi was saying, "What kind of furniture are you looking for here!"

To Lin-chi, "I am no one but myself" is a theory, a philosophy. All those *sutras* are the furniture of Buddhism. The rosary, the bowl are the furniture of Buddhism. "I am no one but myself" is like this glass. Why say it?

No wonder Lin-chi gave him a HO! like thunder. Lin-chi wanted to crush all those magnificent conceptions with his shout.

Why didn't the monk show Lin-chi real existence instead of saying "I am no one but myself"? Why didn't he hit Lin-chi with his staff?

Actualizing Zen is different from conceiving it. I hope everyone has a real actualization of it.

XVII

Lin-chi arrived at Ming-hua's temple, and Ming-hua questioned him, "What are you doing in all this coming and going, coming and going?"

Lin-chi said, "Wearing out my straw sandals."

Ming-hua asked, "For what, after all?"

Lin-chi said, "Old fellow, you don't even know what you are talking about!"

SOKEI-AN SAYS:

Ming-hua's pedigree is also unknown.

This story sounds good. It seems Lin-chi had once been to see Ming-hua, and has come back again. So Ming said, *"What are you doing in all this coming and going, coming and going?"* Good! Waking in the morning and sleeping in the evening and working all your life along and dying in your old age! What are you doing! What would you say? "I make money?" Well, show me. Of course, you cannot. You have a life and then die. Then you return and die again. What do you do?

Lin-chi said, *"Wearing out my straw sandals."* Very good. I am eating my food. That's all.

Ming-hua then asked Lin-chi, *"For what, after all?"* Ming fell into his own question. It's the same as coming and going. He forgot what he was talking about.

Lin-chi said, *"Old fellow, you don't even know what you are talking about!"*

XVIII

When Lin-chi was on his way to Feng-lin, he met an old woman. The old woman questioned him, "Where are you going?"

Lin-chi said, "I am going to Feng-lin."

The old woman said, "Feng-lin is absent from the temple just now."

Lin-chi asked, "Where has he gone."

At that, she started to leave, but Lin-chi called after her. She turned her head and Lin-chi struck her.

SOKEI-AN SAYS:

Lin-chi's pilgrimage was very long. On the way he met an old woman who accosted him and asked him where he was going. In the old woman's view, he was just a youth.

Lin-chi lifted up a corner of his umbrella hat and looked at her and said, *"I am going to Feng-lin."*

"Oh," she said, "I'm very sorry, but *Feng-lin is absent from the temple just now."*

"Where has he gone," asked Lin-chi. *At that, she started to leave.* The old woman took a nasty Zen attitude; she showed him her back, walked a few steps and demonstrated her "going," as in the koan: Where have you come from, and where do you go?

How would you answer?

Lin-chi understood, of course. "Ha! She's trying to show me some Zen. All right! I'll give her a demonstration," and he called after her, "Look here!"

She turned her head and Lin-chi struck her!

I think this old woman woke up, all right. Of course, Lin-chi did not hate the old woman. If she were a Zen student, she would not have turned her head. She would have just gone. Her attitude wasn't a true Zen attitude; it was drama, nothing but drama.

We do not need a drama. We need real life. We do not need a stage. We need a house and food. Among Zen students there are many who take such an attitude, so their Zen is nothing but drama. The real thing is not there.

XIX

Lin-chi arrived at Feng-lin's temple. Feng-lin said, "There is one thing I want to talk to you about. Can we?"

Lin-chi said, "Why gouge out perfectly good flesh?"

Feng-lin said, "The moon over the sea shines serenely without casting a shadow. The forlorn fishes stray from their way."

Lin-chi said, "If the moon over the sea casts no shadow, why do the forlorn fishes stray from their way?"

Feng-lin said, "Seeing the blowing wind, I know the sea is running. At the sport of the waves, the sailing boats flutter their sails."

Lin-chi said, "The moon shines alone above a hushed land. A sudden laughter bursts heaven and earth."

Feng-lin asked, "Though your tongue throws light upon heaven and earth, can you speak a word at this juncture?"

Lin-chi said, "If on your way you should meet a swordsman, better offer him your sword. If he is not a poet, better not offer him your poem."

At that, Feng-lin yielded. Lin-chi then expressed his thoughts in an ode:

"The Great Way bears no resemblance to anything
It proceeds at will in all directions
Even a sudden spark cannot surpass it
Or lightning penetrate it"

Later, Kuei-shan asked Yang-shan, "If even a sudden spark cannot surpass it or lightning penetrate it, how did the sages of the past do something for others?"

Yang-shan asked, "What do you think?"

Kuei-shan said, "They are only words and have no significance."

Yang-shan said, "I don't agree with you."

Kuei-shan asked, "Then what is your view?"

Yang-shan said, "Officially, even a needle cannot be admitted there, but in private, horses and carriages are permitted to drive through."

SOKEI-AN SAYS:

This section of the *Record* is very peculiar; Lin-chi is usually not so poetic, but this is just another aspect of his personality.

When Lin-chi arrived at Feng-lin's temple, Feng-lin asked him, *"There is one thing I want to talk to you about. Can we?"* "There is one thing" is a Chinese idiom meaning, "*Here* is one thing." *Here* is immanent, not *there!*—not somewhere else.

Where is this *here* [touches knee], or *here* [touches shoulder]? You might answer that your consciousness is really *here.* Well, where is your consciousness? *Here* is one thing, but can we talk about it? We cannot grasp or talk about it. In Zen, occasionally a master will express himself in a poem, but more often a master will hit his student with his staff, or shout. One really should not add feet to a snake.

Lin-chi said, *"Why gouge out perfectly good flesh?"* We do not need to talk about it. *Here* is one thing [extends arm]. It is apparent, vivid, no one will doubt this. *Here* is one thing—all cosmos. We cannot look at this outside of the cosmos. We are part of it. We cannot add to the cosmos. We cannot take away from it. Though we may "explain" this cosmos in a million words, we do not change any part of it. Before we talk about it, it changes. Before Buddha, before Plato, this was perfect. There was the answer; there was the conclusion. There was realization.

Why so much talk about it? Why gouge out perfectly good flesh? Why gouge out perfect flesh and fit it in again? Why do unnecessary work?

From the Zen standpoint, why lift the glass *purposely* when it is usually here on the tray?

Lin-chi denied discourse, but Feng-Lin-chi thought this young monk is some adept—well, maybe; maybe he's not so marvelous. He comes from Huang-po, so he might not be so adept at expressing Zen in words.

So Feng-lin took his weapon, poetic expression, and brandished it and said, *"The moon . . ."*—of consciousness—*"over the sea shines serenely without casting a shadow.* In Buddhism, the sun is the symbol of present consciousness, and the moon is the symbol of the subconscious. We observe moon consciousness from sun consciousness, and vice versa. But in Zen, we do not take this symbolic attitude. In our meditation, the moon of pure consciousness serenely shines over the sea of this deep, bottomless, boundless consciousness "without casting a shadow." Not even a dot will cast a shadow on this sea.

Then, as Feng-lin says, *"The forlorn fishes stray from their way."* In daily life, when two or three bits of mind-stuff come up, they control your life. But Feng-lin-says the moon shines serenely without casting a shadow. This is his Zen attitude.

Lin-chi said in response, *"If the moon over the sea casts no shadow, why do the forlorn fishes stray from their way?"* This consciousness is so bright, it will not permit any stray fish to appear. It will not permit a chance for mind-stuff to come up and go astray. This power governs the entire ocean of consciousness.

Feng-lin said, *"Seeing the blowing wind, I know the sea is running. At the sport of the waves, the sailing boats flutter their sails."* When the nightingale sings, we know that spring has come. For Feng-lin, the whole movement is natural—all according to nature.

Lin-chi is saying he didn't come of his own will power, so he is not himself. There is no man in the universe. My stomach is not my self, for I do not digest my food. My body is not my self, for I am not responsible for its life. My nails, my hair are not my self. The functioning of my brain is not my self.

Then where is my self? There is no "my self." All is nature. This is Feng-lin's Zen attitude.

If you ever go to Japan you will see rivers covered in sails, as you do when you go to Long Island Sound. When the wind blows, you can see the whole field of sails turn with the wind, all at once a thousand sails—so beautiful to look at!. This is how Feng-lin explains the power of nature.

Lin-chi said, *"The moon shines alone above a hushed land."* In the state of Utah, there is a desert—nothing else, just a moon in heaven and silent. You only hear the chugg, chugg, chugg of your heart. It's a hushed land—just one consciousness.

In the hushed land of *dharmakaya*, *"A sudden laughter bursts heaven and earth."* Laughter? Because the universe is a *living* being, it shouts at any time, and doesn't just take the "natural" course. Nature uses its natural willpower, not necessarily to wait. It is nature's power. This is Lin-chi's aspect.

Feng-lin is taking the attitude that everything is with nature, but Lin-chi is saying, "Oh . . . yes, there is the power of nature, but there is *this* power as well. This is Lin-chi Zen.

It seems Feng-lin became impatient. He really showed his real nature, the heart of a Zen master.

Feng-lin asked Lin-chi, *"Though your tongue throws light upon heaven and earth, can you speak a word at this juncture?"* We don't need to speak so poetically. Say something.

If Feng-lin were Huang-po or Te-shan, Lin-chi would give a shout. But Lin-chi knew this old monk. There was no use in slapping his face, so he suggested. *"If on your way you should meet a swordsman, better offer him your sword. If he is not a poet, better not offer him your poem."* This means, "If you were a swordsman, I would offer you my sword; but you are a poet, so I won't offer you my sword of consciousness.

This is Lin-chi actualization. When we actualize reality, we do not need philosophy, symbolism, or anything else—just actualize it. That is enough.

And *"At that, Feng-lin yielded.* Reality can be observed from two angles, subjectively and objectively. But after all, these are nothing but words. Whatever you call it, it is only a name that has nothing to do with reality itself [struck gong]. Gonngggggg . . . that is all; we can add nothing to it.

From the human standpoint, we call it a sound, but this is just from our own angle. If we stand upon the absolute viewpoint [struck gong], *that* is all, and that *is* all. Saying more than that is trying to add legs to a snake. But here Lin-chi added an unnecessary leg by expressing himself in an ode:

> *"The great Way bears no resemblance to anything*
> *It proceeds at will in all directions*
> *Even a sudden spark cannot surpass it*
> *Or lightning penetrate it"*

Buddhism is really crystallized in the Zen school; that is why we consider Zen the school of Buddha himself. While other schools depend upon the *sutras*, Zen depends upon one's own consciousness. We do not care for words, for we wish to *actualize* our faith and to articulate *this* reality in our daily acts.

If one should ask you the taste of water, how can you explain it? You can only tell him to drink. He might ask you if it tastes like wine, or lemonade, or soda; and you would have to say no, it's like none of these. You can slap his face or shower him with a bucket of water, but you cannot speak about the great Way. If you say it is the "absolute," this is just a word and limits the meaning. But if you do not speak a word, it can become clear.

As Lin-chi put it, "The great Way bears no resemblance to anything." This is the Tao, the Way. It is also the Dharma. The great Way is like nothing else; it is absolute and is free to move in every direction at once, through every corner of the universe at the same moment, going in a myriad directions. A great poet of China said:

> *My soul is like a moon of autumn night*
> *It reflects upon a clear pool*
> *It has no resemblance to anything*
> *How can I explain it to you?*

Perhaps Lin-chi borrowed some words from this poem.

Later, Kuei-shan asked Yang-shan, "If even a sudden spark cannot surpass it, or lightning penetrate it, how did the sages of the past do something for others?" So how did he teach? If you speak, it is like adding legs to a snake; if you try to show it, it is like selling water from a river—it's quite useless. All the sages from the Buddha to Huang-po, how did they handle this?

Yang-shan was a sagacious young monk, so he tried to get the teacher to speak first, *"What do you think?"* Such conversations are like looking at a menu—you are still hungry.

Kuei-shan said to Yang-shan, *"They are only words and have no significance."* *Yang-shan said, "I don't agree with you."* Such effrontery!

Kuei-shan then asked, *"Then what is your view?"* Yang-shan said, *"Officially, even a needle cannot be admitted there, but in private, horses and carriages are permitted to drive through."* Yang-shan is suggesting the *dharmakaya* aspect to indicate the absolute [raised staff]. You point from the front gate, the reality that is undemonstrable—noumena. Trying to explain it is like trying to scratch crystal with cotton. But, there must be some aspect of this reality, a private aspect of the great Way.

It's like someone who is familiar with a situation, as a king's soldiers are familiar with the people entering the front gate. One soldier whispers to another at the gate, and it opens so everyone can go through. But if they go to the "official" gate, not even they are allowed in. [Sokei-an tapped the bowl lightly with the baton and smiled.] *This* is the hint!

If you struggle to *place* yourself in reality, you will fail. *You are one with it already*. This is the private aspect that you must understand. Then you can enter the gate.

When you take *sanzen*, you will have a koan based on this conversation, and you will apprehend it by your own effort. I can only throw light upon it.

XX

Lin-chi arrived at Chin-niu's temple. Chin-niu recognized Lin-chi coming. Holding his staff sideways, he solemnly sat at the gateway. Lin-chi tapped the staff with his hand three times and entered the monks' hall and seated himself in the first rank. Chin-niu entered the hall, saw him, and said, "The interview between host and guest should be held with a certain formality. Where have you come from that you offer me this affront?"

Lin-chi said, "Old Master, what are you saying?"

Chin-niu attempted to open his mouth, but Lin-chi hit him.

Chin-niu fell back. Again Lin-chi hit him.

Chin-niu said, "Today, I did not have the advantage."

SOKEI-AN SAYS:

When Lin-chi-chi arrived at Chin-niu's temple, Chin-niu recognized him. "Ah, that one has something." Lin-chi didn't have the begging monk's attitude or air about him. "I've been hearing about a monk from Huang-po's place breaking into many master's huts. This must be the one".

Rumor spreads a thousand miles in a short time, so all the monks at Chin-niu's place must have been talking about Huang-po's disciple. So Chin-niu decided to test him.

Holding his staff sideways, he solemnly sat at the gateway. Lin-chi tapped the staff with his hand three times and entered the monks' hall. Chin-niu barred his way with his staff held across his knees. Chin-niu wanted to know what Lin-chi had to say. But Lin-chi just tapped Chin-niu's staff three times and then entered the monk's hall.

Now, if you were Lin-chi, what would you do? Would you salute or introduce yourself? Or would you ask the man before you, "Are you Chin-niu?" Lin-chi just tapped his staff, so Chin-niu followed him into the hall.

This is an open fight. They looked at each other, and at that moment they were in the battle of Zen. Lin-chi had guts of iron. He came slowly, tapping the staff of this master three times and entered the monks' hall. This was Lin-chi attitude at this moment: he recognized the circumstance but not the soul. When a physician operates upon a patient, he recognizes the circumstances of the situation, and does not recognize the person's soul. To the doctor, the man is just a human body, that is all—he is not a person; he is just a disease. This was Lin-chi's attitude.

Then what happened? Lin-chi seated himself in the first rank, as though he were the master of the temple. As Chin-niu entered the hall, he saw Lin-chi in his chair. Naturally, Chin-niu had no place to sit. So Chin-niu said to him, a stranger, *"The interview between host and guest should be held with a certain formality. Where have you come from that you offer me this affront?"* You must understand Lin-chi is not doing this blindly. It is a battle.

Then Lin-chi said, *"Old master, what are you saying?"* Lin-chi is still the master of the temple.

Then Chin-niu opened his mouth, so Lin-chi hit him. Lin-chi beat the tar out of the king! Now, he was king of the universe.

This is *the* Lin-chi style of Zen. It is not personal. There is no elder or youngster, no man, no teacher, no disciple, rich or poor. Only truth exists—Zen existence. That is all.

Then Chin-niu said—this is the wonderful part, Chin-niu is about to swallow everything at once—*"Today, I did not have the advantage."* Of course not; from the first, Chin-niu was a failure. Why should he come to the gate and sit there waiting for Lin-chi? Why not wait in the hall?

The master took the place of a plain plank in front of the door. Rinzai took the place of the master from the very beginning. This is Zen acumen, a quick mind and accurate decision—tap, tap, tap. And he went and took the master's place.

Later, Kuei-shan questioned Yang-shan, "Was there any gain or loss in the contest of the honorable ones?"

Yang-shan said, "If there was any gain, both were the gainers. If there was any loss, both were the losers."

Lin-chi won the battle, but Kuei-shan is the umpire. He will decide the game. (Kuei-shan, of course, did not speak as I speak with you.) As the story was carried into Kuei-shan's temple, Kuei-shan asked Yang-shan about it.

"Was there any gain or loss in the contest of the honorable ones?" Of course, and as I explained to you, Lin-chi gained the advantage. Chin-niu didn't have an advantage from the beginning—or so thought his disciples . . . but Yang-shan didn't see it that way.

Yang-shan said, *"If there was any gain, both were the gainers. If there was any loss, both were the losers."* Both are the master, and both are the not the master—there is only one soul in the universe.

I think you will see this when you observe Lin-chi's koan of the Four Standpoints. Sometimes I recognize the soul but not the circumstances; sometimes I recognize the circumstances but not the soul; sometimes I recognize them together; sometimes not together.

Discourses
I-X (a)

I

Counselor Wang, the governor of the prefecture, and members of his ministry requested the Master to address the assembly from the lecture platform. The Master ascended to his seat and said: "Today, compelled by circumstances beyond my control, I have yielded to ordinary human concerns and have taken this seat. If I were to demonstrate the great matter according to the tradition of the patriarchs' school, I could not open my mouth, and there would be no place for you to find a foothold. Nevertheless, earnestly entreated by the governor today, how can I conceal the principle of our school? If there is here an adept warrior who can array his battle line and unfurl his colors, let him appear and prove himself to the assembly!"

A monk asked, "What is the fundamental principle of Buddhism?"

The Master gave a HO!

The monk bowed low. The Master said, "This kind of monk is worthy of conversing with me."

A monk asked, "Master, of what house is the music you play. From whom have you inherited your style of Zen?"

The Master said, "When I was at Huang-po's temple, I questioned him three times, and I was hit three times."

*The monk was bewildered. Thereupon, the Master gave a
HO! and struck him, saying, "You cannot drive a nail into the
empty sky!"*

SOKEI-AN SAYS:

There are many dialogues in philosophy, those of Plato, Confucius,
and others, but the dialogues of Lin-chi are the most important from the
Zen point of view.

*Counselor Wang, the governor of the prefecture, and members of his
ministry requested the Master to address the assembly from the lecture
platform.* Lin-chi didn't want to speak, but he was beseeched by the
governor to do so, so he accepted.

*The Master ascended to his seat and said: "Today, compelled by
circumstances beyond my control, I have yielded to ordinary human
concerns and have taken this seat. If I were to demonstrate the Great Matter
according to the tradition of the atriarchs' school, I could not open my
mouth, and there would be no place for you to find a foothold.* Lin-chi is
saying that from the first and real point of view it's of no use. He cannot
say a word. There is no heaven to look up to or sun to disappear. Even
Buddha himself calls out for help in such a case. You can see that Lin-chi
is taking a very lofty attitude. He does not care for salvation. Only human
beings call their own work salvation. Such a thing is of no use.

Lin-chi cannot show you the wholeness of Buddhism, but by
showing a part, he is demonstrating the whole. When the Buddha held
up a flower, he was showing a part to demonstrate the whole. *This* is the
demonstration of Zen. But we degrade it to the second, third, and fourth
degree. Blind men in robes go through their whole lives without seeing
true religion. From the first standpoint, he cannot speak a word, so when
he closes his mouth, everything disappears. Even Buddha himself is afraid
in that situation!

There is nothing to speak about beside this present moment. Any
time, any moment, gives you access to IT. But usually we degrade the
manifestation to the second, third, and fourth degree. Thus, blind men
in robes may go through their whole lives without seeing true religion.
To refer to himself as a mountain monk is to belittle himself, the usual
politeness of the time.

From the first degree standpoint Lin-chi would not say a word. He would shut his mouth and everything would disappear.

An emperor once asked a master to speak about the teaching of the *Prajnaparamita Sutra*. The Master ascended to the high seat, struck the lectern, and descended.

"What was that?" asked the emperor.

"Your Majesty," said the Master, "the lecture is over."

But Lin-chi on this occasion came down to the second degree of Zen and said—

"Nevertheless, earnestly entreated by the governor today, how can I conceal the principle of our school? If there is here an adept warrior who can array his battle line and unfurl his colors, let him appear and prove himself to the assembly!" A monk asked, "What is the fundamental principle of Buddhism?" The Master gave a HO! This is the usual Lin-chi answer.

The monk bowed low. The Master said, "This kind of monk is worthy of conversing with me." You must understand this bow. Lin-chi decided to be gentle with the monk.

You have heard many dialogues between Lin-chi and the monks over these last two years. These discourse have been the most interesting and most difficult to understand. There are five or six more pages to translate and then these lectures will be over. I thank you all for attending.

A monk asked, "Master, of what house is the music you play." This tune is inaudible. Zen is transmitted from eye to eye and from soul to soul.

"From whom have you inherited your style of Zen?" There is no self-made Zen in the world. Our understanding must stand on an historical foundation. This monk is asking Lin-chi: "Whose heir are you?" It seems the monk knew Lin-chi quite well.

The Master said, "When I was at Huang-po's temple, I questioned him three times, and I was hit three times." You all know this story.

Zen masters do not usually answer questions. They slap a monk's face or squeeze his neck. Or if he does not understand, we throw him out the window!

An actor once asked his master how to enter cosmic consciousness. He was intending to perform it on stage.

His master asked him, "Can you smile naturally, at will?"

The actor said, "Usually, but not all the time."

"Can you sneeze naturally, at will?"

"No," said the actor.

"Go home and practice this for three years."

After three years he returned to see his master, and he sneezed perfectly, at will.

The master asked him, "Did you enter into cosmic consciousness?"

The actor laughed. Foolish question! Cosmic consciousness is all about us. We are born in it. Can you get *out* is the question!

Lin-chi had inherited his Zen from the three blows of Huang-po.

The monk was bewildered. He was aghast, dumbfounded. He was no fool.

Thereupon, the Master gave a HO! and struck him, saying, "You cannot drive a nail into the empty sky!" He struck the monk and gave his HO! at the same time. Quick as lightning, no explanations. Lin-chi is the essence of philosophy and religion.

A distinguished lecturer asked the Master a question, "The three vehicles and the twelve divisions of the teachings reveal Buddha's nature, do they not?"

The Master said, "No one has ever ploughed this wild field!"

The lecturer said, "How could Buddha have deceived people?"

The Master asked, "Where is Buddha?"

The lecturer was speechless.

The Master said, "Is it your intention to deceive me before the governor? Go! Go! You hinder the others from asking questions!"

SOKEI-AN SAYS:

This lecture-master was not a Zen master. He may have been one of the scholar-monks of a different sect who were supported by the governor, in which case it is understandable that he was apparently not very pleased to have Lin-chi in his territory but rather considered him an enemy. Presenting himself before the governor and his staff, he was showing where he stood when he asked such a scholastic question.

The Three Vehicles are the *shravakayana, pratyekabuddhayana,* and *bodhisattvayana*. In the time of Ashoka, the Buddha's teachings were divided into twelve "baskets": poetry collection, philosophical collection, stories, metaphors, and so on. These writings are studied by scholars and are believed to reveal the truth of his teachings.

Zen students—in my Hinayana period I took monks' training—observe the stages of human mind and emotion, not by studying books, but in their daily practice. In the morning we would, as honorable beggars, visit ten houses. Next morning it would be ten other houses. We must accept anything put into our bowls—raw food, little grains of rice, maybe dirty, never prepared. We would take everything back to the monastery. It was for the monastery we were begging. Its name was written on the bowls as an introduction for us. We were instructed: "You must walk like an elephant. You must not look at anyone's face. You must not think of anything at all." One day we might get a few yen with the uncooked food. Sometimes we were very hungry. Maybe a woman would say, "I think I have seen your face before." We would answer, "I saw your face but I have no memory of it." This is our study of the Three Vehicles' Twelve Divisions of the Buddha's teaching.

I am sure the lecture-master failed to understand Lin-chi's remark: *"No one has ever ploughed this wild field!"* The "wild field" was this lecture-master's mind, covered with weeds and bushes, harboring snakes and toads. Such minds must burn up the trash to find the real soil underneath. The lecture-master must have been terribly disconcerted at Lin-chi's remark. His reply, "How could the Buddha have deceived people," shows his mind was still in the stage of the Three Vehicles' Twelve Divisions. The lecture-master ignored Lin-chi's remark.

All of a sudden Lin-chi showed his real sword. His "Where is Buddha?" came like a clap of thunder rending the sky.

This type of religious teacher is not to be found in the West. Lin-chi makes no demonstration of kindness or compassion. From beginning to end, from head to foot, he was completely honest. When we handle a Zen student, we do not care how he feels emotionally. That does not concern us. We just want him to *realize* something. If you are going to talk about Buddha-nature, you must know firsthand where Buddha is.

The Master also said, "This gathering of Buddhists is being held here today for an important matter. If there are any more questions, come forward and ask them. Quickly! But the moment you open your mouth, you already have nothing to do with it. Why? Have you not heard what Shakyamuni said: 'The Dharma exists without name; it is not dependent upon causation or relation.' But you are unable to have faith in this, and therefore you have this confusion today. Perhaps I am annoying the governor and his staff and obscuring the buddha-nature of others. I had better retire."

Whereupon the Master gave a HO! and said, "You who have little faith in your hearts will never have a day of rest. I thank you for having stood so long."

SOKEI-AN SAYS:

When Lin-chi says "today," "today" has some significance. "This moment" or "this instant" also is not any other instant. There is no other moment to the human soul. It is always this moment only. It is a very important moment—just this moment (striking his brass bowl). If you do not understand "this moment" you die, this lifetime is not yours, you are not living in your life, in your own nature. You are just eating and sleeping and your life is not yours. You enjoy someone else's life, you suffer someone else's life. You come into this life like a dreamer. You go away like a dreamer. Many are like this, pursuing one thing after another. The most important thing to them is the next day, for unimportant matters are very important to them while the main thing is not noted.

The "main thing" brought to the attention of the audience is an often-used word or term, written in Chinese as literally "one great matter."

The "great matter" of the Dharma-assembly is for us "to realize Buddha's Wisdom." The Buddha said, "I struggled for six years for one great matter.

In the myth of Avalokiteshvara, wisdom divides itself into many bodies and they make contact with each other and feel each other and know each other and enjoy each other. Avalokiteshvara was alone in the universe. All alone. He could not see himself for IT was absolute. It was so lonesome he could not see himself for a long, long time, so he tore himself into many and then they felt each other, they knew each other, they could see each other.

If we do not know our existence, we are not existing. We must see each other and know each other. If you are a blind woman and get married, you can not see your husband. With your hands you can feel him, you can touch him, you can know him, but you can never see him.

If there are any more questions, come forward and ask them. Quickly! Hurry up! Life is short. He was like a great general. Of course, the period when he was in North China was one of civil war. There was not a single peaceful day. Since it was wartime, people liked to see monks like Lin-chi. He fitted that time in China. He was impatient and showed his naked sword. He was honest. When he touched another, the other bled.

However—

"The moment you open your mouth, you already have nothing to do with it." You have lost the moment of actual awareness. As soon as you try to talk about it, you have nothing to do with it. I take a drink of water. You ask me how it tastes. If I answer "cold" it has nothing to do with the actuality of my experience of it being cold. The taste gets away before I can talk about it. When you ask a question you have already lost the reality.

Why? Have you not heard what Shakyamuni said: 'The Dharma exists without name; it is not dependent upon causation or relation.' But you are unable to have faith in this, and therefore you have this confusion today." If you can understand this, you know Buddhism. Your head exists without a name; your hands exist without a name; your feet exist without a name. I ask you, Do you have faith in God? You say, yes. Then I ask, What is this? [Holds out *hossu*.] You answer, I do not know. I ask you, What is God? Then you say a million words about this God. God exists without a name of course! He does not depend upon causation or upon relation. If you do not think the name, it still exists.

The law of causation, you might say, is that everything exists perpendicularly; and the law of relation says everything exists horizontally. [Sokei-an uses *hossu* to demonstrate.] How did I come into this world? Perhaps my father ate some shell of a vegetable. It became a part of him, and perhaps it went into my mother's womb for nine months, and then I came into the world. This is causation [holds *hossu* upright, turning it quickly to horizontal], and this is relation.

If there is no causation and relation, you think you do not exist, and when you try to seek some particular point you do not strike that particular point but some other. You do not blame yourself when you fail. You blame your father, you blame your mother, or your children, or communism or something. Never do you blame yourself. Reality exists in this moment without causation or relation. You always look at things as good or bad, never look at things as they are—not good *or* bad. You think the mosquito bad. But the mosquito thinks he is a mosquito, that is all.

A monk once asked, "Originally the universe was pure existence. From this pure, monotonous existence, how did heaven and earth appear?" This is the answer: Who is the questioner? Who is the one who answered? Do you know? The monk says this way [holding *hossu* in one direction], so he is answered in this way [holding *hossu* in the other direction]. The fencer hits so you answer in the opposite symmetrical direction. Nothing else to do. Observe the universe this way; the universe is simple.

Perhaps I am annoying the governor and his staff, and obscuring the buddha-nature of others. I had better retire." Lin-chi looked down and observed all their expressions—all masks and nobody home. Lin-chi must have felt it was not worthwhile to talk all this high philosophy. His idea is too big for them, too deep. So Lin-chi felt sorry.

*Whereupon the Master gave a HO!—*everyone perhaps jumped from his seat, but no one understands; why?—*and said, "You who have little faith in your hearts will never have a day of rest. I thank you for having stood so long."* They didn't have chairs in the temples. They stood in the lecture hall with hands crossed on their chests. So it was a long, long time.

II

One day the Master entered the city of Ho-fu. When Counselor Wang requested the Master to take his seat upon the lecture platform, Ma-yu appeared and asked the Master a question: "The Great Compassionate One has a thousand hands and a thousand eyes. Which eye is the main eye?"

The Master said, "The Great Compassionate One has a thousand hands and a thousand eyes. Which eye is the main eye? Speak! Speak!"

Ma-yu pulled the Master down from his seat and sat upon it
himself. Approaching him, the Master said, "How are you?"
Ma-yu was bewildered. The Master pulled Ma-yu off the
seat and sat upon it himself. Ma-yu left. The Master descended
from his seat.

SOKEI-AN SAYS:

This dialogue reminds me of the Zen of Fa-yen Wen-i [885-958],
a famous master of the ninth century. Fa-yen's Zen was quite peculiar.
If one asked him, "What is this?" [holding out rod], he extended it and
said, "What is this?" His koans are difficult to pass. When questioned,
he answered with the same question. For example: "The original state is
pure; how do the mountains and rivers appear?" His answer was the same.
"The original state is pure; how do the mountains and rivers appear?" If
one asked him "What is the one?" he answered, "What is the one?" If a
teacher writes the number "1" on a board and asks the pupil what it is, the
pupil will answer, "One." If you writes the number "2," the pupil will say,
"Two." If you look at his Zen in this way, there is nothing to talk about. He
observed all mental states as phenomena. If the mental state is limited, he
pointed it out—"This [raising *hossu*] is your mental condition." For Fa-yen
there was no difference in the two incidents; he observed one incident
and a succession of incidents as part and as whole. All is phenomena
and there is nothing to discuss. One incident [held *hossu* vertical] and
another incident [held *hossu* horizontal] and again another [held *hossu*
at an oblique angle] are all just states of phenomena. Thinking and trying
to find an answer is just phenomena, and when one does give an answer,
it is also just phenomena. Fa-yen looked at everything as incidents of
phenomena—as physical and metaphysical incidents. All is phenomena.

This conversation between Ma-yu [n.d.] and Lin-chi is very similar,
and Lin-chi understood Ma-yu before he opened his mouth.

One day the Master entered the city of Ho-fu. When Counselor Wang
requested the Master to take his seat upon the lecture platform, Ma-yu
appeared and asked the Master a question: "The Great Compassionate One
has a thousand hands and a thousand eyes. Which eye is the main eye?"
The Great Compassionate One is Avalokiteshvara.

The Master said, "The Great Compassionate One has a thousand hands
and a thousand eyes. Which eye is the main eye? Speak! Speak!" Lin-chi
was given this question by Ma-yu. He answered with the same question.

Lin-chi is one eye. Ma-yu is one eye. I, myself, am one eye, and you are one eye. Which is the true eye?

When Soyen Shaku came to this country a long time ago to attend the great World Parliament of Religions meeting in Chicago, it was the first time a Zen master had come here to this country, and no one paid much attention to him because of the other dignitaries. Later Soyen went to France. One day in a park he met a Japanese gentleman who said, "Zenji, you must be in the picture of that artist who is sketching this area." "How can you observe in such a way?" said Soyen, "He is in *my* sketch, for he is on the ground that *I* am observing."

You are the main eye in the picture you are observing. In Christian terms everyone is the child of God. Each has the Christ within him. Of the thousand hands within each eye of Avalokiteshvara, the eye is the Christ, and the other nine hundred ninety-nine are the Holy Ghost.

Ma-yu pulled the Master down from his seat and sat upon it himself. I think all the followers of Lin-chi must have been watching very carefully to see what he would do. As Ma-yu pulled him from the altar, Lin-chi did not give the usual shout but watched as Ma-yu took the seat. Ma-yu was showing Lin-chi that he was the main eye—I am the Christ, you are the Holy Ghost. Now it is Lin-chi's turn!

Approaching him, the Master said, "How are you?" A ticklish moment! Lin-chi is showing that he is the main eye.

Ma-yu was bewildered. The Master pulled Ma-yu off the seat and sat upon it himself. Ma-yu left. The Master descended from his seat. Ma-yu did not shout but hopped out of the temple. Lin-chi descended—one eye disappears and all eyes disappear!

This dialogue demonstrates Zen very clearly—no discussions about "monism," "pluralism," and so forth. Just take the seat and descend from the seat. Zen was very crude at that time. It is through this kind of expression that we can observe that kind of Buddhism that is a very plain type of religion.

If we are one of the thousand hands of Avalokiteshvara, we do not need to speak of ego or non-ego. We *know* our true place and our true occupation. We do not have to give up our own position and say, *I* am non-ego!

I cannot say more about this. I hope you will realize this "position."

III

The Master ascended to his seat and said, "Enthroned upon your heart of red flesh is a true man of no rank. He is always going in and coming out of the gates of your face. Anyone who has not yet proved this, behold!"

A monk came forward and asked, "What about the true man of no rank?"

The Master descended from his seat, grasped the monk, and said, "Speak! Speak!"

The monk tried to say something, but the Master pushed him back and said, "What a muckraker this true man of no rank is!"

The Master then returned to his quarters.

SOKEI-AN SAYS:

This is a very good example of Lin-chi's Zen. It is the morning of Zen in the Tang dynasty. It has not yet matured. The monks expressed it in a crude fashion.

The Master ascended to his seat. He entered the temple and walked up to the altar. The altar, a platform, is about a foot up from the floor. Upon this platform is a square chair upon which Lin-chi seated himself. He took his shoes off and placed them before the chair and sat cross-legged. Two young monks came from both sides and chanted the opening sutra to open the discourse. Then hot water was offered in an earthenware cup to the Master. He took it, placing it beside him, and the monks withdrew. Then he began his address and said—

"Enthroned upon your heart of red flesh is a true man of no rank. He is always going in and coming out of the gates of your face. Have you every met this true man? He goes in and comes out of the gates of your faces. You, all those monks, and all of you here [indicating audience]. This is Lin-chi's Buddhism, his God. He is not remote and strange. He does not sit upon the clouds of heaven. He is not meditating at the trunk of the Bodhi Tree. He is not sleeping in the state of nirvana. He is vivid, always coming in and out of this gate [indicates own face] and living upon the flesh that is the true man. No Buddha, no God, but true man.

Anyone who has not yet proved this, behold!" Do you understand this true man? Have you met him? Have you proved the one who is existing upon your own heart? You must meet and behold him.

Lin-chi said you do not need many words to explain Buddhism, and you do not need to study all the thousands of *sutras*. If you do not understand, hearing *this*, there is no use giving you any religious instruction.

Lin-chi says, "Behold!" He is inviting trouble. All the monks watching him knew he came from Huang-po Mountain. He is a strange monk. He opens his mouth wide and says, "Behold!" He speaks as though no one in the world knows Buddhism. He is saying, If anyone has the courage, let him appear and ask a question. Hmmm, something must happen, some storm, some thunder. Lin-chi appeared with his naked sword, without philosophy or scholastic words. He is a Zen master. His *body* is Buddhism. He is original substance. That is his strength.

A monk came forward and asked, "What about the true man of no rank?" The Master descended from his seat. Lin-chi came down from his seat and approached the monk. The monk had guts enough to stand still and wait for Lin-chi. He didn't know what the Master would do. If you know Lin-chi's style, it is difficult to stand your ground. You do not do it instinctively. But perhaps this monk knew only the superstructure of Buddhism, if any at all. Lin-chi—

Grasped the monk, and said, "Speak! Speak!" If you know what the true man is, say a word!

The monk tried to say something, but the Master pushed him back and said, *"What a muckraker this true man of no rank is!"* The monk was not so bad; he tried to say something. He struggled to keep his balance. He tried to show the Master the true man upon his heart. He was not dumbfounded or bewildered, but too slow. When one's Buddhism is just on the lips—chi-chi-chi, like a sparrow,—when a master grasps him he doesn't know what to do.

The Master then returned to his quarters. When you kill a man and see his blood, it is not necessary to kick the corpse. You just go.

This is one of the most famous discourses in the *Record of Lin-chi*. To demonstrate Buddhism in this fashion, a Zen monk need not take fifteen minutes, while the reader of books could take three years and not express as much. What a waste of time!

IV

The Master ascended to his seat. A monk came forward and bowed. The Master gave a HO!

The monk said, "Venerable one, you had better not attempt to fathom me."

The Master asked, "Tell me, just where did the HO! alight?"

The monk gave a Ho!

Another monk asked, "What is the fundamental principle of Buddhism?"

The Master gave a Ho!

The monk bowed. The Master asked, "Would you say it was a good shout or not?

The monk said, "The petty thieves are all defeated."

The Master asked, "What was their offense?"

The monk said, "It has been forbidden to commit the same crime again."

The Master gave a HO!

That same day, when the head monk of the eastern quarter and the head monk of the western quarter met each other, they simultaneously gave a HO!

A monk asked the Master, "Of the two, which was the host and which was the guest?"

The Master said, "Host and guest were apparent at a glance. If you wish to understand what I mean by 'host' and 'guest,' you had better ask the head monks."

The Master descended from his seat.

SOKEI-AN SAYS:

Zen in Sanskrit means meditation, quiet contemplation. Buddhism is founded upon meditation. In primitive Buddhism, no prayer was offered to God; meditation takes the place of prayer in other religions. While Christians kneel down to pray, Buddhists sit cross-legged and enter into meditation. But today there are many sects in Buddhism which have an objective God somewhere outside, so they pray to that God. But the Zen student does not believe in offering prayer in any direction of the universe; there is no word to use and nothing to pray for. Therefore, they meditate. They do not call the name of the absolute and ask its help and its mercy! This Christian prayer is quite natural, but it is childish, too. The Zen student strives for his own religious experience, and for this he will feel gratitude and offer thanks. But he has nothing to say, nothing to ask for, and nowhere to search for God. We realize the almighty power in this actual existence, in all existence, and we call it reality. We know the reality in all the phenomena that we observe, and we feel time and space. We call it actual reality.

Absolute reality is the reality out of which all these colors, sounds, and forms are created by our own senses. The Zen faith is founded upon this reality. We call it by many names. When philosophically we name it reality, it is like a void. But we feel it directly as absolute being; our entire sentient feeling is in it, and when we move it is by that power, and when we speak, it is the voice of that absolute being that we call absolute reality.

The Buddhist must take a very objective attitude. He may ask a question of a master and receive just a shout—HO! You might feel offended, but you must not take such an emotional attitude. There is no emotion in it. It is a simple abstract HO!; that is all. With it, the Master expressed the wholeness and the vitality of absolute being.

The Buddha expressed this in absolute silence. But his silence is different from what we usually think of as silence—the Buddha's silence is not silence. By his silence he spoke volumes of words! Later, in the Zen school of China, the masters used both silence and the shout. All your understanding will be experienced in silence when you answer your koans. Some will express silence in a poem and some with a shout. A Zen student will not use philosophical terms. It is different from other types of Buddhist expressions. It is in this record that you will understand Zen as expressed in the Tang dynasty.

The Master ascended to his seat. A monk came forward and bowed. The Master gave a HO! This could crush an ordinary monk, giving him a shout before he has even asked his question. In Japanese fencing there is a method called "sudden stroke." The combatants face one another with their swords drawn between them. Then comes a quick shout and they commence to fight. The sudden stroke is to strike before the opponent can commence to strike. Lin-chi's shout is like this.

The monk said, "Venerable one, you had better not attempt to fathom me." This monk had guts. He did not jump but calmly made his statement. Lin-chi's shout is like a needle that probes the mind of the monk. Then the monk takes the same attitude. According to the ability of each, Lin-chi will sound out his mind.

We all do this in daily life. If you are a manager, a new man appears and you shout, "What do you want?" He will immediately take an attitude. With that attitude revealed, you fathom his personality. Chinese fishermen throw a branch of leaves upon the water and when the fish gather underneath, they bring them up in a net. Lin-chi's shout is like this; he want to understand the monk with it. In this line, the monk is evading Lin-chi. He is hiding—"Don't try to fathom me!" But it was no use. Lin-chi's eye was clear.

The Master asked, "Tell me, just where did the HO! alight?" The monk *gave a HO!* This is good discourse. The monk was not an amateur, but a real Zen student.

A doctor in Japan was studying Rinzai [Lin-chi] Zen. One day he went to a temple of the Soto school, where the master was giving a lecture. After the lecture the doctor approached the master to ask a question. Knowing that the doctor came from the Rinzai school, the master suddenly gave him a blow and said, "How dare you approach me!" This Rinzai student apologized and retired. Shame! He took it psychologically—in the ordinary sense. Abominable! Had he been my student, I would have struck him again!

But this monk is good. He gave a HO!—the Master's sound.

Another monk asked, "What is the fundamental principle of Buddhism?" Blind monks make a queer Buddhism out of their ignorant minds.

The Master gave a HO! This is the profound principle of Buddhism.

The monk bowed. The Master asked, "Would you say it was a good shout or not? This question is a hook! If you answer it, you are certainly hooked!

The monk said, "The petty thieves are all defeated." Meaning, all the thoughts rooted in man's mind. That is, "I have nothing to say good or bad."

The Master asked, "What was their offense?" What is wrong? Why have they lost their battle? Where did they make a mistake?

The monk said, "It has been forbidden to commit the same crime again." Lin-chi has committed it once and now tries the same method again. The monk is trying to make Lin-chi keep quiet.

The Master gave a HO! This type of shout is most terrible. Lin-chi cares nothing for good or bad at this moment—it has no meaning. I hope that some day you will understand these Zen attitudes. They are most useful in daily life.

That same day, when the head monk of the eastern quarter and the head monk of the western quarter met each other, they simultaneously gave a HO! In this one HO! time, space, and this moment are one. There is one experience of one being—time, space, being. And the fourth—the moment? It is not quite the same—it is one yet two; and one must be a loser.

A monk asked the Master, "Of the two, which was the host and which was the guest?" Which is the winner and which is the loser?

The Master said, "Host and guest were apparent at a glance." This is an important point that you will observe in *sanzen*. This principle of Zen must be attained first in *zazen*.

"If you wish to understand what I mean by 'host' and 'guest,' you had better ask the head monks." How do you ask these two at the same time? Which do you ask first?

The Master descended from his seat.

V

The Master ascended to his seat. A monk asked, "What is the fundamental principle of Buddhism?"

The Master raised his flywhisk. The monk gave a HO! The Master struck him.

Another monk inquired of the Master, "What is the fundamental principle of Buddhism?"

Again the Master raised his flywhisk. The monk gave a HO! The Master also gave a Ho! The monk was bewildered. The Master struck him.

The Master then addressed the assembly: "The one who serves the Dharma does not avoid the loss of body and soul. For twenty years I was with my late master, Huang-po. Three times

*I questioned him about the fundamental principle of Buddhism,
and three times he favored me with painful blows from his stick;
but they were like strokes of mugwort. Nowadays, I would like to
have another dose of the stick. Who will administer it for me?"*

*Just then a monk came forward and said, "I will administer
it for you!"*

*The Master held out his stick to him. The monk tried to take
it, but the Master struck him.*

SOKEI-AN SAYS:

In these dialogues there is no trace of human reason. They are free
and lightning fast. It was said of Master Lin-chi that he attained Zen
under the rod of his teacher Huang-po, so through his *rod* one can
understand Zen easily. But anyone who tries to understand his Zen
through philosophy will fail to find any trace of Lin-chi's mind. This
is true. His mind is emancipated from philosophical and traditional
Buddhism. It is therefore typical Zen. He acts with an empty hand and
an empty mind—holds nothing, like a bird taking flight through the sky.
He moves in multifold directions—selects no special way. In daily life our
minds must be like that.

*The Master ascended to his seat. A monk asked, "What is the
fundamental principle of Buddhism?" The Master raised his flywhisk.* This
is the principle of Buddhism. The Buddha raised the golden blue lotus;
Chu-chih raised his finger; Hakuin raised his hand; Wu-men raised his
cane. Do *you* understand this principle? If you do, you will understand Zen.

But sometimes the Buddha raised nothing—just kept silence. After a
visitor had retired, Ananda would sometimes say, "O Lokanatha, I do not
understand why you gave no answer." And the Buddha would say, "Oh
yes, Ananda, I answered." "But I did not hear your answer." "When I was
quiet, said the Buddha, "the whole universe spoke one hundred thousand
words." Ananda put his hand behind his ear and said, "I cannot hear it."

Ananda's answer was very good. Not hearing, he heard the million
voices of the universe—the voices of silence. I once read Mme. Blavatsky's
book *The Voice of Silence*. I do not know if she really heard or not. If she
heard and could describe it, it proves that she never heard. If she really
heard—she would not have written that book!

The monk gave a HO! The Master struck him. The monk understood,
so Lin-chi immediately hit him. "Good, you understand." No moment

between question and answer. This is the height of Zen conversation. The type of Zen dialogue, *mondo* in Japanese, which I am taking to the West comes from this summit.

We are Lin-chi's disciples, but our expression is somewhat different. Lin-chi's Zen is more abstract than the Zen of today, which is more concrete—nearer to reality.

Another monk inquired of the Master, "What is the fundamental principle of Buddhism?" Again the Master raised his flywhisk. The monk gave a HO! But this time Lin-chi does not strike. Hmmm. The monk expected the rod, but Lin-chi did not strike.

The Master also gave a HO! The monk was bewildered. The Master struck him. It is like the special training of a samurai in Japan—lose your attention, and he will cut you down.

The Master then addressed the assembly: "The one who serves the Dharma does not avoid the loss of body and soul." Like the young monk who takes a vow to serve the Dharma. He will go into burning fire or water. They have that courage.

"For twenty years I was with my late master, Huang-po. Three times I questioned him about the fundamental principle of Buddhism, and three times he favored me with painful blows from his stick." It was in Lin-chi's three questions that his teacher handed him the principle of Buddhism that had been handed down from generation to generation—a flame transmitted from one candle to another. This flame I, *osho*, am giving to you. It cannot be spoken. It is not written. It is eye to eye, heart to heart.

"But they were like strokes of mugwort." Mugwort is a weed that has a strong stem that snaps as you pass through a field. Lin-chi was so eager and sincere that he did not feel the pain of the rod of his teacher.

Nowadays, I would like to have another dose of the stick. Who will administer it for me?" Many Zen teachers feel so. When I was a child my father scolded me. Then I would look into his eyes and see true love. Today that type of love is almost obsolete.

Just then a monk came forward and said, "I will administer it for you!" The Master held out his stick to him. The monk tried to take it, but the Master struck him. This monk was blind. It was apparent that Lin-chi would strike him. But he did not strike the monk; he and the monk are the same person! Without this realization, there is no salvation in Zen.

VI

The Master ascended to his seat. A monk asked, "What happens to the one who stands upon the blade of the sword?"

The Master said, "Beware! Beware!"

The monk was disconcerted. The Master struck him.

Another monk asked the Master, "Whenever the layman of the stone cave was treading the pestle, he would forget he was moving his feet. Where did he go?"

The Master said, "Drowned in a deep pond!"

Then the Master said, "When you come here, I do not misjudge you: I know where you come from. If you come in some fashion, you have strayed from the Way. However, if you do not come in some fashion, you have bound yourself without a rope. You had better not judge haphazardly. Your understanding or your lack of understanding are alike a misunderstanding. Speaking thus, I submit myself to your criticism. I thank you for having stood so long."

SOKEI-AN SAYS:

These dialogues so far and the parts to follow are very important. Lin-chi really makes clear to us his Zen and his Buddhist attitude.

The Master ascended to his seat. A monk asked, "What happens to the one who stands upon the blade of the sword?" This means standing upon actual reality—the topmost position in daily life. Why is it expressed in such a fashion, as if in the midst of battle?

The Master said, "Beware! Beware!" The monk did not expect such a response. Although he was *talking* about standing upon the blade of a sword, he never thought that it was the moment upon which *he* was standing! Lin-chi's view was different: At every moment, whether on the battlefield or asleep in bed, that is the time upon the blade! So he said: "Beware! Beware!"

The monk was disconcerted. The Master struck him. This was so sudden! The monk stood aghast; he never suspected that *that* moment was the top of the blade. This is a koan.

Another monk asked the Master, "Whenever the layman of the stone cave was treading the pestle, he would forget he was moving his feet." Once during the Tang dynasty Buddhism was persecuted by the emperor of

346 | SOKEI-AN SASAKI

China. The temples were burned and the images were destroyed. Many monks disrobed and retired to stone caves on the western edge of China. The layman the monk is referring to is a layman who forget he was putting his foot down on the shaft of a pestle that was pounding rice in a very large mortar. He was so engrossed in deep thoughts thinking of Zen, he forgot he was moving his legs. In the mind of a great pianist, the piano entirely disappears. Thus the mind of the layman forgot he was pounding rice. His mind was moving with the action of the pestle and was not artificially pounding rice. This indicates something great is working here.

"Where did he go?" The Master said, "Drowned in a deep pond!" The layman of the stone cave was not existing, but this answer is very clear even though it is very hard to understand the Master's idea.

Where did the layman of the stone cave go?—"Ah, he is drowned in the deep pool of meditation." This is not good, but there is another shade of meaning and very delicious if you can taste it. I hope you can understand this. Lin-chi's viewpoint really corresponds to this layman's viewpoint of Zen. I cannot explain further, fearing I would put an explanation on this marvelous part.

Then the Master said, "When you come here, I do not misjudge you."— If you come here, I see you as possessing everything—nothing is lacking. You possess everything that nature bestows upon you.

"I know where you come from." I immediately understand from what angle of Buddhism you come. I will immediately discover it.

"If you come in some fashion, you have strayed from the Way." If you come in the fashion of the layman soaking himself entirely in the world of formlessness, *you* are not existing and this mortal world is not existing, even this moment is not existing. Nothing is existing.

"However, if you do not come in some fashion, you have bound yourself without a rope." Almost everyone is bound with this rope that does not exist. Philosophy binds up the mind. Both Christian and Buddhist minds are bound up with this and that. All ropes have no existence if you really understand. We each bind one another with these ropes. Your notions bind your life as a human being, and you bind yourself and others.

"You had better not judge haphazardly. Your understanding or your lack of understanding are alike a misunderstanding." Really, from such a stage, it is better not to judge. Your understanding of the pure formless stage is to think you are God. Bound or not bound is not yet the true

stage. Lin-chi broke the shell of the usual religious stage and showed himself as a free man. You cannot imitate this; it must come naturally.

"Speaking thus, I submit myself to your criticism. I thank you for having stood so long." This dialogue shows the height of Lin-chi's understanding. In these short lines, we are given the important point of Buddhism. I hope you understand.

VII

The Master ascended to his seat and said, "There is one who lives on an isolated peak who cannot find a path to descend. Another at a crossroads has neither front nor back. Of the two, which stands before you and which stands behind you? Do not take either to be Vimalakirti or Fu Ta-shih."

The Master descended from his seat.

SOKEI-AN SAYS:

"There is one" is important. Who is that one? Is this one man or God? Why is the peak single, and where is it? If I ask you, "What is the principle of Buddhism?" you cannot say a word, and thousands of sutras cannot explain it. This isolated peak must be reached before attaining buddhahood.

And there is another at a crossroads that has neither front nor back that is like a monster. *"Standing at the crossroads."* Standing at the center of Columbus Circle, for instance, with no front and no back. Strange. What is this curious spirit? How is he different from the one who lives on an isolated peak and cannot find a way to descend?

There are two viewpoints here. Do you know which of these stands before you? Do you know which stands behind you?

Lin-chi gave an interesting koan. If you understand it, these two viewpoints become one. When you stand upon the mountain peak, you are really standing at the crossroads. But which stands "before" and which stands "behind"? How do you answer this koan? Lin-chi says not to take either to be Vimalakirti or Fu Ta-shih. Who are they?

Vimalakirti was a great Buddhist layman, and Fu Ta-shih was a famous Taoist. Vimalakirti was such a great disciple of the Buddha that Shariputra and other great disciples were defeated by him in discourse. He had two children who later became monks. Once he was asked to interpret the *Prajnaparamita Sutra*. His answer was "Prajna," and then he retired. He was asked about his answer and said, "The lecture is over."

So who is this strange one? You must not take this as two standing upon the mountaintop or at a crossroads. Don't look around. If you do I will hit you! These are koans and not difficult ones. Lin-chi's koans are very mild, like sweet candy.

The Master descended from his seat.

VIII

The Master ascended to his seat and said, "There is one who is forever on his way yet has not left home, and there is another who has left home but is not on his way. Of the two, who deserves to be supported by men and who by devas?"

The Master descended from his seat.

SOKEI-AN SAYS:

What is the this "home" Lin-chi is talking about? Who is it that is "on his way"? He stays in his home, yet he is moving around.

I recall a famous story: A messenger from hell came to a monk and said, "Well, your time is up. You must come with me. Yama, the king of the dead, awaits you. "What? Well, I have been so busy in my life that I have had no time to attain enlightenment. Please wait three days, and then I will go with you." The messenger said, "Well, I don't know. I had better ask Yama." When the messenger told this to Yama, he yelled, "What have you done? Go back quickly before he attains enlightenment!" In the meantime the monk meditated hard for three days and attained enlightenment. The messenger searched through the temple, peered into every face but couldn't find the monk. He had disappeared like a candle flame in the sunshine. The flame was there, but no one could find him. He was not himself. He was IT.

If one takes an egotistic attitude, it is absurd. It is like the story of Atlas. Without him the world still stays in place. After all there is *no* self. If you really understand, there is just one divine power. It is in my fingertip, the tip of my tongue. There is no Sokei-an!

In these dialogues Lin-chi expresses himself crudely. He is no poet, but he has disclosed almost the entire Buddhist faith.

IX

A monk asked the Master, "What is the first principle?"

The Master said, "The impression of the Seal of the Three Fundamentals will become distinct. Before you are aware of any doubt, host and guest are distinguishable."

The monk asked, "What is the second principle?"

The Master said, "How could Manjushri permit Wu-chao to ask questions! However, [Manjushri's] expediency is not at variance with his absolute wisdom."

The monk asked, "What is the third principle?"

The Master said, "Behold the puppets manifested upon the stage! Their jumps and jerks depend upon the man behind."

The Master also said, "Each principle comprises three sections, and each section comprises three points. There is direct expediency and direct utility. How do you understand them?"

The Master descended from his seat.

SOKEI-AN SAYS:

In this dialogue Lin-chi is disclosing his three principles. They are very important to Zen students. However they are difficult to grasp. I shall give an explanation, but if you cannot understand do not blame me.

The three principles of Buddhism are *dharmakaya, sambhogakaya, nirmanakaya*—called the *trikaya,* the three bodies. In Christianity they are the Father, Son, and Holy Ghost. Everything has these three principles. For example fire: first there is air, *dharmakaya*; then the fire itself, *sambhogakaya*; and then it's utilization, *nirmanakaya*.

Dharmakaya is the infinite, omnipotent, invisible body. It is omnipresent darkness. *Sambhogakaya* is the body of consciousness, the consciousness revealed when the body separates itself by its own force and makes a union. *Nirmanakaya* is the transforming body—man, woman, dog, cat. In man it is the iceman, policeman, politician, artist.

Three principles of Lin-chi are, however, a little different.

A monk asked the Master, "What is the first principle?" The Master said, "The impression of the Seal of the Three Fundamentals will become distinct. Before you are aware of any doubt, host and guest are distinguishable." The "three fundamentals" are *dharmakaya*, *sambhogakaya*, and *nirmanakaya*. What is the seal? When you receive mail, you see the stamp of the post office—place and date. The "seal of the fundamentals" shows the trikaya at once. One seal that shows the three fundamentals—*dharmakaya*, *sambhogakaya*, and *nirmanakaya*—clearly. What is it? It is the second when you realize that you are these three fundamentals. It is as clear as the impression of a seal. Do you know this moment? Have you experienced it? At the moment they become clear, at *that* moment, you *become* the seal of the three fundamentals.

You must prove this for yourself. It is absolute, relative, and mutable. It has no past, present, or future. It has no space or time. Yet it has duration, expansion and motion. It has beginning and end, is changeable at every moment. Today, here; tomorrow, there—visible, invisible. All these phases become very clear to you at once, like ice, steam, and water are clear to you.

Such an experience must come to your own consciousness, which is enlightenment. Such an experience does not come to your physical body but to your wisdom body. This is the first enlightenment. You see these three at once, in one second. You see your omnipotent body and your omnipotent consciousness and realize your present condition. Your wisdom mind sees through these three fundamentals—God, Christ, and Holy Ghost become clear. *That* is enlightenment.

What is this "seal"? It is the self—just as the staff is the seal, but you do not realize it before you have seen its impression. You must stamp this staff upon your own mind, and it will become the impression. Zen teaches you this. Hibernating in meditation is *not* Zen. As Lin-chi says, "Host and guest are distinguishable."

Today we have very useful technical terms of philosophy, such as subject, object, and so on, but Lin-chi had no such handy expressions. He spoke of host and guest. The consciousness that observes that all is host, and that all phenomena are guest. Before one thinks about something, before one analyzes it, it becomes clear, clear as object and subject. I think in your own experience when you pass the first koan, you will know subject and object—in one moment. They are one. In this sound [bangs *hossu*] is both subject and object.

The monk asked, "What is the second principle?" The Master said, "How could Manjushri permit Wu-chao to ask questions! However, [Manjushri's] expediency is not at variance with his absolute wisdom." Manjushri is the bodhisattva of intrinsic wisdom, The wisdom that we normally have is not intrinsic. It is acquired wisdom. When you go to school you gather acquired information. But if you want intrinsic wisdom you must break the shell of your acquired wisdom that is concealing your intrinsic wisdom. You must chisel off the insignificant part of the mind to discover the intrinsic wisdom that is yourself. That is your true nature. The other is like the thorn of a rose stuck in your flesh which you quickly pull out. However, the mental thorn you leave in your mind for a long time. Everyone has Manjushri in himself.

When you come to Zen you bow, not to the wooden image, but to this Manjushri in yourself. But as there was a living Buddha, so there was a living Manjushri. He has never died. He is still living. Hmmm.

Once there was a monk called Wu-chao who believed that Manjushri Bodhisattva was still living on a mountain in Tibet. He was determined to go and see him. One day he climbed up the mountain but could not reach the peak. Having climbed all day, he decided to stay through the night. The sun fell into the Western horizon and the sky became dark. Suddenly an old man with a long white beard appeared who was feeding a cow. So suddenly did the old man appear, Wu-chao didn't know if the old man was real or not. He approached the old man and said, "I came up this mountain to find Manjushri. Do you know where he is?" The old man said: "Well, the sky is dark now and the mountain is pitch black. If you come to my hermitage and spend the night, I'm sure in the morning you will be able to find him."

Wu-chao followed the old man, and they entered a temple. It was a beautiful temple. The old man made tea and poured it into a cup made of a certain kind of transparent and precious glass made in China at that time. The old man then asked Wu-chao a question: "Do you have this in your country?"

This is a deep question, of course. The old man is talking about transparency. It was a cup so clear you could hardly believe it was there. The old man is, of course, referring to the omnipresent body, the *dharmakaya*. "Do your have this in your country?" means "Do you understand?"

Wu-chao said, "Decidedly no. *We* do not have it." A beautiful answer. Had he said, "Yes, we have it," he would not have understood the *dharmakaya*. If you say you have it, it is not omnipresent!

The old man said, "Well, what are you using in everyday life?"

Wu-chao took the cup and drank—utilization. This is *nirmanakaya*. So in the Zen school, we do not open our mouths. In the shades of conversation there is deep meaning.

At dawn the old man, Manjushri, disappeared, and Wu-chao was led away from the temple by a beautiful child. The child led him to the edge of the mountain. It was dawn and the morning star was in the sky.

Wu-chao asked the child the name of the temple, and the child said, "The name of the temple is written on the eaves of the gate. Look there if you wish to know."

Wu-chao turned to look and suddenly realized there was no gate and no temple where he had slept the night. There was nothing at all—no stone, no image. Nothing.

Wu-chao turned again and there was no child. He was standing alone—the omnipresent body!

So: *"How could Manjushri permit Wu-chao to ask questions! However, Manjushri's] expediency is not at variance with his absolute wisdom."* In that conversation Wu-chao had asked Manjushri a question: "How many monks are in your temple?" Manjushri said: "Three, three, three—three yesterday, three tomorrow." How can one ask absolute wisdom a question? Words are relative; the absolute cannot be conceived by words. As for expediency, Wu-chao made the temple, created consciousness, created the transparent cup—creates all experiences. He creates all from nothing—absolute nothing—*dharmakaya*.

Then Manjushri threw out all expediency as though blowing out a candle flame, and Wu-chao suddenly understood intrinsic wisdom. This is true expediency. Manjushri knew that Wu-chao would attain enlightenment in the morning. You cannot gain wisdom without some pain, some looking ahead.

The monk asked, "What is the third principle?" The Master said, "Behold the puppets manifested upon the stage! Their jumps and jerks depend upon the man behind." The stage is *nirmanakaya*; the puppets are you, me, everyone; the man behind is *dharmakaya.*

The Master also said, "Each principle comprises three sections, and each section comprises three points. There is direct expediency and direct utility. How do you understand them?" This part is not very important. But I shall say a little.

Lin-chi before becoming a Zen monk was a student of the *Avatamsaka Sutra.* Students of the *Avatamsaka* classify everything into parts and divisions, while the Zen monk grasps all the points at once.

In this line Lin-chi has divided each principle into three sections, and each section into three points. Hmmm, like this: The plant must have three stems, each stem having three smaller stems, which have three flowers each. We do not care about this. We see a beautiful dandelion; that is all.

The three sections are the root, the bud, and the flower; or, dormancy, appearance, and realization:

Dormancy is latent; it is non-appearance. When Shakyamuni held up the blue lotus, it was concealed, undemonstrable. It was before sun and moon, before the creation of the universe. When he held up the blue lotus, all the disciples looked but did not understand. Then Mahakashapya looked, and he smiled. The Buddha never spoke a word. This is the first transmission in Zen. I hope that some Zen student reaches this point. He may not be able to express it or demonstrate it, but it is the conclusion.

Immanuel Kant spoke of this undemonstrable state. When you pick a beautiful young iris plant from your garden and you know it will have a flower in three or four months, where is it now? Where, for that matter, are the dead? In heaven? Hell? You know that they are somewhere, but you cannot prove it

Ananda was with the Buddha for thirty years, yet he did not attain a thing. All the other disciples had become enlightened, but he did not. Yet, *that* was Ananda's greatness. He did not grasp anything because there is nothing to grasp. Therefore, he was enlightened.

The second section cannot be talked about, but it can be proved at any moment. You know your dead father is living here [touches his body]. Buddha is always with me. Christ ascended, but you prove the wound prints on your own body. You will see immediately the body of Christ who has the marks of the nails in his hands and feet; you will feel the wound in the side. If you cannot prove it in your own body, you are not a Christian. This is the beginning; you are initiated when you feel and know the cross upon your heart. When you eat, it is the body of Christ; when you drink, it is his blood. You prove his communion in your own body. Initiation is wonderful. All Buddhists enter here—Ah! *This is That!* Heaven and earth shine at once in this initiation.

Realization is enlightenment when it is proved in your own body. Through eye and ear you realize everything. Then you really come into physical existence, into daily life, and you will find heaven wherever you stand. It is as if you had gone all over the world and returned to your own chair—"Ha! This is the chair that I was looking for!" And you have found your own position between heaven and earth. You know your destiny. Whatever center you have, you must know these three sections:

The monk abandons all and becomes the sky. He enters a monastery.

He is initiated, finds Buddha in himself. Heaven and earth shine.

He comes back to his own village, sees family and friends. He is not a demigod, he is a man. He walks among them and speaks about his understanding.

Lin-chi analyzed one Zen into three principles; this really is enough. We do not really need such structures in Zen, but it can sometimes be helpful. The three points are: 1) mystery in mystery; 2) mystery in body; 3) mystery in word.

What is the mystery? Everyone says Zen is mystical. From the Zen student's standpoint it is not mystical, but from the outside it seems to be so. The world is not a mystery if you understand it.

Hakuin showed his hand to many questions that he was asked. If one were to ask him, "What is the universe?" he would probably show you his hand rather than give you an explanation. But if you asked him why he showed his hand, he would probably say: "Well, if you don't ask me a question, I don't show you my hand. I show my hand because you ask me a question." Of course, when Hakuin shows his hand, it is not a hand. Buddha held up a lotus flower before his disciples, and when he showed this lotus, it was not a lotus. Might you say he showed the universe? Why use a hand? If you ask me what the universe is, I do not show you anything, nor do I speak a word. You must not ask me any more questions, because I showed you the universe already. You saw the universe—there is no answer. If I say something, it is not the universe anymore. I am adding something. It is as though I am adding legs to a snake. The universe does not need any explanation. Endless sky, multifold directions; this is the universe. What is the universe? My answer is this [assumed meditation posture]. But if you ask me no question, I assume no posture. If Hakuin had not been asked a question, he would not have shown his hand. If Buddha had not been asked a question, he would not have shown the lotus flower. Before you ask a question and before you answer is the mystery of mystery, the first point. This means before anything happens—before the sun and moon were created; before the electron and proton were created; before the knowable. No one could understand such a stage. It is impossible to observe by this mortal standpoint. If we give it up, this mortal standpoint, who could observe such a state? No one could. But it is a mystery that we know there is such a stage. It is the mystery in a mystery. The enlightened did not realize that state, but the unenlightened one is naturally manifesting that state. Buddha could not communicate that state, but the badger and the fox are manifesting that state because they came from there. He is not aware of that state so it is inconceivable to him. So whatever he does is inconceivable to him.

The willow branch sways at the mercy of the wind, dropping its branches, but it does not know it is in that unknowable condition. It is manifesting it. The cat meows, the dog barks, humans chatter philosophy, but they do not know what they are speaking about. They never know on what standpoint they are speaking about *that*. So, while they do not know the standpoint on which they stand, they manifest themselves unconsciously, and that unconscious manifestation is the mystery. The dog in the city will scratch the sidewalk unknowingly—you call it instinct. If he digs into the ground, it seems to us there is a reason, but on a city sidewalk? Where is the instinct? It's a mystery. But if any dog knows why he is digging into the sidewalk, it is not a mystery anymore. So man speaks of heaven and earth and God and the demon. Though he speaks, he knows nothing. This is the first point, the mystery in the mystery.

The second point is the mystery in the body. You understand it directly—the unknowable stage. You are in it. You feel it is infinite. You feel it is constituent to your own mind. When you are thinking, you are not in it. But when you are thinking nothing, you are within it. Shift your mind here and there and you are not in it. But return to silence, and you feel it; you prove you are in it. Even though you know it, you cannot speak a word. You say "ah," "infinite," "omnipresent"—whatever word you use, you limit that mystery. So you extend your hand, or you raise a lotus. It is better than speaking. But when you grasped it, you were not thinking anymore. The silent one is not an idiot.

Bodhidharma came to China. Sitting cross-legged he spoke no word for nine years. Do you think he was an idiot? The second point is: if you know it, you cannot speak about it.

The third point is the mystery in a word. Why can't you speak? When you know the "home" of the universe, you know "home" is not a very good word. If you understand this [show *hossu*] or this [meditative posture], why not speak? Because you are just observing it through your wisdom—the whole body does not yet understand it. When your heart and soul understand, why can't you speak a word? Speaking a word will not destroy that "home." Speak if you wish. Though you understand, you cannot speak a word; you are not quite free. You fear something. You fear you might lose that understanding. It is not loseable; it is always with you, in your hand. Though you speak, it will not slip away when you speak it in poetical form, philosophically, in drawing, in painting, in music. This is the third point. If you understand this much, your daily life will be happy, and there will be nothing that can bother you. When you understand nothing, you will understand Chao-chao's "MU." Then you cannot speak anymore. But *your* nothingness is not true nothingness; it is just the "nothingness" in your brain. It is a conception. When you understand true nothingness, you can dance, sing—anything.

These are the three points of Lin-chi, after which—

The Master descended from his seat.

X (a)

In an evening's gathering, the Master addressed the multitude: "In some instances, I take you away from the surroundings. In other instances, I take the surroundings away from you. In yet other instances, I take away both you and the surroundings. In still other instances, I take away neither you nor the surroundings."

A monk asked the Master, "What do you mean by 'take you away from the surroundings?'"

The Master said, "When the spring sun rises, flowers brocade the earth. A child's tresses droop like white tassels."

The monk asked, "What do you mean by 'take the surroundings away from you?'"

The Master said, "The king's command has been spread throughout the land, and the lord of war has laid the dust of battle in the dominions outside the wall."

The monk asked, "What do you mean by 'take away both, you and the surroundings?'"

The Master said, "Ping and Fen have severed their connection with the homeland and hold themselves aloof."

The monk asked, "What do you mean by 'take away neither you nor your surroundings?'"

The Master said, "When the king ascends to the jeweled palace, the peasants in the fields rejoice, singing his praises."

SOKEI-AN SAYS:

This section of the *Record* is not easy to translate into a foreign language. The meaning is somewhat obscure. Even a Chinese scholar finds it difficult to understand the meaning that does not appear on the surface. If you are not a Zen master, it is almost impossible to grasp the technicalities behind the words. This address is another very important discourse by the Master. It is called the Four Standpoints, and they are important to all Zen students, and to all people.

In an evening's gathering, the Master addressed the multitude: "In some instances, I take you away from the surroundings. In other instances, I take the surroundings away from you. In yet other instances, I take away both you and the surroundings. In still other instances, I take away neither you nor the surroundings." Today we have better terms than "you" and "surroundings" in philosophy. We have "subject" and "object". Lin-chi is saying that in certain circumstances he takes away the subjective standpoint from the objective standpoint. "I" am subjective, and my "surroundings" are the objective. He takes you, the living man, person, mind, the subjective from objective matter. When a doctor operates on the human body that has been given ether, it is just a body; there is no "person" there, even when he is operating on his own wife! There is only a body.

When I walk in the streets of New York. I do not enjoy looking at people's faces. Why must I look, and why bother looking at them? There is nothing to gain. In a small village in which you are living generation to generation, you cannot do this; you cannot ignore anyone. But in a big city like New York it is quite different. New York is like a desert, a vast pile of material that seems almost a ruin. No human soul is living when I walk the streets, but my surroundings, the buildings, are still there. I've just taken the people away. That is the first standpoint. I cannot move my hand, but some universal power moves my hand; so with speaking. So with thinking—it is all universal power. If you call this God, there is no man. All is God, and there is no man. The tedious work of your brain is not done by human power; it is done by the power of God. But you take the human attitude and you bother it. You struggle because you do not know this great power is carrying you in its great current. But when you understand your circumstances and your own limitations, you do not struggle.

A monk asked the Master, "What do you mean by 'take you away from the surroundings?'" The Master said, "When the spring sun rises, flowers brocade the earth. A child's tresses droop like white tassels." There is no human being in the world. All is just one power, one universal power. There is no man. Man cannot think anything, though he thinks he is thinking. Man operates what has been operated by some great power already. When I find an answer in thinking, it was not my answer; it was always there; it was intrinsic. I just struck it, as the old miner strikes a vein of gold that was always there. Truth *is* always. I struggle through earth and sand and finally I come to the vein of gold. Truth is always there when we reach it. Therefore, anything I think is not my thinking. It is always there by nature. From this viewpoint there is no subjective standpoint. Why must you put "you" into it? You must not take a personal attitude when you think.

The monk asked, "What do you mean by 'take the surroundings away from you?'" The Master said, "The king's command has been spread throughout the land, and the lord of war has laid the dust of battle in the dominions outside the wall." There is no man and there is no god, as well. Some Zen student once asked his master, "If neither god nor man exists, what is existing?" The master said, "A donkey peeps into the well." A very deep well! The Zen student thought this a marvelous answer and told it to another Zen master who said, "I would rather say that the well peeps at the donkey!" Nothing can be said. There is a Chinese expression: "The carpet and the table legs are saluting each other." This means neither you nor your surroundings. Such expressions are used because there is no way to say it.

When you meditate in the stage of formlessness, you realize there is nothing but infinite space. In that infinite space you find duration. The space is height, width, and depth, and now duration, time. So we call time the fourth dimension. Though you find the multifold directions, if you do not count time, it is three-dimensional. But in meditation, you are in the center of this multifold space. It is like the Bodhisattva Avalokiteshvara and his thousand arms; like the sun and its multifold directions of light. Then you feel duration. It has no directions—north, south, east, or west. You are in the same space, but duration is there. Therefore, multifold space and duration is the fourth-dimensional space. This is the Zen standpoint, and modern science will agree.

When the surroundings are taken away, you feel an infinite space surrounding you. Then you find duration in the stage of formlessness. Consciousness can be prove by perception, but in the emptiness of formlessness, there is nothing to perceive. So space and consciousness cannot prove each other. Therefore, both are annihilated. You have come into absolute nothingness—that which cannot be expressed in words. It is this important standpoint, the third point of Lin-chi that is expressed in the "donkey and the well, the well and the donkey"—a typical Zen expression. When you arrive at this "nothingness," strangely enough you will suddenly understand that *everything* is there. *This* is experience! By this you prove absolute existence. You look again at the universe. It is so near to you now. The Christian calls this "resurrection." It is a very important point to us. You will come to see the entire universal existence. You will not call it "matter" or "spirit," but say *This is That*.

The monk asked, "What do you mean by 'take away both you and the surroundings?'" The Master said, "Ping and Fen have severed their connection with the homeland and hold themselves aloof." You and your surroundings are there untouched. First, no spirit. Second, no matter. Third, neither spirit nor matter. Fourth, spirit and matter. This is what is left in each of the four standpoints. If you have attained these four, you have really attained all standpoints.

Now I will explain Lin-chi's words more clearly.

To the first question: *A monk asked the Master, "What do you mean by 'take you away from the surroundings?'" The Master said, "When the spring sun rises, flowers brocade the earth. A child's tresses droop like white tassels."* Here, in the entire surroundings, there is no man, no soul. But Lin-chi, instead of denying a soul, says: *"A child's tresses droop like white tassels"*—like an old man. There is no such thing! He is telling you there is no soul. There is the willow tree. The weeping willow will droop like tassels in a land where flowers brocade the earth. There is no man, only surroundings.

There are many ways to understand this poem and many monks have given their interpretations, but I follow my teacher, and he followed his teacher and his teacher followed Hakuin generations before me.

The second question: The monk asked, *"What do you mean by 'take the surroundings away from you?'" The Master said, "The king's command has been spread throughout the land, and the lord of war has laid the dust of battle in the dominions outside the wall."* In China, "inland" means "inside the wall"; the "dominions" are outside. In the Tang dynasty, China was the largest empire in the world. Inland was controlled by the emperor; outside the wall was controlled by the warlord. So here, there is no land, no surroundings, just the power of man. Inland is under the power of God, and dominion is under the power of man.

In meditation, the *alaya*-consciousness is under the power of God and this present consciousness is under the power of my self. Hmmm, both are my self, and both are God, but both are power. It is from this second standpoint—taking away the surroundings, leaving the self alone—that Lin-chi gave his wonderful HO! I do not give this elucidation twice in my life, so do not forget it!

The third standpoint is: *The monk asked, "What do you mean by 'take away both, you and the surroundings?'" The Master said, "Ping and Fen have severed their connection with the homeland and hold themselves aloof."* Ping and Fen were two states outside the wall that revolted against the Imperial power and declared their independence. They were entirely shut off from the mainland; just as though god had no connection with God. It is like a man saying, "Well, goodbye God!" How could man do so? It is the third standpoint,. you will give the answer in *sanzen.*

The monk asked, "What do you mean by 'take away neither you nor your surroundings?'" The Master said, "When the King ascends to the jeweled palace, the peasants in the fields rejoice, singing his praises." Here, man recognizes the power of God, and he rejoices. He recognizes both powers. When we observe the entire universe, we feel some great power deeper than our own. Then we come back to our own consciousness and feel the relation with it. Now this active and everlasting life can flow out from this consciousness and the struggle of human life is ended.

You must acquaint yourselves with all these standpoints, and you must express them in your own experience.

Pilgrimages (b)

XXI

When Lin-chi was facing his end, he seated himself and said, "After my death, do not let the eye of my true law disappear!"

San-sheng advanced from the group and said, "How could I let the eye of the Master's true law disappear?"

Lin-chi said, "Hereafter, if someone should question you about it, how would you answer?"

San-sheng shouted, "HO!"

Lin-chi said, "Who would have thought the eye of my true law would disappear in this blind ass!"

Having spoken thus, Lin-chi, sitting erect, revealed his extinction.

SOKEI-AN SAYS:

It was the custom in China, when a Zen master was approaching death, for him to seat himself in his usual place and enter great nirvana—he did not die lying down.

When Lin-chi-chi said, *"After my death, do not let the eye of my true law disappear!"* he meant the eye of the "womb" or the "entrance to the "mental womb." *Garbha* means "womb," and the "eye" is the entrance to this womb. When the soul is in an inferior stage of consciousness, like a *preta*, the soul of this *preta* will enter into the womb and come forth in the form of a *tiryagyoni*, a horizontal-goer or animal. The *preta* may have two hands and two feet, even walk perpendicularly, but now the *preta* belongs to the animal kingdom. And from the gate of the womb of the animal, he may be conceived as a human being, and then as a *deva*, a spiritual being.

These two eyes are two gates of the womb of *deva* through which we enter into the world that the animal cannot know. This is the conception of primitive Buddhism. In this conception, there are five different beings who progress from one womb to the next. Interesting hypothesis!

As a baby looks at the inside of the mother's womb, so we look at the blue sky, the bright sun. We do not know from whence we come nor where we are going. Our eye sees the light, but our soul is still in darkness. All who live in this unenlightened state are living in the womb of the world, the *garbhadhatu*. There are many wombs: Padma Garbha, Lotus Womb; Vajragarbha, Diamond Wisdom Womb, and others. To the Buddhist the womb is a holy place.

The Eye is a very important part of the Dharma or Law. When Shakyamuni held the blue lotus up before the multitude, no one understood. But among them was a monk, Mahakashyapa, who looked and smiled. The Buddha looked at him and said, "You, Mahakashyapa, to you I hand my Eye of the True Dharma." *That* is the beginning of Zen.

Shakyamuni Buddha had two great disciples, Ananda and Mahakashyapa. Ananda transmitted all the words of the Buddha because of his wonderful memory. The teachings from the lips of the Buddha are what we now call the *tripitaka*, the poetry, allegory philosophy, and precepts. All was received by Ananda and transmitted word for word. He said, "All this I will hold and transmit to be passed from generation to generation to the end of the universe!"

Mahakashyapa was the transmitter of esoteric Buddhism—that never expressed in words by the Buddha. It was Mahakashyapa alone among the multitude who understood the Buddha's meaning when he held up the blue lotus flower. And the Buddha said, "Uphold my true Dharma. Do not let it disappear." So Mahakashyapa handed it down through twenty-eight generations in India. From India it came to China, and then to Japan. Today we have many Zen masters, many branches of Buddhism, but all are true branches of the Buddha's teaching. It is transmitted as a flame by many torch-holders. The power of the light differs in strength, but the fire is the flame of Shakyamuni Buddha himself. It cannot be given in words, but passes from heart to heart, soul to soul, eye to eye.

I am explaining Buddhism through my lips, but I cannot transmit the esoteric teachin—the meaning.

When San-sheng, Lin-chi-chi's oldest disciple, said, *"How could I let the eye of the Master's true law disappear?"* he was talking about the Buddha's True Dharma.

In Zen, the True Law, the true Dharma, is in your own mind. You do not get it from a teacher but through meditation. I receive you in my Zen room, and I listen to your answer. I may acknowledge it, but I do not teach you anything. There is really nothing to teach. Everything is attained by your own effort. I cannot eat your food for you. Your enlightenment depends upon yourself. And I must compare it with the True Law that was attained by the Buddha, Lin-chi, Soyen Shaku, and Sokei-an. So you come to me and express your understanding, and I observe it. You try to meet the mind of the master who gave you a koan. It is a *universal* answer. But when you attain it, it is yours. There are guideposts on the road, milestones. "Ah! This is a highway, not a byway!"

Lin-chi said, *"Hereafter, if someone should question you about it, how would you answer?"* Humph! Lin-chi-chi is very direct. He points a sharp sword.

San-sheng gave a HO!, a Zen expression transmitted to Lin-chi-chi from Huang-po.

Then *Lin-chi said, "Who would have thought the eye of my true law would disappear in this blind ass!"* The blind ass is also a Zen expression. It sounds as though Lin-chi-chi was displeased. A mule is bad enough, but blind as well!

Having spoken thus, Lin-chi, sitting erect, revealed his extinction. Because this eye of the true Dharma is not like *this* or *that*, San-sheng gave the HO! of Lin-chi. It was showing Hakuin's hand, or Chu-chih's finger.

You may remember the story of the youngster who, when questioned by Chu-chih, held up his finger, and had it cut off. The boy attained enlightenment at that moment.

Lin-chi "revealed his extinction"—he entered nirvana.

There are many records of Zen masters as they passed into nirvana. At Daitokuji, a temple in Japan, you may still see the blood-stained robe of the founder, Daito, who after many years of being unable to sit in the lotus posture because of a stiff leg, as his death approached, broke his leg, seated himself, and passed into nirvana.

This passing of Lin-chi is one of the great records.

XXII

The Master's name was I-hsuan. He was a native of Nan-hua in Ts'ao. His family name was Hsing. When he was a child, he was already different from others, and when he became a young man his filial piety was well known throughout the vicinity. After shaving his head and taking his vows, he frequented the lecture halls where he mastered the vinaya and studied the sutras and shastras. One day all of a sudden, he said with a sigh, "These scriptures are curative prescriptions for the salvation of the world, not the principle of the esoteric law that has been handed down outside the canon." Thereupon he changed his robe and roamed about. First he studied with Huang-po; then he visited Ta-yu. These incidents and words are described in this record of his deeds.

After receiving sanction from Huang-po as the heir of his Zen, Lin-chi went to Hopeh. There he lived in a small temple on the shore of the Hu-t'o River, at the southeast corner of the capital of Chen Province. The temple was called "Lin-chi," which means "on the shore of the river," according with the lay of the land.

By that time, P'u-hua was already there. Feigning insanity, he would mingle with the crowds. No one knew whether he was a sage or not. When Lin-chi arrived, P'u-hua befriended him, and when Lin-chi's mission began to prosper, P'u-hua cast aside his coffin and disappeared. This tallies with the prediction of Yang-shan, a little Shakya.

Unexpectedly the temple was burned in a fire caused by war, so the master abandoned it. Grand Marshal Mo Chun-ho then gave up his own house inside the town wall and made it into a temple. Designating it with the old name, "Lin-chi," he asked the Master to occupy it.

Later, Lin-chi swept his sleeves behind him and went south to the prefecture of Ho. The governor of the area, Wang, entreated the Master to remain as his teacher. Before long the master moved to Hsing-hua Temple in Ta-ming Prefecture, where he lived in the Eastern Hall.

One day all of a sudden the Master, without having been ill, gathered the skirts of his robe, seated himself, and finished

his dialogue with San-sheng. Then he died in silence. It was the
tenth day of the first month in the eighth year of Hsien-t'ung
[867] in the Tang dynasty. His disciples built a pagoda for
his body in the northwest corner of the capital of Ta-ming
Prefecture. The emperor decreed that he be given the posthumous
name Zen Master Hui-chao (Illuminating Wisdom). His pagoda
was called Cheng-ling ("Translucent Soul").

Joining my hands and bowing low, I have recorded in brief
outline the life of my master. I am his humble heir Yen-chao of
Chen Province.

SOKEI-AN SAYS:

For a long time I have been giving a commentary on the *Record of*
Lin-chi, but now we are coming to the last chapter. Lin-chi's posthumous
name is Hui-chao. The posthumous name of the first patriarch of our
school in Japan is Daishi. These names were given by the emperor.

Filial piety is not a duty but pure love. Nor do we feel it as
compensation. It is the love of a child for his parents, or the love of the
parents for their child. In Confucianism this is filial piety, the first
cardinal virtue of man. It is said in that teaching that you received your
body and your hair and your skin from your parents. To keep this free
from harm is the first piety of the child toward his parents. So when
I was a child if I went out and fought a bad boy, returning scratched
and bleeding, my mother would say, "Did you read the first line of the
Confucian '*Classic of Filial Piety*?'"

After shaving his head and taking his vows, he frequented the lecture
halls where he mastered the vinaya *and studied the sutras and* shastras. In
the temples the Zen master gave short lectures five times in a month. The
rest of the time it was meditation.

In Zen temples the student is first required to meditate upon his
mind-stuff. He will think something logically, philosophically. For
instance, "Where is mind? It is not outside, so it must be inside." One
day he will come to the question, "Why this inside and outside? There is
really no inside and no outside. Then, where is the mind?" If he denies
the outside, he must deny the inside as well. All being is relative existence.
He thinks in this fashion, following a logical train of thought. He must
not fall into the pit of superstition. This is the first meditation. Then he
will come to the conclusion: "All this is stuff coming from the outside.

This mind-stuff has not real existence." Then the student will begin to question, "Who is thinking? What is my self?" He will come to the conclusion that none of this mind-stuff is himself, but, "The master who thinks is myself!"

Now he will begin to analyze that self—*rupa*, the body; *vedana*, feelings, senses and perception; *samjna*, the thinker; *samskara*, the dreamer; and *vijnana*, consciousness. He will see that his fundamental consciousness not only dreams but digests his food and keeps the balance of this body: something drops into his eye, and the eye closes.

In meditation we analyze five different qualities of consciousness and seventeen stages of *vijnana*. Finally we discover eighteen different *shunyatas*, "nothingnesses."

What is meditation? The scientist analyzes indirectly, with a microscope, but we analyze directly with ourselves, the living apparatus. We sit in *zazen*, observe the mind-stuff flowing like weeds; we become consciousness itself. At last we are "ourselves." And we take this attitude into daily life.

This is the practice in Zen temples, but in the "lecture shops," they "speak" about Buddhism, just as I am now doing!

Lin-chi mastered the *vinaya*, all the Buddha's commandments and precepts, and made researches in *sutras* and *shastras* (the *abhidharma*), the philosophical aspect of Buddha's teaching.

One day all of a sudden, he said with a sigh, "These scriptures are curative prescriptions for the salvation of the world, not the principle of the esoteric law that has been handed down outside the canon." That is, the esoteric aspect of the teaching, which is quite different.

Thereupon he changed his robe and roamed about. First he studied with Huang-po; then he visited Ta-yu. These incidents and words are described in this record of his deeds. This I have described to you in previous lectures.

After receiving sanction from Huang-po as the heir of his Zen, Lin-chi went to Hopeh. I will repeat this story which came before: Lin-chi came to the mountain where Huang-po was teaching Zen. He arrived in the middle of the summer session and left before the session was over. So Huang-po drove him from the temple. However, Lin-chi returned and finished the session. Then he begged Huang-po to permit his departure.

Huang-po questioned "Where do you go?" Lin-chi said, "I will go south of the river, or I will go north of the river."

Huang-po seized Lin-chi by the chest and slapped his face. Lin-chi grabbed Huang-po and slapped him back. Huang-po called his attendant and said, "Bring Po-chang's *zenban* (board used in meditation to prop oneself up). Lin-chi said, "Attendant! Fetch me fire. I will burn it." Huang-po said, "Rather, take it. If you keep that, no one can doubt your attainment."

Lin-chi received it and departed. Then he went around China, met many Zen masters, and finally came back to Hopeh. Hopeh is famous today as the place of a Japanese invasion.

This "sanction" from Huang-po means that Lin-chi was ordained his successor. In the Zen school, no one can call himself a Zen master without a teacher's sanction; nor, in the Zen school, can one give a koan and receive an answer from a student without his teacher's sanction.

There he lived in a small temple on the shore of the Hu-t'o River, at the southeast corner of the capital of Chen Province. The temple was called "Lin-chi," which means "on the shore of the river," according with the lay of the land. "Lin" really means in Chinese "peeping in," so the name actually means "peeping on the shore of the river."

By that time, P'u-hua was already there. Feigning insanity, he would mingle with the crowds. No one knew whether he was a sage or not. When Lin-chi arrived, P'u-hua befriended him, and when Lin-chi's mission began to prosper, P'u-hua cast aside his coffin and disappeared. This tallies with the prediction of Yang-shan, a little Shakya. P'u-hua, a Zen master at that time, was going about town ringing a bell and chanting: "If you come from the bright angle, I will hit you on the bright angle; if you come from the dark angle, I will hit you on the dark angle; if you come from all angles, I will smite you like a hurricane!"

I think you are familiar with another crazy monk in China, Hotei. He is a familiar carving today, sometimes carried as a good luck piece. Over his shoulder is a large knapsack; he has a big stomach, a loose robe, and is always laughing. He used often to sit upon a certain bridge; if one wished to know the weather, he would go there and observe Hotei. If he wore rain shoes, it would rain; if he wore straw sandals, it would be clear. Hotei did not teach anything at all. If a rich man passed, Hotei would tap him on the shoulder and say, "Give me a penny!" In Hotei's time, under the strong power of the emperor, there was no hope of doing anything to improve conditions or of promulgating any new idea. How different from the condition here in America today! You can do so much. Stretch your hand in so many directions. You do not know which to do! In the Tang dynasty even the religious teacher was not able to do anything to improve the life of the human being; he just made sure of his own salvation, lived in his understanding, and helped those who came to him by pointing the way.

So there were such monks as Hotei, living in desperation, physically, who could do nothing better than to take the Buddhist attitude of salvation. Of course, this attitude is still taken by Buddhists today.

I do not quite agree with the way Christianity is promulgated. The missionary comes to save your soul, but does he? I don't think so. He should understand that you have to save yourself by your *own* faith. To ease your soul is just like eating your food. No one can do it for you. And when, by your own exertion, you accomplish your own salvation, you will choose your own type of life—be it simple, comfortable, or as a hobo. It's your own choice!

In Japan today, there are many monks who are doing nothing but living. That is all. Of course, there is some teaching in the temples, but it looks strange from the outside,. All the monks are meditating. The laymen are working, and even the teachers in the winter are just keeping warm against the storms. No wonder the Christians say, "Look at those monks. There is no religion in Japan!"

Sometimes I shrink back in alarm from the American teachers who say there is no teaching in the Orient. I like the monk's attitude regarding the soul. He takes three to four years to meditate, to analyze his own mind and his own consciousness. The scientist today analyzes the nerves of the dead man's brain. Our analysis is more direct. We use *this* mind to analyze *this* mind, and *this* soul to look into *this* soul. Instead of the physical eye, we use the inmost eye; with this we analyze the mind activity, grades of consciousness, the capacity and intention of the soul. To do this by oneself, that is our meditation. We do not care about the heavens of Theosophy!

And so all those sitting monks are trying to find the secret of their own minds. Then each, through his own experience, will understand the other. There is no need for words. I am sure you have seen the picture of the two old monks standing with brooms among the fallen leaves. The two disheveled hermits are looking at each other and roaring with laughter. There is nothing to say, nothing to think about. They are free to laugh! That was their life. From such a viewpoint, you might think this life is not worth living. This, however, is another mental attitude.

There is this story. One day a rich man invited P'u-hua to dinner, and he asked Lin-chi to come with him. Just as the dinner was set before them, P'u-hua said to Lin-chi: "One hair will swallow the ocean; a grain of poppy-seed contains the universe!" Whereupon, Lin-chi stood up and kicked over the beautiful food! They went away without the dinner.

But the next day they were invited again. I think the rich man was sorry that because they argued, they had no food. Again they sat at the table and the fine food was served. And again, P'u-hua asked another question of Lin-chi: "How do you like this dinner compared with the one we received yesterday?" Once more, Lin-chi arose to his feet and kicked over the table. This was his answer, "Well, yesterday's dinner was beautiful and today's dinner was beautiful." And he went back to the temple without eating for the second time!

I hope they were not hungry, for certainly they had eaten the universe!

It is said that just before P'u-hua died, he stood in the street and begged for a robe, but he refused those that were offered him, saying "I am not looking for *this* kind of robe!"

The news of this came to Lin-chi who understood the meaning and looked for a coffin. (Coffins in China are rather like a barrel, and can be nailed at the top.) When P'u-hua returned to the temple, Lin-chi showed him the coffin. P'u-hua was very much pleased, "Oh, I like this robe!" and he put it on his head, and walked out of the temple saying, "I will die today at the East gate."

Several people followed him, but on arrival, he said, "Well I do not feel like dying today. Come tomorrow, to the Western gate."

The next day, they all went to the Western gate, and the same thing happened. For the third time they followed him. This was to the South gate, and as P'u-hua repeated the performance, no one followed him on the fourth day.

At the North gate, P'u-hua met a man whom he asked to nail him into his coffin. The man did so, but immediately ran and told this to the townspeople. Then many people rushed to open the coffin, but they could find nothing inside! Like Christ disappeared in the sepulchre. Everyone heard a bell ringing in the sky, fainter and fainter until it ceased.

You will find the snakeskin but not the snake! *This* kind of snake skin [indicates body] is the most interesting! You live sixty years or so, then cast aside this skin, and disappear! No one knows where you went.

I wrote nine books in my foolish days, but I do not keep them because they are snake skins. So these lectures are also being cast aside, I will not repeat them!

So P'u-hua cast aside his coffin, as his body. And the bell sounded—ting . . . ting . . . ting, in the sky. (Like the angel who found that Christ had disappeared from the sepulchre.)

So Lin-chi became prominent and P'u-hua disappeared!

When Lin-chi went to see Kuei-shan, someone said of P'u-hua: "This one has a head but no tail!"

It is told that Yang-shan conversed with a Hindu monk who had the power to pass through the sky. Yang-shan asked, "From where do you come?"

The Hindu said, "From India."

Yang-shan asked, "When did you leave?"

"This morning."

"This morning? Why did you take so long?"

"Well, I was looking at the scenery."

Yang-shan said, "Perhaps you know supernatural power, but you do not know Buddhism! *I* know Buddhism."

Then the Hindu monk bowed, saying, "I came from India to see Manjushri, but I have seen this little Shakya!"

Unexpectedly the temple was burned in a fire caused by war, so the Master abandoned it. Grand Marshal Mo Chun-ho then gave up his own house inside the town wall and made it into a temple. Designating it with the old name, "Lin-chi," he asked the Master to occupy it. Civil war is the usual state of affairs in China. There has been no peace throughout its history, just as there has never been a day in Japan without some tremor in the earth.

In this period Northern and Southern China were fighting on the shores of the Yangtze River. This was the same war that destroyed the town of Chin, where Lin-chi lived, and burned down this temple. Therefore, he abandoned it and lived for about twenty years in his small temple on the river. In the end, Lin-chi also abandoned this temple that peeped into the river.

Later, Lin-chi swept his sleeves behind him and went south to the prefecture of Ho. The governor of the area, Wang, entreated the Master to remain as his teacher. Before long the master moved to Hsing-hua Temple in Ta-ming Prefecture, where he lived in the Eastern Hall. In China, each town and each house is usually surrounded by a wall, behind which the owner will build a temple. It is like the mind of a Chinese gentleman; his smile is a wall behind which he will make a temple. From the Buddha's time, kings and dignitaries converted their own residences into temples, which they then offered to certain teachers. In Japan as well. Many temples were once rich villas—Daitokuji and Nanzenji were all once imperial villas.

A great military officer had carved two big characters in wood. "Lin-chi" framed this and hung it on top of the temple gate. All the Zen students in China call this the mark of Zen Master Lin-chi. Lin-chi accepted, staying in Hsing-hua two or three years until the temple was destroyed by fire, and then going to a temple of his own disciple. As the Chinese say, "The father came into the son's house." I'm sure that around Lin-chi's quarters were many bronze vases in a garden and many old pine trees. He lived there quietly and alone until the end of his days.

In Zen history, it was not unusual for a monk to leave his temple from ten to fifteen years. The Zen master has three rules to observe: 1) he shall not unpack his possessions, no matter how many years he lives in one place; 2) he must keep his umbrella hat on the wall; 3) he must keep his straw sandals prepared.

One day all of a sudden the Master without having been ill, gathered the skirts of his robe, seated himself, and finished his dialogue with San-sheng. This interview is recorded in the previous lecture. To Lin-chi's question, San-sheng answered with a HO! Lin-chi said, "How can the true eye of my Dharma disappear in this blind mule!" and entered into everlasting *samadhi.* The principle of Lin-chi's Zen is in this HO! When he shouted, it was like a thunderbolt. I cannot explain it further. When you study koans, you will find four different HO!s. So it must have pleased Lin-chi to hear this shout from his disciple before he died.

Then he died in silence. It was the tenth day of the first month in the eighth year of Hsien-t'ung in the Tang dynasty. His disciples built a pagoda for his body in the northwest corner of the capital of Ta-ming Prefecture. The emperor decreed that he be given the posthumous name Zen Master Hui-chao (Illuminating Wisdom). His pagoda was called Cheng-ling

("*Translucent Soul*"). The passing of a Zen master is not death; it is *samadhi*. Therefore, Buddhists never cremate a Zen master's body. The tower is still there—a tile tower. Soyen Shaku went there and found it.

Joining my hands and bowing low, I have recorded in brief outline the life of my master. I am his humble heir Yen-chao of Chen Province. I have been translating this record from the Chinese for two and a half years, and it is now finished.

Glossary

abhidharma: early Buddhist discourses on philosophy and psychology.

akasha: all-pervasive space; the two types are: 1) corporeal space, part of the six *skandhas*; and 2) eternal space, one of the six elements.

alaya-consciousness (alayavijnana): eighth consciousness; basic or "storehouse" consciousness.

anasrava: state of non-leakage or discharge of afflictions and passions from the mind.

arhat: sage or saint who has attained release from the cycle of death and rebirth, the highest state in early Buddhism.

asrava: state of leakage or discharge of afflictions and passions from the mind.

Avalokiteshvara: the enlightened being (*bodhisattva*) of compassion and mercy.

Avatamsaka Sutra: The Flower Garland Sutra; the basic text of the Hua-yen school of Buddhism; it teaches the equality and mutual interpenetration of all phenomena in the universe—that the human mind *is* the universe

bodhi: insight, wisdom, or awakening.

Bodhidharma: (dates uncertain) was said to have arrived in China during the reign of Emperor Wu Ti of the Liang (r. 502-49) and is traditionally regarded as the twenty-eighth Patriarch or successor in the Indian lineage to Shakyamuni Buddha, and the First Patriarch and founder of Ch'an in China.

bodhisattva: enlightened being who seeks buddhahood for the benefit of others.

Brahma: Vedic god representing the absolute.

ch'an (J. zen): Chinese word for *dhyana,* a Sanskrit word basically meaning meditation.

citta: seat of the intellect.

deva: an angel or god who lives in heavenly realms.

Dharma: universal principle, teaching, phenomenon, mental content.

dharmadhatu: realm or world of existents (dharma) or law; the absolute and physical universe.

dharmakaya: "body of *dharma,* "body of law"; the essential mind of Buddha; one of the three bodies of the *trikaya.*

dhyana: tranquil meditation; absorption into reality; contemplation, meditation.

Diamond Sutra (Vajracchika-prajnaparamita-sutra): a condensation of the wisdom (*Prajnaparamita*) sutras, translated into Chinese in 400 C.E. by Kumarajiva (334-413), China's greatest translator of Sanskrit texts.

eight consciousnesses (parijnana): 1-5) the five sense-consciousnesses: seeing, hearing, smelling, touching, tasting; 6) *manas* (*mano-vijnana*), the intellectual function: knowing, judging, conceiving; 7) *klista-manas (klista-mano-vijnana):* discriminative and calculating consciousness, the cause of egoism and individualizing, which is defiled by the germs or seeds (*bija,* data or impressions) of the eighth consciousness; 8) *alayavijnana:* the "storehouse" or basic consciousness that retains the seeds or germs of all phenomena.

Eightfold Path: practices leading to the cessation of suffering: 1) right view; 2) right thought and purpose; 3) right speech; 4) right conduct; 5) right livelihood; 6) right effort; 7) right mindfulness; 8) right concentration.

five skandhas: the five aggregates, heaps, shadows, or "scales" of consciousness that comprise a human being: 1) *rupa:* the body, the five senses, and outer existence; 2) *vedana:* feelings, perception; 3) *samjna:* thoughts, conceptions; 4) *samskara:* mind-elements, mental formations; 5) *vijnana:* consciousness.

four great elements: earth, water, fire, air.

Four Noble Truths: 1) suffering; 2) the origin of suffering; 3) the cessation of suffering, and 4) the path towards the cessation of suffering, the *Eightfold Path.*

Hakuin Ekaku (1686-1769): noted Japanese Zen master of the Tokugawa period from whom present-day Rinzai lines in Japan trace their descent.

Hinayana: "small vehicle"; early Buddhism.

hossu: flywhisk.

hrdaya: heart, mind, or soul

kalpa: incalculable period of time between the creation and recreation of the world.

koan: (J., C. *kung-an*) "case" given to students by Zen masters for contemplation or observation.

Ma-tsu Tao-i (709-788): Chinese Zen master of the Tang dynasty.

Mahaprajnaparamita Sutra: See *Prajnaparamita Sutra*

Mahayana: "great vehicle" of Buddhism; later Buddhism.

manas: active, thinking, and calculating mind.

Manjushri: the enlightened being of Wisdom.

Mara: personification of the passions that interfere with enlightenment.

maya: phenomenal world of illusion, deception, and hallucination; also the mother of Shakyamuni (Queen Maya); and the goddess (Maya) who creates illusion.

nirmanakaya: "body of transformation"; one of the three bodies (*trikaya*) of Buddha.

paramitas: the perfections practiced by a *bodhisattva* "to reach the other shore" (nirvana).

prajna: highest wisdom or insight.

pratitya-samutpada: The twelve stages or links (*nidanas*) in the chain of existence are 1) old age and death; 2) rebirth; 3) existence; 4) grasping; 5) love, thirst, desire; 6) receiving, perceiving, sensation; 7) touch, contact, feeling; 8) the six senses; 9) name and form; 10) the six forms of perception, awareness or discernment; 11) action, moral conduct; 12) ignorance.

pratyekabuddhas: "solitary enlightened ones"; adherents of the Hinayana sect who gain nirvana due to their insight into the twelve *nidanas*.

pratyekabuddhayana: "vehicle," or teaching, of *pratyekabuddhas*.

preta: see *six realms*.

roshi: (J.) "old teacher"; commonly used to refer Zen masters.

rupa: the body, five senses, outer existence; one of the *five skandhas*.

samadhi: state of perfect absorption into the object of contemplation; a state of non-dual consciousness.

Samantabhadra: "Bodhisattva All-pervading Goodness," who embodies the wisdom of essential sameness.

sambhogakaya: "body of bliss"; one of the three bodies (*trikaya*) of Buddha.

samjna: thought, conception; one of the *five skandhas*.

samsara: eternal round (transmigration) of birth-and-death within the six realms of existence.

samskara: mind-elements and mental formations; one of the five *skandhas.*

sanzen: (J.) private koan interview with the master.

Shaka: (J.), Shakyamuni, the historical Buddha.

Shariputra: one of ten chief disciples of Shakyamuni Buddha.

shravakas: "listeners"; adherents of the Hinayana sect who seek enlightenment for themselves alone and can only attain nirvana by listening to the teaching.

shravakayana: "vehicle" or teaching of the *shravakas.*

shunyata: emptiness, nothingness, transparency.

Shurangama Sutra: a tantric sutra translated into Chinese by Paramiti in 705 CE; it was popular in China during the Tang dynasty.

six paramitas: 1) generosity (*dana-paramita*); 2) discipline (*shila-paramita*); 3) patience (*kshanti-paramita*); 4) energy, or exertion (*virya-paramita*); 5) meditation (*dhyana-paramita*); 6) wisdom (*prajna-paramita*).

six realms (gati): various modes of *samsaric* existence in which rebirth occurs the realm of desire (*kamadhatu*) consisting of three lower states (*naraka*: hell beings, *preta*: hungry ghosts, and animals, and three higher states (humans, *asuras*: angry demons or demigods, and *devas*: gods or heavenly beings).

six supernatural wisdoms: 1) ability to transform the body; 2) ability to see anything; 3) ability to hear all sounds and understand all speech; 4) ability to mind read; 5) knowledge of all previous existences; and 6) complete knowledge of dispassion.

sutra: discourse attributed to the Buddha.

tathagata: "thus come," "so come"; one of the ten titles of Buddha.

three bodies: see *trikaya.*

three karmas: karmas of deed, word, and thought.

three worlds (tridhatu): the world of desire (*kamadhatu*), the world of form (*rupadhatu*), and the realm of formlessness (*arupadhatu*), the highest realm.

three treasures: "three jewels" of Buddha, Dharma, and Sangha.

three vehicles (triyana): three classes of Buddhist teaching: *shrvakayana*, *pratyekabuddhayana*, and *bodhisattvayana.*

transmigration: the eternal round within the *three worlds.*

trikaya: dharmakaya, sambhogakaya, and *nirmanakaya.*

tripitaka: the "three baskets" comprised of discourses attributed to the Buddha (*sutras*); early Buddhist discourses on philosophy and psychology (*abhidharma*); and monastic rules and regulations governing the communal life of monks and nuns (*vinaya*).

Tushita Heaven: fourth of the six heavens in the realm of desire, dwelling place of the future Buddha.

twelve divisions of the canon: 1) sermons; 2) metrical pieces; 3) prophecies; 4) *gathas*; 5) impromptu or unsolicited addresses; 6) narratives; 7) stories of the Buddha's past lives; 8) expanded sutras; 9) miracles; 10) discourses by question and answer; 11) parables and metaphors; and 12) dogmatic treatises.

vedana: feelings, perception; one of the *five skandhas.*

vijnana: consciousness; one of the *five skandhas.*

vinaya: monastic rules and regulations governing the communal life of monks and nuns.

Yama: god of hell.

zazen: (J.) seated meditation.